# 1,000,000 Books

are available to read at

www.ForgottenBooks.com

Read online
Download PDF
Purchase in print

ISBN 978-1-5276-4685-8
PIBN 10877659

This book is a reproduction of an important historical work. Forgotten Books uses
state-of-the-art technology to digitally reconstruct the work, preserving the original format
whilst repairing imperfections present in the aged copy. In rare cases, an imperfection in
the original, such as a blemish or missing page, may be replicated in our edition. We do,
however, repair the vast majority of imperfections successfully; any imperfections that
remain are intentionally left to preserve the state of such historical works.

# 1 MONTH OF
# FREE
# READING

## at
## www.ForgottenBooks.com

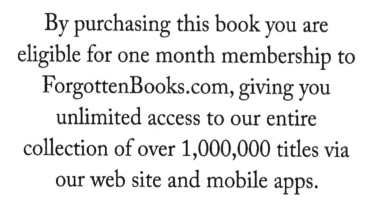

By purchasing this book you are eligible for one month membership to ForgottenBooks.com, giving you unlimited access to our entire collection of over 1,000,000 titles via our web site and mobile apps.

To claim your free month visit:

www.forgottenbooks.com/free877659

English
Français
Deutsche
Italiano
Español
Português

# www.forgottenbooks.com

**Mythology** Photography **Fiction**
Fishing Christianity **Art** Cooking
Essays Buddhism Freemasonry
Medicine **Biology** Music **Ancient**
**Egypt** Evolution Carpentry Physics
Dance Geology **Mathematics** Fitness
Shakespeare **Folklore** Yoga Marketing
**Confidence** Immortality Biographies
Poetry **Psychology** Witchcraft
Electronics Chemistry History **Law**
Accounting **Philosophy** Anthropology
Alchemy Drama Quantum Mechanics
Atheism Sexual Health **Ancient History**
**Entrepreneurship** Languages Sport
Paleontology Needlework Islam
**Metaphysics** Investment Archaeology
Parenting Statistics Criminology
**Motivational**

# DISCOURSES

ON

VARIOUS SUBJECTS

RELATIVE TO THE

# BEING AND ATTRIBUTES OF GOD,

AND HIS WORKS

IN

CREATION, PROVIDENCE, AND GRACE.

BY ADAM CLARKE, LL.D., F.A.S., &c. &c.

VOL. II.

New-York:

MELRATH & BANGS, 85 CHATHAM-STREET.

SOLD BY J. EMORY & B. WAUGH, *New-York ;*—TOWAR, J. & D. M. HOGAN, *Philadelphia ;*—ARMSTRONG & PLASKITT, *Baltimore ;*—CROCKER & BREW-STER, *Boston ;*—WILLIAM WILLIAMS, *Utica ;*—CHARLES HOLLIDAY, *Cincinnati.*

*Stereotyped by James Conner.*

1831.

2<sup>3</sup>97
2<sup>5</sup>-1

$2^3 97$
$2^5 - 1$

# TABLE OF CONTENTS.

# SERMONS.

―――

## SERMON XVII.

―――

## ON THE DECALOGUE, OR TEN COMMANDMENTS.

―――

EXODUS, Chap. xx. ver. 1—17.

1. And God spake all these words, saying,
2. I am the Lord thy God, which have brought thee out of the land of Egypt, out of the house of bondage.
3. Thou shalt have no other gods before me.
4. Thou shalt not make unto thee any graven image, or any likeness of any thing that is in heaven above, or that is in the earth beneath, or that is in the water under the earth:
5. Thou shalt not bow down thyself to them, nor serve them; for I the Lord thy God am a jealous God, visiting the iniquity of the fathers upon the children unto the third and fourth generation of them that hate me,
6. And shewing mercy unto thousands of them that love me, and keep my commandments.
7. Thou shalt not take the name of the Lord thy God in vain; for the Lord will not hold him guiltless that taketh his name in vain.
8. Remember the sabbath day to keep it holy.
9. Six days shalt thou labour, and do all thy work:
10. But the seventh day is the sabbath of the Lord thy God: in it thou shalt not do any work, thou, nor thy son, nor thy daughter, thy man-servant, nor thy maid-servant, nor thy cattle, nor thy stranger that is within thy gates:
11. For in six days the Lord made heaven and earth, the sea, and all that in them is, and rested the seventh day; wherefore the Lord blessed the sabbath day, and hallowed it.
12. Honour thy father and thy mother: that thy days may be long upon the land which the Lord thy God giveth thee.
13. Thou shalt not kill.
14. Thou shalt not commit adultery.
15. Thou shalt not steal.
16. Thou shalt not bear false witness against thy neighbour.

17. Thou shalt not covet thy neighbour's house, thou shalt not covet thy neighbour's wife, nor his man-servant, nor his maid-servant, nor his ox, nor his ass, nor any thing that is thy neighbour's.

———————————————

THE two first verses of this chapter contain the preface which shews the authority by which these commandments are given, and the obligation of the people to obey :—

*And God spake all these words,* ver. 1.

It has been conjectured, and not without great plausibility, that the clause אלה כל הדברים את *eth col hadebarim ha-elleh*— " All these words," belong to the latter part of the concluding verse of the preceding chapter, and should be read thus :—*so Moses went down unto the people, and spake unto them* ALL THESE WORDS. That is, he delivered to them that solemn charge, not to attempt to come up to that part of the mountain on which God manifested Himself, in His glorious Majesty, *least He should break through upon and consume them.* When Moses, therefore, had gone down, and *spoken all these words,* and he and Aaron had re-ascended the mountain, then the Divine Being, as Supreme Legislator, is majestically introduced thus :—AND GOD SPAKE, SAYING. This gives a dignity to the commencement of this chapter, of which the above clause, if not referred to the speech of Moses to the people, deprives it. Our most ancient version, the *Anglo-Saxon,* reads in the same way, ᵹod ᵹᵱᴂc þuᵹ—*God spake thus;* which is the whole of the verse in this version, (and without the *and,*) which makes the whole of this introduction more peremptory and authoritative.

The giving of the law on Mount Sinai, was the most solemn transaction which ever took place between God and man: and, therefore, it is introduced in the most solemn manner. In the morning of that day in which this law was given, (which many learned chronologists suppose to have been May 30, in the year of the world 2513, before the Incarnation 1491, that day being the *Pentecost,*) the presence of Jehovah became manifest by thunders and lightnings,—a dense cloud on the mountain,—and a terrific blast of a trumpet,—so that the whole assembly was struck with terror and dismay. Shortly after, the whole mount appeared on fire; columns of smoke arose from it, as the smoke of a furnace; and an earthquake shook it from top to base; the trumpet continued to sound, and the blasts grew longer, and louder and louder. Then JEHOVAH, the sovereign Lawgiver, came down upon the mount, and called Moses to ascend to the top, where, previously to His delivering this law, He gave him directions concerning the sanctification of the people. See Exod. xix. 16, &c. From the awful manner in which the law was introduced, it is no wonder that at first view it was deemed the ministration of terror and death. 2 Cor. iii. 7. Appearing rather to drive men *from* God, than to bring them *nigh* to Him. And, indeed, from this solemn fact, we may learn, that an approach to God would have been for ever impracticable, had not Infinite Mercy found out the *gospel scheme* of salvation. By this, and this alone, we draw nigh to God: *for we have an entrance unto the holiest by the blood of Jesus.* Heb. x. 19. Even the Apostle of the Gentiles was deeply struck with this terrific display of God's majesty, though contemplating it in the *mild light* of the glorious *gospel.* "For," says he, "ye are not come unto the mount that might be touched, and that burned with fire; nor unto blackness, and darkness, and tempest; and the sound of a trumpet, and the voice of words; which voice, they that heard, entreated that the word should not be spoken to them any more: for so terrible was the sight, that Moses said, I exceedingly fear and quake:—but ye are come unto mount Sion, and unto the city of the living God, the heavenly Jerusalem; and to an innumerable company of angels; to the general assembly and church of the first-born, which are written in heaven; and to God the Judge of all, and to the spirits of just men made perfect; and to Jesus, the *Mediator* of the *New Covenant,* and to the *Blood of sprinkling,* that speaketh better things than *that of* Abel." Heb. xii. 18—24.

The *obligation* of the people to *hear* and to *obey,* is founded on ver. 2. *I am Jehovah thy God, which have brought thee out of the land of Egypt, out of the house of bondage.* As יהוה *Jehovah,* He is the Fountain and Cause of all being: there was nothing *before* Him, for He had no beginning: there can be nothing after Him, for He is eternal, and can have no end. And as He is the cause of all being; the creator of heaven and earth, as He had already manifested Himself to this people; so He is the preserver of all that He has made. Of all that is good and excellent, He is the cause: without Him nothing is good, nothing holy, nothing strong. He has, from His nature and being, absolute right over all that He has made: and is, necessarily, the Lord and Governor of all things, animate and inanimate, spiritual and material. He alone has *authority* and *power* to *save* and to *destroy* :— to bring into being, or annihilate that whith He has already created. He is the *First*, and He is the *Last:* He is the *Beginning* and the *End:* the Uncreated, Self-sufficient, Omniscient, Omnipotent, Omnipresent, Creator of all things, and Father of the spirits of all flesh. *For His pleasure they are and were created.* As they were brought into being by His omnipotent *will*, so they continue to exist during His *pleasure.* Under such a Sovereign, man is not left to a state of *indifference*, whether he will obey or disobey; as if these were *indifferent things.* He *must obey* and shew his allegiance, if he regard his own welfare: he *may* disobey, and shew thereby his spirit of rebellion: and thus, the postherd of the earth enters the lists with the Almighty. In subjection and obedience, all good is secured: in disaffection and rebellion, all good is forfeited. Man *may* CHUSE *life* or *death*,—a *blessing* or a *curse:* and, according to his *choice*, for God *compels* nothing on this head, will be his state in time and eternity ; a state of misery or a state of happiness; and both ineffable. A just consideration of this subject is imperious on man: and why? God made him. He is Jehovah, and governs all things: and obedience to His will is the highest interest of man.

But, in addition to His *right* over them, as Creator and Sovereign, He says, *I am* THY *God ;*—אלהיך *Eloheyca.* There is something in the term אלהים *Elohim*, that is peculiarly interesting to *man.* It is allowed by wise and learned men, to signify, God in covenant with man :—God having undertaken to raise man from his fall, and restore him from sin, degradation, and misery, to that state of glory, holiness, and excellence, from which he had fallen. And, indeed, all this is implied in the bare idea of God ;—the Good One ;—the best of Beings ;—He who is as benevolent as He is just ;—as beneficent as He is powerful ;—He who is the supreme and satisfying Good of all intelligent beings ;—who.

though He be infinitely just, delighteth not in the death of a sinner; and who, though infinitely perfect and happy, and therefore needing nothing that He hath made, delighteth in the salvation of man.

He to whom God says, *I am thy God*, in this peculiar sense, has reason for eternal exultation.  And that He had shewn himself to be God, the good Being, to Israel, he adds : *which have brought thee out of the land of Egypt, out of the house of bondage*.  I need not here enter into the ancient history of the Israelites, and of their 430 years servitude in Egypt, where they were at all times ill used, and towards the latter part of their sojourning there, most cruelly oppressed; these things are well known.  From that land, in which the true God was not acknowledged—where they had no means of grace, and no spiritual or intellectual advantage of any kind;—out of this place of *slavery*,—this *house of bond-men*, God, by a strong and mighty arm, redeemed them; and was now actually guiding them to a land where they were to eat bread without scarceness; where God alone should be their *King ;*—where they were to have the essence of *civil liberty ;* —and, with all other good things, the *means of grace*, and the *hope of glory*.  All these were obligations of the highest kind, and reasons why they should receive His laws immediately from Himself; and take them for the regulators of their heart, and the rule of their conduct.

There are two points of view under which this Law of God appears both singular and important.

1. It is the most ancient code or system of law ever given to man.

2. It was written in *alphabetical* characters, invented by God himself; as it is most probable that, previously to this, no such characters had been known in the world.

1. It is the most *ancient* code or system of law ever given to man.  All the nations of the earth have been unanimous in the opinion that the *first code* of law must have come from heaven : and so necessary was a Divine origin for those laws, to which all were to render obedience, that the great legislators of antiquity were obliged to pretend that from some *god* or *goddess* they received, by inspiration, the laws they pro posed to the people, to whatever *form* of government they

chose to apply them. The intercourse which Moses had with Jehovah, was soon known among all the nations of the East; —and from them the Greeks and Romans received the information. Hence the pretensions of *Numitor* among the ancient *Romans;—Lycurgus* and *Solon* among the *Greeks;* —*Zeratusht* or *Zoroaster,* and *Menu,* among the *Persians;* —and *Mohammed* among the *Arabians.* But no laws have been proved to be divine and rightly attributed to God, but those given by *Moses* to the Jews, and by Jesus to the Gentiles. The oldest record in the world is the *Pentateuch.* It is the simplest, the purest, and the most comprehensive of all that has ever been delivered to men. Christ's *Sermon on the Mount* is the *Comment* on the Mosaic code.

2. These laws were written in *alphabetical* characters, invented by God himself; as it is most probable, that before the giving of the two tables of stone written by the finger of Jehovah, there were no alphabetical characters of any kind known to man.

In the early ages of the world, letters would have been of little use. Men living then to a great age, and nigh to each other, transmitted instructions down to posterity by *word of mouth.* This is what is called *tradition—i. e.* transmitting from hand to hand the facts necessary to be remembered: but when the age of man became shortened, when kingdoms and commerce were established, and the inhabitants of the earth were greatly multiplied, and consequently scattered over the face of the earth, then the use of alphabetical writing became necessary. And seasonably, as Dr. A. Bayley observes, in supply of this want, we are told, that God, at Mount Sinai, gave unto a chosen people, laws inscribed with His own hand. " No time seems so proper, from which to date the introduction of *letters* among the Hebrews as this: for, after this period, we find continual mention of letters, reading, and writing, in the now proper sense of those words: *And it shall be when he* (the king) *sitteth upon the throne of his kingdom, that he shall* WRITE *him a copy of this law,* IN A BOOK—*and it shall be with him, and he shall* READ *therein all the days of his life.* Deut. xvii. 18, 19. *And Moses* WROTE *this Law, and delivered it to the Priests, the sons of Levi.* Deut. xxxi. 9. The first time we meet with any mention of writing, is in Exod. xvii. 14.; *And the Lord said to Moses,*

WRITE *this for a memorial in a Book.* But it is evident, that either this passage is introduced here, instead of Deut. xxv. 17. by way of *anticipation,* or that by the words סמ זאת זכרון בספר *kethob zoth zikkaron ba-sephar*—" Write this for a memorial in a book," was intended only a *monumental* declaration of the defeat of Amalek, by Joshua, by some action or *symbolical* representation : for, it is immediately subjoined, *And Moses built an altar, and called the name of it* יהוה נסי YEHOVAH-NISSI—*The Lord is my banner.* Moses, it is said, *επαιδευθη, was educated* in all the wisdom of the Egyptians— in all the learning of which they were possessed ; but it is manifest he had not learned of them any method of *alphabetical writing,* otherwise there had been no occasion for God's act and assistance, in writing the two tables of the Law ; no need of a miraculous writing : had Moses known this art, the Lord might have said to him, as he often does afterwards, *Write thou these words.* Exod. xxxiv. 27. *Write on the stones the words of this law.* Deut. xxvii. 3. *Write ye this song for you.* Deut. xxxi. 19. Possibly it might not be going too far to say, that neither *letters* nor *language* were a *natural discovery;* and that it was impossible for man to have invented either : for, 1. Reason may shew us how near to an impossibility it was that a just and proper number of convenient characters for the sounds in language, should be *naturally* hit on by any man ; for whom it was easy to *imitate* and *improve,* but not to *invent.* 2. From the evidence of the Mosaic History, it appears that the introduction of writing among the Hebrews was not from man but God. 3. There are no vestiges of letters subsisting in other nations, *before* the delivery of the Law on Mount Sinai ; nor then among *them,* till long after. See Dr. A. Bayley's Four Dissertations ; Diss. I. p. 33.

That God actually wrote the ten Commandments on the two tables of stone, seems evident, beyond doubt, from the following texts :—

" And the Lord said unto Moses, Come up to me into the mountain, and be thou there ; and I will give thee tables of stone, and a law, and commandments WHICH I HAVE WRITTEN, that thou mayest teach them." Exod. xxiv. 12.

" And He gave unto Moses upon Mount Sinai, two tables

of testimony, tables of stone, WRITTEN WITH THE FINGER OF
GOD." Exod. xxxi. 18.

"And Moses went down from the mount, and the two
tables of testimony were in his hand; the tables were written
on both their sides. And the tables were the WORK OF GOD;
and THE WRITING WAS THE WRITING OF GOD, graven upon
the tables." Exod. xxxii. 15, 16.

" These words (the ten Commandments) the Lord spake
in the mount, out of the midst of the fire, of the cloud, and of
the thick darkness, with a great voice: and he added no
more: and HE WROTE THEM upon two tables of stone."
Deut. v. 22.

Nothing can be clearer than these texts; and it seems
quite impossible to give them any other meaning than that
to which they are applied in the preceding observations: and
from them we learn, that alphabetical characters were the invention of God; and that the first piece of alphabetical writing was that of the *ten commandments*, written by the finger
of God on Mount Sinai, upon two tables of stone.

The laws delivered on Mount Sinai, have been variously
named; in Deut. iv. 13. they are called עשרת הדברים *ésereth
ha-debarim*—THE TEN WORDS.

In the preceding chapter, ver. 5. God calls them את בריתי
*eth beriti*, MY COVENANT; *i. e.* the agreement He entered into
with the people of Israel, to take them for His peculiar people, if they took Him for their God and portion. IF *ye will
obey my voice indeed,* and KEEP MY COVENANT, *then shall ye
be a peculiar treasure unto me.* And the word *covenant*
here, evidently refers to the *laws* given in this chapter, as is
manifest from Deut. iv. 13.—*and he declared unto you His*
COVENANT, *which He commanded you to perform, even* TEN
COMMANDMENTS.

These Commandments have also been called the MORAL
LAW, because they contain and lay down rules for the regulation of the *manners* and conduct of men.

Sometimes they have been termed התורה *ha-thorah*, THE
LAW, by way of eminence, as containing the grand system of
spiritual *instruction, direction, guidance,* &c. as the radical
meaning of *thorah* signifies.

Often it is called the DECALOGUE, Δεκαλογος, which is a

literal translation into Greek of the עשרת הדברים *ésereth ha-debarim*, or TEN WORDS of Moses.

Among divines these Commandments are generally divided into what they term the *first* and *second* table.

The *first table* containing the *first, second, third,* and *fourth* Commandments, and comprehending the whole system of THEOLOGY, the true notions we should form of the Supreme Being; the reverence we owe, and the religious service we should render to Him.

The *second table* containing the remaining *six* Commandments, and comprehending a complete system of Ethics, or moral duties, which man owes to his fellows; and on the due performance of which, the *order, peace,* and *happiness* of society depend. By this division, the FIRST table contains our *duty* to GOD: the SECOND, our *duty* to our NEIGHBOURS.

This division, which is natural enough, refers us to the grand PRINCIPLE, *Love to God* and *Love to man;* through which *both* tables are observed. 1. Thou shalt love the Lord thy God with all thy heart, soul, mind, and strength. 2. Thou shalt love thy neighbour as thyself. On these two hang all the law and the Prophets. Matt. xxii. 27—40.

### THE FIRST COMMANDMENT.

#### Against Mental and Theoretic Idolatry.

*Thou shalt have no other gods before me,* ver. 3.

לא יהיה לך אלהים אחרים על פני *lo yehieh leca Elohim acharim ál panai,*—"There shall not be to thee, strange gods before, or in the place of me." It is worthy of notice, that each *individual* is addressed here, and not the *people collectively*—though they are all necessarily included—that each might feel that he was bound for *himself*, to hear and do all these words. Moses laboured to impress this personal interest on the people's minds when he said, Deut. v. 3. "The Lord made this covenant with *us*, even *us*, who are all of *us* here alive this day." To *us*, called Christians, to every one of us, are these words directed also, and to our children and children's children. All are concerned here: the supreme Lawgiver utters His commands, not relative to religious rites and ceremonies, but to spiritual and moral duties—duties which we must fulfil both to God and man, if we wish to be happy in this world, and in the world to come. We must therefore lose sight of the *Ritual Law* of Moses, in this we are not concerned; we have to do with that unchangeable moral law, which belongs to all mankind, in all countries, in all states and conditions of life, in all the ages of the world: —given by the Sovereign of heaven and earth, to all the human beings that constitute His subjects and family on the habitable globe.

After having recalled to their remembrance His mercy in visiting them in Egypt, and His power manifested in bringing them out of a state of servitude as degrading as it was oppressive; and this by a series of acts plainly descriptive of His eternal power and Godhead;—he now commands them to acknowledge no other being as God, but Himself. As the word אחרים *acharim* means *strange* or *strangers*, we may consider it here as implying, thou shalt not acknowledge, not only the *strange gods* of a *strange people*, but also, any god or pretended power, with which thou art *unacquainted*—no one who has not given thee such proofs of his being, power and goodness, as I have done, in delivering thee from the *Egyptians*—dividing the *Red Sea*—bringing *water* out of the rock—bringing *quails* into the *desert*—sending *manna* from *heaven* to feed thee—giving the *pillar* of *cloud* and of *fire*, to direct thee in the wilderness by *day*—to be a *light* to thee by *night*—and to cover thee from the ardours of the sun when shining in the might of his strength. By these miracles, God had rendered Himself *familiar* to them; they were intimately *acquainted* with Him, and the operation of His hands: and therefore, with great propriety, He says, " Thou shalt have no strange gods before me;" על פני *ǎl panai*, or *peney*—in my *presence*—or in the place of those *manifestations* which I have made of myself.

This commandment prohibits every species of *mental* idolatry—We must not attempt to form conceptions of the Supreme Being as if confined to *form*, to any kind of *limits*, to any particular *space* or *place:* as JEHOVAH, He is in every respect inconceivable ;—no mind can grasp Him ;—He is an Infinite Spirit ;—equally in every place, and in all points of duration ;—He cannot be more present in one place than another, because He fills the heavens and the earth, though the *manifestations* of His presence may be more in particular places and especial times. His working shews that He is *here* and *present*; though He would be no less present, were there no *apparent working*. He is not like man, though, in condescension to our weakness, He represents Himself often as possessing *human members* and *human affections*. When a thing is said to be done by the *finger*, the *hand*, or the *arm* of God, this only points out *degrees of power* manifested in performing certain works of *mercy, providence, deliverance,* &c. And these *degrees of power* are always in *proportion* to the work that is to be effected. The *finger* may indicate a comparatively slight interference, where a miracle is wrought; but not one that is stupendous. The *hand*, one where great power is necessary, accompanied by evident skill and design. And the *arm*, one in which the mighty power of God comes forward with sovereign, overwhelming, irresistible effect. When the *shoulder* is attributed to Him, it points out His almighty, sustaining power,—maintaining His government of the world, and of His church,—supporting whatever He has made;—so His *heart* represents His *concern* for His own honour, for the welfare of His followers, and for the afflicted and distressed.

This Divine Being we must sanctify in our hearts:—that is, we must separate all transitory, material, and particularly earthly things, from the notion we form of Him. We cannot conceive *what* He is, and *how* He is. It is enough for all the purposes of devotion and faith, that we can acknowledge Him, as the Cause of all being;—infinitely perfect in Himself, —needing nothing that He has made,—supporting all his creatures,—willing the perfection and happiness of all His intelligent offspring, for whom He is especially concerned; for He made *man*, in His own image, and in His own likeness.

But as this God is inconceivably great, holy, just, good, and merciful, how shall we come into the presence of His holiness and justice, seeing we have sinned and have rebelled against Him? It is true, the consideration of His goodness and mercy may encourage us; but still, what right have we to expect that He will give the preference to the claims of His goodness and mercy, rather than to those of His holiness and justice? Here the doctrine of a Mediator must come in. *Sacrifice* was appointed to the Israelites, as the medium of approach to this most awful and glorious Being. That sacrificial system was a type of the Incarnation, Passion, Death, and Atonement of our Lord and Saviour Jesus Christ. And, as to us there is only one God, so there is only one Mediator between God and man: we approach, therefore, this Infinite Spirit, through Him who hath lain in His bosom, and hath declared Him, and made Him known to mankind.

This commandment also forbids all inordinate attachment to *earthly* and *sensible* things :—*i. e.* things that are the objects of our senses, and for the possession of which our appetites and affections are intensely occupied.

As God is the Fountain of happiness, and no intelligent creature can be happy but through Him, whoever seeks happiness in the creature, is necessarily an idolater, as he puts the *creature* in the place of the Creator; expecting *that* from the gratification of his passions, in the use or abuse of earthly things, which is to be found in God alone.

Thus we find, that the first commandment in the Decalogue, is divinely calculated to prevent the misery of man, and to promote his happiness, by taking him off from all false dependence, and leading him to God himself, *the Fountain of all good.*

### THE SECOND COMMANDMENT.

*Against Making and Worshipping Images.*

*Thou shalt not make unto thee any graven image*, ver. 4.

As the word פסל *pesel,* which we translate *graven image,* signifies in its root, to *hew, carve, engrave,* &c. it may here signify any kind of image, either of *wood, stone,* or *metal,* on which the *axe,* the *chisel,* or the *graving* tool, has been employed. This commandment includes, in its prohibitions, every species of idolatry practised in Egypt. For a particular description of the different objects of religious worship among the Egyptians, I must beg the reader to refer to my Comment on the *ten plagues of Egypt,* and particularly to the concluding observations at the end of Exod. xii. *Image worship* is a positive breach of the first command. It attempts to humanize God, and fills the miserable idolater with the opinion that God is like to himself, if not altogether so : and *image worshippers* in general have no other idea of God than that of a gigantic man, of amazing dimensions, of vast strength, wisdom, and skill; no other kind of being having any such strength or wisdom. Hence, among the Roman Catholics, God is represented as a very grave, venerable old man, with a *triple crown*, (which, however, their popes borrow,) to signify His sovereignty over *heaven, earth,* and *hell; angels, men,* and *devils,* being subject to Him." All these, as well as the *triple crown,* their · symbol, have the popes of Rome, by their doctrines, traditions, and pretensions, arrogated to themselves. They have the keys of both worlds; they open and no man shutteth; they shut and no man openeth! It is a matter of the highest astonishment, that the blasphemous pretensions of these individuals should have been acknowledged, and conceded to them for so long a time, by all the powers of Europe! They have raised up and put down emperors and kings at pleasure. Have absolved, as in a moment, all their officers and subjects from the most solemn oaths of allegiance, and their obligations of obedience :—and for all this they have given them indulgences, purgatory, transubstantiation, image-worship, worship of the Virgin Mary, as queen of heaven; saints and angels as mediators and intercessors; prayers for the dead; and uncertain and contradictory *traditions*, in place of the BIBLE! All these must be received on their authority; and he who disputes their authenticity is a *heretic* :—*i. e.* one that the church of Rome orders to be *burnt alive* :—and those who reject their authority, incur the Divine displeasure, and if not reconciled to them and their church, shall be banished from the presence of God, and the glory of His power, to all eternity! What blasphemous pretensions! What gross idolatry!

*Or any likeness that is in heaven above, or that is in the earth beneath, or that is in the water under the earth,* ib.

To have the full spirit and extent of this commandment, we must collate this place with Deut. iv. 15—19. " Take ye, therefore, good heed to yourselves; (for ye saw no manner of similitude on the day that the Lord spake unto you in Horeb, out of the midst of the fire;) lest ye corrupt *yourselves*, and make you a graven image, the similitude of any figure, the likeness of male or female, the likeness of any beast that is on the earth, the likeness of any winged fowl that flieth in the air, the likeness of any thing that creepeth upon the ground, the likeness of any fish that is in the waters beneath the earth: and lest thou lift up thine eyes unto heaven; and when thou seest the sun, and the moon, and the stars, even all the host of heaven, and shouldest be driven to worship them and serve them." This is, in the first place, directed against the idolatry of *Egypt*. All who have even a slight acquaintance with the ancient history of Egypt, know that Osiris, and his wife Isis, were supreme divinities among that people. Their images were objects of adoration, and were multiplied throughout the land. Several of those images, of a very high and remote antiquity, with various mythologic emblems, now lie before me;—and which had been doubtless objects of adoration;—some of them are thickly covered over with hieroglyphics; and, could they be deciphered, would, no doubt, cast much light on the history of those persons, their deification, and the worship paid to them. Some of these images are cut out of *marble*, others out of *sand-stone*, and others out of *schist*. Among these also, are the *Anubis* or barking *dog;* the *Cercopithecus* or *monkey;* and the *Ibis* or *stork*. Some of these are modelled of *clay*, and baked in the fire; others *carved* out of *cedar*, lately brought from the tombs of the kings in Upper Egypt; and others formed from *brass*. Not only the *dog* and the *monkey* were adored, but also the *ox* and the *cow*. The *ox* was sacred, because they supposed that Osiris took up his residence in one of these animals. Hence they always had a living ox, which they supposed to be the habitation of the deity; and they imagined that on the death of one he entered into the body of another, and so on successively. This famous *ox-god* they called *Apis* and *Mnevis*. Here every species of idolatry is forbidden. By the *male* and *female*, *Osiris* and *Isis* may be intended: for, to these they paid divine honours. By *any beast*,—the dog, the monkey, the cat, and the ox, are intended. By *the fowl that flieth in the air*,—the *ibis*, or *stork*, the *crane*, and the *hawk;*—for these were all objects of Egyptian idolatry. By *that which creepeth on the ground*,—the *crocodile, serpents* in general, and the *scarabeus* or *beetle*, may be intended, for all these were objects of Egyptian adoration. *The likeness of any fish*,—all *fish* were sacred animals in Egypt. One called *oxurunchus*, had a temple, and had divine honours paid to it. See Strabo, lib. xvii.

Another fish called *phagrus*, was worshipped at Syene, according to *Clemens Alexandrinus*, in his *Cohortatio;* and the *lepidotus*, and *eel*, were objects of their adoration, as we learn from *Herodotus*, lib. ii. cap. 72.

In short, *Oxen, Cows, Sheep, Goats, Lions, Dogs, Monkeys,* and *Cats :*—the *Ibis*, the *Crane*, and the *Hawk :*—the *Croco-dile, Serpents, Flies*, and the *Scarabeus* or *Beetle :*—the *Nile* and its *Fish :*—the *Sun, Moon, Planets*, and *Stars :*—*Fire, Air, Light, Darkness*, and *Night :*—*Onions, Leeks*, and other horticultural productions; were all objects of Egyptian idolatry, and all included in this very *circumstantial* prohibi-tion as it stands in Deuteronomy: and very forcibly in the general terms of the text, *Thou shalt not make unto thee any graven image, or any likeness of any thing that is in the* HEAVENS *above*, or *that is in the* EARTH *beneath, or that is in the* WATER *under the earth.* And the reason of this is very evident, when the various objects of Egyptian idolatry are considered. But it is not directed solely against Egyptian idolatry—but against all idolatry, whether found among the *savage tribes* in North America—the worshippers of the *visible heavens* in China—the devotees of *Brahma, Siva*, and *Mahadeo* in Hindostan—the followers of Budhoo in Ceylon, and Java and Ava—or the corrupt Christians in the Church of Rome :—against all these, and all like them, has God sent forth the SECOND *Commandment.*

There is something remarkable in the 23d verse of this chapter, that should be noticed here : *Ye shall not make with me gods of silver, neither shall ye make unto you gods of gold.* In ver. 3. it is commanded, *Thou shalt have no other gods* BEFORE *me*, אל פני *al panai*—But here they are commanded, Ye shall not make with me gods of silver, or of gold, אתי *ithi*, WITH *me*, as emblems or representatives of God; in order, as might be pretended, to keep the displays of His magnificence in memory. He would not even have a costly altar :—on the contrary, He ordered one of earth, or plain turf, to be erected, on which they should offer those sacrifices, by which they should commemorate their own guilt, and the necessity of an atonement, by which they might be reconciled to God.

*Thou shalt not bow down thyself to them, nor serve them,* ver. 5.

Two things, in addition to what is mentioned above, should be noted here. 1. They shall offer no mental adoration to images. 2. They shall perform to them no religious service.

1. Thou shalt not bow down thyself to them; מחוּה אל להם *lo tishtachoch la-hem*—Thou shalt not *prostrate thyself* to them, in any act of adoration; kneeling down, putting the head between the knees, and touching the earth with the forehead, was the common form of religious adoration. Ye shall conceive no idea of their capability to hear, help, or save you; they are nothing but the block, stone, or metal, which you see: from them you never received help, and to them you are under no obligation.

2. Thou shalt not serve them; ולא תעבדם *velo taâbdem*—Thou shalt not honour them with any religious rite—such as *sacrifice*, offering, &c.; for this is one of the acceptations of the verb עבד *âbad*, and in Exod. xii. 25, עבדה *âbodah*, signifies *religious service*, such as God required of the people—and in this sense it is often used. Hence we find that prostration, kneeling, prayers, mental adoration, offering candles, frankincense, &c., or performing pilgrimages, to saints, angels, images, &c., is flat idolatry, and point blank against the *letter* and *spirit* of this commandment.

To countenance its image worship, the Roman Catholic Church has in some cases left the whole of this second commandment out of the decalogue, and as a second command, she has omitted it in all her Formularies, Catechisms, Missals, and Church books that I have seen; and to keep up the number of TEN commandments, she has divided the *tenth* into *two*, contrary to the whole spirit and sense of this law, that speaks only of the objects of *covetousness*.

This omission and division is totally contrary to the faith of God's elect, and to the acknowledgement of the truth which is according to godliness. The verse containing this second command is found in every MS. of the Hebrew Pentateuch that has ever yet been discovered. There is not even one word of the whole verse wanting in any of the hundreds of MSS. collated by *Kennicott* and *De Rossi*; nor in my own, *five* of which are among the oldest extant. It is in all the ancient *versions*, *Samaritan*, *Chaldee*, *Syriac*, *Arabic*, *Septuagint*, *Coptic*, *Vulgate*, and also in the *Persian*. The *Anglo-Saxon* gives this command with its usual sententious brevity. Ne pinc þu þe aᵹnaᵹene Iɪobaɪ, Ne work thou the graven (or image) gods. Do not make such—and why? Because Ic eom Dꞃihꞇen þin Lꞃoꝺ, I am the Lord thy God.

And by all people and sects, the Roman Catholics excepted, with whom I have any acquaintance, it has ever been considered as the *second commandment.*

*For I the Lord thy God,* am a *jealous God,* ib.

There is scarcely a word of more *ominous* interpretation, than the word *jealousy.* It is a *suspicion* often generated from love, in weak minds, that it is not returned—for love demands love ; and nothing else can be its recompense. It is often ideal, being founded on appearances which, traced to their origin, are found to have no connexion with, nor bearing on, the subject of the suspicion. It is however, in most cases, a real evil to that mind which is exercised with it. One of our poets has described it well :—

> " It is the green ey'd monster that doth mock
> The meat it feeds on,—
> But O, what cursed minutes tells he o'er
> Who doats, yet doubts ; suspects, yet strongly loves !"

But it signifies also, an *anxious care* to preserve a person or thing in a *state* of *purity*—to prevent defection in a person, whose heedless and incautious conduct might lead into transgression, though at first, neither premeditated nor planned. This is what may be called a *godly jealousy*—anxious care to preserve its object from corruption and ruin. Thus, Jehovah was jealous over the Israelites ; and St. Paul jealous over the church of God at Corinth, that he might present it as a chaste virgin to Christ, 2 Cor. xi. 2.

When the Lord says, " I am a jealous God," He shews in the most expressive manner, His love to the people. He felt for them as the most affectionate husband could feel for his spouse. The *covenant* between Him and them was the strong bond which required their invariable attachment to Him ; and bound Him to afford them His continual protection and support. He saw, from that lightness and variableness of their conduct, that they might be easily led astray into idolatry, which was the breach of that stronger than matrimonial bond by which He and they were bound to each other. He was *jealous* for their *fidelity,* because He willed their invariable happiness.

On this gracious principle, He tells them, that *He visits the iniquity of the fathers upon the children unto the third and fourth generation of them that hate Him.* This necessarily implies, IF the children hate Him, as their fathers did, and continue to offend Divine justice, by walking in the same way. For no man can be condemned by the justice of God for crimes of which he never was guilty. This point has been for ever settled by God, in His most solemn declarations by the prophet *Ezekiel,* ch. xviii.

But, as *idolatry* was the same in reference to the breach of the covenant between *God* and the *people,* as infidelity is in reference to the marriage contract between the *husband* and *wife,* idolatry may be principally intended here; and, therefore, the visiting the sins of this kind, may refer to national judgments. By the withdrawing the Divine protection, the idolatrous Israelites were delivered up into the hands of their enemies, from whom, the gods in whom they had trusted could not deliver them. This, God did to the *third* and *fourth* generation, *i. e. successively,* as may be seen in every part of the Jewish history, and particularly in the book of *Judges.* Now God did this, not to punish *to destruction* or *extermination,* but to be the instrument of their amendment. And this became the grand and only efficient means in His hand of their deliverance from idolatry :—for, it is well known that, after the Babylonish captivity, the Israelites were so completely saved from idolatry, as never more to have disgraced themselves by it, as they had formerly done. These national judgments, thus continued from generation to generation, appear to be what is designed in the text, by *visiting the iniquity of the fathers upon the children unto the third and fourth generation.*

Those, therefore, who tread under foot God's commandments, shall be trodden under foot by God's judgments. But, see what He says to *them who love Him and keep His commandments* :—as they have *love* to Him, which is the principle of all obedience, so they *keep His commandments* ;—they *observe* their *nature, consider* their *authority, see* their great *usefulness,* and that it is their *interest* to obey them ; and, therefore, get the Holy Spirit to write them in their hearts, that they may practice them in their lives.

To these it is said, *He shews mercy.* Let it be observed, that even they who *love God* and *keep His commandments, merit* nothing from Him: and, therefore, the salvation and blessedness which they enjoy, come from the mere *mercy* of God.

*Shewing mercy unto thousands of them*, &c. ver. 6.

What a disproportion between the works of *justice* and *mercy* ! JUSTICE works to the *third* or *fourth ;*—MERCY, to *thousands of generations* !

Our blessed Lord might have had reference to this place, when He comprised the fulfilment of the whole law, in *love* to God and man. For, as we have already seen that *love* is the grand principle of obedience, and incentive to it, so there can be no obedience without it. It would be more easy, even in Egyptian bondage, to make brick without straw, than to do the will of God, unless His love be shed abroad in the heart by the Holy Spirit. *Love*, says the Apostle, *is the fulfilling of the law.* Rom. xiii. 10.

We see that this commandment prohibits every species of *external* idolatry; as the *first* does all idolatry that may be *internal* or *mental.* All *false worship* may be considered of this kind; together with all *image worship*, as we have already seen; as well as all superstitious rites and ceremonies. I have no doubt that the gross perversion of the simplicity of Christian worship, by the introduction of various *instruments of music* into churches and chapels, if not a species of idolatry, will at least rank with *will-worship*, and *superstitious rites* and *ceremonies*. Where the *Spirit* and *unction* of God do not prevail in Christian assemblies, priests and people being destitute of both, their place, by general consent, is to be supplied by *imposing ceremonies, noise*, and *show*.

### THE THIRD COMMANDMENT.

*Against False Swearing, Blasphemy, and Irreverent Use of the* NAME *of* GOD.

*Thou shalt not take the name of the Lord thy God in vain*, ver. 7.

The strong reason for obedience to this commandment, is included in itself; THE LORD THY GOD prescribes this. Oppose not His authority, for He is the LORD. Offend Him not, for He is THY GOD. The *first, second, third, fourth*, and *fifth commandments*, are proposed in the same way. " The

LORD THY GOD says, Thou shalt have no other gods before me." " Thou shalt not make to thyself any graven image, &c. for I, THE LORD THY GOD, am a jealous God." " Thou shalt not take the name of THE LORD THY GOD in vain." " Remember the Sabbath day to keep it holy,—for it is the Sabbath of THE LORD THY GOD." None of the other commandments is introduced in the same way. The *four* fifst commandments refer to God himself, and the *fifth* to our *parents*, who stand to us in the place of God, and next Him should be held in the highest respect; and, therefore, they have this peculiar sanction. Because He is the Lord OUR God, therefore we should keep these laws. And because our *neighbours* owe to us, and we to them, help, support, and kind offices, therefore we should keep the remaining five, by which the *whole human family* are bound to each other. All God's commands have a solid reason why they should be obeyed. All, who read as they should, will see this.

As the word שוא *shavé*, which we translate *in vain*, signifies not only *vanity*, a *vain thing*, but also *falsehood*, and a *lie*; the spirit of the commandment is, Do not invoke God to *witness* an *untruth*. He is the God of truth;—the devil is the father of lies and liars. Do not call on Him to pledge His truth to support a falsehood, nor shalt thou use the name of the Lord thy God in a falsehood or untruth. This would be the highest offence! And yet, how often is it committed? The word *in vain*, signifies for *no purpose*, to *no end*,—*uselessly*,—*triflingly*,—*lightly*,—without *respect*,—*irreverently*.

Now, this precept not only forbids all false oaths, but all common swearing, where the name of God is used, or where He is appealed to as a *witness of the truth*. It also necessarily forbids all light and *irreverent* mention of God, or any of His attributes; and we may safely add, that every prayer, ejaculation, and supplication, that is not accompanied with *deep reverence*, and the *genuine spirit of piety*, is here condemned also. So also, is the wicked mode of turning the name of *God*—of the *throne* of His glory, into *interjections*, and words to express *wonder, amazement, surprise*, &c. As *O God! O Lord! O heavens! Good God! O my God!* &c. &c. When it is evident, from the character of the persons, their habits, the nature of the circumstances in which they then were, that their *souls* were as truly without the *fear of*

*God,* as their *tongues* were without *respect* to the *company* or *reverence* to their *Maker.*

But the command may be, and is, broken in thousands of instances, in the *prayers,* whether *read* or offered *extempore,* of inconsiderate, bold, and presumptuous worshippers. To hear the most solemn prayers, expressing the sighing of a contrite heart, the desires of such as be sorrowful, the fervent breathings of the righteous after fuller communion with God; where the person considered not what he said, and had no feelings corresponding with the solemn words he uttered—is to witness an awful breach of the *third commandment,* which God will the more signally punish, because the excellent prayers came from feigned lips. And alas! how few are there who do not break this command both in their public and private devotions. How low is piety in the church of God, when we are obliged to pray in order to escape damnation,—" Lord, cleanse us from our secret faults! and pardon the *sins* of our *holy things!*"

Even *heathens* thought that the names of their gods should be treated with reverence: *Plato* (De Legib. lib. ix.) says, " It is most undoubtedly right not lightly to profane the names of the gods, using them as we do common names, but we should watch with purity and holiness all matters belonging to them."

But let us hear the solemn penalty—*the Lord will not hold him guiltless that taketh His name in vain.* Whatever the person himself may think or hope, however he may plead in his own behalf, and say, " he intends no evil, hopes he is sincere, and thinks it his duty to say the *good words,* which pious and learned men have put in the mouths of those who cannot make prayers for themselves," &c.; yet, if any man, in the above ways, or in any other way, take the name of the Lord his God in vain, God *will not hold him guiltless:*— He will account him *guilty,* and punish him for it. All common swearers, blasphemers, and those who in their prayers, or conversation, take the name of the Lord in vain, I would address in the nervous words of Mr. Herbert,—

" Take not His *name* who made thy mouth, *in vain:*
It gets thee nothing, and hath no excuse:
Pride and lust plead pleasure, avarice gain,
But the cheap swearer through his open sluice
Lets his soul run for nought, and nothing fearing.
Were I an infidel, I would hate *swearing.*"

## Against Profanation of the Sabbath, and Idleness on the other Days of the Week.

*Remember the sabbath day, to keep it holy,* ver. 8.

As this was the most ancient institution, God calls upon them to *remember* it. As if He had said, Do not forget that when I had finished the creation of the heavens and the earth, and all that is in them, I instituted the sabbath; and remember *why* I did so, and for *what* purposes.

The word ‏שבת‎ *shabath*, signifies *he rested*, and hence *shabath*, or sabbath, the *seventh day*, or the day of *rest*, or *rest* simply. In *six* days God created the heavens and the earth, and rested, that is, ceased to create on the *seventh* day; and has consecrated it as a day of rest for man. *Rest* to the body from labour and toil: and *rest* to the soul from all worldly cares and anxieties. He who labours with his *mind* on the sabbath day, is as culpable as he who labours with his *hands* in his ordinary calling. It is by the authority of God, that the sabbath is set apart for *rest* and religious purposes, as the *six days of the week* are appointed for labour. How *wise* is this provision! How *gracious* this command! It is essentially necessary not only to the body of man, but to all the animals employed in his service: take this away, and the labour is too great; both man and beast would fail under it. Without this consecrated day, religion itself would fail, and the human mind becoming sensualized, would soon forget its *origin* and *end*.

Even as a *political* regulation, it is one of the wisest and most beneficent in its effects of any ever instituted. Those who habitually disregard its *moral* obligation, are to a man not only *good for nothing*, but are *wretched* in themselves, a *curse* to society, and often end their lives *miserably.* The *idler* is next to the *sabbath-breaker.* As God has formed both the body and mind of man on principles of *activity*, so He designed him proper employment: and it is His *decree*, that the mind shall improve by *exercise*, and the body find increase of vigour and health in honest *labour*. He who *idles* away his time on the six days, is equally culpable, in the sight of God, as he who *works* on the seventh. The *idle person* is ordinarily clothed in *rags;* and it has ever been remarked in all Christian countries, that sabbath-breakers generally come to an ignominious death.

The appointment of the sabbath is the *first* command ever given to man ; and that the sanctification of it was of great consequence in the sight of God, we may learn from the various repetitions of this law : and we may observe that it has still for its object not only the benefit of the soul, but the health and comfort of the body also.

Because this commandment has not been particularly mentioned in the *New Testament*, as a moral precept binding on all, therefore some have presumptuously inferred, that there is *no sabbath* under the Christian Dispensation. Were there none, Christianity itself would soon become extinct, and religion would soon have an end. But why is not the moral obligation of it insisted on by our Lord and the Apostles ? They have sufficiently insisted on it,—they all kept it sacred, and so invariably did all the primitive Christians ; though some observed the last day of the week, the Jewish sabbath, instead of the first day, in commemoration not only of God's resting from His work of creation, but also of the resurrection of Christ from the dead. But to insist on the necessity of observing it, was not requisite, because none doubted of its moral obligation ; the question itself had never been disturbed ; not so with circumcision and other Mosaic rites. The truth is, it is considered as a *type*. All *types* are of full force, till the thing signified by them take place :—but the thing signified by the *sabbath*, is that *rest* in glory, which *remains* for the people of God, and in this light it evidently appears to have been considered by the Apostle, Heb. iv. As, therefore, the *antetype* remains, the moral obligation of the sabbath must continue, till time be swallowed up in eternity. The world was never without a *sabbath*, and never will be. And there is scarcely a people on the face of the earth, whether civilized or uncivilized, that has not agreed in the propriety of having a *sabbath*, or something analogous to it. But it has been objected, that the sabbath could be only of partial obligation ; and affect those only whose day and night were divisible into twenty-four hours ; and would never be intended to apply to the inhabitants of either of the polar regions, where their days and nights alternately consist of *several*

*months* each. This objection is very slight. The object of
the Divine Being is evidently to cause men to apply the
*seventh part of time* to rest: and this may be as easily done at
*Spitzbergen* as at any place under the equator. Nor is it of
particular consequence where a nation or people may begin
their sabbath observances;—whether it fall in with our, or
the Jewish, or even the Mohammedan sabbath, provided they
continue regular in the observance, and hallow to religious
uses this *seventh part of time.*

In His mercy, the Divine Being has limited our labour to
*six* days out of *seven.* In order to destroy the institution of
God, the *French National Assembly* divided time into *decads,*
and ordered every *tenth* day to be kept as a day of relaxation,
dissipation, and merriment. The offended God wrought no
miracle to bring back His institution; but, in the course of
His providence, He annihilated them and their devices, and
restored the sabbath, in spite of legislative enactments to the
contrary; and the people, bad as they were, rejoiced to be
put in possession of the sabbath which God had consecrated
to rest and religious uses, from the foundation of the world.

But let us remember, as before noted, that while we *rest*
on the *sabbath,* we do not *idle away* the other *six days.* The
Lord commands, *Six days shalt thou labour and do all thy
work,* ver. 9. Therefore, it has been justly observed, that he
who idles away time on the six days, is equally guilty before
God, as he who does his ordinary work upon the sabbath.

No work should be done on the sabbath, that can be done
on the preceding day, or can be deferred to the ensuing week.
Works of absolute *necessity* and *mercy,* are alone excepted.
He who works by his *servants* or *cattle,* is equally guilty as
if he worked *himself*: for God has commanded that both the
cattle, and the *male* and *female servants,* shall rest also. Yea,
the *slave* himself is included; for so the original word עבד
*âbed* often signifies. But in what a state of moral depravity
must those *slave-holders* be, who reduce their slaves to such
a state of wretchedness, that they allow them only the sabbath
day to *cultivate those grounds* from which they are to derive
their subsistence; having no food allowed them but what they
are able to bring out of the earth on that day in which the
supreme Lord has commanded their masters to give them *rest,*
and to require no *manner of labour from them.* Such ene-

mies to God must expect no common judgment from the justice of the Most High, whatsoever countries they may inhabit.

Where men are unmerciful to their own species, no wonder that they have no feeling for the *beasts* that perish. *Hiring out horses,* &c. for *pleasure* or *business, going on journeys, paying worldly visits,* or *taking jaunts* on the Lord's day, are breaches of this law. *Doth God care* for *oxen?* Yes, and He mentions them with tenderness—*that thine ox and thine ass may rest:*—How criminal to employ the *labouring cattle,* on the *sabbath,* as well as on the *other days* of the week! In *stage coaches,* and on *canals,* horses are in continual labour. In general there is no sabbath observed by the *proprietors* of those vehicles. Yet, so tender and scrupulous are some *proprietors,* that they would not on any account do any of these things themselves; but they can be *share*-holders in stage-coaches, wagons, canal boats, &c. &c. where the sabbath is constantly profaned, and from which they derive an *annual profit!* Good souls! ye would not do these things *yourselves;* you only hire *other persons* to do them, and you live by the profit! Take heed that you enter all these things punctually in your *leger,* for the day is at hand in which you must render a strict account. More cattle are destroyed in *England* than in any other part of the world in proportion, by continual labour. The noble *horse,* in general, has no *sabbath.* Does God look on this with an indifferent eye? Surely he does not. *"England,"* said a foreigner, " is the *paradise* of *women,* the *purgatory* of *servants* and the *hell* of *horses.*"

On this head, I conclude with, Reader, remember that thou keep holy the sabbath day—thou needest the rest of it for thy body; and the religious ordinances of it, for thy *soul.* God has hallowed it for these purposes: observe it as thou oughtest, and it will bring health to thy body, and peace to thy mind. So be it! Amen.

### THE FIFTH COMMANDMENT.

*Against Disrespect and Disobedience to Parents.*

*Honour thy Father and thy Mother, that thy days may be long upon the land,* &c. ver. 12.

Hear, ye children :—God has given us only *ten command-*

*ments,* essentially necessary to our happiness in our religious, civil, and domestic life; and one of the *ten* speaks of, and strongly recommends, obedience to parents. Nature and common sense teach us that there is a degree of affectionate respect which is owing to parents, and which no other persons can properly claim. For a considerable time, parents stand, in some sort, in the place of God to their children; and therefore rebellion against their lawful commands has been considered as rebellion against God. This precept, therefore, prohibits not only all injurious acts, irreverent and unkind speeches to parents; but enjoins all necessary acts of kindness, filial respect, and obedience.

We can scarcely suppose that man *honours* his parents who, when they fall *weak, blind,* or *sick,* does not exert himself to the uttermost in their support. In such cases God as truly requires the *children* to provide for their *parents,* as he required the parents to feed, nourish, instruct, support, and defend the children, when they were in the lowest state of helpless infancy. *Honour the Lord with thy substance,* says Solomon, Prov. iii. 9. On this the Rabbins say, *Honour also thy father and mother:* the LORD is to be thus honoured, *if thou have it:* thy *father* and *mother,* whether thou have it or not; for, if thou have nothing, thou art bound to *beg* for them. Nor will the Lord have that given to religious uses which the parents need. Our Lord has exposed, and deeply condemned this conduct. See Matt. xv. 5—9. Mark vii. 10—13.

All the *reasonable* commands of parents, children, while they are under their jurisdiction, should punctually obey. And even in cases where parents have no right to command, (as in matters of *religion,* which refer only to God and the conscience, and in the choice of *partners for life,* in which the parties themselves are alone interested, because they are to dwell together for life,) their *counsel* and *advice* should be respectfully sought, as their *age* and *experience* often enable them to speak oracularly on such a subject. But if the parents and children live in a state of peace and good understanding together, they will seldom disoblige each other in matters of this kind.

Children hate *death* and love *life*—they hope for many days, and the hope of happiness seems to smile continually on *them.*

To this feeling God addresses Himself: *Honour thy father and thy mother, that thy* DAYS *may be* LONG *upon the* LAND *which the Lord thy God giveth thee.* This, as the Apostle observes, Eph. vi. 2. is the *first commandment* to which God has annexed a *promise*, and therefore we may learn, in some measure, how important the duty is in His sight. In Deut. v. 16. it is added by the same spirit, *That it may go well with thee :* we may therefore conclude, that it will go *ill* with the disobedient : and there is little room to doubt, that the *untimely death* of many *young persons* were the judicial consequences of their disobedience to their parents. Most who come to an untimely end, are obliged to confess that *this,* with the breach of the sabbath, were the principal causes of their ruin. Reader, art thou guilty? Humble thyself therefore, before God, and repent.

1. As children are bound to succour their parents, so parents are bound to educate and instruct their children in all useful and necessary knowledge; and not bring them up either in *ignorance* or *idleness.*

2. They should teach them the fear and knowledge of God : for how can parents expect affection or dutiful respect from those who have not the fear of God before their eyes? Those who are the best *educated,* are generally the most affectionate and obedient.

### THE SIXTH COMMANDMENT.

#### Against Murder and Cruelty.

*Thou shalt not kill,* ver. 13.

God is the Fountain and Author of *life*—no creature can give life to another : an archangel cannot give life to an angel —an angel cannot give life to man—man cannot give life even to the meanest of the brute creation. As God alone gives life, so He alone has a right to take it away : and he who, without the authority of God, takes away life, is properly a *murderer.* This commandment, which is general, prohibits murder of every kind :—

1. All actions by which the life of our fellow-creatures may be suddenly taken away, or abridged.

2. All wars for extending empire, commerce, &c.

3. All sanguinary laws, by the operation of which the lives

of men may be taken away for offences of comparatively trifling demerit.

4. All bad dispositions, which lead men to wish evil to, or meditate mischief against, each other; for the Scripture says, *He that hateth his brother in his heart, is a murderer.*

5. All want of *charity* and *humanity* to the *helpless* and *distressed;* for he who has it in his power to *save the life* of another, by a timely application of succour, food, raiment, medicine, &c. and does not do it; and the life of the person either falls or is abridged on this account; he is, in the sight of God, a *murderer.* He who neglects to save life, is, according to an incontrovertible maxim in law, the *same* as he who takes it away.

6. All who by immoderate and superstitious fastings, macerations of the body, and wilful neglect of health, destroy or abridge life, are *murderers;*—whatever a false religion and ignorant superstitious priests may say of them. God will not have *murder* for *sacrifice.*

7. All *duellists* are *murderers*—almost the worst of murderers : each meets the other with the design of *killing* him. He who shoots his antagonist dead, is a *murderer:* he who is shot is a *murderer* also. The survivor should be hanged; the slain should be buried at a cross way, and the hanged murderer laid by his side.

8. All who put an end to their own lives by *hemp, steel, pistol, poison, drowning,* &c. are *murderers*—whatever coroners' inquests may say of them; unless it be clearly proved that the deceased was *radically insane.*

9. All who are addicted to *riot* and *excess;* to *drunkenness* and *gluttony;* to *extravagant pleasures,* to *inactivity* and *slothfulness;* in short, and in *sum,* all who are influenced by *indolence, intemperance,* and *disorderly passions,* by which life is prostrated and abridged, are *murderers:* for our blessed Lord, who has given us a new edition of this commandment, Matt. xix. 18. proposes it thus : *Thou shalt do* no *murder,*—no *kind* or *species* of murder; and all the above are either *direct* or *consequent murders;* and His beloved disciple has assured us, that *no murderer hath eternal life abiding in him.* 1 John iii. 15.

10. A man who is full of *fierce* and *furious passions;* who has no command of his own temper, may, in a moment, de-

stroy the life even of his *friend*, his *wife*, or his *child.* All such fell and ferocious men are *murderers;* they ever carry about with them the murderous propensity, and are not praying to God to subdue and destroy it.

### THE SEVENTH COMMANDMENT.

*Against Adultery, Fornication, and Uncleanness.*

*Thou shalt not commit adultery*, ver. 14.

The word adultery, *adulterium*, has probably been derived or contracted from *ad alterius thorum*—" to another's bed ;" for it is going to the bed of *another man*, that constitutes the *act* and the *crime.* Perhaps the derivation may be yet more simple : *ad alteram*—*to another woman ;* and she known to be the wife of another man. *Adultery*, as defined by our laws, is of two kinds :—*double*, when between *two married* persons : *single*, when one of the parties is *single*, the other *married.*

One principal part of the *criminality* of adultery, consists in its *injustice :*—1. It robs a man of his right, by depriving him of the *affection* of his wife. 2. It does him a *wrong*, by fathering on him, and obliging him to maintain *as his own*, a *spurious* offspring ; a child which is *not* his.

The *act* itself, and every thing *leading* to the *act*, is prohibited by this commandment ; for our Lord says, even *he who looks on a woman to lust after her, has already committed adultery with her in his heart.* For to such there is only *time* and *place* wanting, if the other party be willing, to complete the crime. And not only *adultery* is forbidden here, but *fornication* also ; as we may gather from our Lord's words, Matt. xv. 19. where, producing the commandments in order, He gives a *word* for *each ;* but when he comes to the *seventh*, He gives *two* words to express its sense :—" For out of the heart proceed evil thoughts, murders, μοιχιιαι, πορνιιαι, *adulteries*, *fornications*, thefts, false witness, blasphemies,"] thus shewing that *fornication* was included under *adultery*, in the seventh commandment.

Under this same prohibition, all *impure books, songs, paintings*, &c. which tend to inflame and debauch the mind, are included. And so is that crime, not proper to be named ; and more disgraceful, and in the sight of God and reason, more abominable than all the rest: and against which our laws are so severe, and the public odium more signally excited. I need not spend any time on the fact, that both *adultery* and *fornication* often mean *idolatry* in the worship of God. The reason of this, see in the beginning of this discourse.

### THE EIGHTH COMMANDMENT.

#### *Against Stealing and Dishonesty.*

*Thou shalt not steal*, ver. 15.

Thou shalt not take what is not thy own, and apply it to thy own use. All *rapine* and *theft* are forbidden by this precept: as well *national* and *commercial* wrongs, as petty larceny, highway robberies, house-breaking, private stealing, knavery, cheating, and defrauds of every kind. Also, the taking advantage of a buyer's or seller's ignorance, to give the one *less*, and make the other pay *more*, for a commodity than it is worth, is a breach of this sacred law. All withholding of *rights*, and doing of *wrongs*, are against the spirit of it.

But the word is principally applicable to clandestine stealing, though it may undoubtedly include all *political* injustice and *private wrongs*. And, consequently, all *kidnapping*, *crimping*, and *slave-dealing*, are prohibited here, whether practised by *individuals*, the *state*, or its *colonies*. I greatly doubt whether the *impress service* stands clear here. Crimes are not lessened in their demerit by the *number* or *political* importance of those who commit them. A *state* that enacts *bad laws*, is as criminal before God as the individual who breaks *good ones*.

It has been generally granted, that under the *eighth* commandment injuries done to *character*, the depriving a man of his *reputation* or *good name*, are included: and of a worse robbery than this, no knave can be guilty; and a greater loss no honest man can sustain: hence the correct and nervous saying of one of our best poets, which never suffers by being frequently quoted:—

> " *Good name* in man or woman, dear my lord,
> Is the immediate jewel of their souls:
> Who *steals* my *purse* steals *trash*, 'tis something, nothing;
> 'Twas *mine*, 'tis *his*, and has been *slave* to *thousands*;

But he that *filches* from me my *good name*,
*Robs* me of that which not enriches him,
And makes me *poor* indeed."

But among all *thieves* and *knaves*, he is the most execrable who endeavours to rob another of his character, that he may enhance his own : lessening his neighbour, that he may aggrandize himself.   This is that pest of society, who is full öf *kind assertions* tagged with *buts*.   " He is a good kind of man ; *but*—every bean has its black."   " Such a one is very *friendly ; but*—it is in his own way."   " My neighbour N. can be very liberal ; *but*—you must catch him in the humour."   Persons like these speak well of their neighbours, merely that they may have the opportunity to neutralize all their commendations, and make them suspected whose character stood deservedly fair, before the traducer began to pilfer his property.   He who repents not for these injuries, and does not make restitution, if possible, to his defrauded neighbour, will hear, when God comes to take away his soul, these words more terrible than the knell of death, *Thou shalt not* STEAL.   See under the *ninth* commandment ; and see Sermon **XXI.** on Psal. xv.

### THE NINTH COMMANDMENT.

*Against False Testimony, Perjury, Lying, and Deceit.*

*Thou shalt not bear false witness against thy neighbour,* ver. 16.

Though the word רֵעַ raâh, signifies to *feed* or *nourish,* and is used to express a *friend,* even one who is peculiarly *intimate :* yet it often means any person *living nigh* to another ; one of the *same village—an acquaintance.*   Here it signifies any person,—any human being,—a fellow-creature,—whether he rank among our *enemies,* or our *friends,*—whether he be near, or far off.

Not only *false oaths* to deprive a man of his *life* or of his *right,* are here prohibited, but also, all *whispering, tale-bearing, calumny,* and *slander,* where the object is to bring the neighbour to *pain, loss,* or *punishment.*   In a word, whatever is deposed as a *truth,* which is *false* in fact, and tends to injure another in his body, goods, or influence, is against the spirit and letter of this law.   *Suppressing the truth,* when known, by which concealment a man may be *defrauded* of his *property*, or his *good name ;* or lie under *injuries* or *disabilities*, which a *discovery* of the truth would have prevented, is also a crime under this law.   The conduct of every *liar* and *deceiver*, comes under the ban of this commandment.   The *liar* is always pretending to bear witness to the *truth ;* and yet his testimony is *false.*   A *liar*, who is *known* to be such, is detested of men : a *liar* is always known to be such, by the Searcher of hearts, and by Him is held in sovereign abhorrence.   He who bears a false testimony against even the *devil* himself, comes under the curse of this law, because his testimony is *false.*   God is the punisher of falsehood, though His *enemy* be its object.

### THE TENTH COMMANDMENT.

#### Against Covetousness.

*Thou shalt not covet*, ver. 17. תחמד לא *lo tachemod*—the word חמד *chamad*, signifies an *earnest* and *strong desire* after a matter, on which all the affections are concentrated and fixed, whether the thing be *good* or *bad.*   This is what we commonly term *covetousness*, which word is taken both in a *good* and *bad* sense.   So when the Scripture says, that *covetousness is idolatry :* yet it also says, *covet earnestly the best things ;* so we find that this disposition is sinful or holy, according to the object on which it is fixed.   In this command, the *covetousness* which is placed on forbidden objects, is that which is prohibited and condemned.   To covet in this sense, is intensely to long after, in order to enjoy a *property*, the *person*, or *thing*, coveted.   He breaks this command, who by any means endeavours to deprive a man of his *house*, or *farm*, by some *underhand* and *clandestine* bargain with the original landlord : what is called, in some countries, *taking a man's house and farm over his head.*   He breaks it also, who lusts after his neighbour's wife, and endeavours to ingratiate himself into her affections, by striving to lessen her husband in her esteem :—and he also breaks it, who endeavours to possess himself of the servants, cattle, &c. of another, in any clandestine or unjustifiable manner.   This is a most excellent moral precept, the observance of which will prevent all public crimes : for he who feels the force of the law which prohibits

the inordinate desire of any thing that is the property of another, can never make a breach in the peace of society by an
act of *wrong* to any of even its feeblest members.

Before I conclude, I feel obliged once more to reprehend
the bad faith of the church of Rome : we have already seen
that this church has in effect struck out the second commandment, relative to image worship, that she might have nothing
in the Bible that might directly testify against her idolatry :
and this fearful liberty she has taken in opposition to the original Hebrew, all the ancient and modern versions, her own
accredited versions—the Septuagint and the Vulgate ; and
against the judgment and usage of every other Christian
church on the face of the earth, all of which consider it as a
separate commandment. To colour this deceit, knowing that
God had given TEN commandments, and that *Himself* had expressly named this number, Deut. iv. 13. this church, after
having disposed of the *second*, by joining it to the *first*, in
order to keep up the number *ten*, divided the *tenth* commandment into *two*, against all Scripture, reason, and common
sense ; for the *tenth* commandment contains only *one subject*,
and that absolutely *indivisible* : it is against *covetousness*, and
against that only, as even a child may discern. This commandment divided into *two*, makes the *ninth* and *tenth*, of the
*church* of Rome, thus :—

" Commandment ix.  *Thou shalt not covet thy neighbour's
wife.*

" Commandment x.  *Thou shalt not covet his house, nor
his man-servant, nor his maid-servant, nor his ox, nor his
ass, nor any thing that belongs to him.*"

This division is without a difference : for it is the same
principle that covets the man-servant, the maid-servant, the
ox, the ass, or any thing that is his, as *that* which *covets* the
neighbour's *wife*, as she is most evidently included among the
*any things that are his.* In vindication of this division it
has been stated, that it is thus divided in the Hebrew text :—
it is true that in some of the Masoretic Bibles there is sometimes the space of a letter after the words רעך אשת *isheth
reèca*, " Thy neighbour's wife ;" but this is no authority to
make *two* commandments out of *one ;* and were we to consider
such a *space* as authority to divide a commandment, we
might make three or four different commandments out of the

D

*fourth;* for so many divisions it has in almost all Hebrew Bibles: besides, there are 239 MSS., and with them the *Samaritan*, which have been collated by *Kennicott* and *De Rossi,* that have no space after the above words: and out of *five* ancient MSS. in my own collection, there are *four* which have no such space.   The division is therefore arbitrary and un- authorised: and the making two commandments out of *one,* is *absurd,* in reference to the *sense,* and *sinful* in reference to the *design.*

Having now gone over this Decalogue, and endeavoured to give the true meaning of each precept, it might be thought proper to give the *sum* of the whole in such a way as they might be easily remembered; and readily applied to all parts of our moral conduct.   To do this would not be very difficult, but to do it *better* than it has been done in the common *Catechism* of the Church, would be a task indeed.   As every *adult* may not have the catechism at hand, and those who have learnt it when young, may have unfortunately forgotten it, I shall transcribe it here :—

" *Q.* What dost thou chiefly learn by these commandments?

" *A.* I learn *two* things; my duty towards God, and my duty towards my neighbour.

" *Q.* What is thy duty towards God?

" *A.* To believe in Him, to fear Him, and to love Him, with all my heart, with all my mind, with all my soul, and with all my strength: to worship Him, to give Him thanks, to put my whole trust in Him, to call upon Him, to honour His holy name and His word, and to serve Him truly all the days of my life.

" *Q.* What is thy duty towards thy neighbour?

" *A.* To love him as myself, and to do to all men as I would they should do unto me: to love, honour, and succour my father and mother: to honour and obey the king, and all that are put in authority under him: to submit myself to all my governors, teachers, spiritual pastors, and masters: to order myself lowly and reverently to all my betters: to hurt nobody by word or deed: to be true and just in all my dealings: to bear no malice nor hatred in my heart: to keep my hands from picking and stealing, and my tongue from evil-speaking, lying, and slandering: to keep my body in temperance, soberness, and chastity : not to covet or desire other men's goods; but to learn and labour truly to get my own living, and to do my duty in that state of life unto which it shall please God to call me."

It is no ordinary recommendation of the passages which I have quoted, that when the famous *Doctor Franklin* under-took to draw up a catechism upon moral and economical prin-ciples for the *Americans,* he incorporated the above passages in his work, with very little alteration, as peculiarly excellent.

As obedience to these commandments is so essentially ne-cessary, and they came to us *from* and *with* the *highest au-thority,* and that the fallen spirit of man is not able to observe them in their *letter* and *spirit* without the especial help of God, I do not think that a sincere heart can ever find more suitable expressions to clothe its desires, when praying for such help from God, than are contained in the *Collect* prefix-ed to these commandments, in the introduction to the *Com-munion-service* of our church, which I shall also subjoin :—

" Almighty God, unto whom all hearts are open, all desires known, and from whom no secrets are hid ; cleanse the thoughts of our hearts by the inspiration of thy holy Spirit, that we may perfectly love thee, and worthily magnify thy holy name, through Christ our Lord.    Amen."

And as every man must know that he *has* broken these commandments, and stands in need of God's *mercy* to pardon what is past, and His *grace* to *help* him in the *time* to come, it is with great propriety, that when the minister ends each commandment, the people cry out, " Lord, have mercy upon us, and incline our hearts to keep this law !"    And when the last is read, that they should all join with heart and voice in the following petition, which I must cordially recommend to all my readers,—" Lord, have mercy upon us, and write all these thy laws in our hearts, we beseech thee !"    We have *broken* them, and need *mercy*—we must *keep* them, but shall not do it, unless God *incline* our hearts to do it, and write them *all upon our hearts* by the finger of His power, as that *finger* wrote the originals on the tables of stone !    Amen, so be it, Lord Jesus !

# SERMON XVIII.

## THE LORD'S PRAYER.

MATTHEW, Chap. vi. ver. 5—13.

5. And when thou prayest, thou shalt not be as the hypocrites are: for they love to pray standing in the synagogues, and in the corners of the streets, that they may be seen of men. Verily, I say unto you, they have their reward.

6. But thou, when thou prayest, enter into thy closet, and when thou hast shut thy door, pray to thy Father which is in secret; and thy Father which seeth in secret shall reward thee openly.

7. But when ye pray, use not vain repetitions, as the heathen do: for they think that they shall be heard for their much speaking.

8. Be not ye therefore like unto them: for your Father knoweth what things ye have need of before ye ask Him.

9. After this manner therefore pray ye: Our Father which art in heaven, hallowed be thy name.

10. Thy kingdom come; thy will be done in earth as it is in heaven.

11. Give us this day our daily bread:

12. And forgive us our debts as we forgive our debtors.

13. And lead us not into temptation, but deliver us from evil: for thine is the kingdom, and the power, and the glory, for ever. Amen.

In speaking on this subject, I shall first consider,—

I. The nature of prayer.

II. The object of prayer.

III. The end aimed at by praying.

IV. What we are to avoid in order to pray successfully.

V. Those petitions that contain all that is necessary for the welfare of the supplicant in the Lord's prayer.

VI. The doxology.

I. Of the nature of prayer:—or an answer to the simple, but very important question, *What is prayer?*

Prayer has been defined, " An offering of our desire to

God for things lawful and needful, with a humble confidence
to obtain them through the alone merits of Christ, to the praise
of the mercy, truth, and power of God;"—and " its *parts* are
said to be *invocation, adoration, confession, petition, pleading,
dedication, thanksgiving,* and *blessing.*" Though the *definition* be imperfect, yet, as far as it goes, it is not objectiona-
ble : but the *parts* of prayer, as they are called, (except the
word *petition,*) have scarcely any thing to do with the *nature*
of *prayer ;*—they are in *general,* separate acts of devotion,
and attention to them in what is termed *praying,* will entirely
mar it, and destroy its efficacy.

It was by following this division, that *long prayers* have
been introduced among Christian congregations, by means of
which, the spirit of devotion has been lost : for where such
prevail most, listlessness and deadness are the principal characteristics of the religious services of such people ; and these
have often engendered *formality,* and, frequently, total indifference to religion. Long prayers prevent kneeling, for it is
utterly impossible for man or woman to keep on their knees
during the time such last. Where these prevail, the people
either stand or sit. *Technical* prayers, I have no doubt, are
odious in the sight of God ; for no man can be in the *spirit
of devotion* who uses such : it is a drawing nigh to God with
the *lips,* while the heart is (almost necessarily) far from Him.

The original words in ancient languages, generally afford
the best definitions of the *things* of which they are the signs ;
for as *names* were first given from necessity, and for con-
venience, terms were used which were borrowed from *actions*
by which some remarkable property or properties of the subject were expressed. " For, the imposition of *names* cannot
be considered as arbitrary ; but for some cause, on account
of some eminent property, attribute, or action ; in short, for
some reason appertaining to the thing which bears that name ;
and hence," says a learned philologist, " the *verb* and the *adjective,* between which there is a great affinity, generally point
out the nature of the *noun ;* the one expressing its *action* and
*state,* the other its *property* and *quality.* Hence too, it appears, the *verb* is the proper *radix* or *root* of the word : for
when a *noun* cannot be brought to a *verb,* it will be impossible to have a clear conception of its meaning ; and it will
appear to be a mere arbitrary sign."

Let us apply these observations to the original words of
the text :—*When thou prayest*—Οται προσευχη. The word
προσευχη, *prayer*, is compounded of προς, *to*, or *with*, and ευχη,
a *vow ;* because, to pray aright, a man *binds* himself to God
as by a *vow*, to live to His glory, if He will grant Him his
grace. The verb ευχομαι, signifies to *pour out prayers*, or
*vows*, from ευ, *well*, and χεω, *I pour out*, probably alluding to
the *offerings* or *libations*, which were *poured out before*, or
*on the altar*. As in ancient times, prayers were scarcely ever
offered to the Divine Being, without *sacrifice* or *oblation ;*
hence the *reason* of the word which is used to express *prayer*.
*Sacrifice* was therefore understood to be essentially necessary
to *prayer ;* because the supplicant, conscious of his guilt,
brought a *sacrifice* to make *atonement* for it ; and to this he
joined *fervent prayer*, that the Object of his worship would
accept the sacrifice in reference to the purpose for which it
was offered. And on the other hand, sacrifice always implied prayer,—prayer, that the evils deserved and dreaded
might be turned away ; the transgression pardoned by which
the guilt was incurred ; and divine strength obtained by which
future transgression might be prevented : and all this would
be naturally accompanied with serious *resolutions* to avoid
the evil and choose the good, in future, and to live so as not
to displease Him from whom the supplicant sought so great a
favour :—hence the *vow*.

Now, these *prayers, resolutions*, and *vows*, were all founded on the *merit* of the *sacrifice* which was brought, and not
on account of the mere *act of praying*, or the *words* produced. As prayer, therefore, which necessarily implied the
earnest desire of the heart to receive mercy from the hand of
God to pardon sin, and grace to help in time of need, is ever
accompanied with a due sense of sin, and the supplicant's total
unworthiness of the blessings he requests, knowing that he
has forfeited life and every good by his transgressions, and
cannot depend on any thing that he has *done*, is *doing*, or
can *do*, to atone for his sin ; therefore, he brings his *offering*,
and the *offering* of *sacrifice* is *essential* to the completion or
perfection of his prayer, and the gracious answer which he
solicits. This has been the true notion of prayer, not only
among the *Jews*, but even among all *heathen nations*, where
any sacrificial system prevailed, and should be the notion of

it in all *Christian countries*, where the *passion* and *death* of JESUS CHRIST are considered a *sacrifice for sin*: and this is the light in which they are universally exhibited, both in the *Old* and *New* TESTAMENTS.

A proper idea of prayer, therefore, is, " *the pouring out the soul* before God, with the hand of faith placed on the head of the *Sacrificial Offering*, imploring mercy, and presenting itself a *free-will offering* unto God, giving up body, soul, and spirit, to be guided and governed, as may seem good to His heavenly wisdom; desiring only, perfectly to love Him, and serve Him with all its powers, at all times, while it has a being."

As a man, to pray aright, must be in this spirit, must feel himself *wholly dependent on God*, therefore, prayer is the *language of dependence*: he who prays not, is endeavouring to live *independently* of God: this was the *first curse*, and continues to be the *great curse* of mankind. In the beginning Satan says, " eat this fruit, and ye shall then be as God." That is, ye shall be *independent*: the man hearkened to his voice,—ate the fruit,—sin entered into the world; and notwithstanding the full manifestation of the *deception*, the ruinous system is still pursued; man will, if possible, live *independently of God*: hence, he either *prays not at all*, or uses the *language* without the *spirit* of prayer.

II. Who, or what is the object of prayer?

As the object of *true faith* is GOD, so is HE the Object of *prayer*: but the *word* of *God*, and especially His *promises*, are also the objects of prayer: for it is the fulfilment of the *promises* contained in that word, unto which the prayer of faith must have its eye directed. But even the *Scriptures* are but a *secondary object* of *faith* and *prayer*:—they, it is true, contain God's *truth*; but they cannot accomplish *themselves*: God alone can give them their fulfilment. Both the *understanding* and the *will* are here engaged: for *truth* is the object of the *understanding*; as *good* is the object of the *will*, we *believe* the *truth*, in order to get the *good*. Therefore, the Lord saith, *Take with you words, and come unto the Lord; say unto Him, Take away all iniquity, and receive us graciously; so will we render the calves of our lips;* that is, we shall present Him the sacrifice promised, and give Him due *praise* for the mercy He sends. See Hos. xiv. 2. and Heb. xiii. 15.

GOD, therefore, on His *mercy-seat*, is the *Object* of *prayer;* and to fix the mind, and prevent it from wavering, the supplicant should consider Him under such *attributes* as are best suited to his own state and wants. There are THREE *general views* which may be taken of this divine Object:—*Infinite Wisdom,*—*Infinite Power,*—*Infinite Goodness.* There are few blessings we want that do not come from *one* or *other* of these *three sources:* we are either *ignorant,* and want *instruction;*—*weak,* and need *power;*—*wretched,* and need *mercy.* As we *feel,* so we should pray; and, in order to feel aright, and pray successfully, we should endeavour to find out our state; to discover our most pressing wants; and to find these, we need much *light,* which the *Holy Spirit* alone can impart; hence, strange as it may appear, we must *pray,* before we *begin to pray.* We must pray for light to discover our state, that our eye may affect our heart, in order to go successfully to the great Object of prayer, to get our wants summarily supplied. We must pray first to *see* what we need; and then we shall pray to get our wants supplied.

III. What is the end proposed by our praying?

The *end* is, *to get our souls finally saved;*—to become wiser and better; to answer the *end* for which God has made and preserved us:—*viz.* to love Him with all our soul, mind, and strength, and to live only to glorify Him. The *end* for which Christ came into the world, and shed his blood for us: —*viz.* that we might be saved from our sins,—that we might bear the image of the heavenly Adam, as we have borne the image of the earthly Adam; and shew forth the virtues of Him who has called us from darkness into His marvellous light;—to follow Him not only in His immaculate life, but to *go about doing good;* and as far as we can, live to promote the happiness of our fellow-creatures. In a word, to regain here, that state of holiness from which we have fallen,—the image and likeness of God:—for in this image and likeness we were created. From these we have fallen;—and to restore us to these, the Lord Jesus was incarnated for us, and died; the Just, for the unjust, that He might bring us to heaven.

This is the great and important *end* for which we should

pray, and for which we should live. Life at longest, is but short; and every hour has work for itself;—therefore, there is no time to spare;—not one hour that we can afford to lose: and besides, life is uncertain, we cannot assure ourselves of *one day* or *hour*:—no, we cannot be certain that we shall live beyond the *present moment.* What need have we then to pray; to call incessantly upon God, that the great work for eternity may be speedily completed, that when He doth appear, we may be found of Him in peace, without spot, and without blame, and have an entrance into the holiest by the blood of Jesus. Let us live then in order to die well,—and live well, that we may live to all eternity! No man is fit to live, that is not fit to die: and no man is either fit to die safely, or to live usefully, who is not living to God. Hence the absolute necessity for *prayer*, that we may receive mercy and grace.

IV. What are we to *avoid*, in order to pray successfully ?

Our Lord answers this question, by shewing us that there are *three* evils which we must avoid in prayer. 1. *Hypocrisy.* 2. Mental dissipation. 3. Much *speaking*, or unmeaning *repetition.*

1. HYPOCRISY.—*When ye pray, be not as the hypocrites.* The word *hypocrite*, signifies one who *personates another* —a *counterfeit*, a *dissembler*—one who would be thought to be *different* from what he *really* is :—who, although he is not *religious*, wishes to be *thought* so;—and performs as many duties of it, as he can, and in the most *ostentatious* way, in order that others may be *persuaded* that the *character* which he *assumes* is genuine, and that he is a true *follower of God*, though he has nothing of religion, but the *outside.*

The Jewish hypocrites *loved to pray standing in the synagogues, and in the corners of the streets, that they might be seen of men.* What were called the *phylacterical prayers* of the Jews, were long; and the *canonical* hours obliged them to repeat those prayers *wherever* they happened to be at such hours; and so full were they of a vainglorious hypocrisy, that they are said to have contrived to be *overtaken* in the streets and market-places, by the *canonical hours*, that they might be seen by the people, and applauded for their great and exemplary devotion. As they had no piety but what was *outward*, they endeavoured to let it fully appear, that they might make the most of it among the people. They prayed *standing*, for it would not have answered their end to *kneel* before God, for *then* they might have been *unnoticed* by *men*, and consequently have lost that *reward* of which they were in pursuit—the applause of the multitude. I have seen some Rabbins, the most celebrated in Europe, walk the streets of a great city, uttering in the most solemn manner their prayers, with the head and eyes frequently turned towards heaven, apparently unconscious of those who met them in the streets. These might have been *sincere*, but their conduct appeared very similar to that of their ancient brethren, which our Lord here reprehends.

But persons professing *Christianity* may be equally hypo- critical; though in a different way: all *showy* religion is a *hy- pocritical* religion. Imposing rites and ceremonies, calcula- ted merely to blind the eyes of the understanding, by ex- citing carnal feelings—speaking to the *animal passions* in- stead of to the *mind*, in order to please men, and make their party strong—is *hypocrisy*; abominable hypocrisy in the sight of God. All ministers and others, who study to use fine expressions in their prayers, rather complimenting than pray ing to God, rank high among the *hypocrites*: and instead of being applauded by men, should be universally abhorred by their congregations. That prayer which is the genuine ef- fusion of a heart deeply impressed with its own necessities, and the presence of God, is invariably as *simple* as it is *fer- vent* and *unostentatious*.

2dly. Our Lord warns us against *mental dissipation. But* THOU, *when thou prayest, enter into thy closet*, &c. Though this exhortation may particularly concern *private prayer*, yet there is a sense in which it may be applied to prayers in *public* also. The address is very emphatic and impressive, Συ δι στη προσευχη εισιλθι εις το ταμιιον σου,—*But* THOU, (whoso- ever thou art, *Jew, Pharisee*, or *Christian*,) *when thou pray- est, enter into thy closet*. Prayer is the most *secret* inter- course of the soul with God, and as it were, the conversation of one heart with another. The world is too profane, and treacherous, to be of the party, and in the secret; we must *shut the door* against IT, with all the affairs that busy and amuse it. Prayer requires *retirement*, at least of the *heart*; for this may be properly termed the *closet*, in the *house of*

*God;* which *house* the *body* of every real Christian is; so St. Paul, 1 Cor. iii. 16.    To this *closet* we must always retire, even in public worship, and in the midst of company.    The very eyes should be guarded : they often affect the heart in such a way, as to mar and render unprofitable this most solemn act of devotion.    The objects that they see will present images to the mind, which call off, or *divide* the *thoughts,* and produce that *wandering of heart,* so frequently complained of by many religious people; whose own unguarded eyes and thoughts are the *causes* of those wanderings which spoil their devotions :—I never could understand how any man can have a *collected mind,* or *proper devotion* in *prayer,* who, while he is engaged in it, has his eyes *open,* not indeed fixed on *one point,* but wandering through the house, beholding the evil and the good ;—he *must* be distracted, and his prayers such, unless technical, or got by heart : then indeed he may *say* his prayers, but he cannot *pray* them.    To *fix the heart,* is it not well to get this impression fixed deeply in the mind. " I am praying to that God who, in His infinite condescension, calls Himself *my Father, and He seeth in secret*—every feeling, apprehension, volition, and operation of the heart, is under His eye ?"    A sense of the divine presence has a wonderful tendency to quiet and fix the heart.

3dly.  Our Lord guards us against *vain repetition*—using *unmeaning words,* or words expressing no sense which the heart at the time apprehends.    Saying the *same things over and over again,* generally to *fill up the time,* or, as our Lord states, under the supposition *that they shall be heard for their much speaking.*    Our Lord's words are μη βαττολογησητε, *Do not battologise :* " This word," says an ancient Greek grammarian, " came from one *Battus,* who made very prolix hymns, in which the same idea frequently occurred."    The following observations on this point, by the late very learned Mr. *Gilbert Wakefield,* I have ever admired :—" A frequent repetition of awful and striking words, may often be the result of earnestness and fervour, see Dan. ix. 3—20 : but great length of prayer, which will of course involve much sameness and idle repetition, naturally creates fatigue and carelessness in the worshipper, and seems to suppose *ignorance* or *inattention* in the Deity ; a fault against which our Lord more particularly wishes to secure them, see ver. 8. ;"

.—and he illustrates this from the *Heautontimoreumenos* of *Terence.*

> Ohe! jam desine deos, Uxor, gratulando *obtundere,*
> Tuam esse inventam gnatam ; nisi illos ex *tuo ingenio judicas*
> Ut nil credas *intelligere,* nisi idem *dictum sit centies.*
>
> " *Pray thee my wife, cease from* stunning *the gods with thanksgivings because thy daughter is in safety; unless thou judgest of* them, *from* thyself, *that they cannot* understand *a thing, unless they are told of it* a hundred times."

I have said elsewhere, speaking on this subject, prayer requires more of the *heart,* than of the *tongue.* The eloquence of prayer consists in the fervency of desire, and the simplicity of faith. The abundance of fine thoughts, studied and vehement motions, and the order and politeness of the expressions, are things which compose a mere *human harangue,* not a *humble and Christian prayer.* Our trust and confidence should proceed from that which God is able to *do in us,* and not from what we *say to Him.* " It is abominable," said a Mohammedan, " that a person offering up prayers to God, should say, ' I beseech thee by the glory of thy heavens,' or, ' by the splendour of thy throne ;' for conduct of this nature would lead to suspect that the Almighty derived glory from the heavens, whereas the heavens are *created,* but God with all His attributes is eternal and inimitable."

It was a maxim among the Jews, that, " He who *multiplies prayer,* must be heard."—And this would be correct did it only refer to a *continuance in prayer,* or *supplication :* but the urging the same request, and speaking the some words *repeatedly,* without proper attention and reverence, is that which our Lord condemns, and of which, not only the *heathens,* but *Jews,* and *Mohammedans,* are guilty ; and not a few of those who are called *Christians,* follow their steps.

It is not merely to tell God our wants, or to shew Him our state, that we are to pray ; for He knows this state, and these wants, much better than ourselves.; but to get a suitable *feeling* of the pressure of these wants, and the necessity of having them supplied ; and *this* we obtain by looking into our hearts and lives ; for here particularly the *eye affects the heart,* and from the urgency of the necessity, we feel excited to pray earnestly to God, for his mercy : and our confessing them before Him affects us still more deeply—induces us to be more fervent—and shews us that none but God can save and defend. And it is only to people who feel thus, that God will shew

His mercy. He who obtains this blessing of God, after feeling that he was undone and lost without it, will duly prize it, watch over, and keep it, and give God alone the whole glory of the grace that has brought him into this *state of salvation.*

V. I come now to consider those *petitions* which contain all that is essentially necessary for the present and eternal welfare of the petitioner; which are all comprised in our LORD'S PRAYER.

### THE PREFACE.

*After this manner, therefore, pray ye,* ver. 9.

We learn from Luke xi. 1. that it was in consequence of a request of one of His disciples, that our Lord taught them this prayer;—*And it came to pass, that, as He was praying in a certain place, when He ceased, one of His disciples said unto Him, Lord, teach us to pray, as John also taught his disciples. And He said unto them, When ye pray, say, Our Father, &c.*

*Forms* of *prayer* were frequent among the Jews; and every public teacher gave one to his disciples. Some *forms* were *drawn out* to a considerable *length,* and from these *abridgements* were made: to the latter sort, the following prayer properly belongs; and consequently, besides its own important use, it is a *plan* for a more *extended devotion.*

What a satisfaction is it to learn from God Himself, with *what words,* and in *what manner* He would have us to pray to Him, so that we might not pray in vain. A king who draws up the petition which he allows to be presented to himself, has doubtless the fullest determination to grant the request. This is a most important consideration, and, properly viewed, will tend much to strengthen our faith when we pray to Him who has given us this *form.*

It may be justly said, that we do not consider the *value* of this prayer; the *respect* and *attention* which it requires; the *preference* to be given to it; and the *spirit* in which it should be offered. *Lord, teach us how to pray!* is a prayer necessary to prayer; for, unless we be divinely instructed in the *manner,* and influenced by the *spirit* of true devotion, even the prayer taught by Jesus Christ himself may be repeated without spiritual profit. They are to be pitied who, in their public devotions, *neglect this prayer*.    To say it is not *en-joined* thus, is a pitiful objection.    Christ used it as *it is*, and taught his disciples so to use it.    Though capable of *great extension*, yet there is no evidence that any such *public use* was made of it.    If it contain only the *principles* of *prayer*, and the *model* according to which our prayers should be formed, He who taught knows best what is contained in these principles : and when in simplicity and godly sincerity we offer to Him these very *principles*, in which He will ever recognize His own hand and His own heart, He will not fail to give us those blessings which are included under these petitions, even to their utmost extent.

But even they who use it in their public devotions, seem to use it in the *wrong place:* should we not *begin* our addresses to God with this prayer ?—and then *after that manner, continue* our requests to a reasonable length.    But whether used in the *beginning, middle,* or *end,* let it never be *forgotten.*

Our Father.—It was a maxim of the Jews, that a man should not pray *alone,* but join with the *Church ;* by which they particularly meant, that whether *alone,* or in the *Synagogue,* he should use the *plural* number, as comprehending all the followers of God.    Hence they say, " Let none pray the *short* prayer,"—*i. e.* as they expound it, the prayer in the *singular,* but in the *plural* number.

This prayer was evidently made, in an especial manner, for the *children of God :* and hence we are taught to say, not *my* Father, but, *our* Father.    " The heart of a child of God, is a brotherly heart, in respect of all other Christians : it asks nothing but in the spirit of *unity, fellowship,* and *Christian charity,* desiring *that* for its brethren, which it asks for itself."

The word *Father,* placed here at the beginning of the prayer, includes two grand ideas, which should serve for a foundation to all our petitions ; 1. That tender and respectful love which we should feel for God, such as that which well-bred children feel for their fathers.    2. That strong confidence in God's love to us, such as fathers have for children. Thus, all the petitions in this prayer stand in the strictest reference to the word *Father ;* the three first, to the *love we have for God;* and the four last, to that *confidence* which we have in *the love He bears to us.*    The relation in which we stand to this first and best of Beings, dictates to us *reverence* for His *Person; zeal* for His *Honour; obedience* to His *will; submission* to His *dispensations* and *chastisements*, and *resemblance* to His *Nature:* When we consider that He is *our Father*, to whom we come, and that it is He who bids us *come*, we may indeed come with boldness to the throne of Grace, and expect all that He has promised, and all that we need. O, what a privilege is contained in this consideration!

*Which art in heaven; ὁ ἐν τοῖς οὐρανοῖς*—WHO *art in the heavens.* The word *which*, properly belongs to *things*, though it was often formerly used instead of *who*, which refers to *persons:* but *who* is certainly the most proper in this place, for there is no *ambiguity* in the original *article.* But it is a matter of little moment, in our addresses to that Being who, in His own person, is neither *masculine, feminine*, nor *neuter*. He is *Illud Inexprimabile*,—that Ineffable,—that Inconceivable, as Cicero expresses the Supreme Unknown Being. He has, however, called Himself *Our Father*, and commanded us so to address Him. We see Him, therefore, as our Father, and lose sight of all other distinctions.

*In heaven*,—or, *in the heavens.* This phrase in Scripture seems used to express,

1st. His OMNIPRESENCE.—*The heavens of heavens cannot* CONTAIN *thee*, 1 Kings viii. 27.;—that is, Thou fillest immensity.

2dly. His MAJESTY and DOMINION over His creatures.— *Art thou not God in heaven, and* RULEST *thou not over* ALL THE KINGDOMS OF THE HEATHEN? 2 Chron. xx. 6.

3dly. His POWER and MIGHT.—*Art thou not God in heaven, and in thy hand is there not* POWER *and* MIGHT, *so that no creature is able to withstand Thee.* 2 Chron. xx. 6. *Our God is in* HEAVEN, *and hath done whatsoever He pleased.* Psal. cxv. 3.

4thly. His OMNISCIENCE.—*The Lord's throne is in* HEAVEN: *His eyes behold, His eye-lids try the children of men.* Psal. xi. 4. *The Lord looketh down from Heaven; He* BEHOLDETH ALL THE SONS OF MEN. Psal. xxxiii. 13.

5thly. His *infinite* PURITY and HOLINESS.—*Look down from thy holy habitation, from heaven*, &c. Deut. xxvi. 15. *Thou art the high and lofty One, who inhabitest eternity, whose name is Holy.* Isai. lvii. 15.

So that when we address Him as our *Father*, who is in the *heavens*, we should remember these things as descriptive of the Being, and the attributes of that Being which we address.

### FIRST PETITION.

*Hallowed be thy name!* ver. 9.

This may be considered as a petition with which we begin our prayer.   Now that we are about to address Thee, may we conceive aright of thy Majesty, and come before Thee with the deepest reverence and humility!

The word *sanctify*, literally means *to make holy*.   In this sense we can never apply it to GOD; but the original word *αγιασθητω*, comes from *a*, which signifies *negative*, and *γη, the earth*:—a thing *separated from the earth*, or *from earthly purposes* and *employments*.   As the word *sanctified* or *hallowed*, in Scripture, is frequently used for the *consecration* of a *thing* or *person*, to a *holy use* or *office*; as the *Levites*,— the *first-born*,—the *tabernacle*,—the *temple*,—their different *utensils*, &c.; which were all set apart from every earthly, common, or profane use, and employed wholly in the service of God; so the Divine Majesty may be said to be *sanctified* by us, in analogy to those things;—*viz.* When we in our hearts *separate Him from*, and in our minds, conceptions, and desires, *exalt* Him *above earth, and all created things*. When, in our addresses to Him, we thus *separate* Him from all *human passions*,—from *changeableness, fickleness,* and *caprice*.   When we represent Him to ourselves not *inexorable*, but *easy to be entreated*; not *unwilling*, but *ready* to save: not giving to one *more readily* than to another, who is in the same necessitous circumstances; not as being unwilling *now*, to hear and grant, though He may be willing at some *future time*:—for these things seem to attribute to Him not only *human passions*, but some of the *worst* of those *passions*.   This sanctifying is a thing of great consequence: for improper and unworthy views of God, often prevent or suspend the exercise of *faith;* and we too frequently imagine God to be something like to ourselves;— irresolute in mind, slow to resolve, difficult to be entreated: feeling an unreasonable attachment to *some*, while he feels an abhorrence, equally unreasonable or capricious, of *others*. These views are unworthy of God : He is not like man,—He is not like ourselves. To any praying soul, He is *now*, and *ever must be*, the Fountain of mercy,—the Well-spring of salvation,—always ready to pour out the streams of blessedness to all them that call upon Him; and ever, *ever more ready to hear than wē are to pray, and ever wont to give more than we desire or deserve.*

Farther, God's NAME, signifies God himself, with all the attributes of His Divine Nature,—His power, mercy, goodness, justice, and truth; and this name we may sanctify or hallow,

1st. With our *lips*,—when all our conversation is *holy*, and we speak of those things which are edifying, and meet to minister grace to the hearers.

2dly. In our *thoughts*,—when we repress every rising evil, think chastely, repress all unholy, vain, and disorderly imaginations; endeavouring to have all our tempers regulated by His grace and Spirit.

3dly. In our *lives*,—when we begin, continue, and end all our works to His glory,—having an eye to Him in all we perform; then every act of our common employment will, in His sight, be as an act of religious worship. It is possible so to *eat* and *drink*, that every meal we eat we may feel to be a *sacramental* repast.

4thly. We may *hallow* His *name* in our *families*,—when we endeavour to bring up our children in His discipline and admonition,—instructing also our *servants* in the way of righteousness,—and by having the *Holy Scriptures read*, and *prayers daily offered* in our dwellings. And thus, our *houses* may become *houses of God*,—*tabernacles* or *temples* where prayers and thanksgivings are daily laid upon that altar that sanctifies the gift.

5thly. We *hallow* God's name and *honour* Him, in a particular *calling* or *business*,—when we separate the falsity, deception, and lying, commonly practised, from it; buying and selling as in the sight of the *holy* and *just* God; not mixing superior and inferior articles together, as multitudes do, and selling the mass as pure and unmixed, and of the first quality. How will such dealers appear before God!

## SECOND PETITION.

*Thy kingdom come !* ver. 10.

The meaning of this petition we may collect from the *ancient Jews*, and from their *expectation.* " He prays not at all (say they) in whose prayers there is no mention of the *kingdom of God.*" " Let Him cause His *kingdom* to reign, and His redemption to flourish ; and let the *Messiah* speedily come and deliver His people !" The *kingdom of Christ*, His government in Judea, and His deliverance of them from the Roman yoke, was that which *they* expected : *we* know that the great King of this kingdom is come, and that the government is on His shoulder; and of the increase of His government and kingdom there shall be no end. We should pray that it may increase more and more, for God has promised that it shall be exalted above all kingdoms. Dan. vii. 14—27. And that it shall overthrow all others, and be at last the Universal Empire, see Isai. ix. 7. The *kingdom of heaven* and the *kingdom of God*, mean, (as used in the Scriptures,) the *dispensation of infinite mercy and manifestation of eternal truth by Christ Jesus :* producing the true knowledge of God, accompanied with that worship which is pure and holy, worthy of Him who is its Institutor and Object.

God's government of the world is called His *kingdom*, and it is called so, because it has its *laws*,—all the precepts of the gospel ; its *subjects*,—all who believe in Christ Jesus ; and its KING,—the Sovereign of heaven and earth.

The *kingdom of heaven*, says the Apostle, is *not meat and drink, but righteousness, peace, and joy in the Holy Ghost.* Rom. xiv. 17. It does not consist in the gratification of *sensual passions*, or *worldly ambition*, it is the *government of God* among men, a counterpart of the kingdom of glory upon the earth. It is *righteousness*, without mixture of *sin ;* peace, without *strife* or *contention ; joy in the Holy Ghost—* spiritual joy or happiness, without mixture of *misery.* And all this, it is possible, through the grace of our Lord Jesus Christ, to enjoy here below. " How then does heaven differ from this state?" It makes the RIGHTEOUSNESS *eternal*, the PEACE *eternal*, and the JOY *eternal.* This constitutes the HEAVEN OF HEAVENS. In the world, His followers may have tribulation ; but in Him, they shall have *peace:* and He has spoken these words unto us, that *our joy may be full.* We should pray that *this kingdom* may speedily come into the *nation* at large—into the *whole earth*, into our own *neighbour-hood* and *family*, and into our own *souls.* Ever pray, and constantly look for *this* kingdom,—it is *coming*,—it is *at* *hand*,—it is *among us !*

### THIRD PETITION.

*Thy will be done*, ver. 10.

This petition is properly added immediately after the pre-ceding. For when the *kingdom* of righteousness, peace, and joy in the Holy Ghost, is established in the heart, there is then an ample provision for the *fulfilment* of the divine *will.*

The will of God is infinitely wise, good, and holy: to have it *done* among men, is to have infinite *wisdom, goodness,* and *holiness, diffused* throughout the *universe;* and the *earth* filled with the *fulness of God.*

The *will* of God is the measure of all good ; when that is *done*, every thing relative to the *end* and *perfection* of that *Thing* or *Person*, is accomplished. With respect to the sal-vation of man, let us observe,

1st. That the salvation of the soul is the result of *two wills* conjoined ; the *will of God* and the *will of man.* If God do not *will* the salvation of man, man cannot be saved : if man do not *will* the salvation which God has provided for him, he cannot be delivered from his sins.

2dly. This petition certainly points out a *deliverance from all sin*, for nothing that is *unholy* can consist with the *divine will ;* and if this be fulfilled in man, surely sin shall be eradi-cated from the soul.

3dly. This is farther evident from these words, *as it is in heaven:*—*i. e.* as the angels do it : for they obey with all *zeal, diligence, love, delight,* and *perseverance.*

4thly. Does not the petition plainly imply, we may, through Christ strengthening us, live *without sinning against God ?* Surely, the holy *angels* never mingle *sin* with their *loving obe-dience ;* and as our Lord teaches us to pray, that we may do His will *here*, as the angels do in heaven, can it be thought He would put a petition in our mouths, the fulfilment of which is impossible ?

5thly. This petition, thus understood, certainly overthrows the assertion, "There is no such state of purification to be attained here, in which it may be said, *the soul is redeemed from sinful passions and desires.*" It destroys this objection, for, it is *on earth* that we are commanded to pray, that this *will,* which is our *sanctification,* may *be done.*

6thly. Our souls can never be truly happy till our *wills* be entirely subjected to, and become one, with the will of God.

7thly. How can any person offer this petition to his Maker who thinks of nothing *less* than the performance of the will of God, and of nothing *more* than the doing his *own ?*

Some see the mystery of the Holy Trinity in the *three* preceding petitions :—The *first,* being addressed to the FATHER, as the source of all Holiness.  The *second,* to the SON, who established the kingdom of God upon earth.  The *third,* to the HOLY SPIRIT, who, by His energy works in men both to *will* and to *perform.*

To offer these *three petitions* with success at the throne of God, *three graces,* essential to our salvation, must be brought into exercise : and indeed, the petitions themselves necessarily suppose them :—

FAITH ; OUR FATHER.—For he that cometh to God must *believe* that He is.

HOPE ; *Thy kingdom come.*—For this grace has for its objects, things that are *future.*

LOVE ; *Thy will be done.*—For love is the incentive to, and principle of all *obedience* to *God,* and *beneficence* to *man.*

The man who can with a truly enlightened mind and clear conscience, say, from the bottom of his heart, THY WILL *be done !* has attained to a very high degree of Christian perfection.

### THE FOURTH PETITION.

*Give us this day our daily bread,* ver. 11.

God has made man *dependent* on Himself, for meat, drink, life, breath, and all things !

And as He has given us no promise that we shall live till *to-morrow,* we have only to seek for a *daily* provision ; we should live to-day and trust for to-morrow, knowing that he who lives every *present* day for *eternity,* is always prepared to meet his God.

But the word επιουσιον, has greatly perplexed critics and commentators. I find upwards of thirty different explanations of this word. It is found in no Greek writer before the Evangelists; and *Origen* says expressly, αλλ' εοικε πεπλασθαι υπο των Ευαγγελιστων, *but it was formed by the Evangelists themselves.* The interpretation of *Theophylact*, one of the best of the Greek Fathers, has always appeared to me to be the best, Αρτος επι την ουσιαν και συστασιι αυταρκης,—" Bread necessary for our substance and support ;"—*viz.* that *quantity* and *quality* of food which is necessary to *support* our *health* and *strength,* by being *changed* into the *substance* of our bodies. The word επιουσιον, is compounded of επι and ουσια, *upon* or *above our substance;* that is, the bread that is proper for the support of the human system.

There may be an allusion here to the custom of *travellers* in Asiatic countries, who were wont to *reserve a part of the food given them the preceding evening, to serve for their breakfast or dinner the next day.* But as this was not sufficient for the whole day, they were therefore obliged to depend on the Providence of God for the additional supply. In Luke xv. 12, 13. ουσια signifies what a person has to *live on,* his whole *patrimony,* be it *more* or *less;* and nothing can be more natural than to understand the compound word επιουσιος, of that *additional supply* which the traveller needs to complete the provision necessary for a day's eating, over and above what he had in his possession. See *Harmer.*

After all, the word is so very peculiar and expressive, and seems to have been made on purpose by the Evangelists, in order to express their Lord's meaning, that more than merely *bodily* nourishment seems to be intended by it. Indeed, many of the ancients understood it as comprehending that *daily supply* of 'grace, which the *soul* requires to keep it in spiritual health and vigour. He who uses this petition would do well to keep both meanings in view; for he has both a *body* and *soul* which must depend on, and receive from the bounty of God their support.

To make this more impressive, let us note a few particulars :—

1. God is the *Author* and *Dispenser* of all *temporal* as well as *spiritual* good.

2. We have *merited* nothing that is good at His hands;

and therefore, must receive it as a *free gift*. *Give us to day*, &c.

3. We must *depend* on Him *daily* for support: we are not permitted to ask any thing for *to-morrow*: give us *to-day*.

4. That petition of the ancient Jews is excellent—"Lord, the necessities of thy people Israel are many, and their knowledge small, so that they know not how to disclose their necessities: let it be thy good pleasure to give to every man what sufficeth for food." Thus they expressed their *dependence*, and left it to God to determine *what was best and most* suitable. We, also, must ask only what is necessary for our support, God having promised neither *luxuries* nor *superfluities*. Daily support for our bodies, and daily support for our souls, is all that we need, and this we should pray for ; and this we have reason to expect from a bountiful and merciful God ; and then leave it to Him to employ that body and that soul as He pleases. We are His servants ; He calls us to labour : and no man will expect his servants to fulfil their task if they have nothing to eat. God, our heavenly Master, will give us bread for both worlds.

### THE FIFTH PETITION.

*And forgive us our debts, as we forgive our debtors*, ver. 12.

There is a little difference between this petition as it stands *here*, and that in the parallel place, Luke xi. 4. Here it is, *Forgive us our debts,* αφες ημιν τα οφειλημα ημων—*forgive us our debts*, or, *what we owe to thee ; as we forgive our debtors,* τοις οφειλεταις ημων —those who stand indebted to us —understanding in both cases, that both were *insolvent :—we* are indebted to *thee*, but we cannot pay ; we are totally insolvent ; if thou exact, we must be cast into the everlasting prison of hell :—*our debtors* are *insolvent* ; they have neither *money* nor *goods ;* if we go to the extremity of the law, we may arrest their persons, sell them and theirs, or put them in prison for life. *We* are touched with *compassion* for *them*, and therefore *forgive* them the debts they owe us. Be thou moved with compassion to us—we can pay thee *nothing of* the mighty debt we owe, therefore, in thy mercy, forgive our debts to *thee !*

In the gospel of Luke it stands, και αφες ημιν τας αμαρτιας

them—and *forgive us our* sins—*our transgressions* of thy *law*, which expose us to thy curse. But the next clause agrees in substance with the text in *Matthew*, και γαρ αυτοι αφιεμεν παντι οφειλοντι ημιν—*for we also forgive every one that is indebted to us*; that is, all that are *insolvent* and cannot pay, to such we *forgive the debt*, and do not, as the *law* would authorise, sell the person, or throw him into prison, where he must lie for life.

In cases of *debt*, where the person was insolvent, the law empowered the creditor to *sell the debtor, and his wife, and his children, and all that he had*, to pay the debt. Matt. xviii. 25. Or to *throw the debtor into prison*, where he was to be detained till *he had paid the uttermost farthing*. Matt. v. 25, 26. xviii. 34.

*Sin* is here represented as a *debt* which we have contracted with God: and as our sins are *many*, they are represented as *debts*—whatever we have *done, said,* or *thought,* against the holy law of God, is a *sin:* or in other words, *evil thoughts,* including *unholy* and *disorderly passions—evil words,* whether *blasphemous* against *God,* or injurious to our *fellows: evil acts,* whether against the *letter* or *spirit* of the *law,* or *against both,*—are *sins, transgressions of the law;* and consequently *debts* to divine justice. God made man that he might live to His glory, and gave him a *law* to walk by: and if, when he does any thing that tends not to glorify God, he contracts a debt with divine justice, how much more is he *debtor,* when he *breaks* the law by *actual transgression!* By the law of his creation, man is bound at all times and places to love God with all his soul, mind, heart, and strength—and this *love,* which is the *principle* of *obedience,* must lead to every *thought, appetite, purpose, word,* and *deed,* by which God may be glorified—and this *every man owes to his Creator;* and this he could *have done,* had he never *fallen* from God by a transgression which he might have avoided. Ever since his fall, even the *thoughts of his heart have been evil, and that continually;* and his *words* and *actions* have borne sufficient evidence of the depravity of his heart. Man is *wholly sinful,* and in all his *acts* a SINNER; hence his *debt*—his *inconceivable debt* to his Maker. From these things the reasonableness of endless punishment, has been argued: " All the attributes of God are reasons of obedience; those attributes in their

number, as well as in their nature, are *infinite :* every sin is
an *act of ingratitude* or *rebellion* against all these attributes;
therefore, sin is infinitely sinful, and deserves endless·punish-
ment." It is enough that the sinner is incapable of helping
or renewing himself; if he pass through the time of *probation*
without seeking and finding the salvation of God, and die in
his sin, where God is he can never come—he is incapable of
glory :—and as his sinful nature *continues* its operations even
in the *place of torment*, these are *continual reasons* why that
punishment should be *continued.* When we can prove that
the gospel shall be preached in hell, and offers of salvation,
free, full, and present, be made to the *damned,* then we may
expect that the *worm* that *dieth not,* shall die ; and the *fire*
that is *not quenched,* shall burn out !

We are taught in this petition to ask the forgiveness of our
sins and debts : our Lord does not tell us to *fall down before*
*the feet of our heavenly Master,* and say, *have patience with*
*me, I will pay thee all.* No. Of this payment, there is no
hope : the thing is impossible. Man has nothing to pay :
and if his sins and debts be not *forgiven,* they must be
charged against him for ever, as he is absolutely insolvent,
and so completely ruined in his moral constitution, that he is
*past work.* If he be forgiven and set up anew, and his *moral*
*health restored,* then he may, and will *work,* as a proof that
his Lord has had *mercy upon him,* and not only pardoned his
offences, but has healed his spiritual diseases. Thus he will
work, *not to merit heaven,* for this he must have as a *free gift ;*
as the kingdom of God, which is of infinite value, cannot be
purchased with *his money*—indeed he has none—what he
has is his Lord's ; and no man can purchase God's glory, by
God's *grace. Forgiveness* and *glory* must come from the
*free mercy* of God in Christ :—and how strange is it,—we
cannot have the *old debt* cancelled, without contracting a *new*
*one* as great as the old ! But the *credit* here is transferred
from *justice* to *mercy !*

While *sinners,* we are in debt to infinite *justice ;* when
*pardoned,* in debt to endless *mercy :*—and as a continuance
in a state of grace necessarily implies a continual communication of *mercy,* so the debt goes on increasing *ad infinitum !*
Strange economy in the Divine Providence, which by rendering a man an infinite *debtor,* keeps him eternally *dependent*

on his Creator! How good is God! And what does this state of *dependence* imply? A union with, and a participation of the Fountain of eternal goodness and felicity!

But there is a *condition* which God requires, in order to the *forgiveness of sins;* not an *equivalent* for his transgression:—of this man is incapable:—*Forgive our debts, as we forgive our debtors.* It was a maxim among the ancient Jews, that no man should lie down on his bed, without forgiving them that had offended him. *Forgive,* says Christ, *and ye shall be forgiven—for, if ye forgive not men their trespasses, neither will your heavenly Father forgive yours.* That man condemns himself to suffer eternal punishment, who makes use of this prayer, with *revenge* and *hatred* in his heart. He who will not attend to a *condition* so advantageous to himself (remitting 100 *pence* to *his* debtor, that his own *creditor* may remit him 10,000 *talents*) is a madman, who to *oblige* his neighbour to suffer an *hour,* is himself determined to suffer *everlastingly!*

This condition of *forgiving our offending neighbours,* though it cannot possibly *merit* any thing, yet it is *that condition,* without which, God will pardon no man. The goodness and indulgence of God towards us, is the pattern we should follow in our dealings with others. If we take men for our exemplar, we shall err, because our *copy* is a *bad one,* and our lives are not likely to be better than the *copy* we imitate. We should follow Christ, and be merciful as our Father who is in heaven is merciful—surely he who wishes to learn to write, cannot complain of the fairness of his copy! Let us put a case here:—Reader, hast thou a *child* or *servant* who has *offended thee,* and humbly asks forgiveness? Hast thou a *debtor,* or a *tenant* that is insolvent, and asks for *a little longer time?* And hast thou not forgiven that *child* or *servant?* Hast thou not *given time* to that *debtor* or *tenant?* How, then, canst thou ever expect to see the face of a *just* and *merciful* God! Thy *child* is *banished,* or *kept at a distance:* thy *debtor is thrown into prison,* or thy *tenant is sold up:*—yet the *child* offered to *fall at thy feet;* and the *debtor* or *tenant,* utterly insolvent, prayed for a *little longer time,* hoping that God would enable him to *pay thee all:* but to these things the *stony* heart and *seared* conscience paid no regard! O monster of ingratitude! Scandal to human na-

F

ture, and reproach to God! Go, and if thou canst, hide thy self—even in *hell*—from the face of the Lord! Learn, therefore, to *give* and *forgive*—and never turn away thy face from any poor man, so the face of God shall never be turned away from thee.

### THE SIXTH PETITION.

*And lead us not into temptation*, ver. 13.

The word πειρασμον, may be here rendered *sore trial*—from πειρω, to *pierce through*, as with a *spear*, or *spit;* used so by some of the best Greek writers. *Bring us not into sore trial*, i. e. *do not suffer us to be thus tried*—this is a mere Hebraism, where God is represented as *doing* what He only *permits to be done;* the word not only implies *violent assaults* from *Satan*, but also *sorely afflicting circumstances*, none of which we have yet grace enough to bear. This place was so understood by several of the primitive fathers, who have added some such words as these, *quam ferre non possimus*, " which we cannot bear."

The word *temptation* is generally taken to express a strong excitement *to sin;* but if the *leading of God* be considered *literally* here, this sort of *temptation* cannot be meant. St. James settles this point; *Let no man say, when he is tempted,* πειραζομενος, *I am tempted of God,* (απο του Θεου πειραζομαι ;) *for God cannot be tempted with evil, neither tempteth He any man.* Jam. i. 13. Therefore *trials* and *difficulties* must be here intended,—things which may come in the ordinary course of providence, and which the petitioner has not fortitude to meet, nor strength to bear; and which God can either turn aside, or give extraordinary strength to support. Taking the word in its *common acceptation*, and that *lead us not* is to be understood, *do not permit us*, to be overthrown by any devices of our adversaries, whether *men* or *devils;* we are to observe, that the prayer is not *do not permit us to be tempted*. This God will not answer to any man, for *temptation* is a part of our *Christian warfare;* and Jesus, our Lord and Pattern, was *tempted*, and sorely tempted too; and has, by His temptation, shewed us how we may foil our adversary, and glorify our God in the day of such a visitation. The original is very emphatic, και μη εισενεγκης ημας εις πειρασμον, and lead us not in, into temptation. The word εισενεγκης, comes from *αοφμω*, *to bring* or *lead in*,—and this is compounded of *ας, into*, and *φιρω, to bring*, or *lead*; taking this kind of *double entry* into consideration, there is room enough for the criticism that states, " *into* is more than *in* ;"—a man may be tempted, and *in* a state of temptation, without entering *into* it : entering *into* it, implies, giving way, closing in with, and embracing it. That man has *entered into* a *temptation*, who feels his heart *inclined* to it, and would act accordingly, did *time, place*, and *opportunity* serve. Christ was *tempted* even to *worship the devil*; but He *entered* not *into* any of the temptations of His adversary ;—the prince of this world came and found nothing in Him—no evil nature *within*, to join with the evil temptation *without*. Now, a man may be on the verge of falling by some powerful and well circumstanced sin—he may be *in* it; but the timely help of God may succour him, and prevent him from *entering into it ;*—and thus a brand is plucked from the burning. He was *heated*, yea *scorched* by it, but was saved from the desolating and ruinous act. This may be one meaning of this most important petition : and thus the poet,—

" O, do thou always warn
My soul, of *danger near :*
When to the *right* or *left* I turn,
The voice still let me hear,
*Come back !* *this* is the *way ;*
*Come back !* and walk *herein ;*
O may I *hearken* and obey,
And *shun the path of sin.*"

We see the *progress of temptation* in the case of *Achan*, and his *entering into* it. 1. *He saw a rich Babylonish garment, and a wedge of gold.*—There was no sin in simply *seeing* it. 2. *When he saw it, he coveted it.*—Here he *felt* the temptation, it began to gain possession of his *heart*. 3. *He took it.*—Here he *entered* fully *into* it, but conscious of his iniquity, and afraid of exposure and punishment; he, 4. *hid it among the stuff,*—hid it in such a way that it could not be found out, but by God himself. We see from this, and many other cases, that temptation may come,

1. As a *simple, evil-thought.*
2. A *strong imagination*, or impression made upon the imagination by the *thing* to which we are tempted.
3. *Delight* in viewing it, with the opinion that, if *possessed*, it would be *useful.*

4. *Consent* of the will to perform it. Thus *lust* is conceived, *sin* is finished, and *death* is brought forth. Jam. i: 15.

Our Lord's advice to His disciples, Matt. xxvi. 41. may be an illustration of this petition—*Pray that ye enter not into temptation, the spirit indeed is willing, but the flesh is weak.* " Ye may be tempted; do not *enter into it :* for though your hearts may be now *right* with God, and ye are willing to go even unto prison or death for my sake, yet the *flesh* is weak : it may be overcome—my power only can save you : but this cannot be expected where the means are not used : therefore *watch* and *pray*, or your fall is inevitable." *O Lord, let us fall into no sin!* Amen.

### THE SEVENTH PETITION.

*Deliver us from evil*, ver. 13.

Ρυσαι ἡμας απο του πονηρου—*Deliver us from the devil*, or *wicked one.*

*Satan* is expressly called ὁ πονηρος, *the wicked one*, Matt. xiii. 19 and 38; compare with Mark iv. 15., Luke viii. 12. This epithet of *Satan*, comes from πονος, *labour, toil, sorrow, misery*, because of the *drudgery* that is found in the way of *sin*, the toil and *sorrow* that accompany and follow the commission of it, and the *misery* which is entailed upon it, and in which it ends. This is a good description of him who *seeketh rest and findeth none*—who *goes about* as a *roaring lion*, seeking whom he may devour; of him who can truly say—" Where'er I go is hell; myself am hell." And all they who are his children partake of his nature, and of his restless *wretchedness*—the wicked are like the *troubled sea* that can *never rest*, but is always *casting up mire and dirt.* To be *delivered* from the *paw of this lion*, is no small mercy; to have him bruised under our feet, is a *great triumph.* Rabbi Judah was wont to pray thus : " Let it be thy good pleasure to deliver us from impudence and impudent men : from an evil man, and an evil chance : from an evil affection, an evil companion, and an evil neighbour; from *Satan*, the destroyer, from a hard judgment, and a hard adversary !" I have remarked among the simple, honest inhabitants of the counties of *Antrim* and *Londonderry*, in *Ireland*, that the common name for the *devil* or *Satan*, was *The Sorrow :* a good sense of the original word, *ὁ πονηρος*, the *wicked one*, the *evil one*, the SORROW. He who is *miserable* himself, and whose aim is to make all others so. Where *sin* is there is *sorrow*. Deliver us from the *evil*, *toil*, *labour*, *sorrow*, and *misery* of *sin!* Lord, hear the prayer!

*Deliver us—ρυσαι ἡμας*, a very expressive word—*break our chains—loose our bands—snatch, pluck* us from the evil and all its calamitous issues. The word *deliver* seems to imply that we are already in the hand, or less or more under the power of the *adversary*. It is an awful thing to be either *under the power of evil*, or in the *hand of Satan*. How earnestly should we offer up this petition to God, that we may be saved from a danger so imminent; that being deliver-ed out of the hands of our enemies, we may serve God in righteousness and true holiness before Him, all the days of our life! Amen.

Some make but *one petition* of the *two* latter; they appear to me to be *sufficiently distinct*—the *former* leads us to pray against *excitement to sin*—the *latter*, against the *consequence* of having *given place to the devil*. It is a different thing to pray against solicitations to sin—and to pray to get the thoughts of our hearts cleansed by the inspiration of God's holy Spirit: the *first* says, *May we sin against thee no more!* —the *second* says, *Deliver us from the power, condemnation, and pollution* of the crimes which we have already commit-ted! They are very different petitions: and this considered, there are doubtless *seven petitions* in the Lord's Prayer.

### THE DOXOLOGY.

*For thine is the kingdom, and the power, and the glory, for ever. Amen.* ver. 13.

The whole of this *Doxology* is rejected by *Wetstein, Gries-bach*, and the most eminent critics, as being omitted by many ancient MSS., *versions*, and *fathers*. The authorities on which it is rejected, may be seen in the above writers. *Gries-bach* seems perfectly convinced that it never made a part of the sacred text, originally.

Now, as this *Doxology* is at least *very ancient*, and was in use among the *Jews*, as well as *all the other petitions of this excellent prayer*, it should not, in my opinion, be left out of the text, merely because some *manuscripts, ancient versions,* and *ancient ecclesiastical Greek writers,* have omitted it ; and because those which retain it, write it *variously.*

It may be considered as giving a reason for the preceding petitions. Thou canst *do* all that we have requested ; for *Thine is the kingdom*—that kingdom, the coming of which thou hast commanded us to pray *for.* See *this* explained under the *Second Petition.*

*And the power ;*—that *energy* by which this kingdom is raised up, governed, and maintained—the *power* that *rules over all,* and can do all things.

*And the glory ;*—honour and praise shall redound to Thee in consequence of having established the kingdom of grace, by the gospel, upon earth, in sending thy Son to bless us, by turning us away from our iniquity, and setting up the kingdom of righteousness, peace, and joy in the Holy Ghost, in the hearts of them who believe. To THEE *alone* all this shall be ascribed, for THOU art the *universal King,* in the *universal kingdom,*—THOU art the *almighty* Ruler in heaven, earth, and hell. To THEE appertains the *glory* of having made both worlds, of sustaining them by the word of thy power, and of having redeemed mankind by the blood of thy Son.

*For ever ;*—εις τους αιωνας, *to the for evers,* or, as some authorities have it, νυν και αει και εις τους αιωνας των αιωνων, *now, and for ever, and for ever and ever,*—or, *to ages of ages,*—or, *to the evers of evers.* In such cases we often use *for ever* and *ever,*—or, *for evermore.* The first *ever,* taking in the whole duration of *time ;* the second *ever,* all the *eternity* that is to *come.* The original word, αιων, comes from αει, *always,* and ων, *being,* or *existence.* This is Aristotle's definition of it.

There is no word in any language that more forcibly points out the grand characteristic of eternity,—that which *always exists.* It is often used to point out a limited time, the *end* of which is not known. But this use of it is only an *accommodated* one ; and it is the grammatical and proper sense of it, which must be resorted to in any controversy concerning its scriptural meaning.

We sometimes use the phrase *for evermore*—*i. e. for ever and more ;* which signifies the *whole of time,* and the *more,* or interminable duration beyond it.

*Amen.* This word is Hebrew, אמן *aman,* and signifies

*faithful,* or *true.* The word itself implies a confident resting of the soul in God; with the fullest assurance that all these petitions shall be fulfilled to every one who prays according to the directions given here by our blessed Lord; to whom be ascribed the kingdom, the power, and the glory, for ever and ever! Amen.

An old English divine has given the following illustration of the Lord's prayer, which is well worth the reader's attention :—

*Our Father,* Isai. lxiii. 16.

| | |
|---|---|
| By right of creation, | Mal. ii. 10. |
| By bountiful provision, | Psal. cxlv. 16. |
| By gracious adoption, | Eph. i. 5. |

*Who art in heaven,* 1 Kings viii. 43.

| | |
|---|---|
| The throne of Thy glory, | Isai. lxvi. 1. |
| The portion of Thy children, | 1 Pet. i. 4. |
| The temple of Thy angels, | Isai. vi. 1. |

*Hallowed be Thy Name,* Psal. cxv. 1.

| | |
|---|---|
| By the thoughts of our hearts, | Psal. lxxxvi. 11. |
| By the words of our lips, | Psal. li. 15. |
| By the works of our hands, | 1 Cor. x. 31. |

*Thy kingdom come,* Psal. cx. 2.

| | |
|---|---|
| Of Providence to defend us, | Psal. xvii. 8. |
| Of grace to refine us, | 1 Thess. v. 23. |
| Of glory to crown us, | Coloss. iii. 4. |

*Thy will be done on earth, as it is in Heaven,* Acts xxi. 14.

| | |
|---|---|
| Towards us without resistance, | 1 Sam. iii. 18. |
| By us without compulsion, | Psal. cxix. 36. |
| Universally, without exception, | Luke i. 6. |
| Eternally, without declension, | Psal. cxix. 93. |

*Give us this day our daily bread,* Isai. xxxiii. 16. Psal. civ. 14.

| | |
|---|---|
| Of necessity, for our bodies, | Prov. xxx. 8. |
| Of eternal life, for our souls, | John vi. 34. |

*And forgive us our trespasses,* Psal. xxv. 11.

| | |
|---|---|
| Against the commands of Thy law, | 1 John iii. 4. |

Against the grace of Thy gospel,         1 Tim. iii. 13,

*As we forgive them that trespass against us,* Matt. vi. 15.

By defaming our character,            Matt. v. 11.
By embezzling our property,           Philemon 18.
By abusing our persons,               Acts vii. 60.

*And lead us not into temptation, but deliver us from evil,*
                    Matt. xxvi. 41.

Of overwhelming affliction,           Psal. cxxx. 1.
Of worldly enticements,               1 John ii. 15.
Of Satan's devices,                   1 Tim. iii. 7.
Of error's seduction,                 1 Tim. vi. 10,
Of sinful affections,                 Rom. i. 26,

*For thine is the kingdom, and the power, and the glory, for*
                    *ever,* Jude 25.

Thy kingdom governs all,              Psal. ciii. 19.
Thy power subdues all,                Philip. iii. 20.
Thy glory is above all,               Psal. cxlviii. 13,

                *Amen,* Ephes. i. 11.

As it is in thy purposes,             Isai. xiv. 27.
So it is in thy promises,             2 Cor. i. 20,
So be it in our prayers,              Rev. xxii. 20.
So it shall be to thy praise,         Rev. xix. 4.
                    BERNARD'S *Thesaurus,*

HEYDON-HALL, MIDDLESEX,
        *Oct.* 3, 1828,

# SERMON · XIX.

## THE TRAVELLER'S PRAYER.

### LITURGY OF THE CHURCH OF ENGLAND.

O Lord, our heavenly Father, Almighty and everlasting God, who hast safely brought us to the beginning of this day; defend us in the same with thy mighty power; and grant, that this day we *fall* into no *sin*, neither *run* into any kind of *danger;* but that all our doings may be ordered by thy governance, to do always that is righteous in thy sight : through Jesus Christ our Lord.  *Amen.*

## ADVERTISEMENT.

PERHAPS it may be necessary to state, that the ensuing discourse, most certainly of a singular kind, owes its origin to the following circumstance :—

On Dec. 17, 1817, I was providentially called to take a journey from Liverpool to Hull, in company with an intelligent and pious friend.  Being alone, we had on the way some useful conversation, relative to the circumstances of such religious people as were obliged to pursue their business by frequent journeys both by *sea* and land, in which no privacy could be enjoyed ; and where, consequently, that *daily walk,* which a Christian should observe towards his Maker, was often so unavoidably interrupted, that it was next to impossible to have a recollected mind, or a heart regularly turned to God by prayer and supplication.

In our discussion of this subject, we both agreed, that to have a *solemn form of well chosen words,* by which the mind could fully express itself, in reference to its circumstances, without the labour of looking for suitable expressions, must be of great utility ; and to both of us, the *third Collect for Grace*, in the Liturgy of our excellent Church, appeared to contain both the *ideas* and *words*, which above all others, were best suited to such occasions, and in which every Christian heart could join.

On that occasion, I termed this Collect *The Traveller's Prayer ;* and from that day formed the resolution, whenever I should be able to command a sufficiency of time, to write a short discourse upon it, not only to recommend this very suitable and comprehensive *form*, for this very purpose ; but also to explain the import and force of every expression, that they who should use it in such pilgrimages, might have the full benefit of it, by praying not only with the *spirit*, but with the *understanding* also.

The purpose then made, and of which I have never lost sight, one day's rest, after the fatigues of a long sea-voyage, and land journey, has given me an opportunity to fulfil : and judging that the prayer, *thus considered*, may be as profitable to others as it has been to myself, I venture to make it public : and, I have no doubt, that every *serious reader* will heartily join with me in praying that the many thousands of those who are exposed to the inconveniences and perils of travelling by land and by water, and the suspension more or less of religious duties through such journeyings, may be enabled to avail themselves effectually of the *prayer* itself, and of this little help towards a better understanding, and more extensive use of it : and that there may be in this case, as in all others, a *continuity* in that *thread* of devotion which should run through the whole *web* of life : so that in all the day, that may constitute the years of their pilgrimage, they *fall* into no *sin*, neither *run* into any kind of *danger*.

May His presence and blessing be the reader's portion ! and after the *journey of life* is ended, may he have an abundant entrance into the Holiest by the blood of Jesus, where *sin* can never come, and where *danger* can have no place !

---

1. WITH the business of life there are many untoward and hurrying circumstances connected, which, in their natural operation, are unfriendly to personal piety ; and therefore re-

quire much watchfulness and prayer, that while we are, as duty binds us to be, *diligent in business*, we may also be *fervent in spirit*; that while we are serving ourselves, we may not forget to *serve the Lord*. Where the favour and blessing of God are, there are necessarily peace and safety: and where His blessing is not, there is no health—no prosperity.

2. In order to *obtain* this blessing, and *secure* this favour, there must be not only a very humble reliance on His mercy and protection, but also fervent supplication for the grace necessary to enable us to pass through things temporal, so as not to lose those that are eternal.

3. Even in the use of *lawful things*, we may lose our souls: for lawful things may be used unlawfully, and thus, that which was intended to be a blessing, may become a snare; and eventually a curse. He who is not aware of this dangerous possibility, will not watch against it; and therefore *his fall* is unavoidable. How necessary then is the wise man's advice, *Acknowledge Him in all thy ways, and He will direct thy steps*. Let us take care first, that the *way* be right— that the business or employment by which we endeavour to get our bread, be just and honest:—that it be a *lawful* business—one *useful* to society—one that, in the course of His Providence, God may smile on: and let us see that in the *way* or *manner* of our conducting it, there be neither *avarice* nor *falsity*.

4. When, on examination, we find all is right, not only as to the business, trade, or calling, by which we hope to gain the necessaries of life for ourselves and those who are dependent on us; but also, that we are endeavouring with a pure conscience to conduct the *lawful* business *honestly*, without guile or deceit, we are authorised to expect God's blessing; and consequently success in our honest labour. But for all this God must be inquired after to do it for us;—that is, to bless and prosper our lawful endeavours, so that we may be able to provide things honest in the sight of all men. For, remember, that it is the Lord that giveth thee power to get wealth.

5. All these considerations strongly shew the absolute necessity of prayer to Him who is the Creator and Governor of all things, and the Disposer of all events. " But how can we *pray*, or be spiritually collected, while travelling day and

night in stage-coaches, where the company is as miscellane-
ous as the roads they take in journeying through life."—Nor
have we less disadvantages in steam-packets, merchants' ships,
and such like conveyances, when we go to transact our business on the coasts of the sea, or from continent to continent,
on the deep waters.—I grant that all these things are unfriendly to the spirit of piety: and this is the concession
with which I set out.    But still they are not insuperable hin-
derances; and, *pray* we must, or not prosper.    Many pious
persons, in these circumstances, have deplored the unsuitable-
ness of *time, place,* and *company,* to prayer; a total want of
*privacy,* with various causes of distraction breaking in every
minute, so that the mind is incapable of working up its
thoughts into any thing like orderly and regular supplication,
and in such a state, disturbed thoughts can only form themselves into unconnected words and sentences, with which,
how sincerely soever intended, the mind is generally dissatis-
fied: and thus the perplexity is increased.

6. If ever a *form of sound words* were necessary, it must
be in such a case as this: a *form,* short, simple, and terse,
where the mind is saved the labour of composing the words
which the heart at once feels to be the just types of its desires, and by which it can come at once unto the Lord, and
present before Him its necessities and most fervent desires;
being saved the trouble of searching for suitable words to
express its wants and wishes.    Such is the *form* which appears as a motto to this discourse, but which is, in fact, the
*text* on which the whole is intended to be built.    As I wish
to benefit the antiformalist as well as him who pleads for its
use and importance, I only wish the former to go with me
but a little way in the present case, and I have no doubt, if
his heart be right with God, he will soon find that in his journeyings through the maze of this world, in the secular business of life, he will be glad to find such a help to his devotion
so near at hand.

This short prayer divides itself into the following parts, or
portions;—

I. A solemn address to the Supreme Being:—

" *O Lord, our heavenly Father, Almighty and everlasting
God.*"

II. An acknowledgment of His care and providence in preserving our life :—

*" Who hast safely brought us to the beginning of this day."*

III. A strong petition, to be preserved, during the day, from sin and hurtful accidents :—

*" Defend us in the same with thy mighty power ; and grant, that this day we fall into no sin, neither run into any kind of danger."*

IV. Supplication for guidance through the secular business of the day, that it may be wisely and righteously transacted :—

*" But that all our doings may be ordered by thy governance, to do always that is righteous in thy sight."*

V. All these petitions, and the expectation of their fulfilment, are grounded on Him who, in all the services of the Church, is represented as the great sacrificial Offering; and through whom alone, God's gifts and mercy can be communicated to mankind :—

*" Through Jesus Christ our Lord. Amen."*

I. A solemn address to the Supreme Being.

" O Lord, our heavenly Father," &c.

In considering the above divisions, it will be necessary to examine the import of each word, that the mind may duly apprehend the idea, or precise meaning intended to be conveyed by it.

1. The Supreme Being is here addressed by a title that is intended to point out His *dominion* and *sovereignty ;—viz.* LORD. *Power* belongs to Him, who is the object of our worship; and power *exercised* in the way of *dominion* or government. He is the *Creator*, and consequently the *Preserver* of all things ; as He has sovereign rule, so He has sovereign right. He upholds all things by the word of His power; and has an absolute right to dispose of them, and govern them as He pleases. All beings are under Him and depend upon Him ; and it is He alone that gives life and breath to all things. He has way every where, and the purposes of His will all things serve. As we would feel the deepest reverence in approaching the presence of the King, so at least should we feel in approaching the Majesty of the heavens and the earth. I need not add, that reverence and godly fear should penetrate the heart—that we should feel our obliga-

tions to, and dependence upon Him; and that though we have authority to *pray*, for this He has given us; we have no authority to *command*—we are the *creatures* coming into the presence of the *Creator*; and *subjects* approaching the throne of the *King*. The exclamation O, is the expression of the petitionary spirit; and by a proper consideration of the Being we thus address—*O Lord!* the soul is brought into the spirit and attitude of a supplicant.

2. If we have not some endearing conception of this august Being, superadded to that of His *Majesty*, His terrors may well make us afraid:—confidence cannot be excited by the bare contemplation of *Majesty* and *supreme authority*: to come with boldness to the throne of grace, we must be convinced that He who sits on it, has a friendly disposition towards us, and in evidence of it, has commanded us to ask that we may receive: therefore, with great judgment, have the excellent compilers of our Liturgy, or public Service, added here, *Our heavenly Father.* A proper *choice* of *terms* is of wonderful use when the speaker wishes to address himself to the conscience and heart; and the judicious *collection* of such terms gives them additional expression and force, and so it is here. The Divine Majesty is first presented to our view, and before Him we are constrained to *bow*. While awed by His presence, and trembling before Him, we hear Him proclaimed by that most endearing of all names and relations, *Father!*—What! is this *Sovereign*, this most *tremendously glorious*, and *transcendently magnificent Being*, my FATHER? Does He call me His son, His child? Is that dazzling throne, the throne of *Grace?* That *seat* of *majesty*, the seat also of *mercy?*—of good will, of tender care, of gracious solicitude and parental affection! Yes: THOU art OUR FATHER: for such pity as a father sheweth unto his children, such pity hath the Lord for them that love Him. He is not merely *a Father*, or, the *Father of the spirits of all flesh;* but he is OUR *Father*—one whom we may confidently call our *own*, and claim as *our own;* for Himself acknowledges us for His children.

3. But He is *our heavenly Father.* From an *earthly* father, we have derived, in a secondary way, our being; and by such we have been fed, clothed, defended, fostered, and protected. The *hand* that *led* us, was a hand of *tenderness:*

the *voice* that *cheered* us, was the voice of *affection* and *love*.
He girded us when we knew him not : we were objects of
his *solicitude* when we could not call him by that endearing
name. We smiled through the effects of his parental kindness, when we could not comprehend that it was from him,
under this God and Father, that we derived the happiness
which was expressed by that smile. Well, all that this our
tenderly affectioned and beloved earthly father did for us, was
a proof of the love of our heavenly Father towards us—for
it was from *Him* that our *earthly father* derived his parental
tenderness, and through His bounty alone was he enabled to
feed, clothe, and protect us. Then, with what confidence
may we draw nigh to Him. Our *earthly fathers* were both
limited in their knowledge, and limited in their means :—they
often wished to succour us when it was out of their power—
to feed us, when they had not the means—their *love* extended to *all* our wants and necessities, but their *hand* could reach
but to a *few* : but here, we are introduced to our " heavenly
Father," whose *love* is ever *ardent*—ever *operative,* whose
*all-seeing eye* ever affects His *heart*, and His *loving heart* ever
dictates to His *Almighty hand.* And to shew this efficiency,
the same wisdom, piety, and good sense, of our reformers,
already mentioned, have most properly added here, what
qualifies and confirms the whole,—

4. " Almighty and everlasting God."

We have already seen what is implied in the character of
the Supreme Being, as " THE LORD, and *our heavenly Father.*" We now come to consider more particularly His
power as it immediately concerns ourselves. We see in the
course of the world, that there are multitudes of moral and
natural evils which nothing but Almighty power can restrain,
turn aside, or destroy : and that there are many good things
of both kinds, absolutely necessary to the preservation, comfort, and salvation of man, which no less a power than *Omnipotence* can produce and establish. Now, it is ever necessary in order to our confidence and faith, to have the conviction, that He who is our *heavenly Father*, is the *Almighty
and everlasting God. Almightiness*, is that from which all
*might* or *strength* must be derived ; and in which, all *might*
*or strength* is *included.* Every *rational* and *intelligent* agent
has a degree of *power*. All *animate* beings have also a

measure of might, which they have liberty to use or exert at any time, and in what measure they feel necessary. Every particle also of *inanimate matter* has a degree of force, though unconscious of it, which it is ever exerting under a particular direction, which learned men, for want of knowing a better name, have agreed to call *attraction* or *gravity*. By this principle, all portions of matter *adhere;* and this is called the *attraction of cohesion:* and by this they *tend to each other*, so as to form a grand whole, about the centre of which, at unequal distances, all particles of matter are collected; and this is simply termed *gravitation* or *attraction*. The *horse* has strength to *run;* the *ox* to *draw*; the *lightning* to tear the *oak;* the *sun* to influence all the other *bodies* in our system; and the *earth* has *vegetative energy* to produce the *grass* which grows for the cattle, and the corn which grows for the service of *man:* and *man* has *strength, wisdom*, and *skill*, to employ all these in his service, and direct their powers and influences to his *use*. Now, all these mighty powers and energies God has not only made, but *directs* and *manages*, both conjunctly and separately—all are ever in His grasp, subsist and exist by Him—He *rides* on the whirlwind, and directs the storm—He quells the raging of the seas, He sits upon the water floods, and remaineth a King for ever. Yea, He *rides upon the heavens as upon a horse*—manages all their powers and influences, howsoever varied, combined, or acted upon by each other, in their almost untraceable motions, revolutions in their respective orbits—the velocities by which they travel from imperceptibly *slow*, to incomprehensibly *swift*.

Now, fellow-traveller, this is God; thy "heavenly Father!" And this is a sketch of the *Almightiness* which shall ever, as far as is necessary, and in every requisite proportion, be exerted for thee, while thou puttest thy trust in Him, and acknowledgest Him in all thy ways.

5. There is only one point more necessary to be considered on this head—that this Almighty God is *everlasting*. Our *earthly* fathers are dead:—they have endured but a time, and could not continue by reason of *death:* but thy *heavenly Father* is *everlasting*—He is *eternal*—He is without beginning of days, as without end of time. As His Being knew no commencement, so it shall know no end. As His *kingdom* is *infinite*, so His *power* is *eternal*. And if any

thing farther be necessary to impress just sentiments of his parental relationship to thee, behold it in the word GOD, which signifies the GOOD *Being*. He who is good of Himself, in Himself—and the Cause of all the good that is in the heavens, and
in the earth, in angels and in men. The fountain of all *good*,
whether natural or spiritual—of all the good that ever was,
and ever will be, to all eternity.

II. An acknowledgment of His care and providence in preserving our life :—

" Who hast safely brought us to the beginning of this day."

1. *Life* itself is a wonder, and in its principles, inexplicable:
its preservation is not less so. Apparently it depends on the
circulation of the blood through the heart, the lungs, and the
whole system, by means of the *arteries* and *veins ;* and this
seems to depend on the *inspiration* and *expiration* of the *air*,
by means of the lungs. While the *pulsations* of the *heart*
continue, the *blood circulates* and *life* is preserved. But this
seems to depend on *respiration*, or the free inhaling of the
atmospheric air, and expiration of the same. While, therefore,
we *freely breathe ;* while the *lungs receive* and *expel* the *air*, by
*respiration* or *breathing ;* and the *heart* continues to *beat ;*
thus circulating the blood through the whole system,—life is
preserved. But who can explain the phenomena of *respiration ?* And by what power do the lungs separate the oxygen
of the air, for the nutrition, perfection, and circulation of the
blood ?—And by what power is it that the heart continues to
*expand* in order to *receive* the blood ; and *contract*, in order
to *repel* it, so that the circulation may be continued ; which
must continue in order that life may be preserved ; why does
the heart not get weary, and rest ? Why is it that with *incessant labour*, for even *threescore* and *ten years*, it is not exhausted of its physical power, and so stand still ?—These are
questions which God alone can answer satisfactorily, because
life depends on Him, whatsoever *means* He may choose to employ for its continuance and preservation. Hence with great
propriety does the *traveller*, (and indeed so should *all others*,)
thank Him, for having *safely brought them to the beginning*
*of* any *day.*

2. *Night* also is a season of danger,—it is the season from
which our cares and attention to self-preservation are excluded.
*Self-preservation*, which is called the *first law of nature*, oc-

cupies much of our time during the course of the *day*—our *eyes* and *ears* watch for us, and our *hands* and *feet* ward against danger. *Caution* and *foresight* are ever on the alert, in order to descry and avert any evil that might tend to injure or destroy life : but in the night-season, *eyes, ears, hands, feet, caution,* and *foresight,* are all inactive, and fall under the common state of inaction which possesses all the members of the body. God alone can preserve us from the *violence of the fire,* the *edge of the sword,* the *designs of wicked men,* the *influence of malevolent spirits,* and the various *natural obstructions* and causes of the *cessation of the action of vital functions,* which might put an end to life.—He who carefully considers these things, will wonder that his *life* is safe at *any time;* and much more, that it is preserved during the course, even of a *single night.*—While we slumber, God neither slumbers nor sleeps. He is the watchman not only of Israel, but of the whole human race, because He is the Father of the spirits of all flesh,—of all mankind.—He hates nothing that He has made : but *man,* on account of that dignity with which He has endowed him, He pre-eminently loves. To thank God for our *preservation* in the course of the *night,* and for bringing us *in safety to the beginning of a new day,* is at once a duty, as rational and proper, as it is Christian. Our preservation at *any time,* our preservation at *all times,* is the effect of God's mercy : and for this, on the return of recollection, after the slumbers of the night, we should feel especial gratitude ; for had we died in any previous night of our life, could we have died safely ? Fellow-traveller, ask this question at thy heart and conscience, and then see whether thou canst refrain from thanking the *Almighty* and *everlasting God for* bringing thee to the beginning of the day ! Thou art still alive ; and though in a *stage coach* or on the *great deep,* thou art still alive in the land of the living—in a state of probation —in a place where thou canst *pray,* and acquaint thyself with God, and be at peace, that thereby good may come unto thee.

III. A strong petition to God, to be preserved, during the day, from sin and hurtful accidents :—

" Defend us during the same with thy mighty power ; and grant, that this day we fall into no sin, neither run into any kind of danger."

1. Dangerous as the *night* season may appear, for the

above reasons, the *day* is in fact no less so. Though in the night we can take no care of ourselves, yet we are less exposed to the *bustle of life*, which gives birth to so many kinds of dangers.—The labours of the day, in several of the avocations of life, are performed in perilous situations. *Mining*, in which hundreds of thousands are employed, is a tissue of dangers:—in every moment, life is exposed to imminent and various deaths, by what is called the *fire-damp*, and the *falling* of parts of the pit on the miners. Those who travel by *land*, or by *water*, are not less exposed. By *common stage-coaches*, accidents are not only frequent, but often mortal: weekly accounts from public registers, are full of details of such calamitous events. Those who travel by *water* are yet more exposed than those who travel by *land*. On *sea*, there is never more than a few inches of plank, between any man and death. In a *sudden squall*, a ship may easily *founder*:—in a *gale* blowing on a *lee-shore*, she may soon be *dashed to pieces*, and every hand lost. A ship may *spring a leak*, which no industry or skill may be able to stop; and after incredible labour of the crew, fill and go to the bottom, and every person be consigned to a watery grave. In cases where the weather has been *dark* and *tempestuous* for *several days*, so that no observation could be taken, and the *reckoning*, because of the conflicting and *thwarting tides*, has been necessarily *imperfect*. In a hazy state of the atmosphere, the ship may make land in a *breeze* or *gale*, either by *night* or *day*, and be suddenly dashed in pieces:—some of these perilous states I have witnessed.— Besides these, there is a multitude of other dangers, which unavoidably accompany a sea-faring life; and which in numerous cases, are destructive of human life:—what need of an Almighty Preserver! For those who go down to the sea in ships, and occupy their business in *great waters*, should they not pray to God that He may defend them with His *mighty power!* for no less a defence can avail, when He raiseth the stormy wind, which lifteth up the waves of the sea, so that they mount up to the heaven, and go down again to the depths, and their soul is melted with trouble: and the poor seamen reel to and fro, and stagger like drunken men, and are at their wit's end.—What need, I say, have such to cry unto the Lord in their trouble, that He may bring them out of their distresses, by making the storm a calm, so that they may be

brought safely unto their desired haven?—Through the whole
of life's maze, there are dangers :—the *changes and chances*
of this mortal state are numerous; and neither by day nor
by night, by land nor by water, can we be a moment safe,
but under the direction and defence of the mighty power of
God.

2. But, that against which we should direct our most fervent prayer, is *sin*.—This is more perilous, and more destructive than all the possible calamities which may occur on the
land, and the more awful deaths which may meet us on the
ocean. But what is *sin?* Let us understand this well, that
we may see the propriety of praying that the mighty power
of God may so defend us that we fall not into it.

Sin is the transgression of God's law—it is the doing any
thing which God has forbidden; or leaving undone what He
has commanded us to do. Either the *doing* in the one case,
or the *not doing* in the other, is here called *falling into sin.*
—In this petition, reference is made to a hidden *gin, trap* or
*snare;* or to a *pit* in the ground, over which *rushes* or *reeds*
are artfully laid, so that the deception may not be *easily discovered;* and the heedless traveller falls into it before he is
aware, and is so entangled that he cannot get out.—Sudden
temptations to *anger,* by which quarrels are provoked, and life
endangered or destroyed, may be construed among those *mortal falls.* There may be temptations also to *drunkenness,*
and various kinds of *debauchery,* from which no *traveller* is
exempt; and by which any may *fall,* if not *defended by the
mighty power* of the Lord. I need not instance temptations
from "her whose house inclineth unto death, and her paths
unto the dead :—for she hath cast down many wounded, yes
many *strong men* have been slain by her: for her house is
the way to hell, *going down* to the chambers of death." With
such, the path of the traveller is often most grievously in-
fested—and the sin is more easily besetting, when a man is at
a distance from his own house, and where he is not met by the
eye either of *acquaintance* or *friend.* Many fall into sins
when they are *abroad,* to which they have neither *temptation*
nor *incentive* when they are at *home.* Let none, therefore,
despise councils of this kind : howsoever well armed, there
are deceptions and dangers in the way; and if not to the very
*grosser vices,* yet to others, by which the soul may equally

suffer; and the letter as well as the *spirit* of the prayer is, *grant that* THIS DAY *we fall into no* SIN : and the *night also*, may be safely included in the petition.

2. The prayer is extended not only to defence against sin, but against all kinds of *hurtful accidents :*—" Neither run into any kind of danger."

The *dangers* into which we may *run*, are widely different from those already mentioned. I have spoken of two kinds already; those which we may meet with in travelling by *land ;* and those which may occur in travelling by *water ;* but the *running into any kind of danger*, may refer to any thing that may occur in our walks in *the streets* or *lanes* of *any city* or *large town*. I have known persons in endeavouring to run out of the way of carts and coaches, actually run into the way of danger. I have known one who, walking along the parapet, was crushed to pieces by a cart wheel against the wall. I have seen a woman, striving to see the raree show of an illumination, fall from a garret, and dashed to pieces on the pavement. I have seen a man who had got too much liquor, riding furiously, his horse fell, and he was killed on the spot. I have seen another who, getting on forbidden ground, was shot dead on the spot. I have known another who fell over a bank, and was dead before he could be taken up. In short, I have known many who *ran into various kinds of dangers*, and have paid for their imprudence, temerity, or what was called the *accident*, by the loss of their life. On what I have seen, as well as on what I have heard, I see the great necessity of using such a prayer as this in every part of the walk of life—*grant that in this day we run into no kind of danger :* and in crossing the streets of London, or other large cities and towns, let us remember the proverb, that " there are always 200 yards more of room *behind* a coach, than *before* it ;" of this many are sadly unmindful, and run across public streets, before horses and carriages driving at full trot ; and not a few have either lost life or limb by this folly.

IV. Supplication for guidance through the secular business of the day, that it may be wisely and righteously transacted :—

" But that all our doings may be ordered by thy governance, to do always that is righteous in thy sight."

1. The *governance* of God, is a subject of mighty importance ; and concerns every human individual.

What God has *created*, He *upholds* : what He *upholds*, He *governs*. Without Him nothing is wise, nothing is holy, nothing strong. Many suppose that God governs the world by *general laws*—or rather, that He has imposed, what they call *general laws*, and left them to govern the world, with which He does not intermeddle. That this notion is absurd, will at once appear, when we consider, 1st, That all *generals* are composed of *particulars* ; and if He govern the *generals*, He must also govern the *parts* of which they are composed. 2dly, That if there be laws which He has imposed on the universe, whether they be *general* or *particular*, they must have their *action* and *efficiency* from HIMSELF, and whatever be the *mode* according to which He governs, He, Himself, must be the *energy*, by which the government is administered ; and therefore it is not *general* nor *particular laws* which govern the world : but the great, wise and holy God, governing according to a *particular mode* of His own devising ; and according to which, He is disposed to work.—Properly speaking, He governs not by either *general* or *particular laws*, but by His own infinite wisdom, adapting His operations to all those circumstances and occurrences which are ever before Him ; and ever under His direction and control—" from seeming evil still oducing good—and better still in infinite progression." As all matter and spirit were *created* by Him, and all that He has created, He *upholds*, so all *matter* and *spirit* are *governed* by Him. Every thing therefore is under His continual *superintendence* or *governance* : and as that *governance* is *wise, holy,* and *good ;* so whatever is governed by it, is governed in the *best manner,* and conducted to the *best end.*

2. This *governance* of GOD, is the *model* of all perfection in government ; and all that is conducted by this model, must be what is *useful* and *good* to the *whole ;* and beneficial to the *individual.* God, in His government of the world, has for object the *benefit* and *salvation* of men. They whose *doings* are *ordered, i. e.* arranged and directed, by His government, must aim at *His glory,* and the welfare of their *fellow creatures ;* and their whole conduct must *tend* to promote glory *to God in the highest ;* and on *earth, peace* and *good will* among men.

3. As God's *governance* is *righteous;* so every work of man, which is formed on that *model*, must be righteous also. *Be ye holy, says the Lord, for I am holy;* i. e. in other words, Let all your *doings be ordered by His governance, that ye may always do that which is righteous*, not in the estimation of *man* merely, but in the *sight* of the Lord.—Let not this be the case *occasionally* or on *select* occurrences, but *always;* in all times, places, and seasons. For the spirit of the Christian religion does not enjoin *occasional acts of piety*, merely; but a whole life of justice, integrity, truth, and righteousness. In short, we should have the very thoughts of our hearts cleansed by the inspiration of God's Holy Spirit, that we may perfectly love Him, and worthily magnify His name. And we shall never act thus till we get under the divine *governance;* and *begin, continue,* and *end,* every work to His glory, and the benefit of mankind. Then, and then only, shall all our doings be ordered by His governance; and then only, shall we do that which is righteous in His sight.

V. All these petitions, and the expectation of their fulfilment, are grounded on Him who, in all the Services of the Church, is represented as the great sacrificial Offering; and through whom alone, God's gifts and mercy can be communicated to mankind : hence we conclude by saying,—

"Through Jesus Christ our Lord. Amen."

1. God never dispenses either gifts or graces, but on some sufficient reason to justify His conduct; though He owes not any account of His conduct to man. But why is it that He should become our *Father?* Why is it that He should *take care of us day and night?* Why is it that He should *preserve us from sin and danger?* Why is it that He should *guide us by his governance*, and so influence us by His grace and Spirit, that we may do *that which is lawful and right in His sight?* —These things He does promise; and why should He bind Himself to do these things for *us*, who are debased by sin, and whose best desert is Hell!—who have rebelled against Him, and have not hearkened to the voice of the Lord our God, to walk in the ways that He hath set before us?—*Why?* He does all these things for us through Jesus Christ our Lord. The word *through* signifies here, not *by* Christ as an agent; but *on account* of Christ;—*for the sake* of Him—on account of His *worth, worthiness* or *merits :*—and why? This Christ,

took our nature upon Him, became man, died in our stead, and thus bore the punishment due to mankind, in His own body upon the tree.—He was delivered for our offences ; and rose again for our justification. God was pleased with this, and He is pleased with all those who believe in this Christ as having died to make an atonement for their sins, and thus reconcile them to God. There is no good in man but what God's mercy puts in him ; therefore, it is not for *man's sake*, on *man's account*, or for *his worth*, or *merits*, that God does these things for him: but for the sake of Jesus Christ our Lord. But who is this person for whose *sake*, or *merits*, God does all these things for man ? He is called *Jesus Christ our Lord ! Jesus* is a *Hebrew* word, and signifies him that *saves*.— This is the interpretation of it given by the angel of God, who foretold His birth—*His name shall be called* JESUS, *for He shall save His people from their sins*, Matt. i. 21. But the word signifies also a *preserver*—that is, the person who *having saved, preserves* those in the *state of salvation* who depend upon Him—so that the word Jesus signifies one who saves men from sin ; and who preserves them in that state of salvation.

2. The word *Christ* is *Greek*, and is the same as *Messiah* in *Hebrew*, and both signify the Anointed One, or the Anointer. In ancient times, Prophets, Priests, and Kings, had *oil* poured upon their heads, in token that God had appointed them to their respective offices. Now, *oil* was an emblem of the *Holy Spirit ;* of His gifts, and of His graces : and when a man was anointed with oil, in the name of the Lord, for any of the above offices, it was supposed that the *Holy Spirit* rested up on him in the gifts and graces necessary to qualify him to fulfil the *office* to which he was appointed by the Lord, whether it was that of *priest, prophet,* or *king*. For the good sense of mankind, in ancient times, as well as the direct revelation of God, taught them that no man could fulfil the office of a pro- phet, either by *preaching* or *predicting future events*, unless endowed by this spirit of wisdom and understanding :—that no man could worthily execute the priest's office, either by offering sacrifice to God for the people, or making intercession for them, unless influenced by that Holy Spirit which sancti- fied every sacrifice and gift, and communicated the *power* of *intercession* and *prayer*.—Nor did they suppose that any *king*

could decree justice and judgment, or properly *administer the laws*, unless the discernment and unction of that *Holy Spirit* of the Lord rested on him. *Christ*, in whom the fulness of this Spirit dwelt, was appointed to be the *Prophet, Priest*, and *King*, of the human race. As a *Prophet*, He declares to and teaches man the will and counsel of God.—As a *Priest*, He offers His own body on the cross as an atonement for the sin of the whole world.—As a *King*, he reigns over the whole earth by His power, and in the hearts of all true Christians by His Spirit.

3. He is called also, *our Lord*—This title I have already explained; it signifies *governor—supreme potentate :*—and He *governs the church*, and *rules* the *hearts*, affections, and desires, of all His children. Man has no *worthiness* for which he can claim any thing from the God of justice ; therefore, whatever he receives, it must be for Christ's sake. And this truth is so great and important that all, or nearly all the prayers in our Liturgy, are thus concluded :—every grace and gift of God's Spirit is asked " for Christ's sake." For His *sake, repentance, faith, pardon* of sin, *holiness* and *heaven* are requested of God—" for *Jesus Christ's sake*," or, " through *Jesus Christ our Lord*." We have an entrance to the Holiest by His Blood. And because of the infinite merit or worth of His sacrificial offering for the sins of men, God can be just, and yet the Justifier of him who believeth on Jesus :— He who thus believes, had been previously a rebel against God, but is now turned to Him with a truly penitent and believing heart.

To ratify and confirm these several petitions, we add the word *Amen*, the meaning of which I come now to explain.

*Amen*, is a mere *Hebrew* word, and signifies *faithful*, or *true ;* and when used at the end of prayer, implies a confident resting of the soul on God, with the fullest assurance that the petitions which have been offered according to His will, shall be all, most graciously and punctually fulfilled.

As therefore, the word has reference to the *truth* and *faithfulness* of God, so it has also to the *sincerity* of the person who ends, and, as it were, *seals* his petitions with it. If the heart be not *concerned* in the petitions, the *Amen* is of no use. God will not ratify, by a fulfilment, prayers which our *hearts*

H

cannot be said to have offered at the throne of grace. But when *right words* are used, and the lips have not uttered them till the heart have weighed the import of each expression, then the whole may be justly presumed to have entered into the ears of the LORD *our heavenly Father;* and that He will turn aside the evils which threaten us, and grant us those good things which we have sincerely asked in the name, and for the *sake* of

JESUS CHRIST OUR LORD.

# SERMON XX.

## DEATH UNAVOIDABLE.

2 SAMUEL, xiv. 14.

14. For we must needs die, and *are as water spilt on the ground, which cannot be gathered up again; neither doth God respect any person : yet doth he devise means, that his banished be not expelled from him.*

THE circumstances in which these words were uttered, as well as the remote, but direct cause whence these circumstances flowed, must be considered, in order to see and to feel the weight and importance of the maxims laid down in the text.

In the eleventh chapter of this book, the inspired writer, 1st. Gives us a very circumstantial account of David's transgression with Bathsheba, the wife of one of his captains, and the criminal means he used to hide his transgression, which, as intended, brought about the death of this brave man. 2. The notice taken of those criminal acts by the God of justice and purity, in chap. xii., and the divine threatening relative to the judgments which God would send, or permit to fall on himself and family, as proofs of the depth of his guilt, and of the high and just displeasure of that sovereign Lord, whose authority he had despised, and whose laws he had broken.

The message of God was sent to David by the prophet Nathan, and was delivered in a few, simple, but dreadfully appalling words. *" Wherefore hast thou despised the com-*

*mandment of the Lord, to do evil in His sight?  Thou hast
killed Uriah the Hittite, with the sword, and hast taken his
wife to be thy wife, and hast slain him with the sword of the
children of Ammon.  Now, therefore, the sword shall never
depart from thine house:—I will raise up evil against thee,
out of thine own house:—for thou didst it secretly: but I
will do this thing before all Israel, and before the sun."*  See
ch. xii. 7—12.

The fearful and appalling effects of David's double crime,
and the denounced judgments of the Almighty, we shall soon
see fulfilled in the horrible *rape* of *Amnon,* on his *half-sister;*
in the *fratricide* of Absalom, who treacherously murdered the
ravisher of Tamar, who was *his* full sister; the *expulsion* of
the *murderer* from the favour of his father, and his banishment from the Israelitish court; and subsequently, the *rebellion* of this wicked brother, and unnatural son, against his
own father; the total overthrow of the *thoughtless multitude*
which he had drawn into the vortex of his rebellion; and his
own *tragical death,* when fleeing from the battle in which he
was defeated.

On these subjects, too awful and revolting in their nature
and circumstances, it would be improper to dwell; to mention
them in connexion with the fact on which the text is founded,
is quite sufficient: and from them we shall draw this inference
only, that while they shew the horrible depravity of the human heart, and the long suffering, just judgment, and unmerit-
ed mercy of Jehovah, their detail in the Sacred Writings is
an illustrious proof of the truth of those divine records: for
who, that intended to deceive, by fabricating a religion which
he designed to father on the purity of God, would have in
serted such an account of one of its most zealous advocates,
and previously its brightest ornament!  God alone, whose
character is impartiality, has done it, to shew that His religion,
the truth of which is demonstrated by its own intrinsic and
influential purity and excellence, will ever stand independently
of the conduct of its professors.

It was during the time of Absalom's banishment from the
Israelitish court, that the transactions mentioned in this chapter took place.  Absalom, plotting deep designs of treason
and rebellion against his too fond parent, saw that unless he
was reinstated in his favour, and brought back to court, he

could not possibly execute them ; applied to Joab, the gene-
ralissimo of his father's forces, to use his influence with the
king, to effect his restoration :—after a great deal of reluc-
tance, evidenced on the part of the general, he at last under-
took the negociation. And, that he might appear as little in
it as possible, employed a sensible widow of Tekoa, (a little
city in the tribe of Judah, about twelve miles from Jerusalem,)
to use the prominent features of her own case, and embellish
them according to the circumstances of the case which she
was instructed by him to represent to the king—in order that
he might, without knowing her design, or in the least suspect-
ing her cunning, pronounce a solemn decision, which would,
by fair construction, apply to the case of Absalom, and thus
oblige David to recal his son from banishment.

Being admitted to the king's presence, she uttered a cry of
distress, *Help, O king!* and being encouraged to open her
case, made, in substance, the following statement :—" I am a
desolate widow ; and my husband at his death left two sons :
these in an unfortunate disagreement quarrelled, and one was
slain. My late husband's family rose up and demanded the
slayer to be delivered up to them, that he might pay with his
life, the life of his brother whom he had slain ; as the law had
provided that the *nearest a-kin* to him who was. slain, should
avenge his death, by slaying the murderer. This being my
only son, and the sole heir and representative of the family,
if he be destroyed, the inheritance is lost, and to my deceased
husband, there shall not be either name or posterity left in
Israel."

The king, affected with the case, told her that he would
give orders to the proper officers to consider her appeal. As,
in such a case, *delay* would be most likely to bring about discovery, and thus defeat the whole design, the widow affecting to be much alarmed for the safety of her remaining son,
and seeing that David hesitated to decide, and promise to save
the life of her son, supposing that he did so lest the not
bringing the offender to the assigned punishment might appear to reflect on the administration of justice in the land ;—
to remove all such scruples from his mind, she very cunning-
ly, and with great address, cried out, " Let the iniquity of
rescuing him from the death that I allow he has deserved, be
visited on me, and my father's house, and the king and his

throne be guiltless, if this should be found to be a case to which the royal clemency should not have been extended." To pacify her, the king told her, that if the next of kin still continued to urge his claim, founded on the law, to bring him before him, and he would so settle the matter, that he would in future relinquish his claim. The widow, seeing that this would not bring the business to such a bearing that it would issue in the conclusion she wished, affected the greatest alarm, lest the avenger of blood should instantly avail himself of the authority of the law to slay the murderer, prayed the king to issue his mandate to prevent this, and to give her his solemn promise that all proceedings relative to this affair might be stopped.

The king, increasingly affected with the case, and the widow's importunity, instantly pronounced her son's pardon, and confirmed it by a solemn oath—*As the Lord liveth, there shall not one hair of thy son fall to the earth !*

The widow having now taken all the preliminary steps she had projected, and having arrived at that conclusion with the king that she wished for, thus discloses her purpose, and applies and enforces her request with what is called the *argumentum ad hominem,* (a mode of reasoning by which a man is pressed with consequences drawn from his own principles or concessions, to admit what his opponent contends for,) which she expands in the following manner :—" Is not the king himself blameable ? Does he act a consistent part ? He is willing to pardon the meanest of his subjects, the murder of a brother, at the instance of a poor desolate widow; and he is not willing to pardon his son Absalom, whose restoration to favour is the desire of the whole nation ! Is that clemency to be refused to the king's son, the hope of the nation and apparent heir to the throne, which is shewed to a private individual, whose death or life can be of consequence only to one family ?"—" Why, therefore, dost not *thou* recal thy banished child ?"—Whatsoever there is done, should be done *quickly:* all *must die ; God has not exempted any one from this common lot:*—though Amnon be dead, the death of Absalom cannot bring him to life, nor repair this loss. Besides, Amnon for his crime justly deserved to die, and thou in his case didst not administer justice. Horrible as this ᷉atricide is, is it not a pardonable case ? Was not the crime of Amnon the most flagitious?—and the offence to Absalom, (the ruin of his beloved sister,) indescribably great? Seeing then that the thing is so, and that Amnon can no more be re-called to life, than *water spilt upon the ground can be gather-ed up again;* and that God, whose vicegerent thou art, and whose example of clemency as well as justice, thou art called to imitate, *devises means that those who are banished from Him* by transgression and sin, may not be *finally expelled* from His mercy and His kingdom:—remember, then, the Lord thy God, restore thy son to favour; pardon his crime, as thou hast promised to restore my son, *and the Lord thy God will be with thee;* He will shew thee His mercy, and grant thee His salvation.

That such argumentation was conclusive and successful, need not be stated; Absalom was recalled; but while *mercy* triumphed, *justice* had its claims, and was respected: though the legal guilt of his crime was pardoned, he was permitted to return to Jerusalem, and yet his father very properly re-fused to admit him either to his confidence or presence, till he should have more proof of his humiliation; and therefore he was ordered *to go to his own house:—for the king said, let him return to his own house; and let him not see my face,* ver. 24.

Though the argument in the text is as elegant as it was well timed, artfully conducted, and successful, yet we must lose sight of it as referring to the case of *Absalom,* and consi-der it as containing indisputable maxims applicable to occur-rences which are in continual train, and to facts which are universal, and which concern and should interest every hu-man being. In this general way the widow of Tekoa herself uses it :—*For we must needs die, and are as water spilt on the ground, which cannot be gathered up again; neither doth God respect any person: yet doth he devise means, that his banished be not expelled from him.*

From these assertions I shall,

I. Draw the general conclusion, that death is *unavoidable,* for the reasons which I shall adduce.

II. That no *state* or *condition* of man can exempt him from it.

III. That all men are in a state of *exile* or *banishment* from God.

IV. And that notwithstanding the justice of their banishment, God has found out *means* for their *restoration*.

I. Death is unavoidable : *we must needs die :* that is, there is a *necessity* why death should bring all mankind under his empire.

The term *necessity*, from the Latin *necessitas*, requires, in such a connexion as this, *definition*. Our best Lexicographers, without attempting to point out its component parts, give it this general definition—*cogency, compulsion, inevitable consequence ;* that state of such things as must be as they are, and cannot possibly be otherwise, without implying a contradiction ; and therefore cannot cease to be what they are, and as they are, unless they be annihilated, or undergo an essential alteration of their nature : and therefore it has been derived by grammarians from *non cessans esse, not ceasing to be* what it is ; because, if it did *cease to be what it now is*, that which it was *ceases to exist.* Sometimes it signifies *need, want, poverty*—that *without which* we cannot live, or be comfortable in life ; such as *air*, to inflate the lungs— *power* of contraction and dilatation of the *heart*, in order to the circulation of the blood, without which we cannot live— *food*, without which we can at no time live comfortably, and must totally cease to live, if proper aliment be not supplied. Thus the man's *death* was *necessary* or *unavoidable*, because he had no *food*—his *lungs* collapsed, and he could not *breathe* —his *heart* ceased to receive and convey the blood, and therefore he died ; and could not, in such circumstances, *but die.* His death was *necessary* or *unavoidable*, because he *wanted* what was *necessary* or *needful* to support life. And he may be said to be under a *double necessity* of dying, who not only *wants* what is *needful* to support life, but is also *in*, or *under* the influence of circumstances which, from their own natural operation, would *inevitably deprive him of life.* The unavoidableness of death is that which is here intended by, *we must needs die :* there is a necessity for it :—

1. Because we are now naturally mortal, and cannot live always.

2. The Author of life, who has the supreme authority over us, has most positively declared to men, *ye shall surely die.*

3. Because the very means of life tend remotely to destroy it.

4. Without death, the resurrection of the body, and its ultimate immortality, cannot take place, nor be insured.

Therefore, *we must needs die*, in order to become immortal —in order to bear the bitter pains of an eternal death—or to enjoy the fulness of an eternal joy and felicity at the right hand of God.

With any other acceptations of the word *necessity*, my subject is not concerned. I leave, therefore, *absolute necessity, physical necessity, moral necessity, casual necessity, fatality, compulsion, free agency, &c.* to their relative subjects.

Then, 1st. *We must needs die*, because we are naturally *mortal;* and cannot, in our present connexions and circumstances, live always. But it may at once be asked, *Whence* does this *necessity* arise?

That God made man *conditionally* immortal, cannot, I think, be reasonably doubted. Though formed out of the dust of the earth, his Maker breathed into his nostrils the breath of life, and he became a living soul: and as there was then nothing *violent*, nothing *out of its place*, no agent too *weak* or too *slow*, on the one hand; or too *powerful* or too *active*, on the other; so all the operations of nature were duly performed in *time*, in *quantity*, and in *power*, according to the exigencies of the ends to be accomplished. So that in *number, weight*, and *measure*, every thing existed and acted, according to the unerring wisdom and skill of the Omnipotent Creator. There could, therefore, be no *corruption* or *decay:* no *disorderly induration*, nor preternatural *solution* or *solubility* of any portions of matter. No *disorders* in the *earth* :—nothing *noxious* or *unhealthy* in the *atmosphere.* The vast *mass* was all *perfect* :—the *parts* of which it was composed equally so. As He created, so He upheld all things by the word of His power : and as He created all things, so by Him did all things *consist.* Thus expressed by the Apostle, Και αυτος εστι προ παντων, και τα παντα εν αυτω συνεστηκε, Coloss. i. 17., *And He is before all things; and by Him, all things stand together :*—cohere, keep their respective places, and accomplish their appointed ends. And among these MAN :—every *solid* had its due consistency,—every *fluid*, its proper channel :—some for support and strength, others for *activity* and *energy;* and the various fluids to conduct to every part the necessary supplies, and to furnish those *spirits* by whose natural and regular agency, life, under God, is sustained.

I have stated that man was created *conditionally* immortal: for God, who had a right to impose on him, as a free agent, what *conditions* He thought proper, and that line of duty, which, as a *subject* to his SOVEREIGN, he was bound to observe, said, when He placed him in the garden of Eden, *Of every tree of the garden thou mayest freely eat ; but of the tree of the knowledge of good and evil, thou shalt not eat of it ; for in the day thou eatest thereof thou shalt surely die ;* מות תמות *mot tamut, i. e. Dying thou shalt die :* Thou shalt then lose the *principle* on which thy *immortality* depends ;—thou shalt, on the breach of this precept, *begin to die,—thou shalt ultimately return unto the ground, for out of it wast thou taken ; for dust thou art, and unto dust thou shalt return.* This simple, plain, easy condition, on which depended his immortality, he broke ; and thus forfeited his right to the blessing with which he was naturally endowed ; and thus corruption and decay, and a disorderly course of nature, were superinduced : the *air* that he breathed became unfriendly to the continual support of life : the *seeds* of *dissolution* were engendered in his constitution, and out of these, various diseases sprang, which by their repeated attacks, sapped the foundation of life, till at last the fruit of his disobedience verified the judgment of his Creator ; for, after living a dying life, it was at last terminated by death.

Now, as all have sinned, so death passed upon all men : therefore, " *we must needs die,* and are as water spilt on the ground, that cannot be gathered up again."

2dly. The Author of life, who has the supreme authority over us, has most positively declared to sinful men, *Ye shall surely die.*

We have seen that death had no place among the works of the Creator, at the beginning. It was threatened as an evil, when the test of obedience was given to man. Had it been a thing *natural* or *unavoidable,* why should it be mentioned as the *penalty of transgression ?* Why should it be intimated that such a thing should take place, should they be disobedient, that must have taken place in the order of natural cause and effect, whether they were obedient or not ? Neither pain, disease, exhausting labour, nor any of the ills of life, that are the fore-runners and concomitant causes of death, are spoken of at all, but as things whose existence was *possible*, and only *certain*, if disobedience took place. Before sin entered into the world, it was simply threatened as a cautionary measure, to prevent the fall to which a free-agent was exposed—*In the day thou eatest of it, thou shalt surely die.* When *sin* entered into the world, then *death* entered by sin: and it was not till after this fatal and ruinous ingress, that God said to the first mother, *I will greatly multiply thy sorrow and conception:—in sorrow thou shalt bring forth children; and thy desire shall be to thy husband, and he shall rule over thee.*

Nor was our offending first father to be treated with greater indulgence: for to him, thus said the Lord:—" *Adam, where art thou? Hast thou eaten of the tree whereof I commanded thee that thou shouldst not eat?* Because thou hast eaten of the tree of which I-commanded thee, saying, Thou shalt not eat of it: cursed is the ground for thy sake, (בעבורך *baábureca*, on thy account, or because of thee;) in sorrow shalt thou eat of it all the days of thy life: thorns also and thistles shall it bring forth to thee; and thou shalt eat the herb of the field; in the sweat of thy face shalt thou eat bread, till thou return unto the ground: for out of it wast thou taken: for dust thou art, and unto dust shalt thou return."

Now all this clearly proves not only that there was no death before sin, but also that there was no *predisposing cause* of death—nothing that, in the course of nature, could bring it about. The ground was fertile, and it seems there were neither noxious nor troublesome productions from the soil; and the benediction of the Most High rested upon the earth, mountains, hills, plains, and valleys: but when *sin* entered, what a change! The globe becomes stubborn and intractable; noxious and troublesome weeds have their full growth; though the husbandman exerts all his muscular force in painful and exhausting labour, his toil is ill repaid; *thorns* and *thistles*—every genus, family, and order, of injurious plants, spring up with rapid speed, into destructive perfection; and often, when the labourer is about to fill his arms with the productions of a painfully earned harvest, a *blight* vitiates the grain;—*tornados* and *tempests* shake it out of its husk, and give it to the fowls of the air, or tear up the stalks from the root, and scatter them to the winds of heaven; or *land-floods* carry off the shocks which stood nearly ready to be housed; and thus the hope of the husbandman perishes. By these, and by various other means, does the righteous God fulfil the purposes of His justice, and accomplish his declaration—*in sorrow shalt thou eat of it :* for on thy account, the earth itself is cursed. Thou shalt return to the ground whence thou wert taken. Thou hast forfeited thy natural happiness and immortality—death spiritual has already entered thy soul, and the death of thy body shall soon succeed—THOU SHALT DIE! Thus spake the God of justice and unchangeable truth. He who alone could create, and who alone can destroy. He spoke—His word was *fate !*

Therefore, *we must needs die*, though He is not the Author of death, nor has pleasure in the destruction of the living.

3dly. *We must die*, because, in the present order of things, the *means of life* tend ultimately to destroy it.

In the order of Divine Providence, there are two kinds of aliment, from the consumption of which man is to derive his support—*vegetables* and *flesh ;* and to prepare each for his digestive powers, his jaws are furnished each with a complete set of *teeth*, variously configured for their respective purposes ;—some for *cutting*, some for *tearing*, and some for *grinding ;* hence, divided by anatomists into *three* classes :— 1. *Dentes incisores*, or *cutting-teeth*, what we would call the *biting-teeth*, which have their place in the front of the mouth. 2. *Dentes canini*, the *dog-teeth*, or those by which we rend and tear tough substances, such as *flesh ;* and these are situated on each side of the incisors. 3. *Dentes molares*, or *grinding-teeth*, mill-stone teeth, called also *double teeth* and *grinders*, by which we reduce *seeds*, *vegetables*, and *flesh*, into their smallest parts, that when taken into the stomach, they may be more easily acted on by its muscles and the juices it contains. But notwithstanding this merciful *provision* of necessity, and *provision* for its supply, so far has mortality seized upon the whole frame of man, that, in general, the decay of the teeth renders the mastication of the food imperfect, so that it is ill or imperfectly digested in the stomach; on this account the *chyle* extracted from the food is neither in sufficient quantity to repair the wastes of nature, nor is it sufficiently elaborated to afford a wholesome blood, and the various fluids necessary for the preservation of the human frame;—hence, indigestion, and the various crudities that torment the bowels, independently of the evils which the *stomach* itself—the whole *internal canal,* the *kidneys,* the *liver,* the *lungs,* and the other *viscera*—suffer; which impede their operations, and are unavoidably sapping the foundations of life. The *heart* itself, though the strongest and naturally healthiest of all the viscera, partakes of the general lethal calamity; the blood is languidly received and transmitted; its stimulating property impaired, the circulation in the fine or *capillary vessels,* in the extremities, becomes very torpid; the smallest are soon stopped or obliterated: hence, the nourishment of such parts being very imperfect, the *feet* and *legs* become cold, feeble, and rigid; and the *hands* and *arms* palsied. The *eyes* partake of the general imperfection: the humours and muscles that constitute their principal substance, become *opaque,* flattened, and lose their vigour. In short, to follow the beautiful metaphorical description of *Solomon,* they that *look out of the windows are darkened;*—the *sound of the grinding is low,* teeth being decayed;—the *scalp* or skin of the head becoming thin, the juices necessary to nourish the *hair* fail, so that it falls off. *The silver cord—* the whole nervous system—*is loosed;* and hence that direful train of those mental and corporeal maladies that often make life a burden. The *golden bowl*—the *brain,* the origin of the nerves, and as is supposed, the *place* where *reason* keeps its seat, where *thought* and *reflection* are formed—*is broken,* rendered unfit to perform its functions with requisite vigour. *The pitcher is broken at the fountain*—the *vena cava,* which brings back the blood to the *right ventricle* of the heart. The *wheel is broken at the cistern*—the great *aorta,* which receives the blood from the *left ventricle,* to distribute it to the different parts of the system—ceases to receive, and the other to impart it; the *pulse* necessarily ceases, the *lungs* collapse and cease to respire, the blood is no longer *oxidized,* all *voluntary motion,* as well as *sensation,* cease—and the man dying, even through the means of life, so many years, now dies! *Then the dust returns to its dust,* and *the spirit,* finding its clay tenement no longer habitable, *returns to God who gave it;* see Eccles. xii. 2—7. Man, therefore, cannot continue by reason of death: howsoever warded off for a time, it finally triumphs, for the counsel of the Lord shall stand; thus, WE MUST NEEDS DIE, *and are as water spilt on the ground.*

4thly. We must die, to become immortal.

As death of any kind is a *violence* and *imperfection* in nature, it could not have existed in the beginning. God had created no living thing, with a *necessary* liability to death: it could have been no part of his design; *decay, corruption,* and *dissolution,* could not affect any of His works, as proceeding from His hand: yet we see that this primitive state did not continue: now, innumerable diseases affect animal life; even the brute creation are liable to them, and these, sooner or later, terminate in death. It is the same with the *human* being; man, like to them, has his *infancy, youth, mature age, old age, decrepitude,* and *death. Cursed is the earth for thy sake,* is a mighty vortex which has involved the whole *animal* creation. The *creature* we find *is subject to vanity;* yea, *the whole creation groaneth, and travaileth together in pain, until now.* Rom. viii. 20—22. *Sin* entered into the world, and *death* by sin; and this did not affect our first parents only, but the whole of their posterity; for *sin hath reigned unto death from Adam to Moses :* as the Apostle expresses it, *even over them who ' had not sinned after the similitude of his transgression.* Rom. v. 14. And since that time, death has proceeded to abridge life, that he might bring in a *total* destruction—for such is the natural tendency of this evil. But God has been pleased to arrest its impetuosity, and limit its operations; and *three score and ten years* have been assigned by the Sovereign of the world, as that general boundary, beyond which few can pass, and to which, with care, temperance, and piety, all may reach. Adam was permitted to live 930 years; his son Seth, 912; his son's son Enos, 905; Cainan, the descendant of the latter, 910: and generally, after the time of the above Patriarchs, life became gradually abridged; and, although Noah had attained 950 years, and his grandfather Methuselah had reached to the high age of 969, beyond which human life had never been extended: yet, after this, life became progressively shortened, till the limit of *three score and ten years* was fixed by the will and authority of the Author of life. Yet, how few reach it, so prevalent is sin, the fountain of *indolence, intemperance,* and *disorderly passions;* which, as a mighty and overwhelming land-flood, is sweeping away thousands of human beings daily! But how long soever protracted, each man's earthly duration terminates with—*he died*—or, *was slain*—or, *slew himself!* the three horrible *gates* which sin has opened into eternity, through which impetuously rush all the successive generations of men! But are they ingulfed in the great unfathomable abyss for ever? Does *death feed upon them* eternally? Is there no redemption from this awful effect of its ravages? Are we, in the most positive sense of the word, *like water spilt upon the ground, which cannot be gathered up again?* No! there shall be a resurrection both of the *just* and *unjust;* but this is not a necessary consequence of the preceding effects or cause. It springs not from nature, nor by any *law* by which nature is governed. There is no *principle of regeneration* or *revivification* in the putrid corpse, nor in that dust in which it is finally resolved. The resurrection of the human body springs from the *justice* and *mercy* of the supreme Governor. Even a *direct* promise of it scarcely exists in that Revelation which contains the history of the creation and fall of man, and of the various dispensations of grace and justice, by which God governed the world for more than 4000 years; and what does appear in those Sacred Writings *relative* to this, is there by anticipation, for the resurrection of the body is properly a *doctrine of the New Testament,* and comes solely by *Him,* who was delivered for our offences, and rose again for our justification. He alone is the *resurrection and the life:* for since by man came sin and death, by man came also the resurrection of the dead;—for, as in Adam all died, even so in Christ shall all be made alive. Had He not died and risen again from the dead, there had been no resurrection of the dead; all had finally perished;—but now is Christ risen from the dead, and become the first fruits of them that slept. See the powerful reasoning of the Apostle of the Gentiles on this momentous subject, 1 Cor. xv. 12. &c. The promise of a resurrection, is a promise of the New Testament; the doctrine is there alone stated and explained. The *resurrection of Christ* is the basis on which it rests, and the proof of its certainty; for He alone has brought life and immortality to light,—or, as the Apostle has beautifully expressed it,—

*καταργησαντος μεν τον θανατον, φωτισαντος δι' ζωην, και αφθαρσιαν δια του ευαγγελιον.* 2 Tim. i. 10. " He hath counterworked death, and illustrated life and incorruption by the gospel;" whatsoever *undermined* life, to bring about *corruption* and *death*, He hath *countermined;* and from the darkness of death, and his empire of corruption, He hath brought into *full view* that *life*, of which He is the Author; and that *immortality*, which is the consequence of *destroying death*, that last enemy.   So " this corruptible shall put on incorruption, and this mortal, immortality, and then shall be brought to pass that saying, (which darkly intimated what is now clearly revealed,) *Death is swallowed up in victory*."

Now, although many of the things spoken of by the Apostle, belong properly to the state of *genuine Christians*, yet, the general subject includes *all;* as *all must needs die*, so *all* shall *rise again from the dead:*—the human body shall then be built up on indestructible principles, a principle of immortality shall preserve it: it shall no more live by supplies received from the *animal* and *vegetable* creation ; which, as we have seen, while they nourish for a time, are nevertheless planting in our nature the seeds of decay and dissolution. For, as *flesh and blood*, in their present state, *cannot enter into the eternal world*, nor can *corruption inherit incorruption*, all shall arise immortal: for death himself being destroyed, and consequently all the predisposing causes that led to his dominion, there can be no more death, corruption, nor decay: man shall become immortal,—an immortal body must be associated with an immortal spirit, to dwell together in that eternal state, where no change of elements or substance that might affect *identity, form*, or *continuance*, can ever have place.

Now, as all shall arise, and many through their perversity, and obstinate continuance in transgression, have died in their sins, it follows, that of the many *that sleep in the dust of the earth, some shall awake to everlasting life, and some to shame and everlasting contempt*. Dan. xii. 2.  For while " the *righteous* shall shine forth like the sun, in the kingdom of their Father, the *wicked* shall be turned into hell, with all the people that forget God."   Hell is no place of decay or dissolution,—there is an unquenchable fire,—there is a worm that never dies: and the subject on which those agents will act, shall be as deathless as themselves.

To such persons, there shall be an eternal separation from God, and *banishment* from the glory of his power. As the whole man has sinned, so the whole man must suffer; and the vengeance of eternal fire cannot be suffered but by him who is *immortal.* The wicked therefore must die a natural death, that they may be raised immortal, in order to be capable of enduring the punishment due to their crimes: and the righteous must die, and be raised immortal, in order that they may be capable of dwelling eternally in the presence of God, and beholding His glory.

This is not the unwarranted assertion of man; it is the awful decision of the Judge of quick and dead! Hear him! "When the Son of man shall come in His glory,—and before Him shall be gathered all nations,—He shall separate them one from another, as a shepherd divideth sheep from goats,—and He shall set the sheep on his right hand, and the goats on His left,—then shall He say to those on His right hand, Come, ye blessed of my Father, inherit the kingdom prepared for you from the foundation of the world,"—(for which procedure, He gives the reasons,)—"also He shall say to them on His left hand,—depart from me ye cursed, into everlasting fire, prepared for the devil and his angels,"—(and for this decision He gives also the reasons,) and then orders the execution of the unchangeable purpose, in this solemn declaration; Και απελευσονται ουτοι εις κολασιν αιωνιον· οι δε δικαιοι εις ζωην αιωνιον, "And those shall go away into eternal punishment; but the righteous into eternal life." Matt. xxv. 46. The words which point out the *duration* of the state of both these classes, are the same: as the *life* is *eternal,* so is the *punishment.* Men may quibble and trifle *here,* but their desperate criticisms will not be urged *there.* There is no *injustice* in *hell,* more than there is in *heaven.* He who does not *deserve* it, shall never fall into the bitter pains of an eternal death,—and no man shall ever eat of the tree of life in heaven, who has not a *right* to it.—Blessed are they that do His commandments, that they may have a right to the tree of life, and may enter in through the gates into the city, Rev. xxii. 14. The former would not come to God, that they might have life, therefore they *deserve* perdition. The latter gladly accepted

I 2

the pardon purchased for, and offered to all, through His blood, and received the spirit of holiness, to sanctify and refine their souls for the kingdom of heaven ; " they have overcome by the blood of the Lamb, and His testimony, therefore they are before the throne, and they shall walk with Him in white, for they are worthy. Yet still hell was made only for the *devil* and his *angels*, not for *man :* man is an intruder into it ; no human spirit shall ever be found there, but through its own fault. He who refuses the *only means* of *salvation*, is lost. God willed not his death.

Having now considered the general conclusion from the text, that *death is unavoidable,* for the reasons which I have adduced and illustrated ; I return to the subject under the second head.

II. That no *state* or *condition* of man can exempt him from it.

That it has been the study of man for nearly 6,000 years to prevent this generally reputed *great calamity,* needs little proof ;—*life* to man is the dearest thing he can conceive: when exposed to death, every thing is put to stake in order to turn aside the danger, and preserve life.

A being, who has from long experience, a deep knowledge of human affairs, and of the human heart, has said, *skin for skin, yea all that a man hath, will he give for his life :*—and on the same ground is the universal maxim placed, *self preservation is the first law of nature :* and from the same principle sprang the whole *system of physic,* with all pretensions to the *art of healing,* and to the millions of *specifics,* which through successive ages, ignorance and imposture have told the public, would cure all the maladies of man. Every *nostrum,* said in effect to every *patient,* (suffering more from the *botchery* of the *charlatan,* than he did from the *disease* by which he was afflicted) *take this and thou shalt not surely die.*—Time and experience took off the mask ; and the *infallible,* and the *probatum est,* were equally discredited, because they were found equally inefficient.

There was however little respite to poor suffering humanity, for the next bold adventurer, who knew how to practice on the *love of life,* and brought forth his *powders* and *fluids,* fortified with a *list of cases* in which they had been successfully applied, was sure to meet with encouragement : and hence it has been justly said, " Nothing in the history of society is so inexplicable as the proneness to believe in *quackery ;*"—but this may be in part accounted for, from this simple circumstance, that the *empiric* most *confidently promises*, what the *patient* most *ardently desires.* Take this *bottle*—take this *box, and* *ye shall not surely die. Immortality,* in effect, is every where promised : and the *desire* for, and *hope* of *life,* absorb every inquiry ; reason and judgment are *put to sleep,* the man sur- renders himself into the hands of his unknown enemy, his *final* *sleep* soon hushes every complaint, and the GRAVE *covers* a multitude of sins.

All these things are daily occurrences, yet the living lay it not to heart ! Though perhaps few men absolutely expect immortality in the present life, yet they put off death indefi- nitely ; they allow that they are travelling towards it ; but it is a horizon that recedes as they advance. and is ever at the same distance. Death is not *seen* in his *approaches,* nor *felt* in the continual *sap* which he is carrying on under the *founda- tions* of life ! Regular *medicine* has promised much, and done little ; but the *alchemistic chemistry* has promised *more,* and with greater plausibility.

In all ages and countries since the time of Constantine the Great, and many carry it to a much higher antiquity, there has been a class of medical philosophers, well read for their respective times, in *chemistry,* who thought that *nature* tended to bring every thing to perfection, but required the assistance of *art* to enable it to succeed. As to *metals,* they considered *gold* only to be in a state of *perfection.;* that all the other metals were *imperfect,* only because they had not of *themselves* a sufficient energy to bring their respective seeds to maturity. *Silver, lead, tin,* and *quicksilver,* they considered as making the nearest approach to the perfection of *gold ;* and all their labour was directed to find out a *tincture* that would commu- nicate the requisite energy ; depurate and impregnate the comparatively imperfect mass, and bring about a speedy *trans- mutation !* This, called also the *Philosopher's stone,* many of them professed to have *obtained,* and therefore were called *adepts.* From their reasonings on the purifying and transmu- tation of *metals,* which they considered to be a *healing* and subliming of their *diseased nature,* they thought that the *tinc- ture* which brought *them* into a state of health and perfection, might be applied successfully to the healing of all the *diseases incident to the human*, and even *brute* creation; and not only preserve them in health, but continue life indefinitely.    This also they professed to have *obtained*, and they termed it THE *Elixir*, and the GRAND ELIXIR, and roundly asserted that they who used it, before any of the functions of life were essentially injured, would *never die*.    A *violent death* only could affect them ; but the use of the elixir would infallibly repair all the *wastes* of nature, destroy all *contagion*, and ever maintain the *healthiest action* in all parts of the animal machine.    This secret they say all the Patriarchs possessed, and this alone accounts for their extraordinary longevity !  *Arabia, Germany, Holland, France,* and *England,* produced many of those highly learned and favoured men ! from the 12th to the 18th century, who not only attracted the veneration of the *lower classes,*  •  but also the notice of *kings, queens,* and *nobles* of all countries All these had  steadily in view these *two* points, 1. To *trans mute the inferior metals into gold ;* that they might build churches, endow  hospitals, and in a word destroy *poverty !* 2. To heal *infected nature,* procure an *established and unim parable state of health,* banish sorrow and sighing ; and in effect, destroy death ; so that, we *must needs die,* should have no foundation in nature, and might be blotted out of the Bible !

Several of our own countrymen were professing possessors of this  grand secret :—*Friar Bacon, Thomas Norton, John Dastin, George Ripley,* Sir *Edward Kelly, Pearce, the black monk, Starkey, Vaughan, &c. &c :* Even *spirits* were evoked by *John Dee* and others, to assist in the *speedy perfection* of this work !—On the continent, *Nicholas Flammel, Basil Valentine, Sandivogius, Isaac* and *John Holland, Raymond Lully, Artephius,* (who arrived, as it is said, to the age of 900 years,) *J. Pontanus,* and *Theophrastus Paracelsus,* who might have lived still, had  he not neglected to fortify himself by a few drops of the *Elixir,* when he went into a house infected by the plague, by which he lost his life ! I pass by those of modern times, several of whom I have known, who laboured hard, spent much property in the *fire,* and were ever *on the very eve of success,* when " disappointment laughed at hope's career," by the extinction of the fire,—by the carelessness of a servant,—the *oversetting* of a *cup,—breaking* of a *retort*,—or *cracking* of a *crucible*, &c.    But where are now,

"Those mighty masters of the healing art."

They are gone with the years beyond the flood.—*They have returned to the ground from which they were taken ;—Dust they were, and unto dust they have returned !*    After all their pretensions ; after all their labour ; after all their hopes and imaginations ; they arrived at the period, when the words of the *widow of Tekoa*, poured contempt on all their expectations ;—they heard the knell of death, and feeling his dart, were obliged to exclaim, WE also MUST NEEDS *die !*

Some modern political Philosophers, have gone so far as to imagine, that there is a certain perfectability in human nature which, under proper management, might be so exalted, as to induce such a healthy state of the human constitution, that a very great extension of the term of life might be the consequence—that the mind, so intent on its own improvement, would rise above *animal propensities*—feel no desire to propagate the human species; and, consequently, the long extended life of the community, would bring about neither *want* nor *famine*, as procreation would be at least very unfrequent !—This also was soon discovered to be vanity and vexation of spirit ; for—*we must needs die*, met the hypothesis at every turn.

Widely different from all those schemes to avoid death and gain immortality in this life, is that of Mr. John Asgill, a member both of the Irish and English House of Commons, who, sometime about 1700, published and detailed in a book entitled, " An Argument proving that, acccording to the Covenant of Eternal Life, revealed in the Scriptures, Man may be translated from hence into that Eternal Life, without passing through Death :" although the human nature of Christ Himself could not be thus translated ; for it was necessary in the Gospel Economy, that *He* should suffer death.

The leading features of his scheme are the following ; Man, who through his fall is liable to death, is yet by faith in Christ restored, not only to the favour of God, through whom he receives a seed of eternal life, so that he shall never die everlastingly ; but also when the business of life is ended, he shall be *translated*, so that he shall never see death in this state of being: and hence this gentleman was called *translated* ASGILL. The Scriptures on which he chiefly founded his opinion, are—Luke xx. 34—36., *The children of this world marry, and are given in marriage: but they who shall be accounted worthy to obtain that world, and the resurrection from the dead, neither marry nor are given in marriage, neither can they die any more: for they are equal unto the angels, being the children of the resurrection*—and John xi. 25., *Jesus saith unto her, I am the Resurrection and the Life; he that believeth in me, though he were dead, yet shall he live: and whosoever liveth and believeth in me, shall never die.*

This scheme had some peculiar recommendations, as founded professedly on Divine Revelation, and especially on the gospel of Christ, in the exceeding great and precious promises which it gives to genuine Christians. But some paragraphs having been culled from his work, which the House of Commons decided to be "profane and blasphemous," neither of which were ever intended by the honest man, he was in 1707 expelled the British House of Commons, having been previously expelled from the Irish House on account of the same book! He wrote a long defence of himself and his work, in which he says, "He was ejected from the Irish House because he had *too much land:* and from the British House because he had *too little money.*" But after all poor Mr. A. found that HE must *needs die;* and he is now *as water spilt on the ground which cannot be gathered up again.*

I might add here, that there are certain cases in which the prolongation of life would be a *curse.* How many tyrants, and *other* oppressors of suffering humanity, who were like the most destructive pestilence, diffusing over whole regions calamity and death, and whose mad career of human butchery no hand of man could stop, have been arrested by the strong arm of the Almighty, and delivered over to *death,* that the bleeding world might have respite, and the desolate places again become inhabited! Had many years been added to the lives of such men, what might have been the consequence, who can tell! While consternation and death walked before them; and famine and desolation followed in their train; it was some consolation even to think—"These cannot *continue,* by reason of death." But what shouting and triumph were there when it was known—they are brought down,—laid low,—even unto the dust!

Again, were it not for *death,* as an agent in the hand of God,
how fearfully would the *science* of *iniquity* be in many cases
perfected, and the *trade* of *sin* be extended! Some seem to
live only to invent *schemes* of sin, and bring to perfection the
*practice* of transgression. Were the lives of such to be protracted to the extent of those of the Antediluvians, so that
they might have the opportunity of maturing their schemes,
and improving the *modes* and *instruments* of aggression and
spoliation; and of teaching their science to all those who
might be willing to learn (and countless multitudes would be
their pupils;)—*sin* and its *practice* would be multiplied in the
earth, beyond all conception, and to the most fearful extent.
But see the Divine Economy,—wicked men do not live half
their days, limited even as life now is. *Death* is a grand
agent in the hand of the God of justice to stop their career,
blast their plans, and confound their devices. Thus iniquity
is not multiplied in the earth to that overwhelming extent to
which it would have been, had not the life of man been shortened. Was it not on this very principle, that God destroyed
the primitive earth by a flood, and permitted one righteous
family only to remain : the great family of sin being all cut off,—
their infernal arts and diabolical sciences have all perished;
the earth arose anew under better auspices, and life was
abridged, that the fallen principle might not have time to mature
its plans of transgression;—yet, a gracious Creator granted
what is sufficient for all to work out their salvation, to recover
that Divine image which they had lost, and be prepared, by
His mercy, for the enjoyment of eternal glory.

After having proved that *death is unavoidable,* and shewn
the folly of the attempts that have been made to elude it;
I come now to consider what may be called the *reason* by
which the *widow of Tekoa* supports her argument, in reference
to the fulfilment of her request, viz. *God hath devised means
that his banished be not expelled from him.* From which I
shall take occasion to shew,—

III. That all men are in a state of banishment from God.

To see this the more plainly, we must collate the *primitive,*
with the *present state* of man : a few postulates are here necessary : viz. God made man. Whatsoever He has made was
made perfect in its kind : it had nothing *too much*—nothing
*too little ;*—there was no *superabundance,* for that would have

been *useless*, and argued want of *economy*—there was nothing *deficient*, for that would have argued want of *skill*—or of *materials*—or of *effective means*.

All the *various* genera and species of STONES, of *minerals*, of *vegetables*, and *animals*, were perfect in their kinds : for example, *diamonds*, *rubies*, *emeralds*, *sapphires*, &c. were perfect in their kinds ;—so were the different kinds of ROCKS —*granites*, *basalts*, *limestone*, *sandstone*, &c. All the different genera of VEGETABLES—*oaks*, *ashes*, *elms*, &c. All *seeds*, *grasses*, *flowers*, &c. were perfect in *their* kinds. All ANIMALS —*beasts*, *cattle*, *fowls*, *fishes*, *insects*, and *reptiles*, were perfect each in its kind. MAN, the noblest of all, and for whom all these were made, was perfect in *his* kind, composed of *body* and *spirit ;* the *former* was perfect in all its parts; the *latter* in all its powers and faculties. But his spirit was endowed with a peculiar perfection and excellence, for it was made in the *image* and *likeness of* GOD. Gen. i. 26. And this image, according to the Apostle, consisted in *righteousness*, *truth*, and *holiness*. Eph. iv. 24. Now, as between GOD, the Fountain of righteousness, holiness, and truth, and all SPIRITS who are partakers of these excellencies, there must be an intimate *union*, for these properties cannot exist independently of Him,—therefore man was made in *union* with God. In Him he not only lived, moved, and had his being ; but every thing answered the purpose for which God made it. With the will of his Maker, there was a perfect consent in his will—in all its volitions, and in all the acts founded on, and proceeding from those volitions. All that was in him, all that proceeded from him, God beheld to be *very good :* he walked with God, dwelt in God, was *one* with God, and God with him. With his Maker he had the closest *intimacy*, and the strongest *fellowship*. As God is omnipresent,—wheresoever man moved, in all the directions his body could go, and in all the excursions his mind could take, he ever met the Fountain of his being and blessings ; and the Object of all the wishes and desires of his heart.—Between him and his God there was no *distance ;* and there could be none, because of this *sameness of nature :* and had his nature *continued* the same, this union and intimacy must have continued. But—Man being in this honour continued not ;—by the envy of the devil sin entered into the world :—SIN, that which implies the total absence of righteousness, truth, and holiness—and the presence of the evil principle of *wickedness, falsity, and impurity;* from which flowed enmity to God and goodness; alienation of affection and desire from the supreme Good : and transgression of the law of God, as the effect of this alienation and enmity.   Man therefore was no longer in *union* with his Maker, nor could he be, for what concord can there be between *hatred* and *love, truth* and *falsehood, holiness* and *impurity*—in a word, between *Christ* and *Belial.*   As an abominable thing, he was driven out of Paradise, and that act of expulsion was emblematical of his • banishment from the presence of God, and the glory of His power.   All his descendants partook of his apostate nature ; and all evidenced the influence of the body and soul of SIN and DEATH, by transgression against God, and obstinate rebellion :—and thus it has continued through all generations to the present day—all have sinned, and all in consequence are banished from the manifestation of His glorious presence.   He is not in all their thoughts, their ways are not His ways :—heaven is not more distant from the earth, than His thoughts are from their thoughts, and His ways from their ways.   And had not mercy rejoiced over judgement, every human soul would have been *banished* into everlasting fire, to dwell with devils, and damned spirits, *through ages of a hopeless end.*   But such is the *blinding* nature of sin, that man does not see this, his banishment ; and such is its *hardening* nature that he does not feel it.   Yet it is worthy of especial remark, that, as soon as the conscience is awakened, and the divine light shines into the soul, the penitent sees and feels that he has lost his supreme Good, and that he is banished from the presence of his God and Father.   He comes with weeping, and with supplication is he led : he asks the way to Zion with his face thitherward—he *seeks* his forfeited inheritance, and the favour of his Maker ; but so deep is he lost in the wilderness—so far into the strange country has he wandered from his Father's house, that he knows not whither to turn in order to commence a return ; of the success of which, he finds it even difficult to hope : his complaint is like that of the most afflicted of men,—" *O that I knew where I might find him, that I might come even to his seat !—Behold I go forward but he is not there ; and backwards but I cannot perceive him : on the left hand where he doth work, but I cannot*

K

*behold him : he hideth himself on the right hand that I cannot
see him."* Job xxiii. 3—9. Who shall give hope to this distressed soul ? That hope on which faith can legitimately rest ;
—for he acknowledges the justice of his banishment ?—God
alone can give this hope, as we shall see in the next particular.

IV. For He *hath devised means that his banished be not
expelled from him.*

There is something very remarkable and emphatic in the
original, מחשבות חשב *ve-chasheb chasheboth,—*" he hath devised
devices,"—or, " he hath computed computations."　The
word חשב *chashab,* signifies, *to reckon, compute, lay one's
thoughts together, contrive, superadd, meditate, scheme, plan,*
and, to be intently determined on *finding out ways and means*
to accomplish a particular end. It signifies also *to embroider,*
to *superadd* figures. to a *cloth,* on which they were to be exhibited : and this requires *skill* in the *plan, correctness* in the
*outline,* and the production of *effect* by the *arrangement, co-
louring,* and *grouping* of the figures. The word therefore
shews, that there was a *difficulty* in the case, which God alone
could overcome,—that, speaking after the manner of men,
it required a *skill, forecast,* and *energy,* which He alone
could supply ;—a *scheme* which astonished the *prophets* who
predicted the salvation of man ; for " they inquired and
searched diligently, what and what manner of time the spirit
of Christ which was in them, did signify, when it testified be-
forehand, the sufferings of Christ, and the glory that should
follow,—which things the angels desire to look into." 1 Pet.
i. 10, 11. In short, the *scheme* was so *difficult* to execute,
there being so many interests to be consulted, that Jehovah
himself is represented as *struck with wonder,* at the arduous-
ness of the undertaking. *He saw that there was no man,
he wondered that there was no intercessor ;—therefore his
own arm brought him salvation, and his righteousness sustained him.* The *interests* that were involved, were the
*honour of God's justice,* the *exhibition of His mercy,* and the
*recovery of a lost world,* by such means as should *magnify
God's law,* and make it *honourable,—*make a *free course* for
the *current of His mercy* in such a way, as would be consistent with the *requisitions of His justice :* and would be *effectual* to the full and *free pardon* of all the *guilt* of all sinners ;

the complete *purification* of the ingrained *pollution* of all souls, and their *restoration* to the *image of God*, in which they had been created, and the *enjoyment of that heaven* which they had forfeited, and to which they were to be restored on the ground of a *new right*.

1. To effect these mighty purposes, God, in His sovereign love to the world, *devised* the plan of human redemption, by the incarnation and sacrificial offering of Jesus Christ upon the cross, " who made there, by His own oblation of Himself once offered, a full, perfect, and sufficient sacrifice, oblation, and satisfaction, for the sins of the whole world." Thus, *divine justice* was satisfied by a sacrifice offered by Him, who was *God manifested in the flesh*, and *in whom dwelt all the fulness of the Godhead bodily*. In Him, " *Mercy and truth* met together : *righteousness and peace* kissed each other." As *man*, He died for *man :* as Goɒ, the sacrifice was infinitely meritorious. Then, by the preaching of the gospel, the grand *jubilee* was proclaimed, and all the *exiled inhabitants* of the earth were invited to *return* to Him, from whom they had so deeply revolted ; to receive, through the great Sacrifice and Mediator, " an *inheritance incorruptible, undefiled, and that fadeth not away*, reserved in heaven for them who are kept by the power of God through faith unto that salvation, which is ready to be revealed in the last time." And, as He *died for our sins*, so He *was raised again for our justification ;* and, though we *must needs die, and are as water spilt upon the ground, that cannot be gathered up again*, yet in the morning of the general resurrection, *He will change our vile bodies, and make them like unto His glorious body, by that working by which he is able to subdue even all things unto Himself ;* so effectually hath God *devised means that His banished* should not be finally *expelled from Him.* Who then that believes the glad sound, and that by faith presents the true sacrificial Offering at the throne even of *justice*, as well as of *grace*, need *fear death ?* It is the *last enemy*, and even this last enemy shall be *destroyed*. Reader, then look to Jᴇsᴜs ! and when thou hast cast thy burthen on the Lord, look on *death*, and see if it have got *any terrors :*— on the *grave*, and see if it be likely to *triumph*. No—for He hath *swallowed up death in victory.* Reader, He hath

died for *thee;* believe on the Lord Jesus Christ, and thou shalt not perish, but have everlasting life.

2. But although the sacrificial death of Christ be the *grand means* and the *cause* whence human salvation flows, yet there are other *means* which God devises in order to make this effectual: the LAW of God must be published, to shew man His righteousness. It must *enter,* that *sin* may be seen *to abound:* by this law is the *knowledge of sin,* for no man can see his guilty state, and the ruin to which he is exposed, unless he examine his *conduct* and the *workings of his heart* by the *law:* in vain is *salvation* preached, unless sinners are shewn that they *need it.* What are they to be *saved* from? Is it not the *curse* of the law? *Cursed is every one that continueth not in all things that are written in the book of the law to do them.* This curse has fallen on every soul of man, for all have sinned and come short of the glory of God. And who sees the worth of the Gospel who does not know the *exceeding sinfulness of sin!* He who does not preach this *law,* strongly and fully, does not use one of the principal *means* which God has devised that His banished be not expelled from Him.

3. When this is done, and the sinners become terrified, and fearfulness surprises the hypocrites, then Jesus must be announced, as the *Lamb of God that takes away the sin of the world:—*His incarnation,—His agony and bloody sweat,—His cross and passion,—His death and burial,—His glorious resurrection and triumphant ascension,—with His mediation at the throne of God, must be all distinctly and powerfully announced, as proclaiming the *way,* the *truth,* and the *life;* and proving, that *no man can come unto the Father but by Him.* If JESUS be preached *without* the LAW, sinners become either hardened or lost in their own *presumption:* if the LAW be preached *without* CHRIST, sinners are driven into *despair.* Shew Israel that he has destroyed himself: then shew him that in this omnipotent Saviour his help is found.

4. But even all this Scriptural and rational preaching will avail nothing, unless another means of God's devising be superadded, in order to give it effect—the *influence* of the HOLY SPIRIT:—that *Spirit* that *convinces of sin, righteousness,* and *judgment;* that Spirit of *light* and *fire,* that penetrates the inmost recesses of the soul, dragging forth to the

view of conscience the innumerable crimes that were hidden
under successive layers of deep darkness, when through this
luminous, burning agency, the sinner is obliged to cry out,
*What shall I do to be saved! Save, Lord, or I perish!
Heal my soul, for it has sinned against Thee!* When this
conviction of sin is deepened in every part, and utter *self-
despair* has taken full possession of the understanding and
judgment, then that same *Spirit* will take of the things that
are Christ's, and shew them to the broken heart:—it will
excite strong *confidence* in the sovereign availableness of His
merits, who, by the grace of God, has tasted death for every
man; and when, through His mighty working, the penitent
has laid hold on the Hope set before him in the gospel, that
Spirit despatched from the throne of *justice* and *grace*, will
bear witness with his spirit, that the great Sacrifice is accepted
in his behalf, and he shall immediately hear, by no equivocal
voice, *Son, be of good cheer, thy sins are forgiven thee!* On
this news from above, he rejoices with joy unspeakable and
full of glory; finding that he is 'begotten again unto a living
hope; knowing that if he abide in this faith, rooted and
grounded in love, and be not moved away from the hope of
the gospel, having his robes washed and made white by the
blood of the Lamb, he shall soon obtain that inheritance that
is incorruptible, undefiled, and that fadeth not away, which
is reserved in heaven for all the sons and daughters of God.

5. Besides these which are the *grand means* and *cause* of
salvation, God *devises* many others, humanly speaking, of a
minor character, suited to the various complexions and circumstances of men; to bring the thoughtless man to a sense
of his danger, and a conviction of His readiness to save.
Several of these are beautifully detailed by *Elihu*, in his pa-
thetic address to Job, chap xxxiii. 14. :—in *dreams* and *visions*
of the night, He often opens the ears of man and seals his instruction, ver. 15, 16. ;—He reduces his *strength* by *sickness,
chastening him with pain upon his bed,* and the multitude of
his bones with strong pain, and *terrifies* him with the fear of
*approaching death,* ver. 19—22. :—in the course of His gracious Providence, He sends some of His *faithful servants* to
visit him in his sickness, to shew him his sinfulness, and the
*Ransom* which the Lord hath provided for him, ver. 23, 24. :
—thus He delivers his soul from going down to the pit, and

his life sees the light, ver. 28. *Lo, all these things worketh God oftentimes with man, to bring back his soul from the pit, to be enlightened with the light of the living.*

6. In short, there is scarcely an *occurrence* in *Providence,* that has not the same gracious *tendency :* as He is continually pressing every thing into the service of man, in order to his conversion, and causing all things to *work together* for good to them that love Him. And all this *devising of mean°,* and *constructing* that apparently complex and astonishingly contrived *apparatus* of human redemption, justifies and illustrates that strong assertion of the Lord by his prophet :— *Have I any pleasure at all that the wicked should die, saith the Lord God, and not that he should return from his way ana live ? As I live, saith the Lord God, I have no pleasure in the death of the wicked; but that the wicked turn from his way and live :—Turn ye ! turn ye! from your evil ways ! for* WHY *will ye die, O house of Israel.* Ezek. xviii. 23. ; xxxiii. 11.

Thus, reader, it is demonstrated, that though *we must needs die, and are as water spilt upon the ground, that cannot be gathered up again,* and that God respecteth no man's person, *yet doth He devise means that His banished be not expelled from Him.* Then, believe on the Lord Jesus Christ, receive the gift of His Holy Spirit, and thou shalt not perish, but have everlasting life !

Now unto Him that is able to keep us from falling, and to present us faultless before the presence of His glory with exceeding great joy ; to the only wise God our Saviour ; be glory and majesty, dominion and power, both now and ever. Amen.

*March 22, 1829.*

# SERMON XXI.

## TWO IMPORTANT QUESTIONS ANSWERED.

PSALM xv. 1—5.

1. Lord, who shall abide in thy tabernacle? who shall dwell in thy holy hill?
2. He that walketh uprightly, and worketh righteousness, and speaketh the truth in his heart.
3. He that backbiteth not with his tongue, nor doeth evil to his neighbour, nor taketh up a reproach against his neighbour.
4. In whose eyes a vile person is contemned; but he honoureth them that fear the Lord. He that sweareth to his own hurt, and changeth not.
5. He that putteth not out his money to usury, nor taketh reward against the innocent. He that doeth these things shall never be moved.

THAT divinely inspired man who has been called emphatically the *Apostle of the Gentiles,* has informed us that, *Whatsoever things were written aforetime, were written for our learning, that we, through patience and comfort of the Scriptures, might have hope.* Rom. xv. 4. Now, as he speaks here *to* those under the Christian dispensation, *of* those who lived under the Jewish dispensation, and consequently of those Scriptures which were given to Moses and the Prophets, by the inspiration of God; we learn that those Scriptures were not designed for the use and benefit of that people only, but were intended for the edification of both Jews and Gentiles, to the end of time. If, therefore, we were even to suppose that this Psalm were written toward the conclusion of the Babylonish captivity, and that it related to the settlement of the returning captives, in their own land, and pointed out the restoration of the temple worship, and the character of the persons, who should be found fit to be employed in it: yet still, from the authority of the Apostle, we have a right to claim it as designed for us also, and expect from it *instruction*, lessons of patience, comfort, and hope.

But, losing sight of this point, we see that the subject is of the most general utility, and demands the most serious attention of all who believe in the immortality of the soul, and are concerned for their character here, and their future happiness.

*Lord, who shall abide in thy tabernacle? who shall dwell in thy holy hill?* yer. 1.

As it may be necessary to make a little alteration in the translation, it will be proper to introduce the original; the alteration, however, though important, will be very slight: יהיה מי יגור באהלך מי ישכן בהר קדשך —*Yehovah, mi yagur be-aholeca; mi yishcon be-har kodsheca?* " O Jehovah, who shall *sojourn* in thy tabernacle? Who shall *dwell* in the mountain of thy holiness?"

The word *abide* refers to a *permanent* dwelling, a *settled* habitation, which is not the meaning of יגור *yagur*, in the text. It is derived from גר *gar*, or, גור *gur*, to *dwell any where for a time; to inhabit as not in a settled dwelling; to sojourn as a stranger;* and rather means a *temporary lodging*, or a *sojourning*, answering to the *tabernacle*, to which it refers: and the word ישכן *yishcon*, from שכן *shacan*, to *remain, rest, sit still*, or *remain at rest*, is properly enough translated *dwell*, or *abide*, *i. e.* to *rest permanently*, answering to the *temple*, or *holy hill of God—Zion*, to which it refers in the second clause of the verse. Now, for the better understanding of this *twofold question*, we should note the following particulars :—

1. The Jewish *tabernacle*, which was a kind of moveable temple, and was *migratory* with the Israelites, in all their *peregrinations* from Egypt till their *settlement* in the Promised Land, is allowed by all to be a type of the *church militant*, or the state of the people of God in *this world*.

2. *Mount Zion*, or the *mountain of God's holiness*, where Solomon's temple was built, and the divine worship in all its ordinances became *established*, is allowed by the general voice of Jews and Gentiles, to be a type of *the kingdom of heaven*. The *ark*, there became *stationary*, being absorbed in the tem-

ple, was no longer *carried about from place to place,*—and the whole was typical of that *city* that hath *foundations:* of that *rest* that remaineth for the *people of God.*

3. Of the TABERNACLE, which was a *temporary*, and frequently *removed building*, it is said, יגור מי *mi yagur, who shall lodge*, or *sojourn* there? It was not a *resident* or *dwelling-place*, but a place to *lodge in for a time*.

4. On the contrary, the TEMPLE was a *fixed* and *permanent building:* and relative to it, we have the inquiry, ישכן מי *mi yischon*, who shall *dwell*, *abide*, or have his *permanent residence* there?

5. As the TABERNACLE was a sort of *migratory* model of a *temple*, carried about on the shoulders of the priests and Levites, there was no *dwelling* there, for any; they could only *lodge* or *sojourn*, at, or round about it.

6. The TEMPLE being *fixed*, the Priests, Levites, &c. became permanent occupiers; there was no lodging or sojourning; but permanent residence for all connected with it.

7. The TABERNACLE, therefore, is a proper type of the *church militant, wandering up and down, tossed by various storms and tempests;*—the followers of God having here, *no continuing place; sojourning* only, in their state of *probation* on earth, and that only for a short time, in order to acquire a preparation for eternal glory.

8. Also the TEMPLE is a proper type or emblem of the *church triumphant* in heaven. It is the *dwelling-place,*—the eternal *residence* of all who have been faithful unto death:— who are made *pillars in the temple of God, to go no more out for ever.* Here the *wicked cease from troubling, and the weary are at rest.* Having made the above remarks, which are founded on the letter of the Text, we may next observe, that the whole subject resolves itself into two questions:—

I. Who can be considered a fit member for the *church militant* here below?

II. Who shall be made partaker of an endless glory in the *church triumphant* above?

These questions must necessarily be answered together.

I. Who can be considered a fit member of the church of Christ here below?

To this question the inspired writer answers—

*He that walketh uprightly and worketh righteousness, and speaketh the truth in his heart,* ver. 2.

In a word, he is a man that is, 1st. *Upright.* He is an honest man. *He walketh uprightly.*

2ndly. *Just* in his DEED. *He works righteousness.*

3rdly. *True* in his WORD. *He speaks the truth in his heart.*

1st. *He walketh uprightly.* םימת ךלה *holech tammim,* " He who is walking perfectly." He who sets God before his eyes,—does every thing through a right *motive,* in reference to a proper *end;* beginning, continuing, and ending every work so as to have God's blessing *in* it, promote God's glory *by* it, and benefit both himself and his neighbour *through* it. He is not one who makes a *selection* of *duties* or *precepts,* which he finds no natural disposition or propensity to disobey ; omitting those that cross his inclination, or would impair his worldly gains : on the contrary, he has respect to all God's commandments :--should each have a cross in it, he takes up that cross. He knows that the whole forms one great system of *perfection,* and he aims at being *perfect, as his Father who is in heaven is perfect.* He never *stands still ;*—the Text does not say that he *has walked perfectly ;*—so *did Lucifer* in *heaven;* so did *Adam* in *Paradise:* but both afterwards rebelled, and *walked sinfully.* But this man *is walking :* he has *begun to walk,*—*is walking,*—and purposes, by the grace of his God, to *walk on* to *the end:* nor *cease to walk perfectly* until he ceases to live. He takes the *words* of God for the *rule* of his conduct, and His *Spirit* for the director of his heart. He feels himself a *stranger* and a *sojourner* here below, and is constantly *walking on* towards the *kingdom of heaven.* He acts not only according to the *letter,* but also according to the *spirit* of God's law. He knows, he feels, that the law is holy, and the commandment is holy, just, and good. He *walks* according to the *perfections* of God's law, and feels the weight and importance of all its injunctions. In a word, he has *simplicity* in his *intentions,* and *purity* in his *affections.*—He no more *seeks* any *by-ends,* than he *walks* in any *bad way.*

2ndly. *He worketh righteousness.* •

He is not satisfied with a *contemplative* life ; he has *duties* to perform. The law of righteousness has placed him in certain *relations,* and each of these relations, has its particular duties. The word צדק *tsedek*, here, signifies to give *just weight*, —to *render to all their dues*.   1. As he is a *creature* of God, he has *duties* to perform to his *Maker*.   He owes to HIM *reverence* and *obedience*,—his heart is the property of his Creator;  he distinguishes the voice that says, *My son, give me thy heart*,—and this he knows lays him under the obligation to love God with all his heart, soul, mind, and strength; and to serve Him through that love.   This is giving God *His due*. This is *beginning* with the *right principle*, that he may go straight to the *right end*.

2. As a member of *civil society*, he has various duties to perform to his fellows, as they have to him.   He is to love his neighbour as himself.   He is to *direct* him, *instruct* him, *defend* him, and *support* him, when he finds him *out of the way*,—*ignorant* of his *interest*,—*assailed* by *overwhelming forces*,—or *destitute* of the *necessaries* of *life*.   This, all human beings owe to each other.   And having fulfilled these duties to his neighbour, as necessity may require, he has rendered to *him his due*.

3. There are duties which he owes to *himself*.

That his *body* may be in health, vigour, and activity, he must avoid every thing by which it might be injured, particularly all excesses in eating, drinking, sleeping, and the opposite to immoderate sleeping, *sitting up very late*, and rising very early, in order to indulge in some favourite study :—this is *lighting the candle at both ends;* and in this way the taper of life must soon burn out.

That his *soul* may be saved, he must avoid all sin ; all irregular and disorderly passions.   It is a duty he owes to his *soul* to apply to God for that grace which produces repentance, faith, and holiness : and in order to get these blessings, he should *read, watch, pray, hear the word of God preached*, and diligently use all the ordinances of God.   He who acts not thus, defrauds his own body and soul.   But the person described in the Text, *works righteousness*,—gives to all their due,—and thus keeps a conscience void of offence towards *God*, and towards *man*.   He *works*—labours to fulfil all the duties he owes to his Creator, and to his fellows : nor in any of these does he do the work either deceitfully or carelessly ; —he labours so as to bring *purpose* and *energy* to bear on every work he undertakes.

3rdly. *He speaketh the truth in his heart.*

We have already seen that the person who is a proper member of the *church militant*, and is living in a growing meetness for the *church triumphant*, is *upright* in *thought*, and *just* in *deed ;* and here it is asserted that he is *true* in *word :* and to be right in the sight of God, in *thought, word,* and *deed,* affords the highest proof of a soul completely regenerated. He who is so, is a *perfect man.* He is, under this particular, represented as a *true man ;*—in him there is no *false way ;*—he does not speak *one thing,* while he *means another ;*—he professes nothing but what he *feels* and *intends.* With him there are no *hollow friendships, vain compliments,* nor *empty professions* of *esteem, love, regard,* or *friendship.* His *mouth* speaks nothing but what his *heart* dictates. His *heart,* his *tongue,* and his *hand,* are all in unison. *Hypocrisy, guile,* and *deceit,* have no place in his soul. To *speak the truth in his heart,* is a rare qualification ;—perhaps the rarest in the whole assemblage of Christian graces. How seldom do we give a thing its right name ! How often do we *profess* what we do not *feel.* In our transactions with men, how seldom do our *hearts* speak what our *lips* utter. To induce persons to *buy,* do we not speak falsely of the *quality* of the article presented for sale,—assert that it cost *so much,* when our consciences know that such a saying has *ten* or *twenty* per cent. of a *lie* in it ? And when *buying,* do we not underrate and vilify the article, that we may get it the *cheaper.* The wise man mentions such a character,—*It is naught, it is naught, saith the buyer, but when he is gone his way, he boasteth,* Prov. xx. 14. Thus he lied with his *tongue,* when his *heart* spoke the *truth.* He overreached his neighbour, and afterwards *boasted of his knavery.* How common is this vice ! Should ich a man be a member of the mystical body of Christ ! Was such a false spirit ever seen in heaven ! There are various other ways in which a man does not speak the truth in his heart ; but the speeches are not so deeply criminal, because he does not intend to *defraud* his neighbour. In compliments, how much falsehood is spoken :—*e. g.* " How do you, Sir ?—I am infinitely glad to see you." Now it is most probable, 1st, That he feels no gladness on the occasion ; therefore, he does not *speak the truth in his heart.* 2. It is *false,* if even he *feel* glad, to say, that he is *infinitely* so. There is another *pro-*

*fession*, often made in these compliments, which from its very nature, must be void of truth :—" I hope I have the pleasure of seeing you in the enjoyment of the most excellent health."" —" Sir, it is an essential addition to my happiness, to find that it is so." Now all these are *falsities ;* but they are not intended to deceive,—they are used according to custom,— they are either the effusions of a light and frivolous mind,—or are spoken *thoughtlessly.* But will these considerations ex- cuse them ? How does the God of truth hear them ? What does His Spirit say ? *Behold, thou desirest truth in the inward parts :*—and does He not search the heart, and try the ways ! *Thou God seest me !*—should be a subject of frequent medita- tion. Does not our Lord say, *We shall give an account of every idle word, in the day of judgment :* how much more of every *wicked, deceptive*, and *lying* word. In the transactions of life, how many are led, from the experience they have had of the falsity of those with whom they have done business, to *doubt* every man's veracity, and to *suspect* all ! And who can much blame them ;—and yet the feeling is *ruinous :*—it divests them of *charity*, and strikes at the very foundation of *brotherly. love.* Indeed, it goes far towards a dissolution of the neces- sary *bonds of society*, for public confidence is difficult to be supported where such a disposition prevails. But still there are overreaching and lying persons to be found ; and we may deplore that state of society, where there is so much need for *caution* and *watchfulness.* This made the very pious Mr. *Herbert* exclaim,

> Surely if each man saw another's heart,
> There would be no commerce ;
> All would disperse
> And live apart.

But there is a *love that thinketh no evil ;* and the person in the text is he who is in possession of it, for *he speaketh the truth in his heart :* and we may add,

> " *Believes* no evil, where no evil *seems.*"

4thly, *He backbiteth not with his tongue.*
The original is very emphatic, רגל על לשנו *lo ragal ál leshono.* He *foots not upon* (or with) *his tongue.* He is one who treats his neighbour with respect. He says nothing that might injure him in his *character, person*, or *property.* He

forges no calumny. He is author of no slander. He insinuates nothing by which his neighbour may sustain any kind of damage.

The *tongue*, because of its frequent employment in slanderous conversation, is represented in the nervous original, as *kicking about* the character of an absent person : a very common vice, and as *destructive* as it is *common :* but the man who expects to *see God*, abhors it, and *backbites not with his tongue.*

The words *backbite* and *backbiter,* come from the Anglo-Saxon, bac or bæc, *the back*, and bitan *to bite :*—the meaning of which has not altered to the present time. But how it came to be used in the sense it is now, in our language, seems at first view unaccountable ; but it is a metaphor taken from the conduct of a dangerous *dog :* and it is intended to convey the *treble* sense of *knavishness, cowardice,* and *brutality.* He is a *knave* who would rob you of your good name ;—he is a *coward*, that would speak of you in your absence, what he dared not to do in your presence ;—and an *ill-conditioned dog* only, would fly at and bite your back, when your face was turned from him. All those three ideas are included in the term ; and all meet in the *detractor* and *calumniator.* His tongue is that of a *knave*, a *coward* and a *dog.* The Rabbins term the *backbiter* the man with the *three-forked tongue ;*—with it he wounds three persons at the same time—the *man* whom he *slanders ;* the *man* who *receives* the *slander ;* and *himself* who is the *slanderer.*

Of such a person the Roman poet has this celebrated saying :—

> *Absentem qui rodit amicum ;*
> *Qui non defendit, alio culpante : solutos*
> *Qui captat risus hominum, famamque dicacis ;*
> *Fingere qui non visa potest : commissa tacere*
> *Qui nequit ; hic niger est : hunc tu, Romane, caveto.*

HOR. *Sat.* lib. i. sat. 4. ver. 81.

He, who malignant tears an *absent friend,*
Or, when attacked by others, *don't defend.*
Who trivial bursts of laughter strives to raise,
And courts of prating pretulance, the praise ;
Of things he *never saw,* who tells his *tale,*
And *friendship's secrets* knows not to *conceal :*
This man is *vile ;* here, Roman, fix your mark,
His soul is *black,* as his *complexion's dark.*

FRANCIS.

The character in the Text, is wholly different from that censured above, and from all others of a similar nature. He who acts otherwise, has no right to the privileges of the church militant; and none of his disposition can ever see God.

5thly. *He doeth no evil to his neighbour.*

He not only avoids all *evil speaking* against his neighbour; but he avoids also all *evil acting* towards him. He speaks no evil of him, and does no evil to him. He does him no harm ;—he occasions him no wrong. On the contrary, he gives him his *due.* See under the *second* particular : where this subject is largely considered.

6thly. *He taketh not up a reproach against his neighbour.*

The word חרפה *cherophah*, which we translate *a reproach*, comes from the root חרף *charaph*, to *strip*, to *make bare*, to *deprive one* of *his garments :* hence חרף *chareph*, the *winter*, because it *strips the fields* of their *clothing*, and the *trees* of their *foliage :* and by this process, nature appears to be *dishonoured* and *disgraced.* The application to the subject in the Text is easy. A man, for instance, of a good character, is reported to have done something evil :—the tale is *spread*, and the *slanderers*, *whisperers*, and *backbiters, carry it about:* and thus the man is *stripped* of *his fair character*,—of his *clothing of righteousness, truth*, and *honesty.* And yet the whole report may be *false:* or the person, in an hour of the power of darkness, may have been tempted and overcome; may have been wounded in the cloudy and dark day ; and now deeply mourns his fall before God ! Who, that has not the -heart of a demon, would not strive rather to *cover*, than to *make bare* the fault in such circumstances ! Those, who, as the proverb says, " *Feed like the flies, passing over all a man's whole parts to light upon his sores*," will take up the tale and *carry it about.* Such, in the course of their diabolic work, carry the story of scandal, among others, to the righteous man ;—to him who loves his God and his neighbour :— but what reception has the talebearer ? The good man *taketh it not up*, לא נשא *lo nasa*, he will *not bear it*,—it shall not be *propagated* by or from him. He cannot prevent the detractor from *laying it down ;* but it is in his power *not to take it up:* and thus the progress of the slander may be arrested. *He taketh not up a reproach against his neighbour ;* and by this means, the *tale-bearer* may be discouraged from bearing it to another door. If there were no *takers up* of defamation, there would be fewer detractors in the land. If there were *no receivers* of *stolen goods*, there would be *no thieves* : and hence another proverb, founded on the justest principle, " The *receiver* is as *bad* as the *thief.*"     And is not the *whisperer*, the *backbiter*, and the *tale-bearer*, the worst of thieves ?—Robbing not only individuals, but whole families of their reputation :— scattering firebrands, arrows, and death? Yes, they are the worst of *felons* :—Hear the poet who was well acquainted with the human heart :—

> Good *name* in man or woman, dear my lord,
> Is the immediate jewel of their souls :
> Who *steals* my *purse* steals *trash*, 'tis something, nothing ;
> 'Twas *mine*, 'tis *his*, and has been *slave* to *thousands* ;
> But he that *filches* from me my *good name*,
> *Robs* me of that which not enriches him,
> And makes me *poor* indeed.

O how many a fair fame has been tarnished by this most Satanic practice ! But bad as the *accidental* retailer of calumny is, he who makes it his business to *go about to collect stories* of scandal, and who endeavours to have *vouchers* for his calumnies, is yet worse ; whether the stories be *true* or *false,*— whether they make the *simple relation*, or *exaggerate* the *fact,*—whether they present a *simple lens*, through which to view the character they exhibit, or an *anamorphosis*, by which every feature is *distorted*, so that in a monstrosity of appearance, every trait of similitude of goodness is lost : and then the reporter himself takes advantage of his own inferences ;—" O Sir, how bad this is ! But—but, there is worse behind."— This *insinuation* is *like* a *drag net*, gathering as it goes, and bringing every thing into its vortex : the good and the bad, are found in one indiscriminate assemblage.

Suppose the stories to be *true*, or *founded in truth*, what *benefit* does society or the *church* ever derive from this underhand detailing ?     *None*.     There are but few cases ever occurring, where the misunderstanding between the members of the church of Christ, should be brought before *two witnesses*, much less before the *church :* but there are some such, and our Lord orders us to treat these with the greatest caution and forbearance.     On this point, see a sermon of the late Rev. J. Wesley, entitled, *The Cure of evil speaking*

Let us now hear what the Sacred Writings say of the flagitious characters already reviewed; and the various *words* by
which they express them.

1. *Evil speaking*—This is termed βλασφημια, *blasphemy*,
injurious speaking, either against God or man. Our Lord
gives it the following associates, Matt. xv. 19, "Out of the
heart proceed *evil thoughts, murders, adulteries, fornications,
thefts, false witness, blasphemies.*

2. *Whisperers*—The private communicators of scandals
and calumnies; see Prov. xvi. 28. "A froward man sheweth
strife: and a *whisperer* separates chief friends." Prov. xxvi.
20. Where no *wood* is, the fire *goeth out:* so where there
is no *tale-bearer* (or WHISPERER,) the *strife ceaseth:* the original is נרגן *nargan:* of this word, an able Hebraist gives the following definition—"נרגן *nargan;* from רגן *ragan*, to be rancid,
rank, or rusty, as bad butter or bacon." "Hence it is applied
to a mind rankled or exulcerated with discontent, envy, or
malevolence; and which uttereth itself in words suitable to
such *bad dispositions.*" See *Taylor* and *Schultens*, on Prov.
xviii. 8.

The whisperer is called ψιθυριστης in Greek, Rom. i. 30;
where he is coupled with *backbiters, haters of God, despite-
ful, proud, boasters, inventors of evil things, &c.;* see also
ver. 31.

3. *Tale-bearer*—One who had been taken into confidence,
and told *privately*, the secrets of his friend; and makes it his
business to carry them from place to place, and from person
to person, as a pedler his wares. Prov. xx. 19. He that
goeth about as a tale-bearer, revealeth secrets. "הולך רכיל *ho
lic racil*, a slanderer—a defamer; who picketh up stories,
true or false, and details them out to the disadvantage of
others." *Heb.* and *Eng.* Concordance.

4. *Backbiters*—See on ver. 3. and see Rom. i. 30. and 31,
where they are associated with the flagitious characters, mentioned under *tale-bearers.* The backbiter is called in Greek
καταλαλος, *a speaker of evil against another, a detractor.*

5. *Slanderers*—1 Tim. ii. 11. διαβολοι, *devils*, from διαβαλ-
λειν, to *shoot through*, with such fiery darts as the devil uses,
and which the shield of faith only can quench. See Eph.
vi. 16.

6. All these deal in *scandal*, σκανδαλα, *stumbling blocks, of-*

*fences ;* whatever hinders or injures another in his Christian *walk,* or brings any reproach on the cause of Christ. These are the things which He will gather out of His kingdom, and them that do iniquity, and will cast them into the furnace of fire. See Matt. xiii. 40, 41.

All the above, with the whole family of defamers, false accusers, calumniators, detractors, destroyers of the good reputation of others, traducers and libellers, however they may rank here, shall have one lot in the eternal world ; none of them shall become *residents* on the hill of God's holiness ; and should not here be permitted to *sojourn* in His *tabernacle,* or *militant Church.* Reader, pray God to save thee from the spirit and conduct of these bad men : have no communion with them, drive them from thy door, yet labour to convert them if thou canst ; but if they will still continue as disturbers of the peace of society, of the harmony of families, and of the union of Christ's Church, let them be to thee as heathen men and publicans ; " the basest, the lowermost, the most dejected, most under-foot, and down-trodden vassals of perdition."

7thly. *In whose eyes a vile person is contemned.*

This person follows the rule given by our Lord, *By their fruits ye shall know them :* he tries no man's *heart,* for he knows men only by the *fruits* they bear, and thus he gains knowledge of the *principle* from which these *fruits* proceed. As to the *vile person* נמאס *nimas,* mentioned here, his name points him out, " a reprobate, one abandoned to sin"—and justly, נבזה *nibzeh,* he is *abhorred ;* is loathsome, as if covered with the *elephantiasis* or *leprosy,* as the word implies.

He may be *rich ;* he may be *learned ;* he may be a *great man* and *honourable* with his master, in high offices in the state ; but if he be a *spiritual leper,* an *infidel,* a *profligate,* the righteous man must despise him, and hold him, because he is an enemy to God and man, in sovereign contempt. If he be in power, he will not treat him as *worthy* of the dignity with which he is invested—but he will respect the *office ;* and while he respects the *office,* and obeys the law, will despise the *man.* And this is quite right, for the popular odium should ever be pointed against vice, lest vice should be accredited by rank and fashion.

*Rab. Aben Ezra* gives a curious turn to this clause, which

he translates thus—*he is mean and contemptible in his own eyes* :—and it is certain that the original ומאם בעיניו נבזה *nibzeh be-êinaiv nimas*, may bear this translation.   His paraphrase on it is beautiful :—" A pious man, whatsoever good he may have done, and however concordant to the divine law he may have walked, considers all this of no worth, compared with what was his duty to do for the glory of his Creator."   A sentiment very like that of our Lord, Luke xvii. 10.   *So likewise ye, when ye shall have done all these things which are commanded you, say, we are unprofitable servants ; we have done that which was our duty to do.*

Taken in this sense, the words intimate, that the man who is truly pious, who is a proper member of the *Church militant*, and is going straight to the *Church triumphant*, is truly humble : he knows he has nothing but what he has received ; he has no merit ; he trusts not in himself, but in the living God.   He renounces his own righteousness, and trusts in the eternal mercy of God, through the infinitely meritorious atonement made by Jesus Christ.   The language of his heart is—

> " I loathe myself when God I see,
>    And into nothing fall :
> Content that thou exalted be,
>    And Christ is all in all."

8thly. *He honoureth them that fear the Lord.*

This clause is a proof, however excellent Aben Ezra's sentiment may be, that he has mistaken the meaning of the preceding clause.   The truly pious man, while he has in contempt the honourable and right honourable profligate infidel, yet *honours them that fear the Lord*, though found in the most abject poverty ; though like Job on the dunghill, or like *Lazarus* covered with sores, at the rich man's gate.   *Character* is the grand object of his attention : *person* and *circumstances* are of minor importance.

*The fear of the Lord* is often taken for *the whole of religion :* and sometimes for the *reverence* which a holy man feels for the *majesty* and *holiness* of God, that induces him to hate and depart from evil.   Here, it may signify the lowest degree of religion ; that *repentance whereby we forsake sin :* for the fear of God is the *beginning of wisdom ;* and *to depart from* evil, that is *understanding.*   He who fears God, and trembles at His word, is so far a *genuine penitent.*

*9thly. He sweareth to his own hurt, and changeth not.*

This holy man adheres inflexibly to *truth,* and at all risks maintains his integrity. He is not only *true* and *just* in all his *dealings* in the common transactions of life, but often acts to his own injury rather than not fulfil his engagements to others. If at any time he have solemnly bound himself to do so and so, and afterwards find that to keep his engagement will be greatly to his damage, though he and others may clearly perceive that the obligation was made *in error,* and reason would, in such a case, release him from the performance ; yet such reverence has he for *God* and for *truth,* that he will not *change,* be the consequences what they may.

He is also as steady to his *promises* as to his *oath ;* and his bare word once passed, will *bind* him as *solemnly* as any *oath.* Indeed, the thoroughly honest man needs *no oath* to *bind him,* —his character *swears* for him ; we have need only of a little reflection to convince us, that he who will not be *honest* without an *oath,* will not be honest *with* one.

In illustration of the doctrine in this clause, I will introduce one fact, which I had many years ago, from high authority :

His late Majesty, GEORGE *the Third,* was very fond of children :—often in his walks both about *Windsor* and St. *James' Park,* he would stop when he saw an interesting child, and speak kindly and affectionately to it, give it some little toy, or sweetmeat, and often a piece of money. One day observing a little lad about four years old, who seemed to have strayed away from its fellows, he addressed it, and finding it intelligent for its age, he took it by the hand, and led it towards the palace, the child nothing loath. He brought the little fellow into the queen's apartment, and presented it to her, with " Here queen, here is a very nice little boy, that I have picked up in my walk,"—and then addressing the lad, " That's the queen, my dear, bow to her." A chair was immediately brought, the little fellow was seated on it, and in a trice some sweatmeats and fruits were laid before him. Little master felt himself quite at home, ate freely, and endeavoured to answer every question that was put to him. And when he had well eaten, it was suggested, that the child might be missed, and cause anxiety in the family, it would be best to restore him to his play-ground. Before he was removed from his chair, the king took out a *new guinea*, and placed it before him, saying, "Here my dear is a pretty thing which I will give you." The child looked at it for some time, and then with his finger pushed it away on the table, saying, "I don't know it—I won't have it;" and looked indifferently over the table. The king said, "Well, my dear, if you won't have this, what will you have? Come, tell me what you'll have, and I will give it to you." There were several papers of a very important nature then lying on the table, which had lately been brought into the royal apartment:— the child looking earnestly at one, said, "I'll have that pretty picture," and put his hand towards it. The king looked confounded, and hesitated; the queen for a time was equally surprised, but she first broke silence, (the child having then his *pretty picture* in his hand, which was no other than a new *bank-note for a very large amount!*) and said, "He must have it—your Majesty's word is passed; your royal promise cannot be recalled." The king with great good humour assented, with, "Yes, yes, he shall have it." A faithful domestic was called, the child delivered to him, with the injunction, to take him back to the park, find out his play-mates, or nurse, and follow their directions, till he should find the dwelling and parents of the child—nothing of either being known to his Majesty or his domestics. The servant was successful, delivered the child and his *pretty picture* to the astonished father and mother; returned, and gave such an account to the royal pair, as satisfied them, that while his *Majesty had sworn to his own hurt,* and would *not change,* a wise Providence had directed the whole transaction. The story was well known in the royal family, but there is reason to think the family of the child was never mentioned, for I could learn no more of this singular history, than the facts, the substance of which is before the reader. I well know, that George the Third feared God, and held his own word sacred: nothing could induce him to *change* his purpose, when he believed he was right.

The *Chaldee Paraphrast* has given a different rendering of this clause :—*He sweareth to afflict himself, and doth not change* :—*i. e.* he hath promised to the Lord to keep his body under, and bring it into subjection :—to deny himself, that he may not pamper the flesh, that it may not lead him into transgression; and that he may, by *saving* all he can, have the more to give to the poor.

The *Syriac, Arabic, Ethiopic, Vulgate, Septuagint,* and *Anglo-Saxon,* translate the clause thus :—*he sweareth to his neighbour, and doth not deceive him* : as they all seem to have read, רעה *le-hareâ,* to his *neighbour,* instead of רעה *le-harâ,* to his *damage,* or *hurt* ;—the change in the meaning is made by the *points,* for the *consonants* are the same in both words : but the reading in the text is followed by the most judicious commentators.

From the whole we learn that this candidate for heaven is a man of unimpeachable truth, and inflexible integrity, who would rather *suffer* evil than *inflict* it : and will keep his *promise,* at the risk of his *substance* and his *life.*

10thly. *He putteth not out his money to usury.*

*Usury* signifies a certain part of the produce of a sum lent for the purpose of traffic : so, that a man trading with the capital of another, gave not only *security* for the *principal,* but so much *per cent.* for its *use.* This was as *innocent* as it was *just.* But when the *lender,* taking advantage of the *circumstances* of the *borrower,* required *more* for the *use* of the money than it was *worth, usury* then expressed *exorbitant,* or *unlawful* interest, and in this sense is now universally received. An *usurer* is one that lends out cash, at such unlawful and exorbitant interest as he can twist out of the necessities of a distressed applicant : of such a practice as this, no man that fears God can be guilty.

In all times, the Jews were remarkable for *usury,* and *usurious contracts :* and a Jew that is saved from this practice, and the love of money, from which it originates, is, charity may well hope, not far from the kingdom of God.

The word נשך *neshech,* which we translate *usury,* comes from the root *nashach, to bite as a serpent,* and here, must signify that *biting* or *devouring usury,* which ruins the person who has it to pay. " This increase of usury, (see Leigh's note *sub voce* נשך) is called *neshech,* because it resembles the *biting of a serpent ;* for, as this is so *small* at first, as scarcely to be *perceptible,* but the venom soon spreads and diffuses itself till it reaches the vitals ; so the *increase of usury,* which at first is not perceived nor felt, at length grows so much as by degrees to *devour* another's substance." Our laws have wisely fixed the worth of *lent cash* at *five per cent.*; he who takes more, is a *usurer*,—one who takes *unlawful* interest; and the same law has adjudged the usurer on conviction, to forfeit *treble* the value of the money lent. And the Roman laws condemned the usurer to the forfeiture of *four times the sum;* Cato de Re Rust. lib. i. Our Saxon ancestors had a very bad opinion of *usurers ;*—Edward the Confessor, commanded all usurers to leave the kingdom : and if any were convicted of it, all their property was confiscated, and themselves banished from the realm : because, said the law, *Usury is the root of all evil.* If a priest then, were convicted of being a *usurer*, his whole property was seized, and distributed to pious uses. The clause is thus translated in the *Anglo-Saxon Psalter*—reþe feoh hir ne realde to gýtrunge "Who fee his, (property) not giveth to greediness." My old Anglo-Scottish Psalter has the Latin text, *Qui pecuniam suam non dedit ad usuram*, which it renders, He that gaf nout his catel til oker. Now this intimates that the translators had either read *pecudem*, cattle, for *pecuniam*, money, or that *cattle* was the only *money*, or medium of exchange, current in his time and country ; and indeed it has long been customary, not only in *Scotland*, but also in the various *hyperborean countries*, for the peasantry to pay their rents, &c. in *kind :* so many cows, sheep, &c. given to the laird, thane, or earl, for the usufruct of the ground. That there is no mistake in the translation, is evident enough from the *paraphrase*, where the author repeats the words with his gloss upon them : He that gaf nout his catel til oker, bodyly, als cobaytus men dos gastly : that þe seke naght for his gude dede, na mede of this wereld, bot onely of heben.—*i. e* "He who does not use his property in a *secular* sense, as covetous men do in a spiritual sense ; expecting no reward for his good actions in this world; but only in the kingdom of God."

The very unusual word *oker*, in the *Anglo-Saxon* okeþ and þokeþ, in the *Gothic* pokþ in German mucher, and in *Danish* ager, means *produce, fruits, offspring ;, usufruct*, whether of *cattle, land, money*, or even of the *human progeny.* And the word *catel*, may be used here for *chattels*, substance of any kind, moveable or immoveable :—but the word itself appears to be derived from *cattle*, which were from the beginning, the principal substance or riches of the inhabitants of the country,

and tillers of the field.   And it is well known, that the word
*pecunia*, money, was derived from *pecus*, cattle ;  which were
no *longer* used as a medium of commerce, when *silver* and
*gold* came into use.

There is a passage in the *Ploughman's tale* in *Chaucer ;*
when speaking of the worldly and worthless priests of his
day, he uses the term, *cattel-catching*, for *getting money* or *goods.*

> Some on her churches dwelle
> Apparailled poorley, proude of porte ;
> The seven sacramentes thei doen sell ;
> In *cattel-catching* is her comfort.
> Of eche matter thei wollen mell,
> And doen hem wrong is her disport ;
> To affray the people, thei been fell
> And hold hem lower than doeth the Lorde.

The whole of this tale shews the wretched, ignorant, and oppressed state of the people in England, under the *domination* of
the *popish clergy*, in the fifteenth century.   They have been
*emancipated* by the *Reformation ;* and they will richly deserve the same thraldom, should they ever *permit themselves*
to be entangled again under the same yoke of bondage.

11thly. *He taketh no reward against the innocent,*

*Assassinations* were frequent in Asiatic countries,—and a
*despot* had only to say to one of his dependents or slaves, " Go
and bring the head of such a one :"—and the head was immediately brought !—In other cases, one despot was *hired* to destroy another, either by the poignard of the *assassin* or by
*poison.*  Of these acts I could produce many authentic
instances.   And from this Psalm, it does appear, that private
assassinations were frequent in the time of the Psalmist.   But
the person who is here stated to be fit to *sojourn* in *God's
Tabernacle*, and finally to *reside* in the *mountain of His holiness*, is one who takes *no reward against the innocent.*   He
neither *gives* nor *receives* a BRIBE, to prevent justice, or injure
an innocent man in his cause.   The lawyer, who sees a poor
man opposed by a rich man, and though he is convinced in
his conscience that the poor man has *justice* and *right* on his
side, yet takes the *larger fee* from the *rich* man, to plead
against the poor man, does, in fact, *take a reward against the
innocent ;*—and without the most signal interposition of the
mercy of God, is as sure of perdition, as if he were already in
it.   But, because such unprincipled lawyers have been found,
it is most uncandid and wicked, to apply the censure generally :

though they have much in their power, and may deceive without detection, for law admits of *many quibbles*, and is, in many cases, the *pit of the bottomless deep :* yet men of the highest honour and honesty are found in as great proportion among them, as among others : let those of a contrary character bear their blame, and either reform, or prepare to meet the GOD of *justice.*

*Lastly, He that doeth these things ;*—He, in whose character and conduct all these excellencies meet; though still much more is necessary under the *Christian* dispensation,—*shall never be moved ;* he shall stand fast for ever :—he is an upright honest man, fearing God, loving his fellows, and hating covetousness : God will ever be his support : HE shall *dwell* in the holy hill; after having served his Maker here, in his generation.

Thus we have these two important questions answered,— *Who* can be considered "a worthy member of the Church militant upon earth ?" And, *Who*, after life is ended, shall be received into heaven, and be forever with the Lord ! The answer is, The man who, to *faith in Christ Jesus*, adds those *eleven* moral excellencies, which have already been enumerated and explained ; who has been *freely justified through the redemption that is in Jesus;* and has had *the thoughts of his heart cleansed by the inspiration of God's Holy Spirit;* he shall go to heaven—he shall be received into the Paradise of God, and shall see Him *as He is.* Amen.

To conclude, I hope the Reader will not say, " This is *Jewish doctrine*, and teaches salvation by works." I answer, it is God's doctrine, whether it came by *Jew* or *Gentile.* And as to *salvation by works*, there is nothing of it in the *Text*, and nothing in the *Comment.* But it may be answered, " There is here too much strictness—God does not require so much from *poor, weak, fallible* man." I answer, God requires whatsoever His *word requires*—He will not bring *down* the moral law to our *weakness* and *fall*—but He will bring us *up* to it. Jesus Christ came to *raise* us from our *fall*, to *strengthen* us with strength in our soul ; He has made an atonement for our sins, and it is through *His merits alone* that we either get *heaven*, or the *grace* that qualifies us for it. But still you think, " you may get to heaven without all these excellencies." Let your conscience answer the following questions. Will

M

the man that is *not upright*—that *does not work righteousness* —that does *not speak the truth in his heart*—be saved? Will the *backbiter* and *slanderer*—he who *does evil to his neighbour*, and *takes up a reproach against him*—get to heaven? Will he get there, in whose eyes the *vile person is honourable*, and he who *fears the Lord*, *despicable?*—Will he, who *breaks his word*, and *falsifies his oath;*—that is an *oppressive usurer* —takes *bribes* against the innocent, or to betray, and sell his country, at a *general election*—will he get to heaven? If such persons can get to heaven, what honest man would wish to go thither?—And do you expect to go to heaven with all your imperfections on your head?—Then, you are most awfully deceived. But you say, " you have *faith in Christ;*"—well—see that it be *sound*, for the devils *believe* and tremble. Did Christ come to destroy the moral law? Does the gospel require holiness of heart and life? You know it does. And do you believe this word, *Without holiness no man shall see God?*—And what does this Psalm require, but that holiness of *heart* and *life* which the gospel every where requires? Is the *law* against the *promises of God*, or the *gospel* of God against a *holy life?*—Then you must receive the grace of the gospel, that the *law of the spirit of life*, may make you free from the *law of sin and death*.

If you *do these things*, you *shall never be moved;*—you shall go from heaven below, to heaven above :—but if you only *believe them*, and believe the *gospel* the same way, you shall be *driven away in your iniquities*, and go where you shall be *eternally moved* under the *action* of the *worm that never dieth*, and *the fire that is never quenched.* Go now to Christ, that He may purge your conscience from dead works ,baptize you with the spirit of holiness, guide you by His counsel, and at last receive you into His glory. Amen.

*Heydon Hall, Middlesex,*
    *Feb.* 15, 1829.

TO

# RICHARD SMITH, Jun., Esq.

&c. &c. &c.

*Stoke Newington.*

---

Dear Sir,

I HAVE not asked your permission to prefix your name to the following discourse. My reason is simple, and to myself cogent : I ask no patronage, howsoever respectable yours might be to me, and I beg no favours. Gratitude alone impels me, and it is not in the nature of gratitude to ask *permission* to express its obligations. It may be manifested in various ways, but without some kind of *expression*, it cannot exist. By the present mode I take a liberty which, if I asked, you would not grant: it is then to tell my friends and the public, as far as this discourse may go, that you have from the beginning been the steady and practical friend of the Zetland Isles ; that you have helped me to assist them in the most effectual manner, while you peremptorily refused to let your left hand know what your right hand did. It is true, that while your shadow has been extended over those northern regions, you have often been amply repaid by the good news which you heard from that distant land ;—of the prosperity of a work of *life* and *power* unequivocally manifested in the salvation of multitudes, and in the relief and comfort of many widows and orphans, and of many others equally necessitous and destitute. You have *their* prayers, my gratitude, and *God's* blessing. May the light of His countenance shine upon you and yours for ever ! Amen.

There is something singular, if not in the discourse, yet in the *circumstances* in which it was preached.

In the middle of last June, I sailed out of the Thames on purpose to make, probably, my last voyage to the Zetland Isles. Having arrived at Whitby, I was met by a few select friends, who wished to accompany me on my voyage : the

Rev. James Everett, and W. Read, Esq. of Manchester; John Mosely Smith, Esq. of Stockport; Rev. James Loutit, of Windsor; John Campion, Esq. of Whitby, and my second son, Theodoret, hired a vessel, the sloop *Henry*, Captain Greenwood, which we were to have at our command, to sail *where* and *when* we pleased, wind and weather permitting. As I intended to visit at least the different larger Islands in the Zetland group, and the principal *Voes* or *Bays*, I well knew, from former experience, that this would be impossible, unless I had a vessel at my own command. In those Islands there are no public roads; and to travel over hills, through bogs, and to cross different Sounds and Voes in small crazy boats, would not only take up much time, but would be more harassing than it was at all likely my strength of body and state of health could sustain. We had an excellent passage, and our *land-fall* was Sumburgh Head, the south end of the Island of Mainland, to which we steered when we *bore away* from Whitby; and so truly had we kept our course, that we could not say we had lost one foot of way, in a run of between 3 and 400 miles! I will not trouble you with a detail of our operations while passing up the eastern side of those Islands in a direction due north. It is sufficient to say, we first touched at *Lerwick;* then at the Island of *Whalsey; Burra Voe,* in *South Yell; Uya Isle* and *Uya Sound;* and then *Balta Sound,* in the Island of *Unst;* the most northern of this group. While we lay here, giving time to our Captain to change his sand ballast for *chromate of iron,* I travelled over the high hills, composed almost entirely of *Serpentine rock,* with little vegetable soil, and consequently little verdure, and passing *Harold's-wick,* where we left Mr. Everett to preach, I went on to *North-wick,* the farthest Bay north on the eastern side of the Zetland Isles: a little beyond which, on Sabbath morning, July 6, I preached to some hundreds of people, gathered from various places and considerable distances, the following discourse.

The peculiar circumstances in the case I shall distinctly note. 1st. I stood now on the most northern ground under the dominion of the British crown: and on the most northern inhabited part of that ground. And 2dly. On the line of direction in which I then stood, which was nearly due north, there was neither land nor inhabitant to the north pole. 3dly.

In nearly a direct line east, I had Bergen, in Norway, on my right hand; and farther on, north, Spitsbergen; on my left, west, were the *Faroe Isles;* and onward, north-west, *Iceland,* and then *Old Greenland:*—between these, from *Lamba Ness,* the uttermost point north of the Island of *Unst,* not one foot of land, nor consequently one human inhabitant, is to be found on to the north pole:—so that I was literally preaching on one of the *ends of the earth,* beyond which, in that direction, the sound of the gospel can never be heard.

As I had a plain people to address, I endeavoured to make use of the plainest terms, yet still without bringing down Divine things below the standard of their own dignity; and I believe the discourse was made a blessing to many that heard it.

Of the inhabitants of this Island, I can say the same as of all the Isles in Zetland: they are a people with good understanding and good sense; and in kindness and hospitality to strangers, without parallel. If, in outward circumstances and geographical situation, they have generally but *two talents—* if any people on the globe, from the south to the north pole, have made ten out of the two, it is the Zetlanders: nor have I ever met a people who more richly deserve the truth of the gospel—nor a people who more carefully keep, nor more correctly adorn it.

I know you rejoice in their prosperity, and will bless God for their profiting. You have served them as the *Treasurer* of that fund which is employed to build them places of worship; and you have never suffered the work to stand still, even when the Bank was, for a time, exhausted. May your shadow be extended for ever, and may the sun of your prosperity never withdraw its shining! For the sake of Zetland, as well as on many other accounts,

I am, my dear Sir,

Your much obliged, very grateful and affectionate servant,

ADAM CLARKE.

*Heydon Hall, Middlesex,*
*Aug. 23, 1828.*

# SERMON XXII.

## ACQUAINTANCE WITH GOD;
### AND THE
## BENEFITS WHICH RESULT FROM IT.

A DISCOURSE DELIVERED

# IN THE ISLAND OF UNST,

IN

# ZETLAND,

THE FARTHEST NORTHERN POSSESSION OF THE BRITISH CROWN,

*Sunday Morning, July 6th, 1828.*

JOB xxii. ver. 21—23

21. Acquaint now thyself with him, and be at peace: thereby good shall come unto thee.

22. Receive, I pray thee, the law from his mouth, and lay up his words in thine heart.

23. If thou return to the Almighty thou shalt be built up, thou shalt put away iniquity far from thy tabernacles, &c.

MORE important advice than this, was never given to man: nor can any be more necessary at all times, nor be urged with more powerful motives; nor is it possible that the terms of the advice can be explained by clearer directions:

I. The Advice. " Acquaint now thyself with Him."

II. The Motives. "Thereby good shall come unto thee, and thou shalt be built up."

III. The Directions. "1. Receive the law from His mouth. 2. Lay up His words in thy heart. 3. Put away iniquity from thy tabernacles," &c.

The general meaning is this :—By getting an interest in the Divine favour, and in having the soul brought into a state of peace with Him :—thereby, that is, in these *two things*, good will come unto thee. First, from an interest in His favour, thou mayest expect all necessary blessings. Second, from His peace, in thy conscience, thou will feel unutterable happiness. But we must enter more particularly into a discussion of the important subjects contained in these verses, and examine the foundation and principles on which they rest. They require the deepest attention of the head, and the strongest affections of the heart.

Here we have to do with GOD and MAN : the *perfections* of the one; the *imperfections* and necessities of the other. Let us consider both.

1. With *whom* are we exhorted to *acquaint* ourselves? With GOD. *Who* is HE? This is the most difficult of all subjects;—the most sublime of all knowledge;—but supposed to be, in a certain way, level to the apprehensions of men.

1. The Apostle, speaking to the Corinthians, says, *Awake to righteousness and sin not; for some have not the knowledge of God; I speak this to your shame.*

It appears, therefore, that they might have acquired knowledge, or their ignorance could not have been their reproach. There were many advantages which the heathen Greeks possessed ; and by them, through His works, the eternal power and Godhead of the Creator might be known.

2. It is easy to speak *about* or *of* God :—but to shew *what* He is,—how difficult ! We can trace up every being to others of its own kind ;—there is a *concatenation* of *causes* and *effects*.—We can trace an *acorn* to an *oak*,—and that to another acorn, till we come to the *first plant.* We can trace a *child* to its *parents*,—can conceive that these parents were once *infants*, whom we can trace to *their parents*,—and so on, till we come to a *first human pair*;—but, to what can we trace *these?* They did not produce themselves. St. Luke,

in displaying a genealogy, begins at his own times, and goes from *son* to *father*, whom he finds to be the *son* of *another father*, and so on, till 'he comes to the *last father*, in the *ascending* line, who could not be the author of his own being, and therefore, he properly says, Adam, who was the *son of God*.    This Being, therefore, is the Father of the spirits of all flesh.    1. In reference to man, He is the cause of all human existence.—2. And when we examine all other beings, we shall find that He is equally the *cause* of their existence.

3. But *who* is He?    If He be the *Cause* of all being,—He is necessarily *before* all being, and Himself uncaused : this leads us at once into His *eternity*.

4. In ratiocination, the human spirit can go to God, and when it reaches Him, it is lost in eternity,—not the *idea* of eternity, for of this it can form no *idea*.    Nor can *conjecture* or *fancy*, form any idea of any thing when it arrives at God, but *God Himself*, and *certain attributes*, necessarily inherent in him.

' 5. Here then we see God in His eternity, and no excursion of fancy can go beyond this :—and what is the *doctrine* derivable from this?    Has any of those who have written and spoken on the *Being and Attributes of God*, made any *use* of this grand fact?    I think not.    But has it not an obvious meaning, and is it not this,—*In God, human spirits are designed eternally to rest*,—they cannot go beyond Him ; they can ascend by reasoning to Him,—and this is their intended *place*,—the end of their destination,—their final abode.

6. But does the idea of God, *in* His eternity, and the knowledge that He is the *centre* where intelligent spirits can rest, necessarily shew that these spirits *must find happiness there* ? No, not *simply*.

7. But as we find God to be the *Cause* of all being ; and find an infinity of Being endowed with various degrees of various perfections, and know that nothing can give what it does not possess : hence we learn that God must possess *various perfections ;*—and as He Himself is *infinite* and *eternal*, all His perfection must be such :

1. He must be *wise*, and that wisdom infinite.
2. He must be *powerful*, and that power unlimited.
3. He must be *good*, and that goodness unbounded.
4. He must be *happy*, and that happiness infinitely perfect.

Every intelligent nature must be *happy* in proportion to the *degree of its purity and goodness.* God being *pure* and *good,* is infinitely so, and therefore *infinitely happy.*

5. *Benevolence* is a necessary quality of goodness; and a *desire* to communicate itself, necessarily belongs to *intelligent goodness.* 1. Hence God's creation of man, and intelligent natures. He made them like Himself, that they might derive endless happiness from Himself. 2. Man, therefore, may be made a partaker of the Divine nature. It is the *will* of God that it should be so; but man must *acquaint* himself with God that it may be so.

II. Let us look into MAN, and see *his* state. He is not at *peace;* he has not *good.*

1. He has various powers and faculties,—mighty and extensive; but they are in disorder and ruin. As he has not *peace,* men are in a state of *hostility* among themselves. As he is sinful, he has no *good.* He is, therefore, unhappy. He is torn by inward factions,—conflicting passions :—*judgement* and *conscience* at variance with *passion* and *appetite.* He suffers in himself what nations do who are in a state of *warfare.* In the latter case all *confidence* is destroyed ;—*security* of person and property uncertain ;—the *apprehension* of evil takes the place of *hope;*—treasure is exhausted, and the best blood of the land drained out for its defence. Issue as the contest may, there must be long misery and national distress.

*Man* is at war with his *fellows often;*—and *ever* with and in *himself;*—condemning himself in the thing that he alloweth.

2. Yet he has what is called the *hunger of the soul,*—an insatiable desire after peace and happiness. GOOD, substantial good, is the object of his desire ;—he seeks it early and late, he pursues it under various forms and various names :—but in order to get it he minds earthly things—animal pleasures, secular good, and worldly honours ;—these when attained do not gratify, not only, 1. because they are not of the nature of the soul; but, 2. because they are not *eternal.*

In the pursuit of these, life generally is spent; and vanity and vexation of spirit are written upon the whole.

Is the Father of the spirits of all flesh, unmindful of all this? No—His eye affects His heart,—He sees it with concern, because He wills the happiness of His intelligent offspring.

And Hé shews this concern by this Divine oracle,—*Acquaint thyself now with God, and be at peace, and thereby good shall come unto thee.*

That there should be any occasion for such an exhortation as that contained in the first verse of the Text, is a *reproach to man :* that it should be given by the inspiration of the Almighty, proves the *goodness of God.*

In order to understand these points clearly, I shall consider,—

I. What is implied in aequaintance with God?

II. What are the means by which this acquaintance is to be acquired?

III. What are the benefits which result from this acquaintance?

I. What is implied in an aequaintance with God?

The word *acquaint* signifies to gain knowledge of a person or thing, by association, familiar intercourse, conversation, and exact examination. *Acquaintance* signifies the *knowledge* that is acquired by such means. We say that we are *acquainted* with such a *thing, book,* or *country,* because we have examined the *thing*—read the *book*—or travelled through the *country.* When applied to a person, it signifies : 1. We have *heard* of him. 2. Have been *in his company.* 3. Have *conversed* with him. 4. Have not only interchanged *compliments,* but reposed *confidence* in him ; and thus, 5. become *familiar* with him ; and 6. this *familiarity,* supported by frequent *intercourse,* has been heightened into *friendship.* Hence *acquaintance* and *friend* have nearly the same meaning.

An *intimate acquaintance,* is one *thoroughly known :* and a very *particular acquaintance,* is one with whom we not only interchange all the terms descriptive of friendship ; but also all those *affections* which constitute the spirit of friendship : therefore—1. to *hear* of—2. to *associate with*—3. to *hold conversation* with—4. to become *familiar* with—5. to have confident *communication* with—and 6. to *take* and be *taken into friendship* with, a person, are all implied in being *thoroughly* or *intimately* ACQUAINTED with him.

The word used here, which we translate *acquaint,* סכן *sakan,* signifies to *lay up*—as a *treasure :* to procure an *interest in ; —*we *lay up* the *treasure,* in which we have the whole property, right, and interest, that we may have recourse to it whenever we please; and by it supply all our necessities. This notion of the word agrees very well with the spirit of this exhortation : consider that God alone is the never failing Fountain of all good; get an *interest* in Him—secure His friendship and help ; and then no good will be wanting to you. This meaning of the place, was perceived by *Coverdale ;* for in his Bible, (the first ever published in the English language,) he translates, *Reconcile thyself to Him*—get an acquaintance with Him, come into His presence, cease from thy enmity to Him, make supplication to thy Judge—implore forgiveness— pray to be received into His favour ; and *thereby good*—all good essentially requisite to thy present and eternal welfare— *shall come unto thee.*

Having now considered the *meaning* of the word, the import of the exhortation will be the more easily perceived.

I have already stated, " That it is a reproach to man that such an exhortation should be necessary."   That there should be any human beings, where a divine revelation has come, found destitute of the *knowledge of God*, or that are *unacquainted* with their Maker and Redeemer, is a sore evil, and a high reproach indeed ; but it was so, even in a Christian Church, in the time of St. Paul, for he thus exhorts the people at *Corinth :* " Awake to righteousness and sin not ; for some have not the knowledge of God : I speak this to your shame." 1 Cor. xv. 35.

Let us examine this point intimately.

1. To be *acquainted* with God we must, 1. Hear of Him : —and have we not all heard of *Him ?*   Are not His lines gone out through the world ? and His words to the ends of the earth ?   Even to *you* has the word of his salvation been sent : you, who live here on a line a very little to the east of the north pole, between which and you there is not one human inhabitant, nor one foot of known land—you have heard of Him : you have long had His Bible, your forefathers have heard the word at the lips of teachers sent by Him,—have been favoured with the means of grace, and have had such calls to acquaint yourselves with God, that the well grounded hope of eternal glory, might be ministered through those means, according to these calls.   Even these Isles have waited for His salvation ;—it has been long since sent, that in His arm you might trust.   Have we ever duly consi-

dered what a mercy it is to have a Bible—to be able to read it—to hear it read—to have it explained:—what were your forefathers previously to their getting the Bible? Were they not a nation of gross heathens, serving stocks and stones rudely cut out in the forms of *men* and *women*! of the *sun* and the *moon*; of *Thor, Wodin,* or *Odin*; of *Friga* or *Freya*: either imaginary beings, or ancient freebooters, pirates, cut-throats, and general profligates:—and these were worshipped with abominable and cruel rites, uncleanness, and human sacrifices. The principles of their religion we know; they are still extant in Scandinavian books. A very ancient book called the *Edda,* written in the Icelandic language, one of the most correct and important MSS. of which is in my own possession, gives these principles in detail; describes at large the acts of those who were the objects of their religious adoration: uncovers their hell, (the place of the evil being called *Loke*;) and opens the gate of their heaven, (*Asgard,* the habitation of their gods;) and *Valhalla,* the celestial dwellings of their heroes. And what is this latter? According to the *Edda* it is the *Hall of Odin,* where his followers are to spend their duration in quaffing ale out of the skulls of their enemies! and those very skulls out of which they had formerly drunk the blood of their owners! Is it not an infinite mercy that *you* and your neighbours, the *Norwegians, Danes, Icelanders,* and *Swedes*—the remains of the *Gothic* and Scandinavian tribes—have been saved from this cruel and degrading superstition, by receiving the *Bible* instead of the *Edda,* by which they and you have been taught the knowledge of the true God! Your fathers worshipped in these mountains, over whose summits of serpentine rock I have this morning travelled, and to the north of which we now stand, and imbibed instruction from their *scalds,* poets, and priests, in those inhuman and diabolic arts, by which they were taught to rob, plunder, butcher, and enslave their fellow men! *Now,* the peaceable words of the Gospel of Jesus, succeed to the ferocious strains of the *Volu Spa,* and the dying *song of Lodbrog!* Now, they and you have learnt that the Son of Man is come, not to destroy men's lives, but to save them. Ye have heard of Him who is the Lord God, merciful and gracious, long-suffering, and slow to wrath; forgiving iniquity, transgression, and sin. Be ever thankful for that mercy that has turned you from so deep a darkness, to a light so truly marvellous.*

* The *Edda*, referred to above, is a work in the Icelandic language, and contains the Mythology, and complete religious system of the ancient *Scandinavians*, the people who occupied the kingdoms called *Norway, Sweden, Denmark*, and the *Islands* dependent on those countries.    Among those isles the *Zetland* isles were numbered : from them they were peopled, and from them received the same religious system as that of their neighbours. *Unst* being the nearest both to *Iceland* and *Norway*, was no doubt *first peopled;* and the settlers brought their native *paganism* with them.

There are *two* books called *Edda* :—the *first* compiled by *Sæmund Froda*, an Icelander, who was born in 1056. This work consists of a number of *ancient poems*, on mythological subjects, the chief of which is—1. The *Volu spa*, or the *prophecies* of the *virgin Vola.* 2. The *Havamaal*, or *Divine Discourse ;* and 3. The *Runa Pattur Othins*, or *magical* chapter of *Odin*, or the magical works which can be performed by the use of the *Runic characters.* Of these metrical pieces, there are thirty-six in all, in this poetical *Edda.*

The second Edda is all in *prose*, and is a collection of the mythology, theology, and philosophy of the *Scandinavians*, made by the very learned *Snorro Sturlesson*, about A. D. 1215. This also is in Icelandic. An edition of *this* was printed at Copenhagen, in 4to, 1665, by a Danish lawyer, *Resenius*, in the original *Icelandic*, with a *Danish* and *Latin* version, and copious notes.

An edition of the *Rhythmical Edda*, that of *Sæmund*, was undertaken at Copenhagen, and the first vol. 4to, published in 1787, which was followed by a second vol. in 1818 :—a *third is promised.* To the second vol. there is a *copious* and useful *glossary.*

From these volumes, the whole system of the very ancient *Scandinavian Idolatry*, may be gathered.

The following may give a general view :—

1. *Odin* or *Woden*, their supreme God, is there termed, " *The terrible and severe deity ;*—the *father of slaughter ;*—who carries *desolation* and *fire ;*—the *tumultuous and roaring deity ;*—the *giver of courage* and *victory ;* he who *marks* out *who shall perish in battle ;*—the *shedder of the blood of man*, &c. From him is the *fourth* day of our week denominated *Wodensday*, or *Wednesday.*

2. *Frigga*, or *Freya ;* she was his consort, called also *Heortha*, mother *Earth*. She was the goddess of love and debauchery—the northern *Venus.* She was also a warrior, and divided the souls of the slain with her husband, *Odin.* From her we have *Friday*, or *Freya's* day ; as on that she was peculiarly worshipped. As was *Odin* on Wednesday.

3. *Thor*, the god of winds and tempests, thunder and lightning ;—he was the especial object of worship in Norway, Iceland, and consequently in the Zetland isles. From him we have the name of our fifth day, *Thor's day*, or *Thursday.*

4. *Tir*, the god who protects houses. His day of worship was called *Tyrsday*, or *Tiisday*, whence our *Tuesday.*

As to our first and second day, *Sunday* and *Monday*, they derived their names from the *sun* and *moon*, to whose worship ancient idolaters had consecrated them.

*Asgard* is their *heaven*, or *court of their gods.*

*Valhalla*, their *paradise*, the seat of *Odin* and his heroes, where they are represented as going through their martial exercises, then cutting each other to pieces, afterwards all the parts healing, they sit down to their feast, where they *quaff beer* out of the *skulls* of those whom they had slain in battle—and whose blood they had before drank out of the same skulls, when they had slain them.

*Niflheim*, or *Evil house*, is their *hell.*

*Loke*, the *Devil*, or *principle of evil.*

*Hela,—Death.* Of whom they give this description. Her Palace is *anguish ;* her Table, *famine ;* her Waiters, *expectation* and *delay ;* her Threshold, *precipice ;* and her Bed, *leanness.*

All who die in battle go to *Valhalla*, Odin's palace, where they amuse themselves, as stated above.

The *Scandinavians* offered different kinds of sacrifices, but especially *human :* and from these they drew auguries by the velocity with which the blood flowed, when they cut their throats, and from the appearance of the *intestines*, and especially the *heart.*

2. But in order to be *acquainted* with God we must *know* *Him* by having *communion* with Him : that man is not an acquaintance of ours, with whom we never kept company :—— nor are we acquainted with that God, with whom we never had *communion.*   And as we cannot be said to be *acquainted* with any person with whom we have never *conversed,* so we cannot be said to have any *acquaintance* with that God with whom we never held intercourse by *prayer.*   He that cometh unto God, must *know that He is,* and that He is the rewarder of them who diligently seek Him.   By *prayer,* we approach the palace of the great King ; and by *faith* we enter into that palace.   We present our petitions, which he graciously receives—He speaks peace to His people, that they may not turn again to folly.   Frequent intercourse with this most holy and gracious Being, brings us to an *acquaintance* with His loving kindness and tender mercy.   They who pray not, know nothing of this God ; and know nothing of the state of their own souls.

3. In an *acquaintance,* such as that which the text recommends, there must be *confidence* :—we would not form an *acquaintance* with a person in whom we could not *confide;* and if we found him to be a person of probity, our confidence would be in proportion to our acquaintance.   It is impossible that we could enter at all into a consideration of the nature of God—of His *goodness, mercy, and love*—without feeling confidence that, from that *goodness* all necessary good might be expected ; all pardon and grace from that *mercy;* and all tenderness and compassion from that *love.*   His promises we should consider as perfectly safe : He is faithful, and cannot deny Himself.   His promises are pledges given to men, which His goodness, mercy, and love will redeem.   Hence, *confidence* in Him produces *faith:* we see from His *power* that He *can* do all things ; and from His *mercy, goodness,* and *truth,* that He will do all that is necessary for those who put

It was a custom in Denmark, to offer annually, in January, a sacrifice of 99 *cocks,* 99 *dogs,* 99 *horses,* and 99 MEN—besides other human sacrifices, offered on pressing occasions, public calamities, &c. in order to turn away the anger of their gods.   Even in England, I fear, our ancestors partook much of the spirit and practice of the same horrible and barbarous superstition.   It is no wonder that we say in our public service, when the Gospel for the day is announced to be read, " Thanks be to God for His holy Gospel."   O what an ineffable blessing has the Gospel been wherever it has been preached !   For more of those superstitions, see the *Edda,—Mallet's Northern Nations—Bartholinus de Causis contempta Mortis,* &c.

their trust in Him. For all His promises are *yea* and *amen*, in our Lord Jesus Christ. Thus, increasing confidence begets increasing faith; and this increasing *faith* is daily obtaining the fulfilment of His promises. He gives grace and glory, and no good thing will He withhold from them that trust in Him, and walk uprightly.

4. This *confidence* will produce a *holy familiarity;* we shall seek for opportunities of increasing our acquaintance with one who is the Sovereign Good: without whom nothing is wise, or holy, or strong: and without whom, we can neither *know* what is *right,* nor *do* what is *holy* and *just.* And this very conviction will tend to increase the spirit and practice of prayer—and consequently our communion with God.

5. *Intimate acquaintance* with a person, engendering mutual confidence, and begetting a pleasing familiarity, is very little short of what is termed *friendship :* nor does there seem to be any difference between *intimate acquaintance* and *special friendship.* But however this may be, we well know, that they who acquaint themselves with God, as above specified, will find Him to be their *Friend,* their highest, chiefest, and *best Friend*—a *Friend* that loveth at all times—that knows the souls of His followers in adversity : that is untouched and uninfluenced by any kind of caprices, and on the permanency of whose friendship we may depend, while in simplicity and godly sincerity, not with fleshly wisdom, but by the grace of God, we have our conversation in the world. Thus, while God is the *Friend* of every true *believer,* of all who have got an acquaintance with Him. every true believer is a friend of God. All these things are implied in being *acquainted* with Him. My brethren, lay these things to heart, and see whether you have received this wise man's exhortation, *Acquaint now thyself with God.*

6. But that translation of the original word, which appears in *Coverdale's* Bible, the first complete Bible ever printed in the English language, must not be overlooked. *Reconcile thyself to Him.* Man is in a state of *enmity* with God : he is a *sinner* against his Maker, a rebel against his Sovereign, he is attainted of high treason, by God's law, and is condemned to death ; and that death he must suffer, if he be not reconciled to the great Lawgiver. Now this *reconciliation* supposes that the man ceases from his rebellious acts, and that with a peni-

tent soul he implores forgiveness from his offended Judge.
We have already seen that *thorough acquaintance* will terminate in *friendship ;*—a union of hearts and hands, where both
parties seek each other's welfare and happiness.   This state
of friendship is impossible where the man is living in a way
which proves his heart to be in a state of *enmity* to God.
Can we suppose that a subject is *reconciled,* or in a state of
*friendship* with his king, who is breaking his laws daily,—
blaspheming his name,—traducing his character,—ridiculing
and despising his government,—teaching others to disobey
the laws,—making as many enemies to the constitution of his
country as he can, and strengthening by all means in his
power, those who are already the enemies of the state ?   Is
not such a one the worst of felons ?   Does he not deserve the
most exemplary punishment?   Should not every peaceable,
honest, loyal man, abhor him ?   Should he not be considered
the nation's disgrace, and a public pest ?   And should he not
be avoided as a dangerous leper, infecting every *place* where
he sojourns, and every *person* with whom he comes into contact ?   All this is readily granted by every person who loves
his own safety, honours the king, and seeks the peace of society.   What then shall we say of the *open sinner,*—of the
" cheap swearer, who through his open sluice, lets his soul run
for nought ?"   Of the *liar*—whose heart is not true to God—
nor his tongue to it—nor his actions to either !   Of the
*drunkard*—who consumes his body, his health, and his substance—who, in the phrensy of inebriation, may kill his
mother—or, in the sottishness of continued tippling, may fall
into a pit, and be dashed to pieces—or fall under a cart wheel,
and be crushed to death?   And what shall we say of the
more *secret sinner ?*   He that *cheats* and *defrauds,* who has
the *false* or *deficient measure,* and the *bag with deceitful
weights ?*   Of the polished *flatterer,* who to promote his own
interest, invests another with a character, the qualities of
which he has never borne ?   Or of the specious *hypocrite,*
who, while he pretends to all *saintship,* is destitute of *holiness*
—whose religion is only a cloak to cover the deformities of
his character ?   Are not all these, (and the catalogue might
be vastly increased,) enemies to God in their minds, by evil
propensities, and in their lives, by wicked works ?   If these
do not get reconciliation to their God, without doubt they shall

perish everlastingly. To such, I cry, be reconciled to Him, that ye perish not.

II. Seeing this *acquaintance* is of such importance, and this reconciliation is so absolutely necessary; and that man, naturally, is blind and sinful, it will be necessary next to inquire, by what means these blessings are to be obtained.

We are not left to our own judgement to devise an answer to this important question :—He who gives the exhortation, has laid down the proper directions ; and they are the best parts of this speech delivered by Eliphaz the Temanite. I shall take them in order.

The *first* advice, in reference to this acquaintance and reconciliation, is : *Receive, I pray thee, the law from his mouth,* ver. 22.

What is the *law* that is here intended? Those who contend that this book was written *before* the giving of the law, say that the *law* here mentioned is the *seven* precepts which Noah, after the flood, delivered to his sons, and they to their posterity. The precepts were in substance, the following :—

1. Obey judges, magistrates, and princes.

2. Avoid all idolatry, superstition, and sacrilege.

3. Avoid all blasphemy, perjury, and irreverent use of God's name.

4. Avoid all incest, and unnatural conjunctions.

5. Avoid all murder, battery, infliction of wounds, mutilations, &c.

6. Avoid all theft, fraud and lying.

7. Eat no blood, nor any portion of animals cut off while the animal is alive. This we find is a custom among the Abyssinians even to the present time.

Others say, the *law of nature* is intended. Those who maintain that the Book of Job was written before the Law of Moses, are driven to such miserable shifts as these to support their hypothesis. I hesitate not to say, that the *law* of God given to the Israelites, by the ministry of Moses, is that which is here intended ; and it is called here by way of emphasis תורה *Torah*, Law ; the real system and source of *instruction*, which contains אמריו *amraiv*, " his words," the words or sayings of God Himself; consequently not the *Noahchic precepts*, nor the *law of nature*, neither of which were ever *written* or *registered* as the words of *God's mouth*. As to the *Noahchic pre-*

N 2

cepts, they are a rabbinical fable : and as to the *law of nature*,
what is it, or what was known of it, till God gave that *law*,
which has been the *source* from which all just counsels, and
right precepts, have flowed.

It is the law, or revelation from God, that must be studied
and *received*, in order to know God, to get acquaintance with
Him in His holiness and purity ; and to know what is the desert of *sin*, and how a sinner is to be *reconciled* to his Maker.
This is to be received, as God's *own words*—as proceeding
immediately from *Himself*, stamped with His authority—and
that law by which every sinner shall be tried.    That law not
only shews the holiness of God, and the sinfulness of sin ; but
also the *means of reconciliation*.    In it the whole *sacrificial*
system is laid down ; and this pointed out the sufferings and
death of our Lord Jesus Christ, as the true Sacrifice prefigured
by the various sacrifices prescribed by the law.    We see in
the immolation and death of the victims under the law, what
every sin deserves,—*viz. death ;* and we see, by the sacrifice
of Christ, that no sinner can expect reconciliation to God, and
remission of sins, but through His offering—for God was in
Christ reconciling the world unto Himself.    And we must receive the law that declares these things, from His *mouth ;*—not
be content with merely *reading* our Bibles, or with the general acknowledgment that this word is a revelation from God ;
we must read and hear it, as if God spake it now *from His
mouth*, to our ears.    Thus we shall feel its authority, and
tremble at His word.    There is a great difference between
simply *reading* the Scripture, and receiving it as *from the
mouth of God.*    What *man* says to us, may mislead us :—do
not take the sayings of men for any thing that concerns the
salvation of your souls : see what God has said :—believe this
alone implicitly.    Do not deceive yourselves by the common
saying, " God is merciful, and we shall fare as well as others."
It is true that God is *merciful ;* but He shews mercy to them
who truly turn to Him ; He will not prostitute His mercy on
them who run on in their evil ways : and as to *faring* as well
as others—if these *others* be like yourselves, living in sin,
without acquainting themselves with God—you will, it is true,
*fare as well as they ;* for the wicked shall be turned into hell,
with all them that forget God.    Nor will the *multitude* of the
damned, alleviate the punishment of any individual in the

wretched mass. *You* need not perish, for God has devised means that your banished soul may not be endlessly expelled from Him.

The *second* direction is, *Lay up his words in thy heart.* The *heart* is often taken to express all the faculties of the soul, especially the conscience and understanding. The spirit of this direction is—Take a serious view of what God has spoken—see that you *understand* it—and if you understand it, endeavour to feel it—Ask conscience whether you be the person of whom God speaks?—whether you have ever repented and turned from those iniquities which God reprehends?—whether God for Christ's sake have forgiven them? —and whether He have given you the *witness of His Spirit*, that it is so?—David says, he hid the word of God in his heart, that he might not sin against Him. Have *you* done so?— Having received the words of His mouth into your heart, do you *retain* them there? If you have received the word of reproof and conviction : if, by it, the Spirit of God have convinced you of sin, righteousness, and judgement, then you are prepared for the next direction :—

Thirdly, *Return to the Almighty.* Our blessed Lord represents a sinner under the figure of a *silly sheep* which has *strayed away from the flock*, and from under the care of the *shepherd*, and has wandered into the *wilderness*, exposed to destruction, not only because it is gone from under the shepherd's eye, but on account of its exposure to destruction by means of ravenous beasts. And for such a stray-sheep, there is no safety, but in being *brought back to the flock*, and again placed *under the shepherd's care.* This direction therefore is of great moment : you must *return to the Almighty.*—Stop, sinner! whither art thou going? Art thou not already on the *precipice ?*—on the verge of destruction ?—A little farther and the gulf is shot, and the horrible pit is closed upon thee for ever !—After stopping and considering, *return to the Almighty* —His parental voice may be still heard—has He not said " Let the wicked man forsake his way, and the unrighteous man his thoughts ; and let him return unto the Lord, and He will have mercy upon him, and to our God, for He will abundantly pardon." Remember who it is to whom you are to return : it is the *Almighty*—He who is *able to save* if you do return : and He who is able to *destroy* if you do *not*. Satan as a roaring lion is going about seeking whom he may devour. If you be a sinner against God and your own soul, you are fair prey for this devourer! *The lion hath roared,* will you not fear? *The Lord hath spoken*—therefore his servants must *prophecy.* They must *warn* the wicked, that they may not have to answer for his blood at the judgement-seat of Christ. But in and through all this, hear the expostulating voice of your heavenly Father :—WHY will ye die, O house of Israel? O Jerusalem, Jerusalem, how often would I have gathered you together as a hen doth her brood under her wings, but ye WOULD not. To refuse such invitations—to stop the ear *against such entreaties*—to harden the heart against such compassionate calls—demand the most exemplary judgements. A *remedy* is provided, but they who sin against that only remedy, must of necessity perish. It is the ALMIGHTY that calls—and none less than the ALMIGHTY can *save;* and remember, that because He is the *Almighty,* He is able to punish ; and, that it is a fearful thing to fall into the hands of the living God.

Fourthly. *Put away iniquity far from thy tabernacles.* You must not only put away your *own sins*—cease from your evil companions—allow yourself no indulgence in any *secret sin*—but you must give heed that iniquity be not *tolerated in* your *tabernacle*—your *household* or *family.* Teach your children, your servants, and all that are connected with you, the fear of the Lord. Let your house be a house of *prayer,* not a den of thieves—let not the idle, the vain, the profligate, or profane, have a place in your domestic establishment. If such be your *neighbours,* hold no intimacy with them. See also that there be no *ill-gotten property* in your house! See that if you have defrauded any, you have made, or will make, immediate *restitution.* See that there be no *trick* or *deception* in the *mode* of managing your business, disposing of your wares, buying from the manufacturer, or selling to the consumer. Most people have not only easily besetting sins in their *constitution,* but also easily besetting sins in their trade and mode of conducting their business. All this must be *put away*—and, as the text says, *put* FAR *away.* Let not your gain have God's curse in it for a canker, because it is not honestly acquired; but see that you have His blessing in your basket and your store, because you have provided things honest in His sight, who searcheth the heart, and trieth the reins.

One great point yet remains ; and with this, Job's friend *Eliphaz*, who gives this exhortation, and these directions, could be but slightly acquainted ; and that is, the return to the Almighty *through the Mediator ;* and the *reconciliation* to Him, through the sacrificial offering of Him who was the Lamb slain from the foundation of the world.

If we take the word הסכן *hasken,* which our translators render *acquaint,* and which *Coverdale,* our earlier translator and martyr, rendered *reconcile,* it will open a rather different sense at first view, though it may lead ultimately to the *same end.* Strictly speaking, no man can *reconcile himself* to God, though he may be said to do so, who uses God's appointed means of reconciliation, in the way that He has Himself appointed. We learn that " God was in Christ *reconciling* the world unto Himself :" and the Apostle gives us to understand that the whole gospel is *a ministry of reconciliation.* See 2 Cor. v. 18, 19, and 20. " All things are of God, who hath reconciled us to Himself by Jesus Christ, and hath given to us the ministry of reconciliation:—to wit, that God was in Christ reconciling the world unto Himself, not imputing their trespasses unto them ; and hath committed unto us the word of reconciliation. Now then, we are ambassadors for Chirst, as though God did beseech you by us ; we pray you in Christ's stead, be ye reconciled to God." A short paraphrase on the above words is all that can be necessary in reference to the translation of our text given by *Coverdale.* God is here said to have reconciled us to Himself by Jesus Christ. As He has given Christ to die for sinners, they have through Him access to God : for His sake and on His account, God can receive them : and it is only by the grace and spirit of Christ, that the proud, fierce, and diabolic nature of man can be changed and *reconciled* to God ; and *by* and *through* this Sacrifice, God can be propitious to them ; for the grace of Christ alone can remove the *enmity* of man. As the word *reconciliation* signifies in the original a *thorough change,* the grand object of the gospel is to make a thorough change in men's *minds* and *manners ;* but the first object is the removal of *enmity* from the heart of man, that he may be disposed to accept of the salvation which God has provided for him ; for the

enmity of the heart is the grand hinderance to man's salvation. Christ, by His offering upon the cross, made *atonement*
for the sin of the world, and thus laid the foundation of reconciliation between God and man. The Apostles, and all their
genuine successors in the Christian ministry, have the *word*
or *doctrine* of reconciliation. They state the doctrine, shew
the necessity of it, and entreat men to accept the mercy
which God has provided for them. The whole of this gospel
ministration is simple, short, and plain, and may be thus sum-
med up :—

1. You believe that there is a God.

2. You know He made and preserves *you*.

3. In consequence it is your duty to love and serve Him.

4. To shew you how to do this, He has given a revelation
of Himself, which is contained in His *law* and *gospel*, which
you are commanded to receive.

5. You have broken this *law*, and incurred the penalty,
which is death.

6. Far from being able to undo your offences, or make reparation to the offended Majesty of God, your hearts, through
the deceitfulness of sin, are blinded, hardened, and filled with
enmity against your Father and your Judge.

7. To redeem you from this most wretched and accursed
state, God, in His endless mercy, has given His Son for you,
who has assumed your nature, and died in your stead.

8. In consequence of this, He has commanded, that *repentance* and *remission* of *sins* shall be preached to all mankind in His name.

9. All who repent of their sins, and return to the *Almighty,*
believing in Christ, as *having died for them,* as a *sin offering,*
shall receive remission of sins.

10. And if they abide in Him by that faith which worketh
by love, they shall have an eternal inheritance among them
that are sanctified. This is the sum and substance of the *doctrine of reconciliation :* and whether this were in the mind
of *Eliphaz,* when he gave Job the exhortation in the text, it
is essentially necessary in every exhortation to *sinners,* constructed on Christian principles. In order then to *acquaint*
yourselves with God, to be *reconciled* to Him, and to be
saved unto eternal life, apply to Him through the Son of His

love, who died for your offences, and rose again for your justification.

III. I come now to consider the *benefits* which result to
man through this acquaintance with God.

They are many and important, and may be seen here,
either in the *text* or *context*.

Eliphaz first makes a general statement—*Thereby good
shall come unto thee.* The preceding words, *Be at peace,*
seem to be rather intended to point out the benefit of the acquaintance here recommended, than any part of the *exhortation* here used. In this way they were understood by translators, both *ancient* and *modern ;* and in this sense I shall
take them.

2. *Good shall come unto thee,*—נהם *baham,* in them; *i. e.*
in acquaintance with God, and the peace or prosperity of
soul which follows. Thou shalt have the supreme good.
1. The *pardon* of all thy sins. 2. The *sanctification* of thy
nature. 3. The *witness of the Holy Spirit* in thy conscience
that thou art born of God, and passed from death unto life.
4. A right to the tree of life, and, through the Blood of the
covenant, to the eternal inheritance.

Peace, שלום *shalom,* signifies, as used in the Bible, prosperity of all kinds : health of body, peace of mind, and prosperity in all lawful worldly affairs: all these are included in
the word *good*—good shall come unto thee—good to thy
body—good to thy soul—good to thy family—good in time
—and good in eternity. To know God in the proper *experimental* sense of the word, is not only to be *acquainted*
with the *Fountain* of *happiness,* but to *drink* of the *water of
life.* To be reconciled to God, is to have a *title* to eternal
glory, and a *right* to the *tree of life :*—to enjoy His favour
is better than the present life, with every earthly blessing
which can possibly be enjoyed. To have *peace* with God,
and peace in the conscience, is to have an ineffable feast, with
quietness and assurance for ever. To have communion with
God, and His Spirit to witness with ours that we are His children, is to have life in its plenitude of satisfaction, and a
glorious prospect of blessedness in that future state, where
neither *natural* nor *moral evil* can ever come. These are
general declarations relative to the happy consequences of

being acquainted with the true God, and knowing Jesus Christ, whom He hath sent.

But Eliphaz enters into a detail of blessings and advantages which should be enjoyed by him who received his word of exhortation.

1. *Thou shalt be built up*—not only the *lapsed state* of thy affairs shall be repaired, and thou shalt have every good that is essentially necessary for thee in this life, but thou shalt have God for thy continual protector.

Though *building up* may in general signify an *increase* of *property*, and especially of *children*, which were considered the chief riches among the Patriarchs, Israelites, and Asiatics in general, and a promise of this kind must be very acceptable; yet the *fortifying* and *protecting* may be that which is here principally intended. In all parts of Arabia, attacks on the *houses* and *property* of individuals were frequent; and to prevent suffering in this way, every house was a sort of *fortification;* a wall being built round the house, too high to be easily scaled, and a very *low door* in that wall, through which an Arab, who scarcely ever dismounts from his horse, could not pass.

The monks of *St. Catherine,* who have a monastery on the top of *Mount Sinai,* dare not even have a door in their monastery—they are literally *built up,* and every thing that is received from below, comes in a *basket* let down from the top of the wall by means of a *rope* and *pulley.* Both persons and goods go and come in this way. To this kind of *building up,* Eliphaz seems to refer. And as this was considered a sufficient protection in a *general* way, yet God's *building up* must be *universally* safe and sufficient. His *providence* is the grand fortification; it is not only a protection, but a source of *support.* The inhabitant shall dwell in safety; his bread shall not fail, and his water shall be sure. From such a tabernacle, the *wicked,* the *practisers of iniquity,* aggression, and wrong, shall be put far away. To such the promise by the prophet, (who also alludes to depredations of this kind,) shall be amply fulfilled : " In righteousness shalt thou be established : thou shalt be far from oppression, for thou shalt not fear; and from terror, for it shall never come near thee." Isai. liv. 14.

In such a country, and in such circumstances, what a support must such a promise be, when the words were known to be spoken by Him who cannot lie. To the case of Job these things strongly apply; he lived in *Uz*, in *Idumea:* and he himself, as well as all his friends, were *Edomite Arabs.* His *oxen* and *asses* had already been carried away by a marauding company of *Sabeans*, a people who dwelt in *Arabia Deserta*, on the east of *Uz.* The Chaldeans, who carried away his *camels*, were a banditti of the same kind.

By promising such protection against such marauders, Eliphaz slyly insinuates his general charge against Job, *viz.* that he must be a bad man, else he could not have been subjected to such losses and disasters.

2. He promises him great *secular prosperity. Thou shalt lay up gold*, &c. Godliness is profitable for all things. The man who in the days of his forgetfulness of, and rebellion against God, spent much property in riotous living: on his conversion to God, ceases from all those evils, and consequently saves that which he before spent and squandered away :—again, the *blessing of God* rests upon him, and on the work of his hands— thus he both *gains* and *saves.* I have known many who thus became *rich;* and while they continued to *help the poor*, and the *work of God*, they *"laid up gold as dust, and fine gold as the stones of the brooks."* And I have known several cases also, in which God *brought back the captivity;* when the good He had placed in their hands, they put in their hearts, gaining all they could, and keeping all they got—in a word, they ceased to help *God's poor* and *God's cause*, and then He withdrew the hand of His help from them, and left them the earth for their portion, or stripped them of that in which they trusted, that they might return to Him from whom they had revolted. Thus God *gave* in *mercy;* and in *mercy* He *took away.*

3. He promises that the Almighty will be the defence both of him and his property—*Yea the Almighty shall be thy defence, and thou shalt have plenty of silver*, ver. 25. In the 23 verse (see under number 1.) he promises him *personal* protection—*Thou shalt be built up:*—but here he promises the same protection for his *goods* and *property*—He shall increase his substance, and God will not permit him to be deprived of it, by disasters in trade, nor by the hand of fraud, deceit, or robbery. It is not to be wondered at, that while a man makes a proper use of God's bounty, the Giver will take care to pre-

serve His own gift. We *lose*, because we do not properly *credit* God's promises ; and we *lose more,* because we do not *plead* them.

4. He farther gives Job to understand, that he shall not only have that *content* and *comfort* that arise from having all the *necessaries, conveniences,* and *comforts* of life at his command, but he shall have the favour of God, and true happiness in the enjoyment of that favour ; *Then thou shalt have thy delight in the Almighty*—Thou shalt feel Him to be thy portion ; for while thy body lives on His earthly bounty, thy soul shall be fed and nourished by that bread that comes down from heaven, and endures unto eternal life, ver. 26.

5. He shews farther, that in consequence of his acquainting himself with God, he shall have great confidence in Him and much communion with Him—*Thou shalt lift up thy face unto God,* ibid. This expresses great confidence ; and especially that which results from a sense of God's mercy, in the forgiveness of sins. It is an old saying, " He who has got his pardon, may look his prince in the face."—*Guilt* felt in the conscience produces *confusion of face:* how can he look up to God, who knows he has been a rebel against Him, and has no evidence that his sin is forgiven, or that God has adopted him into His family ? But when he feels that God has forgiven him his sins—when he has taken fully the exhortation, *acquaint now thyself with Him*—be *reconciled* to thy offended God ; *then,* and not till then, can he *lift up his face to God;* see his Father and Friend in the person of his Judge ; then he has boldness towards God, and shall not be ashamed when he stands even before the judgement-seat.

6. He promises him great success in all his approaches to his Maker ; *Thou shalt make thy prayer unto Him, and He shall hear thee,* ver. 27. The original is very emphatic, תעתיר *taĕtir,* thou shalt *open* or *unbosom thyself*—thou shalt find *freedom* of *access* to the throne of grace, thou shalt have the *spirit of prayer;* for the *spirit of prayer* flows from the *spirit of adoption;* and when the HEART *prays,* GOD *hears;* and it is encouraged to *pray on,* by the *answers* it receives; the Text adds, *thou shalt pay thy vows.* He who enjoys the favour of God, is full of *good resolutions :* and as these resolutions *spring* from God's *grace,* and are *formed* in His *strength,* so they are brought to good effect— the vows of living to Him who has been so merciful and kind

to them, are paid : every new blessing is a new reason why they should love Him more and serve Him better : they feel this to be their duty and their interest ; they *vow* and *pray on*, are supported, and enabled to pay their vows.

7. Such shall have success in all their good *resolutions. Thou shalt also decree a thing, and it shall be established unto thee*, ver. 28. *The liberal man deviseth liberal things : and by liberal things shall he stand*—This is the doctrine of a *Prophet* superior to Eliphaz : but the sentiment is nearly the same with that which the latter here expresses. Loving God with all the heart, and our neighbour as ourselves, is a disposition from which much glory may be *purposed* to the Supreme Being, and much *good* to our fellows. The holy man *decrees both*, and God who was with his *heart* to decree; will be with his *head* and his *hand* to accomplish; and it is truly wonderful to see how much good such persons decree or resolve ; and how much they are enabled to effect ! *Benevolence* and *beneficence* are the component parts of *love :* a genuine Christian incessantly *wills well*, or is *benevolent ;* and according to his power —the means which God's grace and strength furnish—is *beneficent ;* he *wills well*, and he *does well*.

8. The concluding advantage of this acquaintance and reconciliation to God is, the promise of His continual approbation and blessing. *The light shall shine upon thy ways*, ibid. The *light* is God's approbation, 1st. in the *soul ;* 2d. on the *providential path*—Thou shalt never walk in *darkness*—Thou shalt have no uncertainty concerning the blessedness. of thy state—Thou shalt constantly know that thou art of God, by the spirit which He hath given thee.

Those who are acquainted with God, and reconciled to Him, walk in the *light*, as He is in the light :—they have communion with Him, and with all who are like minded, and feel that the blood of Jesus Christ cleanseth them from all sin : so they continue to grow in grace, and in the knowledge of Jesus Christ. They have also His blessing in their basket and in their store ; in the work of their heads, and the labour of their hands. It is the will of God that they should have that measure of prosperity in all their secular affairs, as shall enable them to owe no man any thing, and to provide things honest in the sight of all men : therefore, acquaint thyself with God, and—Let this be done *now*. There is not a moment to lose. Death is at the door. The tabernacle is decaying in all, and with some already in decay. Therefore,

*Acquaint* thyself *now* with Him, because thou mayest have no *other time*, and eternity is at hand.

Let this acquaintance *now take place*, because of the great *happiness* thou mayest receive.

Because of the *perdition* with which thou art threatened.

Thou shalt have *peace*, שלום *shalom*, prosperity :—whatever may contribute to thy present and eternal happiness. Thou shalt have *peace* with God ;—*peace* in thy own conscience ;— and *peace* with every man ;—and *prosperity* of soul at all times.

Thus ends the account of the benefits which result from an acquaintance and reconciliation with God.

Nothing remains now, but to press you to attend more par ticularly to the *exhortation* in the text. And can there be more powerful motives to this, than the wonderful benefits which are the result of this acquaintance? Listen to your own interests, and you will listen to the *text*. Shut not your eyes against the light, and it will shew you how to walk and to please God. It is of God's mercy that you are called to this acquaintance; but though that mercy in itself endureth for ever, yet your *day of probation* may have a speedy end. Hence the text says, " acquaint thyself *now* with Him." The season of *grace* and *life* neglected, all is lost—you have not a moment to lose. No people on earth hold their lives more precariously, than the inhabitants of these northern Isles. You are ever exposed to more dangers, you who go down to the sea in ships, and transact your most laborious business in slight skiffs on the deep waters of these tempestuous seas, than the men who *till the earth* for their subsistence. Above all others you should ever stand ready to meet your God. With Him as your *Father, Friend,* and *Preserver,* you should be deeply *acquainted*—to Him you should be *reconciled* through the blood of His Son.

Slight not the exhortation in the text, and neglect not his, who is come more than a thousand miles by sea and land to second the exhortation, and to beseech you in Christ's stead to be reconciled to God. Love to your souls has caused Jesus Christ to shed His blood for you—and love to your souls and your country, has led your preacher, fast bordering on three score years and ten, to come to the uttermost northern bounds of the British dominions, to shew and prove to you that God loves you, and that He wills you should come to the knowledge of the truth, and be saved with all the power of an endless life. O my friends, my brethren, acquaint *now* yourselves with this good, gracious, and merciful God, and thereby good, ineffable good, will come unto you. Amen.

# SERMON XXIII.

## LOVE TO GOD AND MAN
### THE FULFILLING OF
## THE LAW AND THE PROPHETS.

MATTHEW xxii. 35—40.

35. Then one of them, *which was* a lawyer, asked *him a question*, tempting him, and saying,

36. Master, which *is* the great commandment in the law ?

37. Jesus said unto him, Thou shalt love the Lord thy God with all thy heart, and with all thy soul, and with all thy mind.

38. This is the first and great commandment.

39. And the second *is* like unto it : Thou shalt love thy neighbour as thyself.

40. On these two commandments hang all the law and the prophets.

THE love we owe to God and man, the subject of these verses, is of the very greatest importance, and should be well understood by every man, as we are assured by our Lord himself, that the whole of *religion* is comprised in thus loving God and our neighbour.

But, What is *religion ?*  And, What is the *true* religion ? These are questions that have been *seriously* asked by some who were inquiring the way to Zion, with their faces thitherward ; and earnestly wishing to know how they might escape the perdition of ungodly men : and a similar inquiry has been made captiously by others, from a supercilious incredulity ; taking for granted, that their question could not be solved in a satisfactory manner.  The Christian *religion* is a revelation from God himself, giving a knowledge of His own being, attributes, and works: and of *man*, his nature, present state, and necessities; shewing also the *way* in which the whole human race may have all their spiritual wants supplied, their souls delivered from evil passions, and be made partakers of a divine nature, escape the corruption that is in the world, through evil desire, and being made truly holy, become in consequence contented and happy, and stand in a continual preparation for the blessedness of the eternal world.

But *how* is this religion, this holiness, content, and happiness, to be acquired? " In itself," say objectors, " it seems impossible, in such a state of imperfection and sinfulness as the present is: and whatever may be stated by *theory,* fact and general experience seem to prove that such a state cannot be enjoyed on earth: and if, to be in such a state, be what is termed *true religion,* and no such state is to be found below—then, there is no such thing as this true religion—or—it was not made for the sons of men." But do such assertions as these prove that the objectors have deeply considered the subject? Is it, after the fullest investigation of the question, that they have come to this conclusion! Or, is this an *echo* of the wicked word of a lying world, that knows as little of God as of His religion; and goes on sowing to the flesh, and of it reaping corruption and ruin. But should there be any honest seriousness in such objectors, a proper consideration of our Lord's words in the text will, I hope, lead them to form a different conclusion.

The occasion of this discourse was as follows :—A lawyer, apparently of the sect of the *Pharisees,* who had been present when our Lord had confounded the *Herodians,* ver. 16 —22; and had silenced the *Sadducees,* ver. 23—32; hoping to succeed better than the former, as having a better cause, came forward, questioned him, and said, *Master, which is the great commandment of the law?*

As the word *lawyer,* in its common acceptation among us, may mislead, as it has not the same meaning in the New Testament, it may be necessary to make a few observations upon it.

The word νομικος, signifies a *teacher of the law;* and thus our ancient *Anglo-Saxon* version, æ-lapeop, a *law-teacher,* or a *doctor of the law.* These teachers of the law were the same as the *scribes,* or what Dr. Wotton calls *letter-men,* whom he supposes to be the same as the *Karaïtes*, a sect of the Jews who rejected all the traditions of the elders, and admitted nothing but the written word.   These are allowed to have kept more closely to the spiritual meaning of the law and the prophets, than the Pharisees did; and hence the question proposed by this lawyer, (who in Mark xii. 28. is called *one of the scribes*,) was of a more *spiritual* and *refined* nature than those proposed by the *Herodians* and *Sadducees* already mentioned.   But this question, howsoever good in itself, was not *candidly* proposed by this law-teacher;—*he asked, tempting him*, trying to convict him of ignorance, or to confound him by subtlety.

To connect this the better with the context, and see the situation in which our blessed Lord was now placed, it will be necessary to observe, that we have here exhibited to our view, *three* kinds of *enemies* and *false-accusers* that rose up against our Lord; and the *three* sorts of accusations brought against Him; *viz.* :—

1. The *Herodians*, or *politicians*, or *courtiers*, belonging to Herod, who form their questions and accusations on the *rights* of the *prince* and *matters of state* :—they came forward, with, *Is it lawful to give tribute to Cæsar, or not?* ver. 17.

2. The *Sadducees*, or *libertines*, who founded their question upon matters of *religion* and *articles of faith*, which themselves did not believe.   Hence, they propose a question concerning the *resurrection*, and that provision of the *Mosaic law*, which states, " if a man take a wife and he die childless, his *brother* shall take his widow and raise up a posterity, that shall succeed to the first brother's estate, and to all his rights and privileges."   *Master, Moses said*, &c., ver. 24.

3. The *Pharisees*, whether *scribes* or *Karaïtes*, who were all hypercritical pretenders to devotion, they came and proposed a question on that vital and practical godliness, the *love of God* and *man*, of which they wished *themselves* to be thought the sole proprietors,—*Master, which is the great commandment?* ver. 36.

To this question our Lord immediately answers, *Thou shalt love the Lord thy God with all thy heart, and with all thy soul, and with all thy mind: and thou shalt love thy neighbour as thyself.*

In these two commandments mention is made of *three kinds of love :—viz.* 1. The *love* we owe to GOD. 2. The *love* we owe to our NEIGHBOUR. 3. The *love* we owe tò *ourselves.* These must not be confounded; and to prevent this, a correct definition should be given of each : for the term *love* in relation to GOD, to our *neighbour*, and to *ourselves*, does not present the same sense, though all partake of the same radical idea.

Though we may define the term, which, however, is not very easily done, yet the *thing* is èxtremely difficult : and philosophers, critics, and divines, have spent their strength on it. Scarcely any definition yet given, is sufficiently *simple.* That the *thing* itself has for its *basis* ESTEEM and DESIRE, there can be little doubt. Dr. *South,* whose definition has been admired, has rather described the *effects* than the *principle.* " Love," says he, " is such an affection as cannot so properly be said to be *in* the soul, as the soul to be *in* that. It is the great instrument of nature ; the bond and cement of society ; the spirit and spring of the universe. It is the whole man wrapt up in one desire."

When we see *goodness* and *excellence,* we cannot but *esteem* them ; and the possessor of them seems peculiarly entitled to our *respect.* Aware of the *utility* of such virtues, we cannot but *desire* their acquisition. If the possession of the *person* or *thing* in which these reside, be possible, we earnestly *desire* that possession. *Esteem* and *desire,* produce *anxiety* and *strenuous endeavour* to gain this possession : and the *ardour* of the *desire* will be in *proportion* to the *view* we have of that *goodness* and *excellence,* and the conviction we *feel* of their being *necessary to our happiness.* Hence, indeed, it may be said, *The whole man is wrapt up in one desire.*

But as the term *love* is that on which the whole strength of these commandments rests, it will be necessary to inquire *here* also into its *grammatical* or *literal* meaning, as was found to be expedient in other places.

The word Αγαπη, from αγαπαω, *I love,* is variously compounded and derived by lexicographers and critics. I shall produce those which seem to bear the most directly on the subject. Αγαπη is supposed to be compounded of αγαν, and ποιειν, *to act vehemently,* or *intensely ;* or of αγειν κατα παν, because love is always active, and will *work in every possible way;* for he who *loves,* is with all his *affection* and *desire* carried forward to the beloved object, in order to possess and enjoy it. Some derive it from *αγαν* and *παυεσθαι, to be completely at rest,* or *to be intensely satisfied* with that which he loves; and *this resting completely on it,* because *perfectly satisfied with it,* constitutes essentially, what is called *love.* Others derive it from *αγαν* and *παω,* because a person *eagerly embraces* and *vigorously holds fast,* that which is the object of his affection. Lastly, others suppose it to be compounded of *αγαω, I admire,* and *παυομαι, I rest,* because that which a person loves intensely, he *rests* in with *fixed admiration* and *contemplation.* This shews that genuine love *changes not,* but always abides *steadily attached* to that which is the sole object of its regard.

Our English term *love,* we have from the Anglo-Saxon, loꝼa, or luꝼa, from luꝼan and luꝼian, to *desire, love, favour, cherish:* and both are most probably derived from the *Teutonic,* leben, *to live;* because love is the means, dispenser, and preserver of *life;* and without it, *life* would have nothing *desirable,* nor indeed, any thing even *supportable.* The Latin *amo,* I love, has been derived by *Minshieu,* from the Hebrew חמה *chamah,* to burn, to waste and dry up, parch: and, considering it as an animal affection, having an animal object, this is sufficiently descriptive of its nature and effects; hence these Leonine verses,—

> *Nescio quid sit Amor : nec amor, nec amor, nec amavi,*
> *At scio, si quis amat, uritur igni gravi.*

I do not know what love is; I do not love, I am not loved, nor have I loved. But this I know, that whosoever is in love, is burnt up by a strong fire.

This is the effect of hopeless love, where it is intense and undivided. So the poet, who in the following lines has painted it in a very affecting manner :—

> " She never told her love,
> But let concealment, like a worm i' the bud,
> Feed on her damask cheek : she pin'd in thought;
> And with a green and yellow melancholy,
> She sat like patience on a monument,
> Smiling at grief. Was not this love indeed ?"

If I understand them right, it is in this way, and with this kind of love, that some *ascetic* or *mystical* writers would have us love God.   And under the influence of such a *feeling*, many of them pined till their moisture was turned to the drought of summer, and they died in a sort of languishing ecstasy!  But this is not the love in the Text : it is all intensely *sublime* and *spiritual, pure* and *holy*.   It has nothing *earthly* nothing *animal* or *fleshly* in it.   It is a pure flame that has come from God, changing and refining our whole nature, and returning all its ardours back to Himself; for there is nothing on earth to which it can attach itself as a *source* from which it can derive gratification and contentment.   It is as much *health* to the *body*, as it is *health* to the *soul*.

Whatever may be thought of the preceding etymologies, as being either just or probable, one thing will be evident to all those who know what *love* means ; that they throw much light upon the subject, and manifest it in a variety of striking points of view.

The ancient author of a MS. Greek Lexicon, in the Royal library at Paris, under the word Αγαπη, has the following definition, Ασπαστος προθεσις επι τη φιλια του φιλουμενου—Συμψυχια—A pleasing surrender of friendship to a friend :—an identity or sameness of soul.   This love is a sovereign preference given to *one* above all others, present or absent; a concentration of all the thoughts and desires in a single object, which is preferred to all others.   Now, apply this definition to the love which God requires of His creatures, and you will have the most correct view of the subject.   Hence it appears, that by this love, the soul *cleaves* to, *affectionately admires*, and *consequently rests* in God ; *supremely pleased* and *satisfied* with *Him* as its portion.   That it acts *from* Him, as its *Author ; for* Him, as its *Master ;* and *to* Him, as its *End*.   That by it all the powers and faculties of the mind are *concentrated* in the Lord of the universe.   That *by* it, the whole man is willingly *surrendered* to the Most High; and that *through* it, an *identity* or *sameness* of spirit with the Lord, is acquired—the person being made a partaker of the divine Nature, having the mind in him that was in Christ ; and thus dwelling in God, and God in him.

But how is this love to be applied in the present case, and in what manner?   Why, it occupies the whole man, in all his powers of body and mind : God says, and Christ here repeats it, *Thou shalt love the Lord thy God with all thy heart, soul* and *mind.* In the *parallel* place, Mark xii. 30, the whole passage reads thus, "Thou shalt love the Lord thy God with all thy heart, and with all thy soul, and with all thy mind, and with all thy STRENGTH;" the same word is added in the *parallel* place, Luke x. 27. I shall consider it therefore as a part of the Text, which indeed is supported not only by those two evangelists, but by several MSS., and by the *Syriac* and *Ethiopic* versions. I grant, however, that it is an addition made by our Lord, for it is not in the original Hebrew. With this *addition,* the original runs thus :—Αγαπησεις κυριον τον Θεον του, εν ολη τη καρδια σου, και εν ολη τη ψυχη σου, και εν ολη τη διανοια σου, [και εν ολη τη ισχυι σου.]

1. What then is implied in *loving God with all the* HEART?

The *heart* is generally considered the *seat of the affections* and *passions*—the place of *hopes, wishes, desires, appetites,* and the like :—and he loves God *with all his heart,* who loves nothing in comparison of Him, and nothing but in *reference* to Him : who is ready to *give up, do,* or *suffer* any thing in order to please and glorify Him :—who has in His heart, neither *love* nor *hatred, hope* nor *fear,* inclination nor aversion, *desire* nor *delight,* but as they relate to God, and are regulated by *Him.* No man can love God with his *whole heart,* if the *desire of the world,* the *desire of the eye,* and the *pride of life,* be not separated from it.

Such a *love,* that Being who is infinitely *perfect, good, wise, powerful, beneficent* and *merciful,* merits and requires from His intelligent creatures : and in fulfilling this duty, the soul finds its *perfection* and *felicity :* for it *rests* in the *Source of goodness,* and is penetrated with incessant *influences* from Him who is the essence and centre of all that is amiable ; for He is the *God of all grace.* This is the love which an *intelligent creature* owes especially to its CREATOR ; a *servant* to his Almighty MASTER ; a *son* to his most affectionate FATHER. This *love* is founded on all the attributes of the Deity; includes all sorts of duties, and is binding both on angels and men. It calls forth all the powers and faculties of an intelligent being into action ; and directs their operations to the accomplishment of the most important purposes ; and the attainment of the most excellent ends. To this love of God, all should submit, every thing give place, and to it, every thing should be referred.

He who can thus love his Maker, must have his heart sprin-kled from an evil conscience ; and feel in consequence that Christ dwells in his *heart* by faith, and has rooted and ground-ed him in His *love*.

2. What is implied in loving God with all *the* soul ?

He loves God with all his *soul*, εν ὁλη τη ψυχη, *with all his* LIFE—who is ready to give up his *life* for His sake:—who is ready to endure all sorts of torments, and to be deprived of all kinds of comforts, rather than dishonour God. He who employs life, with all its comforts and conveniences, to glorify Him, in, by, and through all—to whom life and death are nothing but as they come from, and lead to God,—who la-bours to promote the *cause of God* and *truth* in the world, denying himself, taking up his cross daily—neither eating, drinking, sleeping, resting, labouring, toiling, but in reference to the glory of God, his own salvation, and that of the lost world. He lays out his *life* for God ; spends it for God ; and can be a *confessor* or *martyr*, rather than defile his conscience, and grieve the spirit of God by *doing* or *professing* any thing, that is not according to His eternal truth. From this divine principle sprung the *blood of the martyrs*, which became the *seed of the Church*. THEY *overcame through the blood of the Lamb, and their testimony, and loved not their lives unto death.* See Rev. xii. 11.

3. He loves God with all his MIND, εν ὁλη τη διανοια, with all his *intellect*, or *understanding*, who applies himself only to *know* God, and His holy will ;—who receives with submission, gratitude, and pleasure, the *sacred truths* which He has re-vealed to man :—who *studies* neither *art*, nor *science*, but as far as it is necessary for the service of God ; and uses it at all times, to promote His glory. Who forms no *projects* nor *de-signs*, but in reference to God, and to the interests of man-kind :—who banishes as much as possible, from his *under-standing* and *memory*, every useless, foolish, and dangerous *thought ;* together with every *idea* which has any tendency to *defile* his soul, or turn it for a moment from the *Centre* of eternal repose : who uses all his abilities, both natural and acquired, to grow in the grace of God, and to perform His will in the most acceptable manner. In a word, he who *sees* God in all things,—*thinks* of Him at all times, having his *mind* continually fixed upon God,—acknowledges Him in all

his ways :—who *begins*, *continues*, and *ends* all his *thoughts*, *words*, and *works*, to the glory of His name, continually *planning*, *scheming*, and *devising* how he may serve God and his generation, more effectually ; his *head*, his *intellect*, going before,—his *heart*, his *affections*, and *desires* coming *after*. He is *light* in the Lord, and he walks as a *child of the light*, and of *the day*, and in him there is no cause of stumbling.

4. He loves God with all his STRENGTH, who *exerts* all the *powers* and *faculties* of his *body* and *soul* in the service of God ;—who for the glory of his Maker, spares neither *labour* nor *cost*, who sacrifices his body, his health, his time, his ease, for the honour of his divine Master :—who employs in His service, all his goods, his talents, his power, his credit, authority and *influence ;* doing what he does, with a single eye, a loving heart, and with all his might :—in whose conduct is ever seen the *work* of *faith*, *patience* of *hope*, and *labour* of *love*. He never does the works of the Lord slothfully,—lives under the influence of the energy of God's Spirit, and from the *inward working* of God's mighty power, he is ever *striving* to enter in at the straight gate ; brings as many as he can with him, and goes even near, in courage and fervent love, to the brink of the pit, in order to snatch *brands out of the burning*.

Reader, this is the man that loves God with all his *heart, life, understanding*, and *strength*. He himself, by the grace of the Lord Jesus, has been gathered out of the corruption that is in the world,—has truly repented of all his sins,—been justified freely through the redemption that is in Jesus; and continuing faithful to the grace received, has had the very " thoughts of his heart cleansed by the inspiration of God's holy Spirit," so that he has been enabled (as above) " perfectly to love Him, and worthily to magnify His holy name." What he is, he is by the mere mercy and powerful operation of the grace of Christ: it is by His blood he was justified, and by *that* he has been sanctified. Satan is wholly cast out, and all his goods spoiled ;—and his heart is become a temple of the Holy Ghost. He is, in consequence, crucified to the world and the world to him ;—he lives,—yet not *he*, but Christ lives in him. He beholds as in a glass, the glory of the Lord, and is changed into the same image, from glory to glory. Simply and constantly depending and looking unto Jesus, the Author and Perfecter of his faith, he receives continual supplies of enlightening and sanctifying grace, and is thus fitted for every *good word* and *work.*　O glorious state of him who has given God his whole heart; and in which God ever lives and rules! glorious state of blessedness upon earth,—triumph of the grace of his God over sin and Satan !—state of holiness and happiness far beyond this description, which comprises an ineffable union and communion between the ever blessed TRINITY and the soul of MAN.　O God! let THY *work appear* unto thy servants; and the *work* of *our hands* establish upon us! the work of our hands establish Thou it! Amen.　Amen.

The *law-doctor* had asked, *Which is the great commandment in the law?*　Our Lord having stated the commandment itself, adds, *This is the first and great commandment.*

There are several particulars which are usually referred to, in order to shew that this is the *first* and also the *great* commandment.　It is so,—

1. In its ANTIQUITY.—It is as old as the *creation* of man; and was originally written on the human heart.　It is natural for every child to love its parents,—they are the fountain of its being, and the authors of all its comforts and enjoyments. It is naturally led to them for a supply of all its wants; for its defence against dangers, and for all the information it needs relative to outward objects, and the relation in which it stands to them.　Could any child be more sensible of these things than our *first parents*, when they came out of the hands of their Maker?　They knew Him as their Creator; they saw that His bounty had provided for them all the things they needed. They saw Him in every way, great, and glorious, and good: —they felt their relation to Him,—they loved Him with all their powers,—their love was *pure* and *holy*, and it was not, and could not be *divided,*—there was no other object of love; no other claimant of the homage and affections of their hearts. This was, therefore, the *first* and the *great* commandment.　It was the first information they received from God, and the first dictate of their own hearts.

2. It is the first and greatest in DIGNITY.—And this is evident, in its directly and immediately proceeding from God, and referring to Him.　He is its *Author;* and it belongs to that image and likeness of God in which they were created; and it must therefore be the *greatest, best,* and most *useful.*

He gave it to man in the most *perfect* state of his *being*, and the ability to observe it, proved the *perfection* of that being; and it had the most perfect of Beings for its *Object ;* and that most perfect of Beings was pleased with its *exercise.*

3· In EXCELLENCE.—It is the *chief* of all others, because all others are included in it and spring from it; and thus exceeds in its excellence, as the *cause* excels the *effect.* It *excels,* as it is the chief command of both *covenants ;* and contains the very spirit of the divine adoption : *we love Him, because He first loved us.*

4. In JUSTICE.—Because it alone renders to God *His due :* for it prefers Him before all things, and secures to Him His proper *place* and *rank,* in relation to them.   Not to prefer Him to all the works of His hands, would be the height of injustice and ingratitude,—to put any thing in His place, the grossest idolatry.   Being under infinite obligation to God, we owe Him the homage of the *heart*—He is our Author, our Sovereign, and our Preserver.   *Justice* itself says, *love Him in return for His love.*

5. It is the *first* and *greatest,* in reference to its SUFFICIENCY. It is the *fountain,* whence holiness, contentment, and happiness spring.   He that loves God, as has been before described, requires nothing else to make him holy and happy in this life ; and happy and glorious in the life to come.   He whose heart is filled with the love of God, needs nothing else to make him happy.   This alone is *sufficient,*—it is a fulness of *sufficiency.*

6. In FRUITFULNESS.—All *obedience* to God, springs from this ; all *benevolence,* and *beneficence,* have their origin in this also.   It is the very *root* of all the other commandments, and the fulfilling of the divine law.   When love to God is the spring of all human actions, how beneficent, how useful to man, how honourable to God, must those actions be ?

7. It is the *first* and *greatest* in VIRTUE and EFFICACY.— *Virtue* is moral *strength :* it is *mighty* in its *strength,*—it gives *life,* and *form,* and *effect,* to all the operations of body and soul—It is not only the *cause* of obedience, but the *powerful incentive* to all *duty.   The love of Christ,* says the Apostle, (2 Cor. v. 14.) *constraineth us*—It excites to, drives on, and gives *energy* in, every pious, religious, and benevolent

act. By it alone God reigns in the heart; and by it, the human soul is united to God.

8. In EXTENT.—It takes in God, and *all* his *attributes ;* *each* of His attributes is an object of this love. It takes in *all the works* of *His hands,*—it *admires* and *prizes* them, because made and sustained by Him who is its supreme enjoyment ;—it *extends* to *every human being,*—it is concerned for every fallen human spirit,—it loves *them* with a measure of that love which caused Christ to become incarnate, and to pour out His life unto death for their salvation. It is the source of *philanthropy* and *generous feeling,*—"it spreads itself abroad through all the public, and feels for every member of the land." It *extends* to the *lower parts* of the animate creation ; torture, cruelty, unkindness, and harsh usage, never existed in its sphere. It is the origin of all *benevolent institutions ;* and from it, the *social principle* has its origin. And as itself springs from God, so it refers all that is good, wise, excellent, and useful, in the creature, to that Fountain of ineffable goodness.

9. In NECESSITY.—God made man for happiness,—this love is the sole cause of happiness,—where this love is not, there is, there can be, *no happiness.* The whole earth would be a howling wilderness without it ;—man would exist in the most wretched degree of misery,—all the lower animals dependent upon him, would partake in his misery,—he himself would be next to *Satan* in *hopeless wretchedness.* Destitute of that *love,* here commanded, he would be filled with *hate,* its opposite ; for what love fills not in the human *intellect, hatred* and enmity will :—without this, what would human life be ; man would say in overwhelming trials, " *I hate it; I will not live always,—strangling is better than life.*"—Is not its absence the sole cause of all *suicides,* and indeed of the *general sum of human misery!* It is, therefore, *absolutely* and *indispensably* NECESSARY : without it, what would *angels* be ?—FIENDS : what would *men* be ?—BRUTES and DEMONS.

10. It is the *first* and *greatest* commandment in DURATION. The Apostle has decided this point, 1 Cor. xiii. 13. *And now abideth faith, hope, love ; but the* GREATEST *of these, is* LOVE. It must be *continued* through the whole *duration of time ;* and will not be *discontinued* throughout eternity. *Men* live *on it* —*Angels* live *by it.* To make earth habitable, and heaven

glorious, the *love* that God *commands*, must *endure for ever.*
Without it, the *race of man* would not be continued on the
earth; and without it, the *happiness* of *heaven* would have an
*end.*    For all the above reasons, hear, O man, " THOU *shalt
love the Lord thy God with all thy heart, soul, mind,* and
*strength.*    THIS *is the* FIRST and GREAT *commandment."*

Having proceeded thus far, our Lord, the Fountain of love
and goodness, takes occasion to give this *teacher of the law,* a
lesson, which though contained in the old law, was not acknowledged in practice by even the Scribes and Pharisees :—
therefore he adds,—

*And the second* is *like unto it, Thou shalt love thy neighbour as thyself.* This same commandment is found Lev. xix. 18.
*Thou shalt not avenge, nor bear any grudge against the chil
dren of thy people ; but thou shalt love thy neighbour as thyself : I* am the LORD.    But the *Jews,* in our Lord's time, had
rendered this commandment of none effect; they restrained
the meaning of *neighbour,* to those of *their own kindred,* and
*all others* they considered as *enemies,* and thus they quoted
this law, as our Lord testifies !—*Ye have heard that it has
been said, thou shalt love thy neighbour, and hate thine enemy :
—but I say unto you, love your enemies, bless them that curse
you, and pray for them which despitefully use you, and perse-
cute you.* See Matt. v. 43, 44.

The word *neighbour* (in Greek, πλησιον) signifies one that
*dwells near to us,*—from *nae,* or *naer,* near, and *buer* to dwell;
and well translated in the Anglo-Saxon nehƿcan, him that is
*next* to you, or from naeƿ *near,* and ſtanban *to stand,*—he that
*stands near you.*    And our Lord shews that the acts of kindness are to be done to any person in distress, of whatever *nation, religion,* or *kindred,* he may be; and this kindness should
be done to him that is *near* us, either in *person,* or in *proxy,*
or by *report.*    For a man may be near us *personally,—near*
us by his *representative,*—or near us, brought into our *presence,* by *credible report ;*—so that *any human being* may be
that *neighbour* to whom we should do kindness, when once
his case and necessity is *known ;* for he is *with* us, just *before
us,* in the *trust-worthy* report we have received.    If a man
come from the most *distant part of the earth,* the moment he
is *near* you, he has the same claim on your mercy and kindness, that you would have on his, were your dwelling *place*

transferred to *his* native country. And if he be not personally near you, the true representation of his necessitous case, when once brought before you, places him in effect there; and his claims on you are as strong as if he were *personally present.* It is on this very principle that the *New Zealanders*, our *antipodes*, may be our *neighbours*, when we hear of their *dark* and *dismal state*, totally without *God*, and without any *moral good;* and it is on this same principle, that we love them so much, as to contribute to the best of our power, to send them the *gospel* of our Lord Jesus.

This *second commandment* tells us that we should *love our neighbour* (thus understood) *as ourselves.* As this second commandment *is like unto the first*, we see that the *love* of our *neighbour* springs from the *love of God* as its *source*—is found in the love of God, as its *principle, pattern* and *end;* and the love of God is found in the love of our neighbour, as its effect, *representation*, and infallible *mark.* See some observations on this subject in the Discourse on Eph. iii. 14—21. in Vol. I.

This love of our neighbour is a love of *equity, charity, succour*, and *benevolence.* We owe to him, what we have a right to expect from *him.* " Do unto all men as you would they should do unto you," is a positive command of our Lord. By this rule, we should *think, speak*, and *write*, about every soul of man with whom we are concerned—put the best construction upon all the *words* and *actions* of our neighbours that they can possibly bear. By this rule, we are taught to bear with, love, and forgive him, if he have even been *troublesome*, or have done us *wrong.* We should *rejoice* in his *happiness, mourn* in his *adversity;* desire and delight in his prosperity, and promote it to the best of our power; instruct his ignorance, help his weakness, and risk even our life for his sake, and the public good. The Jews thought that all these things should be done to an *Israelite;* that is the *sense* in which they understood the word *neighbour.* Hear one of their wisest, and most learned men, Rabbi *Mayemon*, " A Jew sees a Gentile fall into the sea: let him by no means lift him out; for it is written, *Thou shalt not rise up against the blood of thy* NEIGHBOUR. But this is not thy *neighbour.*" By this wretched construction of the word, a Jew is bound to suffer a Gentile to perish if he see him in danger of death, though he could

easily prevent this !  But *we*, thank God, have not so learned
*Christ.*  In a word, we must do every thing in our power,
and in all, and through all, the possible varieties of circumstances, for our neighbours, which we would wish them to do
for us, were our situations *reversed.*  This, Jesus has taught
—O how far is Jesus and His gospel above even Moses and
his law.

How happy would society be, were this sacred and rational
precept properly observed !  Reader, if *others* do not attend
to it, it is not the less binding on *thee.*  To him who loves God
with all his heart, the fulfilment of this duty is not only *possible*,
but *easy* and *delightful.*  The carnal mind is *enmity against
God*, and to it, every sacred duty is irksome, and every heavenly virtue hateful ;  but when the heart is renewed in righteousness and true holiness, *submission* to God is its element,
and *obedience* its delight.  And with respect to our *neighbour*, let
us ever remember, that the man who would deprive another of
any *temporal* or *spiritual* privilege, which he requires that
man to concede to *him*, is a bad member of civil and religious
society, and is destitute of the love, both of God and man.

Our Lord gives us the *rule* and *measure* of this love, *Thou
shalt love thy neighbour as thyself.*

*Self-love*, as it has been generally termed, has been grievously decried and declaimed against, even by *religious people*,
as a most pernicious and dreadful evil.  But charity would say,
it is to be hoped they have not understood the subject on
which they spoke.  They have denominated that *intense propensity* which unregenerate men feel to gratify their carnal
appetites and vicious passions, *self-love* : whereas it might
more properly be termed *self-hatred* or *self-murder.*  If I am
to love my neighbour *as myself*, and this love *worketh no ill
to its neighbour*, then *self-love*, in the sense in which our Lord
uses it, is something excellent.  It is properly a disposition
essential to our nature, and inseparable from our being ; by
which we *desire* to be happy, and by which we *seek* the happiness we have not, and *rejoice* in it when we possess it.  In
a word, it is " The uniform wish of the soul to avoid all evil,
and enjoy all good."  Therefore he who is wholly governed
by *self-love*, properly and scripturally speaking, will devote *his*
whole soul to God ; and earnestly and constantly seek all his
peace, happiness, and salvation, in Him alone.

But *self-love* cannot make me happy—I am only the *subject* that receives the happiness, but am not the *object* that constitutes that happiness : for it is that *object*, properly speaking, that I *love ;*—and love, not only for its *own sake*, but also for the sake of the *happiness* which I enjoy through it. No man, says the Apostle, ever hated his own flesh ; but he that sinneth against God, wrongeth his own soul; depriving it of present and eternal salvation, and is so far from being governed by *self-love,* that he is an implacable enemy to his own best and dearest interests in both worlds.

We may if we please, call that *self-love,* which causes us to have only *our own interest* in view ;—and that man, a *self-lover,* who cares for nobody—helps nobody—pities nobody :—who is the centre of his own paltry system, and extending his arms to every part of *his circumference,* rakes every thing into the vortex of himself. Of the widow's moans, and the cries of the orphans, he is utterly regardless ;—he *gets* all he can—*saves* all he can—and keeps all he *gets,* and cares not who wants, or who is in misery. I cannot call this man's principle *self-love*—he has no *love* for *himself*—as he *feels no good,* he *does no good*—and as he does no *act of kindness,* he cannot have even the happiness of a dog—for a dog is pleased when he finds he has pleased his master. He is one who in his *heart* and *conduct* is abhorred of God, and despised by all men. Pray for him, but have no connexion with him :—there are not many of his kind on the earth, bad as it is ; O, pray God, that he may never have his fellow.

One word more on this general subject :—when God says, thou shalt love thy neighbour as *thyself,* He does not say, thou shalt love him *better than thyself.* My love to him should cause me to · *divide* my *last morsel* with him ; but should I give him the *whole,* when I had no prospect of any supply ? It would be an *unnatural* act—this would be loving him *better than myself,* which would be as opposite to *law* as to *nature.*

Reader, review the whole of this love to God and man, its nature and its effects—adore God for His goodness in giving thee such a *Law.* This is the religion of Jesus ! Love ME, and love thy FELLOWS. Be unutterably happy in *me,* and be in perfect peace, unanimity, and love, among *yourselves !*— Great Fountain and Dispenser of love ! fill thy creation with this sacred principle, for His sake who died for the salvation of a lost world! Amen.

To give due weight and importance to these commands, our Lord sums up the whole with this strong assertion, viz.—

*On these commandments hang all the law and the Prophets.*

These two commandments are like the first and last links of a chain, all the intermediate depend on them. True Religion begins and ends in the *love of God and man.* These are the two grand links that unite God to man, man to his fellows, and men again to God.

St. Paul says, (Rom. xiii. 10.) *Love worketh no ill to his neighbour : therefore love is the fulfilling of the law.* He who has the love of God and man in his heart, can do no evil to any creature—he cannot avenge himself on his greatest enemy, much less can he injure or kill a man who has never done him ill. On the other hand, if he *love him,* and love him as *himself,* he will do him any kindness in his power. Disobedience to God, arises from the carnal mind, which is enmity to God ; but when the heart is filled with love to God, and the carnal mind is destroyed, then the enmity is destroyed, and obedience is delightful. He cannot be an enemy in his mind to God, by wicked works, who has the *mind* in him which was in Christ—and to such a mind, the *commandments of the Lord are not grievous.* Now all our duties in life refer either to *God* or to man, or to *both :*—there is no *third party* to which we are accountable, or to whom we *owe obedience :*—having therefore the principle of attachment and obedience to God, and of fraternal affection and kind offices to man ;—and the whole of God's word, whether *Law, Prophets, Psalms, Gospels,* and *Epistles,* refers all our actions to God and man,—therefore the love that *fulfils all the commands relative* to *both,* must be the fulfilling of the law :—and thus *on these two great commandments hang all the law and the prophets.*

On another occasion, mentioned by St. Luke, x. 25. &c. a lawyer having asked our Lord, *What he should do to inherit eternal life ?*—when asked by the divine Teacher what was written in the law on this subject : and answering in the words of these two commandments ;—our Lord replied, *Thou hast answered right: this do, and thou shalt live,* ver. 28 ; we may observe, that the *life* which the Saviour of man promises, may be considered as the necessary *consequence*, and the gracious *recompense* of this *love* to God and man.

He, whose soul *rests in God, supremely*, and *intensely satisfied;* who always *lives* to, and ever acts *for* God, must be happy.   God the author and Fountain of *life* and felicity, *lives* in him; he *lives*, therefore, a *spiritual life*, which consists in the union of *God and the soul; as animal life* consists in the union of the *soul and its body*.   The works of righteousness which he performs, are at once the *evidences* and the *functions* of this spiritual life.   He *lives* to all the important purposes and concerns of life, *viz.* to glorify his God, and to do good to man.   He *lives* under the influences of the *life-giving* spirit, and increases daily in love both to God *and* man. The *life* of the wicked may be justly termed an· *ever-living death;* but the *life* of the righteous, is an *ever-living life.*   He *lives* in *death* itself! death is *his:* it is the gate of *eternal life* to his *deathless* spirit.   He shall never die; and he lives where there is no death; he lives through eternity.   He *lives* in Him who only hath *immortality:* and Him he sees as He is.   Penetrated with the rays of His glory, he contemplates His infinite perfections, each of which must beget in him endless wonder, delight, and satisfaction.   Behold, therefore, what manner of love the Father hath bestowed on us, that we might be called the sons of God!   Father of mercies, God of light power, and love! illuminate, quicken, and invigorate the minds of thy people!—let them see the glorious hope of their calling, and never rest,—

> Till transformed by faith divine;
>   They gain that perfect love unknown;
> Bright in all thine image shine,
>   By putting on thy Son.

These are things which the angels desire to look into; how then should men feel!

The pious *Quesnel* says on the text of this Discourse, "This *double* precept, concerning the *love of God* and *of our neighbour*, is the summary of all the divine and positive commandments; the compendious direction and way to salvation; the *Bible* of the *simple* and *ignorant;* and the *book* which even the most learned will never thoroughly understand in this life."

How much need have we to pray to God, that He may open our eyes, that we may see wonders in His law, and open our hearts that we may feel His glorious power rooting out the seeds of sin. With such glorious privileges before us, and within our reach, why will we live in a state of spiritual *non-age?* Shall the present generation be minished from the earth, before the enjoyment of this state of grace become *general* in the Church of Christ !—Are not all things *now ready?* Has not the Blood of the covenant been shed to justify the ungodly, and sanctify the unholy; and can it ever be *more efficacious* in its nature than it now is ?—Does not God *now* wait to be gracious ? Can He ever be *more willing* to cleanse our hearts from all unrighteousness, than He is *now ?* Does He not make it our duty to love Him *this moment,* with all *our hearts, souls, minds,* and *strength ?* And does He not *know,* that we *cannot* thus love Him, till *He has cleansed our hearts* from all unrighteousness ? Then, He must be this moment *willing* to cleanse us if He expect a loving obedience from us, which he knows is impossible, till He have sprinkled clean water upon us, and made us clean !—The spirit and the bride say come ! and let him that is athirst come, and whosoever will, let him come, and take the water of life freely ! Where is the Holy Spirit the Purifier? Where is faith to receive Him. In the sight of His *Omnipotence,* can it be *impossible ?*—In the sight of His *Sacrifice,* impracticable? No !—

> Faith, mighty Faith, the promise sees,
>   And looks to that *alone :*
> Laughs at impossibilities,
>   And cries, *It shall be done !*

See the Discourse on Eph. iii. 14—21, in Vol. I. where there are several observations on this subject.

# SERMON XXIV.

## THE WISE MAN'S COUNSELS TO HIS PUPIL;

### OR,

## THE TRUE METHOD OF GIVING, RECEIVING, AND PROFITING BY RELIGIOUS INSTRUCTION.

### PROV. xxii. 17—21.

17. Bow down thine ear, and hear the words of the wise, and apply thine heart unto my knowledge.

18. For it is a pleasant thing if thou keep them within thee; they shall withal be fitted in thy lips.

19. That thy trust may be in the Lord, I have made known to thee this day, even to thee.

20. Have not I written to thee excellent things in counsels and knowledge:

21. That I might make thee know the certainty of the words of truth: that thou mightest answer the words of truth to them that send unto thee?

I SUPPOSE these verses to contain an address of the wise man to one of his pupils, and to refer principally to instructions which this pupil had already received. I think it probable, that what is here said, is built on that most important maxim, ver. 6. *Train up a child in the way he should go; and when he is old he will not depart from it.* A short paraphrase of this verse, will serve to shew the connexion between it and the teaching in the text. The original of the first clause of this verse, is curious and impressive :—חנך לנער על־פי דרכו *chanac le-nadr ál-pi dareco, Initiate a child at the opening* (mouth) *of his path.* When he comes to the opening of the way of life;—when reason begins to dawn, being just able to walk alone and to choose in a general way, between good and evil; —stop at this point of entrance, and begin a series of instructions, how he is to conduct himself in every step he takes,

Q

Shew him the *duties, dangers* and *blessings* of the path ; give him directions how to *perform* the *duties,* how to *shun* the *dangers,* and how to *secure* the *blessings,* which all lie before him. Fix these on his mind by daily inculcation, till their impression is become indelible : then lead him to *practice,* by slow and almost imperceptible degrees, till each indelible impression becomes a strongly radicated *habit.* · Beg incessantly the blessing of God on all this teaching and discipline : when this is done, you have obeyed the injunction of the wisest of men ; and then you will have strong reason and pointed revelation to support you in the belief, that there is no likelihood that such *impressions* shall ever be defaced, or such *habits* ever be destroyed. God, who has commanded the duty, will infallibly give His blessing, where the work is faithfully performed ; and His seed sown in His own name, will bring forth fruit to the glory and praise of His grace.

Still a frequent recurrence to first principles will be necessary,—the pupil must be examined in reference to his progress in religious knowledge, and practical piety :—he must be reminded of his *duty,*—of the *snares of life*—and of the *use* he has made of the instructions he has received. He must be called to the feet of his Master,—come, *bow down thine ear, and hear the words of the wise !*—Is thy *talent* improved? What hast thou *gained* by *trading?*

Assuming the same ground as that of Solomon, I will endeavour to copy his example, and leaving all *proverbs* and *initiatory instruction,* I shall endeavour to point out,—

I. The *directions* how to profit by that which wisdom has already delivered.

II. The *nature* of the instruction, and the pleasure and profit to be derived from it.

III. The *end* for which it was given, and

IV. Make an appeal to every disciple relative to the matter and importance of the teaching.

V. So illustrate and defend the heavenly teaching, that the mind of the disciple may have the fullest satisfaction, and most plenary evidence of the truth of God ; and the importance of that truth.

VI. See the reasonableness of witnessing and faithfully proclaiming what we *experimentally* know to be of the utmost importance to the welfare of men in general.

I. Solomon addresses his pupil on the profitable use of the lessons which wisdom had already taught.

We might consider the whole subject in these verses, as relating only to the wise man and his disciple; but as we have the highest authority to believe, that *whatsoever was written of old time, was written for our learning*, I shall consider the whole as applicable to the state of religious society at large; shew our advantages, and how we should hear the teachings of wisdom, in order that we may be saved.

1. *Bow down thine ear, and hear the words of the wise.*

A wise man addresses us, and the wisdom of God speaks by his mouth. Not only the wise man's *words*, but his `sentiments` also, which are those of divine wisdom, should be carefully heard. It would be rude to shew inattention to the friendly address of any man, and especially of one famed for science and piety :—and still more so, if age and experience had matured his knowledge, and given him a certain right to speak as a master, and to teach wisdom even among those that are perfect. But it would be criminal to treat with indifference, Him who speaks from heaven; who can not only speak to the *ear*, but to the *heart ;* and thus gives light to apprehend right things, and power to feel and profit by them. Such a Teacher is in every religious assembly, and while He diffuses His *light* to enable us to discern our state in all wants, guilt, and moral diseases, His *power* is present to heal us. Do we really believe that saying, *Wheresoever two or three are gathered together in my name, I am in the midst of them ;—* and that He who is thus present, is the Fountain of wisdom and mercy; without feeling the utmost certainty of the infallibility of His teaching, and at the same time, His great readiness to impart the instruction we need? *Man* may, even undesignedly, mislead us. God can neither deceive, nor be deceived. The advantage of having such a Teacher is ineffably great.

2. He teaches *knowledge.* He gives *doctrines*, not only *true* in themselves, but such as are confirmed by *observation* and *experience.* Whosoever has learned of Him has become wise unto salvation; and not one soul that has followed His directions, has ever miscarried. Is not this consideration sufficient to induce us to come into His presence with *thanks-*

*giving*, knowing that we are not only going to hear the words of Moses, the Prophets, the Evangelists, and the Apostles; but the word of HIM, *by* whom, as well as *of* whom, Moses, in the law and the Prophets, did write.

On this consideration will not your hearts say, Speak, Lord! thy servants wait to hear. He who is the Sum and Substance of their teaching, condescends to become, by the direct influence of His Spirit upon the heart, our immediate Teacher! What a privilege!

3. Seeing we have such a Teacher, should we not hear Him with deep *humility* and *attention?* This is stated by the wise man in the text—*Bow down thine ear, and hear the words of the wise.* Can we for a moment suppose, that we are worthy of such a privilege? Did we ever, or can we ever, deserve it? Have we not sinned against Him, and is not our mental darkness an effect of our *sin?* Deeply humbled should we be in the presence of our Judge; nor can that humiliation be lessened by the consideration that mercy rejoices over judgement, and to it our obligations are about to be transferred? No,—to eternity it must be a subject of *humiliation*, that so great was our *offence*, and so deep was our *stain*, that they required the humiliation of the Creator of the heavens and the earth, to atone for the offence, and wash out the stain: for He humbled Himself—made Himself of no reputation—took upon Him the form of a servant—was made in the likeness of man—became obedient unto death, even the death of the cross!

And all this was absolutely necessary, in order that He might become our *Teacher*, and pour out His *soul* for transgressors. Bow down then thine ear—approach his footstool with the most *respectful reverence*: and while His ministers are teaching you out of His law, and encouraging you out of the gospel, listen to hear *His voice* in your heart, accrediting the words of His servants, and sealing instructions upon your souls. He takes away the veil—diffuses light, and then you will see wonders in His law. But let it be remembered, that no word of God was ever read or heard profitably, where the spirit of humility did not bear rule.

4. The *words of the wise*, must not only be *humbly* and respectfully heard, but they must be *pondered*—i. e. well weighed, and be the subject of careful *meditation*. Hence the

text says, *Apply thine heart unto my knowledge.* *Put thy heart* to this knowledge—let it and thy heart meet—let them meet as *teacher* and *pupil*—the one ready to *give* all instruction, and the other to *receive* it. And remember that you are to meditate on the lessons of wisdom in order to get practical knowledge—knowledge by which you may act, till you know the truth of God, experimentally and savingly.

Under the first particular, I have considered knowledge as implying doctrine. Now, if good and sound doctrine be not fully *understood*, it cannot be experienced; and if not experienced, it cannot be *practised;* and if not brought into practice, it can be of no use. Hence experimental practical religion must be that which the wise man calls *his knowledge;* and this is evident—

II. From the *comfort* or *happiness* which this knowledge brings, *For it is a pleasant thing if thou keep them within thee,* ver. 18.

1. Thus we see that the words of the wise and his knowledge must be kept *within*—in the *mind*—by recollection and reflection, and in the *heart*, by *experimental* spiritual feeling.

2. There is both *pleasure* and *profit* to be derived from attentive hearing; and the words of life must be laid up in the heart—they are a spiritual treasure, and must be treasured *there.*

3. Throughout all the walk and business of life, the words of God bring satisfaction to the mind, comfort to the heart, and sure direction to the steps. These are no mean encouragements; and in hearing the words of life, we should keep all these things in view.

4. The man who thus attends to the teachings of wisdom, shall gain such an experimental knowledge of them, as to be able to speak of them *suitably, pertinently,* and *persuasively.* *They shall withal be fitted to thy lips,* ib. A man who pretends to religion, and has no *experimental knowledge* of it, soon exposes himself. The words of it are not at all *fitted in his lips.* He knows not the *principles* of the *language* of Canaan—its *grammar* he has never learned—and to pretend to speak it, shews not only his own ignorance, but also his hypocrisy and folly. He can neither *suit* the Scriptures to his own state, nor to that of others. He cannot speak *pertinently* on cases of conscience, subtle temptation, or plausible

objections. He can have no power of *persuasion,* because he has no *experience* of the truth. He is not converted, and neither knows the *Bible, himself,* nor his *Saviour.*

In order that the words of the Most High may be pleasant to a man, he must keep them *within* him, בבטנך *be-bitonca—in thy bowels.* The whole *viscera,* which perform the essential vital functions, must feel their influence. The *heart* must beat for God, the *lungs* breathe for Him, the *stomach* and *bowels* perform their respective functions, that, the whole system being in a *healthy state,* there may be an increase and preservation of strength and energy to be employed in the service of God. And even where there is not a good state of health, it is truly wonderful how much suffering is relieved, and how much weakness is supported by the truly healing influence of the life of God in the soul of man. It is no wonder the words of God are *not fitted* to *the lips* of that man, into whose *vitals* they have never been received.

III. Let us now see the *end* which the wise man has in view, and after him the ministers of the Divine Word, by giving these instructions, ver. 19, *That thy trust be in the Lord, I have made known to thee this day.*

1. To know, feel, and acknowledge that God is the Fountain of all good and perfection; that without Him nothing is wise, nothing holy, nothing strong, is a matter of the utmost importance in religion. With Him, we must begin: with Him, we must end. As He is the Dispenser of all blessings, so is He their Preserver: the prayer of faith *receives* the necessary blessings, and they are *preserved* and *increased* by continual *dependance* on Him. Therefore the wise man, and every man who is instructed in the word and doctrine, will propose this grand *end* in all their teachings, *That thy trust may be in the Lord, I have spoken unto thee this day; even to thee.*

2. He who trusts in his own heart, is a fool;—and cursed is the man who trusteth in man, and maketh flesh his arm. In most cases, even our veriest friends cannot help us; and our own strength and wisdom we often find to be inefficient, and of little worth. Our spiritual enemies are wise, subtle, strong, and experienced; they are also innumerable. They have every advantage against us, even considered as *outward assailants:* but when we consider that they have a most

faithful and powerful *party* within us, the weakest of which is stronger than ourselves, what hope is there of our escape! None.    But in the midst of despair we hear that word, *Trust in the Lord for ever; for in the Lord Jehovah is everlasting strength.*    And in the text we are told to put our trust in the Lord; and that it is one grand design of the public ministry of His word, to excite men to put their trust in the Omnipotent.

3. And that such exhortations may be effectual, they are specific and particular—*I have made known to* THEE *this day, even to* THEE.    Every individual is addressed—every person is specified;—*to thee*, who art nearly overwhelmed with despair, from a sense of thy own worthlessness and weakness,— *to thee* is the word of this salvation sent.    Even a more wretched object than the above appears to be singled out. May *I* hope?    May *I* trust in God?    Is there salvation for *me?*—*me*, the chief of sinners—the worst of backsliders? Yes, *even to* THEE, the Saviour of men comes.    He will bless *thee* by turning thee away from all thine iniquities.    HE tasted death for every man, and His blood cleanses from all unrighteousness.

4. But *when* will He shew mercy?    I answer, He is as *specific* in respect to the *time*, as He is to the *person :—to-day*—even now, when thou art calling, mourning, yea, almost *despairing*, He says, *I have made known to thee,* THIS DAY. *Now*, He would have thee *to put thy trust in Him :* for this is the *accepted time*, and *this the day of salvation*.    He has not commanded thee to trust in reference to the *morrow*, because He has not told thee that thou shalt live another hour.    This He has done in *times past,—I* HAVE *made known to thee*,—thou hast *had* those calls often,—and still I wait to be gracious; and, therefore, *make known to thee*, THIS DAY.    The gate of mercy was never closed against the prayer of a penitent: and *now*, the kingdom of heaven is open to all believers.

IV. An appeal is made to the person himself, relative to the matter and importance of the teaching.

1. *Have I not written to thee excellent things in counsels and knowledge?* ver. 20.

Not only general instructions are given in the way of *oral* exhortation, but excellent things have been *penned* and sent to mankind. We have, thank God, a *written* LAW, and a *written* GOSPEL: and copies of these have been multiplied by millions, and they have been translated into almost all the languages of the earth; and have been sent to nearly every nation under heaven.

2. The things contained in this revelation, are said to be *excellent* :—שלשים *shalashim*. And what more *pure, holy, just,* and *good,* than the LAW? And what more heavenly, benevolent, and effectual to the salvation and happiness of men, than the GOSPEL? All these are *excellent,* and every page is fraught with *excellent things.*

3. But as the word שלשים *shalashim,* signifies, THIRD, THRICE, *three times,* in *three different ways,* it has been thought to refer to the *three books* written by *Solomon,* for the edification of men. 1. *Canticles ;* 2. *Koheleth,* or *Ecclesiastes ;* and 3. *Proverbs :* all containing *excellent things* of their respective kinds.

4. Others, understanding the word to refer to the voice of *Divine* WISDOM, suppose that the *three* grand divisions of the Sacred Oracles, are here intended: *viz.* 1. The *Law ;* 2. The *Prophets ;* and 3. The *Hagiographa.* The division called the LAW, or *Sepher Thora,* contained in the *five Books of Moses.* The PROPHETS were divided into the *former,* which included *Joshua, Judges,* the two books of *Samuel,* and the two books of *Kings :*—the *latter,* which included *Isaiah, Jeremiah, Ezekiel,* and the twelve *minor Prophets.* The HAGIOGRAPHA, or *Kethubim,* comprehended the *Psalms, Proverbs, Job, Canticles, Ruth, Lamentations, Ecclesiastes, Daniel, Ezra, Nehemiah,* and the two books of *Chronicles.* In our Lord's time, this division was a little different. He mentions the *three divisions :* 1. The LAW ; 2. The PROPHETS ; and 3. The PSALMS : but under the word *Psalms,* those books which constitute the *Hagiographa* seem to be intended ; though Josephus mentions only the *Psalms, Proverbs, Job,* and *Canticles,* under that division, which our Lord, (apparently after him,) calls the PSALMS. These *three divisions,* as they take in the whole of the Old Testament, include all the *excellent things* of the Jewish dispensation.

5. Others think they have hit the meaning of *shalashim* in the text, by interpreting it of the *three* grand INTELLECTUAL SCIENCES. 1. *Morality,* or *Ethics ;* 2. *Natural Philosophy,* or

*Physics;* 3. *Theology,* or the science of Divine Things, as contained in the Scriptures.   On all these subjects Solomon wrote ; but his Books on Natural Philosophy are lost.

6. To complete conjecture on this *shalashim,* some of the *Rabbins,* and some *Christians* with them, find in the term, *the three senses* of Scripture, 1. The *literal ;* 2. The *figurative ;* and 3. The *allegorical.*   Here are senses enow out of one poor Hebrew word ; and perhaps none of them the true one ; for after all, as we know the term *thrice,* was often used as the term *seven,*—a certain number for an uncertain ; see Amos i. 11., 2 Cor. xii. 8. ; so it may mean here, no more than, *I have written to thee* OFTEN, *very oft ;* so in *Coverdale ;* and as בשלשם *shalashim,* is here interpreted *excellent things,* or *princely things,* such as become a *king* to speak, we may apply it to the *Scriptures,* and the *excellent doctrines* they contain.   Indeed, it would not be difficult to prove that there is not one important *art* or *science* which is not alluded to in the Holy Scriptures, and used there to illustrate and inculcate heavenly truths.

7. We find, that these *excellent, princely,* or *threefold* teachings consist of TWO *grand parts :* 1. COUNSELS,—מעצות *môetsoth,* from יעץ *yaâts,* to *give advice, counsel,* or *information.* These *counsels* shew men *what* they should *know ; advise* them *what* they should *do.*   2. KNOWLEDGE, דעת *daâth,* from ידע *yadâ,* to perceive, or feel by means of the senses and internal perception ; what should be felt, experienced, known to be true by mental perception.   Therefore, *knowledge* here, may signify all that influences the *heart* and *affections,* and in a divine sense, *experimental religion.*   In these few points every thing of importance to man is included.   1. To be *taught* what we should *know.*   2. To be *advised* what we should *do.*   And 3. to be put in possession of the spirit of true religion, and thus experimentally know what we should *feel ;*—to have that mind in us that was in Christ Jesus ;—harmony of all the affections, regulation of all the passions ;—in a word, genuine, solid, unruffled happiness, or that religion thus described by the poet :—

" Mild, sweet, serene, and gentle was her mood ;
Not *grave* with *sternness,* nor with *lightness free :*
Against example, resolutely good ;
Fervent in zeal, and warm in charity."

For more on *knowledge*, or experimental religion, see under first head.

V. All this is done to give men the *fullest satisfaction*, and most *plenary evidence* concerning the TRUTH of God: *That I might make thee to know the certainty of the words of truth*, ver. 21.

1. The words of truth are *Divine Revelation*, or the *doctrines of truth*. 1. Doctrines that are *true* in *themselves*. 2. That came not from *man*, nor from uncertain *tradition*; but from the GOD of TRUTH. And, 3. Are *fulfilled*, and are fulfilling; and are thus *known* and *felt* to be *truth*, by all that believe.

2. These *words*, or *doctrines of truth*, are here said to be *certain—ܘܫ kosheth*, another word for *truth* itself: they are *the truth of truth*,—a most singular mode of explanation— illustrating a thing by *itself*. There is nothing that can be compared with truth. TRUTH is that which is the absolute opposite to all falsity, lie, semblance, deceit, feigning, or fiction, counterfeit, imposture, hypocrisy, and every thing that is contrary to the " strict conformity of actions to things—of words to thoughts." It is what is *absolutely right*, as opposed to what is *absolutely wrong*; and it might be added, it is what is only *good*, as opposed to what is totally *evil*. Even *types*, *representatives*, *metaphors*, and *symbols*, are considered as *falsehood*, when compared with *truth:* witness that remarkable saying of the Evangelist—*The* LAW *was given by Moses : but grace and* TRUTH *came by Jesus Christ.* John i. 17.

3. Most words which express, or point out things of importance, have *synonimes*, or substitutes, by which the same ideas may be expressed ; and we can often say *such word* is the *same* as *such another word :—Strong*, the same as *able ;— Next*, the same as *nearest*, &c. But we cannot say, " *Truth the same as*"—for there is no SYNONIME—we may indeed say, is " *the* same as *verity ;*" but this is saying nothing, as it only gives a *Latinized translation* of the *English term*.

4. TRUTH, therefore, has no *compeer ;*—it is an essential attribute of God. He is THE TRUTH, the *whole* TRUTH, and *nothing* but the TRUTH, (and so in His word.) Producing *existence*, where there was none before, is the *work* of TRUTH. ESSENCE, whether of *spirit* or *matter*, is the effect of TRUTH.

*Ideas* themselves, are not *truths*, but the *semblances* of *entities,* ——and even some *entities,* so called, may be *fictitious,* and perfectly *unreal.* Can a man take up the *idea* of a *stone,* and throw it at the *idea* of a *lion?* But a *stone* is a *true thing,* so is a *lion: i. e.* such things have positive, substantial *existence.*

5. Now, GOD is TRUTH. His is a *true Being.* He is *infinite, eternal, self-existent,* and *independent;*—there cannot be a *second* such; and hence, He cannot be *compared;* for there *is* nothing, there *can be* nothing, *like to Him.* Infinite, eternal, self-existent, and independent, can be spoken of *no other being.* But all these attributes are *true* of HIM. He then is the *only Creator;*—whatever *exists,* exists *by* and *through* Him. Whatever He does is *true,*—it has a *true existence*—it is not *shadow* or *unreal idea.* Whatever He *says* is *true;*—it is *said,* and must *stand;*—it is *commanded,* and must *stand fast.*

6. *Revelation* can come only from Him; for there is no other source of *knowledge.* And His revelation is distinguished from all other *professed* or *pretended* revelations, by its TRUTH, manifested in the *accomplishment* of *predictions,* and the *fulfilment* of *promises.* Pretended revelations, or such as false prophets and impostors bring forward to deceive men, for the gain, honour, or power, which the framers expect, should they succeed, take care not to deal in *promises* of *supernatural good;* as they well know, that they have neither *supernatural powers,* nor can avail themselves of *supernatural agencies.* All *spiritual blessings,* and *unalloyed happiness,* are referred by them not to a *temporal futurity,* but to an *interminable eternity.* But the *revelation* that is *true,* (and, to be true, must come from HIM who is TRUE, and who is the Fountain of *knowledge,*) abounds in *promises,* not merely in reference to an *eternal state,* but for *every fugitive moment of time.* We have in His revelation exceeding great and precious promises; these promises relate to *every human being,* in every *point* of *its duration : faith* apprehends them, and the *true believer feels* them to be *yea* and *amen,* in *Christ Jesus.* Thus, according to His *truth,* God is every moment convincing, converting, justifying, sanctifying, sustaining, or delivering some human being or beings, and thus religion is maintained in the earth; and as no *sword*

is used, no *secular advantages* held out, to induce men to espouse and profess His religion : hence His operations are *known* to be *spiritual*, and are *proved* to be *true*, because they are seen to be *real*.

7. His revelation is called the *truth ;* and in that revelation He is often called *The* TRUE GOD. When His ancient people became *idolaters*, they were said to be *without the* TRUE GOD. 2 Chron. xv. 3. Jeremiah calls Him the TRUE GOD—the *living* GOD, ch. x. 10. And our Lord tells us, that *it is everlasting life to know Him who is the* TRUE *God.* John xvii. 3. And when the people at *Thessalonica* embraced the *gospel* of *Christ,* they are said by St. Paul, to *have turned from idols to serve the living* and TRUE GOD. 1 Thes. i. 9. And St. John assures us, that it was to reveal this TRUE GOD, that Jesus Christ came into the world. *And we know that the Son of God is come,* and *hath given us an understanding, that we may know Him who is* TRUE ; and *we are in Him who is* TRUE, *in His Son Jesus Christ. This is the* TRUE GOD and *Eternal Life.* 1 John v. 20. And of His *revelation* which is called *The Truth,* it is said, that it *endureth to all generations.* Psal. c. 5. cxvii. 2. That it shall act, in reference to all believers, as a *continual* defence—" His *truth* shall be thy *shield* and *buckler.*" Psal. xci. 4. For God's *Law is the Truth.* Psal. cxix. 142. And the *Holy Scripture* is said to be *The Scripture* of TRUTH. Dan. x. 21. And St. John asserts that the Spirit of God, by which this revelation was given, is *the Spirit of Truth,* or το πνευμα της αληθειας, The SPIRIT *of the* TRUTH, whose office it was *to lead* the minds of the Evangelists, εις πασαν την αληθειαν, *into the whole of the* TRUTH, which they were to testify to others concerning Jesus the Christ, and the redemption that is in Him. John xvi. 13. And the *way* in which God will have all men to be saved, is by bringing *them to the knowledge of the* TRUTH. 1 Tim. ii. 4. That is, to send them His revelation, to teach them what they should know and believe : what they should *do*—what they should here *receive*—and what they are to *expect* in an eternal state.

8. These words of truth are *certain*—the *truth,* springing from the TRUTH. They are not of dubious or difficult interpretation ; they point *directly* to the great *end* for which God gave them ; they *promise,* and they are *fulfilled.* He that

pleads them by faith, receives their accomplishment in the spirit and power of divine love. For the Scriptures, the words of truth, as far as they concern the salvation of the soul, are to be *experimentally* understood; and by this experimental knowledge, every believer has the witness in himself, and *knows the certainty of the words of truth.*

VI. From all the above considerations, we may see the reasonableness of witnessing and faithfully proclaiming what we experimentally know to be of the utmost importance to the welfare of men in general.

*That thou mightest answer the words of truth to them that send unto thee.*

1. What is meant by the *words of truth,* see under the preceding *head.*

When the doctrine of salvation by Christ, is distinctly and faithfully preached, it will excite much discussion ; and there will be many inquirers, *What* is this *doctrine ?* Have any persons received the *blessings* we now hear of? *viz.* The remission of sins—the witness of the Spirit—the full purification of the heart? Áre there any persons among our acquaintance, on whose word we can rely, who can conscientiously assert, that they have a *direct witness,* not only from *the words of truth,* but from the *Divine Spirit, in their consciences,* that they *know* and *feel* that God for Christ's sake has blotted out all their sins? Are there any who were well known before, as *hasty, head-strong, proud, peevish, censorious, envious, passionate men,* or *women,* who are become *mild, meek, easy to be persuaded, humble, contented, gentle, benevolent, merciful* to the *persons, property,* and *characters* of their *neighbours,* and of *society* in general; who have got that love—that *Christian charity,* that suffers long, and is kind—that envies not—that is not puffed up—that does not behave itself unseemly—that is not provoked—that thinks no evil—that bears, believes, and hopes all things ? That when *reviled, revile not again*—that when *cursed, bless*—when *defamed, entreat ;*—who are, in a word, *living to the glory of God,* and striving to promote the welfare of man ? *Where* are *such ?* What are the collateral arguments by which you prove that God has done these things, for those persons? Can you shew us that you and they have not misapprehended the meaning of the Scriptures you quote."

2. Inquiries of this kind should meet with the *speediest,* the *mildest,* and most *distinct answers :* and the *doctrine of truth* should be *illustrated* and *supported* by the *words of truth.* St. Peter, 1 Epist. iii. 15, gives some important advice on this head : *Be ready,* says he, *always to give an answer to every man that asketh you a reason of the hope that is in you, with meekness and fear.* Do not permit your *readiness to answer,* nor the *confidence* yóu have in the goodness of your cause, to lead you to answer *pertly* or *superciliously* to any person : defend the *truth* with all possible *gentleness* and *fear,* lest while you are doing it, you should forget *His presence* whose cause you support ; or say aught, that is unbecoming the dignity and holiness of the religion you have espoused ; or is inconsistent with that heavenly temper which the indwelling spirit of your meek and lowly Saviour must infallibly produce.

3. Let all those who believe these great truths, and maintain them in their conversation with religious people, or with cavillers, take good heed that those sacred Doctrines be not blasphemed, through the unsteadiness of their conduct, or the improper government of their spirits. They, above all others, who make such professions, should be careful to maintain good works, and in all things to manifest a right spirit, lest they should be a stumbling-block to the weak.

I shall now, as a curiosity, put down those verses as they exist in the *first translation* of the Bible into English about A. D. 1350.

My sone bowe in thin eer, and heere the wordis of wise men. Lepe to forsoth herte to my doctrine, the whiche fair schal ben to thee whenn thou kepist it in thi wombe ; and schal rebounden in thi lippis, that in the Lord be thi trost. Wherfor and I schal schewen thee it to day. Loo I have discrivede it thre wise in thoughtis and kunnynge ; that I schulde schewen to thee stedfastnesse, and fair spechis of trewth thou schuldist answeren of these thingis to hem that senten thee.

COVERDALE'S Version, 1535, the first printed edition.

"My sonne bowe downe thine eare, and herken unto the wordes of wysdome, applye thi mynde unto my doctrine : for it is a pleasaunt thinge yf thou kepe it in thine herte, and practise it in thi mouth : that thou mayest alwaye put thi trust in the Lorde. Have not I warned thee very oft with counsell and lernynge ? that I might schewe thee the treuth, and that thou with the verite, mightest answere them that laye eny thinge against thee."

1. From this important passage we learn, that God in His mercy has given a *revelation of His will* to man, every way calculated to make him wise, holy, and useful.

2. That this revelation is the *truth,* and the *full truth,* on all the subjects which it embraces ; and contains in itself, the *full evidence* of its authenticity ; and to all that receive it, it is the power of God to salvation. ·

3. That this revelation contains a vast *variety* of *promises,* suited to all *circumstances* of life, and to every *state* in which the human being can possibly be found.

4. That the great *majority* of those *promises,* are for the *present life :* and Divine truth is *pledged* that all these promises shall be fulfilled to them who by faith and prayer seek their accomplishment from God.

5. That this fulfilment is a *standing evidence* of the truth of this revelation :—for every one who asks, receives—who seeks, finds—and to him who knocks, the gate of mercy is infallibly opened.

6. *Experimental religion* is founded upon such *promises ;* —all believers have *practical proof* that His word is *true* from beginning to end. And this shews that religion is still the *same,* and that the privileges of true believers in the present day, are equal to those which were the inheritance of the true Church in those days when *Prophets* and *Seers* proclaimed the *righteousness* of the Lord ; and *Apostles* and *Evange lists* shewed forth the unsearchable riches of the gospel of Christ.

7. That it is the high *duty* and *privilege* of every man to hear the Doctrine of truth and life, to whom God sends it.

8. That no man can profit by it, who does not hear in the spirit of humility ; willingly renouncing his *own wisdom,* that he may receive that which is from *above ;* and his own fancied *righteousness,* that he may receive that which is by the inspiration of God's Spirit ;—that holiness without which none can see God—the true righteousness that is by faith through Christ Jesus.

9. That there is no *state of grace* into which we can be brought that can make us *independent of God,* the Fountain of light and life : for the Holy Scripture speaks to each, that *his trust may be in God :* and the more we know of Him, and the more we are united to Him, the more we shall feel our

dependence upon Him. When Adam ceased to feel and acknowledge his *dependence* on God, he lost his holiness and happiness. Man is not saved but in being *brought back* to his original state of *dependence* upon his Maker.

10. That it is the privilege of every Christian believer to have a *certainty* of the state of grace in which he stands :—to know that God for Christ's sake has forgiven him all his sins, the Holy Spirit bearing witness with his, that he is a child of God.

11. That it is the *duty* of every person, to *spread* as far as he can, the *words of God*, and to inculcate those doctrines by which alone men can be saved :—In a word, to shew the world, as far as his knowledge, means, and influence can reach, that God is loving to every man—that He hateth nothing that He has made—and that Jesus Christ, by the grace of God, has tasted death for every man.

12. That it is the foolishness of folly to pretend to *religion*, if a man do not support his pretensions by a *godly life* :—for, as true religion has its seat in the *heart*, it will produce its holy effects in the *life*—and it is impossible that such a principle can ever lie hid ; for it is the *life of God* in the *soul of man*, producing the pure flame of love to GOD, its Author, and to *man* its chief object,

One of our good old Bishops gives much good advice on this subject, in a few words :—

1. *Come* to *hear* the word of God,

2. Take heed that you *do hear*, when you are *come*.

3. *Remember* what is suited to your state in the word you have heard.

4. Be sure to *practice* what you *remember*.

5. And *continue* in what you *practice*—Thus you shall not receive the grace of God in vain. For if ye be hearers of the word only, and not doers, ye shall deceive your own souls.

Inspirer of the ancient seers,
  Who wrote from Thee the Sacred Page,
The same thro' all succeeding years :
  To us in our degenerate age,
The spirit of thy word impart,
And breathe the life into our heart.

The sacred lessons of thy Grace,
  Transmitted thro' thy Word, repeat,

And train us up in all thy ways,
    To make us in thy Will complete ;
Fulfil thy Love's redeeming plan,
And bring us to a perfect man.

Furnish'd out of thy treasury,
    O may we always ready stand,
To help the souls redeem'd by Thee,
    In what their various states demand:
To teach, convince, correct, reprove ;
And build them up in holiest love.

R 2

# SERMON XXV.

## CHRIST CRUCIFIED, A STUMBLING-BLOCK TO THE JEWS, AND FOOLISHNESS TO THE GREEKS.

1 COR. i. 22—24.

22. For the Jews require a sign, and the Greeks seek after wisdom :

23. But we preach Christ crucified; unto the Jews a stumbling-block, and unto the Greeks foolishness ;

24. But unto them which are called, both Jews and Greeks, Christ the power of God, and the wisdom of God.

## ADVERTISEMENT.

THE substance of the following Discourse was preached at the opening of a chapel in the country in the year 1825. Not only the substance but the plan is the same; but several of the points are considerably expanded, as I wished to speak more in detail on subjects of a nature entirely analogous to those in the text, and which I could not well introduce in an *occasional* sermon. Many attempts have been made to corrupt Christianity ever since its establishment in the world,—and strange to tell, it was its professed *friends* that made them. From its *enemies* it never had any thing to fear, whether they employed their *pens* or their *swords* as instruments of their enmity. It met all malevolence with the meekness of wisdom; and all open persecution with a patience ennobled by fortitude; and thus it quenched the *fire* and blunted the edge of the sword, while the holiness, innocence, and usefulness of the lives of its followers, gave it a continual triumph over calumny and malevolence. None but its *professed friends* could hurt it, and they only in two ways; either by corrupting the general creed by false doctrines, or impairing and degrading the simple apostolic worship by *gaudy rites* and *useless ceremonies*. With *false creeds*, the Christian Church had often to contend; and with *useless* and *worldly ceremonies* it was often encumbered. God, in His mercy, always brought forward means to counteract these corruptions; and *revivals* of pure and undefiled religion were His grand instruments; and these never failed to call back those who were resting on their lees, and sinking into the spirit of the world, to first principles in doctrine, and simplicity in worship. From these two causes, the pure religion of Christ is now in danger; and in the house of its friends, religion has received some alarming wounds. It is fashionable to *split hairs in doctrine*, so as to perplex the simplicity of truth; to bring in strange opinions, which, even allowing them to have the *semblance of truth*, are but *mint and cummin*, to those weightier matters of the law, which they jostle and put aside. The *discipline* of Christianity has been opposed and often supplanted by *rites* and *ceremonies;* which were introduced either by *superstition* or *worldly mindedness.* In no age of the world was Christianity more corrupted than in that of the *school-men*, who were all *hair-splitting* men; and the world wondered at their subtlety and dexterous sophistry, till religion itself became evanescent, and the works of *Thomas Aquinas* were put in place of the Bible. Something like this splendid trifling is now beginning to shew itself in the Christian Church. May the spirit of judgement and of burning, sit upon and refine it! and may it come pure out of the wilderness, having lost nothing but its dross and tin! Even so, Lord Jesus. Amen, Amen.

A. C.

----

THE city of *Corinth*, to whose inhabitants this epistle was directed, was one of the oldest cities of Greece, being founded more than 1500 years before the Christian era. It was situated on the isthmus which connected *Peloponnesus*, or *Achaia*, now called the *Morea*, to the main land. It had what was called the port *Lecheum*, in the gulf of *Lepanto*, on the west ; and *Cenchrea*, in the gulf of *Egina*, on the east. By which it commanded the commerce of the *Ionian* and *Egean* seas, and consequently all Italy on the one hand, and all the Greek Islands on the other. In a word, it embraced the commerce of the whole *Mediterranean* sea, from the Straits of *Gibraltar*, on the west, to the port of *Alexandria*, on the east; with all the coast of *Egypt*, *Palestine*, *Syria*, and *Asia-Minor.*

Being so exceedingly well situated for trade, its riches became immense, and, for a time, these produced great power and great influence ; but in the end, as is ever the case, riches produced luxury ; luxury, effeminacy ; and this, a general corruption of manners. Sciences, arts, and literature, however, flourished much among its inhabitants, and Cicero termed it the *luminary of Greece*—the sun that gave light to all the other states. It was ambitious of power, covetous of wealth, proud of its literature and learned men ; vain of its public edifices, emulous of all that was great and splendid among its neighbours ; and to all these qualities, it added the most degrading sensuality, and the most extensive ever known in the world. Public *prostitution* formed a considerable part of their religion ; they were accustomed in their public prayers, to request the gods to multiply their prostitutes ; and the temple of *Venus* in this city, one of the most splendid of its buildings, had no less than 1000 courtezans, who were the means of bringing an immense concourse of strangers to the place. In the midst of all this corruption, neither their literature nor the arts were forgotten ; in these respects the Corinthians were enriched in all *utterance*, and in all *knowledge* —in *oratory* and *philosophy :*—and although among all the states of Greece, they were the most likely to have rejected the pure and holy gospel of Jesus Christ, yet in this city the Apostle ventured to proclaim his crucified Master, and though single, against their ocean of learning, and unparalleled sink of pollution, he converted multitudes, and founded here a very eminent and flourishing Church, to which he wrote the two epistles which go under his name, and their address. But so powerful are old deeply rooted propensities, till the heart is entirely purified by the grace of God, that he found it difficult to preserve many of them from lapsing into their former practices, which are pointedly noticed, sharply reprehended, and strongly guarded against in these epistles. The doctrine of *Christ crucified*, finally prevailed over all subtlety and corruption ; and, though many *Jews* continued to blaspheme, and *Gentiles* to gain-say, the *cross of Christ*, even at Corinth, became the Christian's glory.

To *whom* he preached, *what* he preached, and *how* he preached at Corinth, the verses just read declare : and to enter fully into these points, I shall,

I. Give the history of what is contained in the twenty-second verse.

II. Explain the doctrine specified in the twenty-third verse.

III. Make an application of the whole, from what is laid down in the twenty-fourth verse.

I. I shall give the history of what is contained in the twenty-second verse, *viz.*:—

*The Jews require a sign, and the Greeks seek after wisdom.*

1st. Here we have *two* nations of people mentioned ; the *Jews* and the *Greeks*.

2d. We have their chief *moral employment* specified : the *Jews* were requiring *signs ;* the *Gentiles* were *seeking* after *wisdom*.

1. However divided and subdivided the habitable globe may now be, originally there was no distinction of nations. As all human beings proceeded from one father and mother, there could be no distinction; natural, moral, or civil, all were one family : children, and children's children, being ever able to trace themselves up to the parent stock ; and as the Creator had given no distinctive marks to any, so it is evident He designed they should consider themselves as one people, all having the same origin, and all referring themselves and their work to His glory, who gave them their being, and appointed them their labour. Had primitive innocence continued, this state would have continued ; for we find that the first divisions and distinctions which obtained, were occasioned by moral differences ; the inhabitants of the world being first distinguished by *character*—the *religious* and the *profane ;* between those who served God, and those who served Him not ; the posterity of Cain, and the posterity of Seth. But even this distinction was not decisively prominent till the confusion of tongues at Babel, in the year of the world 1757 : for previously to this time, all the inhabitants of the earth were of

*one language*, and *of one speech;* and they *journeyed to-gether;* probably having no variety of customs, and but *one mode* of worshipping the living and true God. So much seems pretty evidently intended, by the account given, Gen. xi. 1, &c.; and this, in all likelihood, prevailed generally through the whole of what was called the patriarchal age. The Patriarchs, whose history is given in the book of Genesis, were of the race of Shem; as the family of Cain never grew to any great eminence. An evil seed, however, was propagated in the earth, till God purged it by a flood, which left only *eight* of the primitive inhabitants; all the rest having fallen victims to this scourge of the Lord.

2. Those *moral* distinctions in the end led to *local* differences; and in process of time, the earth became divided between those professing the true religion, and idolaters: and this took place when God brought the descendants of Jacob out of Egypt, and settled them in Canaan:—there they received the law by the ministry of Moses; and in that place, the worship prescribed by God himself was established. The different nations who had previously dwelt in Canaan, were all idolaters; they worshipped the sun, the moon, and all the hosts of heaven: *i. e.* both *planets* and *stars*, and particularly the *former*.

3. The descendants of *Jacob*, alone, had a Divine Revelation. These were called *Israelites*, after Jacob, who had been named *Israel;* and they also obtained the name of *Jews*, from *Judah*, one of the twelve sons of Jacob; this became their national characteristic, and this name they continue to retain.

While they occupied the *Promised Land*, or *land* of *Canaan*, they were the only people on the earth that worshipped the true God. All the others were called *gentes,* the nations, or *Gentiles;* and although the *twelve Jewish tribes* occupied but a portion of land, scarcely so large as England, yet they were considered as dividing the habitable globe with the Gentiles:—and because the *Greeks* became the most remarkable of all the Gentiles, for *genius, science, learning,* and *arts;* and by them these acquisitions were spread over many parts of *Africa* and *Asia*, and over the whole of *Europe;* the term *Gentiles* was absorbed in *them;* and all the dwellers upon earth were spoken of as *Jews* and *Greeks*, as the Apostle does here; and these terms expressed all the people of the world, as well those who served God, and those who served Him not. And this is the distinction which generally obtains in the New Testament.

4. In ancient times, the Gentiles were of little moral note; but they were sufficiently distinguished for their idolatry and wickedness: having received the gospel of our Lord Jesus, they have now arisen to great eminence; and the *Jews,* who have rejected it, though they still continue a distinct people, are generally dwindled down to contempt and insignificance. Here we see the truth of the saying of the wise man:— *Righteousness exalteth a nation; but sin is the reproach of any people.*

5. Perhaps no two people, nationally considered, were ever more *proud:* each was lost in its own *self-esteem.* To the *Greek,* the *Jew* was a *barbarian;* to the *Jew,* the *Greek* was a *dog.* Both held the other in supreme contempt. The *Greeks* considered the *Jews* as worthy of no regard—as the *basest* and *lowest* of the human race: and the *Jews* considered *them* as cast out from the presence and approbation of God, and utterly incapable of salvation; and hence they hated each other with a perfect hatred. The Greeks or Gentiles converted to God, now feel *pity* for the *Jews;* and have frequently offered them the mercies they so richly enjoy; while the *Jews,* continuing to reject the Gospel, treat the others with *contumely* and *disdain.*

6. The *Jews* and *Greeks* were as opposite in their moral pursuits as they were in their national prejudices. The *latter* were in continual pursuit of what they called *wisdom,* Σοφια, *sophia;* and this was divided into two kinds, Σοφια της φυσιᾶς, the *knowledge of nature,* or what we call *Natural Philosophy:* and Σοφια του Θεου, the *wisdom of God,* or rather, as they understood it, that *knowledge* or *learning,* which treats of *spiritual beings;* or, what we call *Divinity.* Not having an infallible teacher, they had no fixed principles: and as there were many pretenders to *wisdom,* who went under the name of φιλοσοφοι, *philosophers,* or *lovers of wisdom,* each of whom made the most specious pretensions to the full discovery of *truth,* and then set up public schools; the whole of Greece was filled with *teachers:* these often disagreeing, they divided into *sects,* and the people in course, were divided into *parties,*

each supporting its favourite teacher. These all professed to be in pursuit of the το καλον, or το αγαθον, what the Roman philosophers called *summum bonum*, the *supreme good*,—that, after which all longed ; and that, without which all knew they could not be happy. But here again the diversity of sentiments brought about much confusion, there being numerous and discordant opinions among the philosophic sects, concerning that in which the *supreme good* consisted !

7. A little before the Incarnation, this *seeking after wisdom*, became fervent and *general ;* and as there was none of sufficient wisdom and authority to say " this is *right*,"—and " this should be the general belief;"—a class of learned men arose, who, supposing that truth was certainly to be found *among* the philosophers, though no one teacher or sect had it *all*, set themselves to *select* out of the writings of the *Academics* and *Peripatetics*—out of the various *sects* that sprung from these—the principles of the true philosophy ; and these were called the *Eclectic* sect. But these had no better success than the *individuals* or *sects*, from whose opinions they formed their *selection :*—all was *hypothesis ;* nothing was proved. *Experimental philosophy* did not exist, and all the energies of the mind were spent in *speculations ;* and he who was most profound, *i. e.* the most *obscure*, and consequently the least understood, was considered the ablest philosopher ! The *summum bonum*, or *supreme good*, in pursuit of which they wasted their oil, and spent their days, eluded their research. Their opinions concerning it were endless : not less than 288, according to *Varro* and St. *Augustine*, are collectible from their writings ;—and yet only *one* of these, if the truth *were* among them, could be true : and as the *supreme good*, can only come from God ; for His favour and a transfusion of His holiness, constitute the supreme good of man ; consequently, not one of those opinions was true, as none of them knew that God, from whom alone this divine gift can come.

*Cicero*, one of the greatest men in the heathen world, scrupled not to say, that " there is nothing in the world, how absurd soever, but has been maintained by one philosopher or other !" Indeed they were not agreed even in their definition of true *philosophy* or *wisdom*. *Epictetus* said it consisted in *three* things :—" 1. The practice of precepts ; 2. The reason of precepts; and, 3. The proof of precepts," But here the question returns; What are the *precepts*, the *practice* of which is enjoined by the definition given above, the *reason* of which is required, and the *proof* of which is demanded? In vain do we talk of *practice*, *reason*, and *proof*: if there be not important *principles*, and there be not a self-evident agreement, fitness, and propriety in the principles, so as to recommend themselves to every man's conscience, in vain do we ask for *practice*, *reason*, and *proof*. And as it is from *truth* alone that such *principles* can be derived, they cannot form *right principles* who have not the *truth*. In short, the teaching of Philosophy had become a means of the emolument of the teacher; and while they boasted to be *free*, they themselves were the *slaves* of various evil tempers and passions; so that it was said, with great propriety, of *philosophy* or *wisdom*, in its several stages,— Philosophy was *impious* under DIAGORAS; *vicious* under EPICURUS; *hypocritical* under ZENO; *impudent* under DIOGENES; *covetous* under DEMOCHARES; *voluptuous* under METRODORUS; *fantastical* under CRATES; *scurrilous* under MENIPPUS; *licentious* under PYRRHO; *quarrelsome* under CLEANTHES; and, at last, intolerable to all men. Thus, *when the world by wisdom knew not God*, it pleased Him, by the foolishness of preaching (of the proclamation of *Christ crucified*) to save them that believed. Yet the *Greeks* continued to *seek after wisdom*.

8. The JEWS, who had received much of their knowledge of God, and the rites and ceremonies of His religion, by the ministry of *angels*, in which miraculous interferences were frequent; at last would credit nothing relative to God and supernatural things, unless confirmed by a *sign*, or some supernatural appearance or fact: hence the saying in the Text, *The Jews require a sign*, and *the Greeks seek after wisdom*. Each of these people professed to have in their various pursuits, their perfection and happiness in view—one seeking this, in the *increase of wisdom*, or the *discoveries of Philosophy*: the other, in the *increase* or *multiplication of miracles*. These required a *sign* or *miracle* to confirm the *truth* of every oracle delivered by the most accredited Prophet; and at last grew so insolent and unreasonable, as to require miracles to support their credence of things already confirmed by miracle!

9. After all their vain glorious boasting, each of these people felt the need of something *greater* and more *certain* than

s

that which they had already received. The Jews had been led to expect a *sovereign ruler*, who should unite *supreme power* with *unerring wisdom*—one like to their ancient potentate *David*; at once a *hero*, a *legislator*, a *prudent governor*, and a *restorer of the purity* and *efficiency* of the Divine worship. This long expected person was spoken of among them by the title משיח *hamasshiach*, the Anointed One, one who was to be especially sent from God, to be to them as above described. From the writings of Moses and the Prophets, they were led to expect this person to come in the power and wisdom of God: but they expected in him a *secular splendour* that ill comported with a *spiritual ruler*, sent immediately from Heaven : and this secular splendour the Apostle seems to have immediately in view in his use of the word Σημειον, *sign ;* and this was the *sign from heaven* which the Pharisees and Sadducees urged Christ to shew them, Matt. xvi. 1 ; " Shew us, by thy assumption of supreme power, and by thy supernatural influence, that thou art the King sent from God, whom our fathers expected ; and in whom alone, we can have confidence." —In answer to this, He calls them *a wicked and adulterous generation, who were ever seeking signs*—σημειον επιζατει, *seeking sign upon sign ;*—but no sign should be given but that of the Prophet Jonah :—that is, the passion, crucifixion, and resurrection, which would appear to them as *weakness,* and utterly *inconsistent* with the character they conceived of Him, should be the grand proofs, that He was the person sent from God who was to give His life for the life of the world : and instead of conquering by the *sword*—human *armies,* or condescending to employ *twelve legions of angels,* He should conquer by the *cross,* to the utter confusion of *human pride* and *vanity ;* and thus He would shew that His kingdom was not of this world.

10. Nor were the *Jews* the sole people who about this time were seeking and expecting a *supernatural leader,* and *instructer ;* the *Greeks* also had their expectations raised in the same way. From the uncertainty of the opinions of their philosophers, and from some almost prophetic intimations given by *Socrates* in his conversation with *Alcibiades,* as related by *Plato,* Alcib. 2. p. 100. edit. Bipont. ; the Greeks felt the necessity of a teacher, that could give them *certain* information relative to the *supreme good ;*—and they were in

high pursuit of this wisdom when the Apostle wrote. The words of *Socrates* on this subject are very remarkable; I will give the substance of them for the information of those who may not have the opportunity of consulting the original: they may be found in the conclusion of the dialogue between *Socrates* and *Alcibiades* concerning prayer, called the *second Alcibiades*.

Socr. You see, therefore, that it is not safe for you to go and pray to God, lest your addresses should happen to be injurious, and God should wholly reject your sacrifice;—It is necessary, therefore, that you should delay till you have learned what disposition you ought to be in, both towards God and men.

Alcib. But how long will it be, O Socrates? And who will be this instructer?

Socr. It is he who careth for you. But as Minerva removed the mists from the eyes of Diomed, that he might distinguish gods from men, so must he first remove from your soul the mist that surrounds it; and then furnish those helps by which you shall be able to distinguish good from evil.

Alcib. Let him remove that mist, or whatever else it be, for I shall be always ready to follow his commands, so that I may become a better man.

Socr. Αλλα μην κακεινος θαυμαστην οσην περι σε προθυμιαν εχει. It is wonderful how greatly he is disposed towards the making you such.

These were lights shining in a dark place; all pointing towards *Him* who is the true light that lighteneth every man coming into the world.

In reference to their moral condition, I have now given—

1. A short history of the *nations* mentioned—the *Jews* and the *Greeks* : 2. Taken notice of their employment in reference to their moral expectations and feelings—*The Jews require a sign,—The Greeks seek after wisdom.* The Apostle next tells us, how he met the requisition of the Jews, and the researches of the Greeks.

II. This will appear from a consideration of the doctrine contained in the 23d verse;—*We preach Christ crucified.*

1. We have already noticed the expectation of the Jews and of the Greeks of a divine Teacher:—God who had excited these expectations, either by His *prophetic word,* as in

the case of the *Jews ;* or by a secret influence in the mind, as in the case of the *Greeks* and other Gentiles; determined to meet them in such a way as would most effectually satisfy them, and promote His own glory.   As man by his wisdom could not find out the *cure* for his own malady, for this was the invention of God ; so the *manner* or *way* in which this remedy was to be applied, must rest with God alone.   As He saves man on his *own terms,* so He will save him in His *own way.*   Not merely to hide pride from man, but be cause he could neither find out the thing nor the way; and God chooses the *thing* and the *way,* because nothing *less,* nothing *else* than what He provided, could have answered the end. God alone knew best what would answer the purposes of His own *justice* and *mercy*—man neither knew the proper nature of God's justice, the extent of his own misery and helplessness, nor the quantum of *mercy* necessary to be applied to meet the ends of *justice,* and to save the delinquent into that state of blessedness and perfection as would best accord with his wants and capacities, and the dignity and honour of God himself.

2. The great Ruler, Lawgiver, and Restorer of lapsed human nature, and of the pure worship of Almighty God, expected by the Jews ; and the unerring Teacher whom the Greeks looked for, as the promulgater of the truth, and settler of all doubts relative to the opinions of the different philosophers ; was the *seed* or *offspring of the woman :*—the Son of a virgin, without the co-operation of man—was He who was intended ; and who, in the fulness of time, was manifested in the flesh.   He was not only the *Messenger of the great design,* (Μεγαλης της βουλης Αγγελος,) but also that Lamb of God who was to take away the sin of the world ; and was, in that counsel, or *design,* slain from the foundation of the world. This Person, in whom dwelt all the fulness of the Godhead bodily, took part of human nature, that He might be capable of redeeming those whose nature He shared :—and there was a *congruity,* if not a *necessity,* that the expiation should be made in the *nature* in which the offence was committed, and the guilt contracted.

3. As sin seems to have entered into the world in the *form* or *spirit* of *pride* and *vain glory ;* and as contraries are to be counteracted by their contraries; the glorious Redeemer

chose to be *born of a woman*—to take upon Him the *form of a servant*—to *humble Himself unto death*, even *the death of the cross*. In these things, by the example of his *humility*, the *pride of man* is abased and confounded, and the necessity of *humiliation of soul*, in order to salvation, fully evinced.

4. But it was not merely to teach *humility* that Christ was *made man*, and *suffered death upon the cross :* it was also, and *chiefly*, to make an *atonement* for sin :—this was pre-figured by the whole of the Jewish ritual, and especially by the whole sacrificial system; all shewing that the *death* of a *human being*, of infinite dignity, was absolutely necessary for the salvation of a lost world. This most glorious person was THE CHRIST—*God manifested in the flesh*—for that WORD *that was in the beginning with God, was made flesh, and tabernacled among men, full of grace and truth*. By this union with man, He, the God-Man, Christ Jesus, was a *human being* of infinite dignity. And the passion and death of this most august Being upon the cross, was the *atonement* required and appointed by the order both of the *justice* and *mercy* of God, for the redemption of man.

5. The Gentiles had also *their sacrifices*, for even the common sense of all mankind agreed in this, that all men had sinned, and could not make reparation by any *works* of righteousness, or rites of religion, for their sin; hence the necessity of an atonement. They all saw that man, in consequence of his sins, and sinfulness, was a worthless being; that he stood in need of innumerable blessings, which were totally out of his reach:—hence to him a *grand sacrifice* was requisite, and that sacrifice should be of infinite worth. Thus it could not only atone for sin, but purchase the necessary blessings for them. So universal was the persuasion, that a *sacrifice* was necessary to make *atonement for sin*, that even the *Gentiles* were not scandalized at the doctrine of *Christ crucified;* it was only at the *circumstance* of Christ's being crucified as a *malefactor :* and the Jews were not stumbled at the *doctrine*, but at the assertion, that Jesus was the *Messiah*, and that, that Messiah was crucified, which they deemed impossible ; as, according to their notions, the Messiah was born to *reign*, not to *suffer* and *die :* and as they had crucified Him through maliciousness, they did not like to an-

swer to God for the blood of an innocent man; for this the Apostles had charged home upon them.

6. It was on this ground that the Apostles preached *Christ crucified* for remission of sin, there being no other way of salvation :—all had sinned, and all must finally suffer and be expelled from God and heaven eternally, or receive the benefit of such a sacrifice as they proclaimed the death of Christ to be : and were most pointed in stating that all who believe in Him as being thus sacrificed for them, should be freely justified from all things; and that the salvation of the soul could be secured no other way, either in reference to the *Jews* or the *Greeks.* And what was necessary *then*, is equally so *now ;* for still, there is no entrance to the Holiest but by His blood. For His meritorious death, no substitute has ever been found : nor, were the thing possible, will God ever invent a new way of salvation, to accommodate the caprices of *Jews* or *Gentiles ;* no, nor of those professing *Christians*, who refuse to acknowledge Christ as a sacrifice for sin. This may appear illiberal, but it can only be in appearance ; for as this is the doctrine which God teaches, it can neither be illiberal nor improper: and there is no mode of interpretation that can turn away the evidence of those numerous Scriptures, which attest that Christ was delivered for our offences, and rose again for our justification ; in consequence of which, we have redemption in His blood, the remission of sins ; and there is no other name given under heaven among men by which we can be saved. Therefore all genuine Christian ministers must continue to preach Christ crucified :—and why *crucified ?* That he might put away sin, by the *sacrifice* of Himself.

7. How this preaching was received, he next informs us : —*It was to the Jews a stumbling-block*, and *to the Greeks foolishness.*

The word σκανδαλον, which we translate *stumbling-block*, signifies, that bit of wood in a trap, called the *key*, or *bridge*, on which, when the animal treads, the spring is set loose, and it falls into the pit, or is seized by the *cheeks* or *grips* of the trap, so that it cannot make its escape, or is strangled by the grips. It signifies also, any *impediments* laid in an open country, where an army, whether of *horse* or *foot*, is expected to march ; which injure the feet so much, that neither man nor horse can proceed in it. It signifies any impediment by which a person is hindered in his journey ;—any thing which causes a man to *decline from the truth*, or from any *right way*, or to *halt* in that way, as a man would do who falls over a *block* in the way, and has his legs so hurt, that he either cannot proceed at all, or only by *halt* or *limping*. In short, any thing that gives what we call *offence*—what displeases a person, so that he will go out of the right road, and become the means of inducing others to depart from it also ;—any thing that opposes a man's preconceived opinion, his predjudices, or caprices, so that he will neither *believe* nor *do* a thing which it was his duty and interest to perform ; but he obeys his caprices, or follows his *prejudices*, even to his own hurt. Thus it was with the *Jews ;* they were carnally minded ; they had no notion of a spiritual kingdom, all must be *secular* and *show*, in their Messiah ;—they could not bear a man, however potent in miracles, &c. if he had not *worldly pomp.* Such a person was not according to their notions of a Messiah, and to associate with him, would be to them *scandalous* and degrading.

8. The preaching therefore of *Christ* or Messiah *crucified*, was such a stumbling-block to the Jews. Jesus came *meek, lowly, poor*, and *mean;* not possessing, and apparently not able to command, any *worldly pomp.* We have already seen, that they expected the Messiah to come like *David* in his glory : an all conquering hero,—a wise legislator,—an able counsellor,—a reformer and supporter of the national religion. But when Christ appeared, though they were astonished at the miracles He wrought, and at the wisdom by which he preached, they yet required a *sign:*—the *token* of earthly dominion ;—the assumption of royalty,—which they supposed to be essentially requisite to the character of the Messiah; they, therefore, refused to acknowledge Him : and as they saw no secular power in Him, they became inveterate against Him ; maligned, persecuted, and at last crucified Him : and to vindicate their iniquitous conduct, they continue, by all kinds of blasphemy, to traduce Him and His religion to the present day. Thus *they have made Him a stumbling-block*—stumbled over Him, fallen, wounded themselves ; and are now no more able to take one step in the way of salvation: and in this wounded condition they have been lying for 1800 years. They are

also caught in the trap which they have laid, and into the pit which they have digged for others.

9. The preaching of the *cross*, or *Christ crucified*, was *foolishness to the Greeks :* and nearly on the same ground, that it was a *stumbling-block* to the *Jews.* Whatever they might have thought of the person of Christ, and the mighty works which He did, had He lived and preached *among* them —they despised the doctrine of His Apostles, because its sum and substance was,—Christ died for you, and rose again from the dead ; and has commanded, that repentance and remission of sins be preached to all nations, (*εις παντα τα εθνη, to all gentiles*) in His name. They could not see how a man crucified at *Jerusalem,* as a *malefactor*, could by his death, redeem them that lived at *Corinth,* at *Athens,* or *Ephesus,* from sin and all evil, and bring them to a state of endless blessedness ! Besides, the preaching of the Apostles was not with the *wisdom of words,* ver. 17.—that imposing show of high sounding, obscure, and many compounded terms, which the Greek poets, philosophers, and orators crowded into their discourses, in order to induce the people to admire them.— These, the Apostles avoided, well knowing that God would destroy the *wisdom of the wise* and *bring to nothing the understanding of the prudent*, ver. 19. and that He would make foolish the wisdom of this world, ver. 20. Had they come with this mighty pomp of *words*, and the doctrines of Christianity had been received, men would have thought, that this *majesty of speech*, had been the grand converting medium : and that nothing but human *eloquence* could be the instrument of converting Jews, and Gentiles, to the religion of Christ :—but God did His work so, that no flesh—no man— could glory in His presence.

10. What incensed the Jews yet more was, the strong assertion of the Apostles, that the death inflicted on Jesus Christ, made Him the grand Offering, and propitiatory Atonement of which their Prophets had spoken, and to which all their legal sacrifices bore testimony ; and that from henceforth no offer of salvation could be made to them, nor promise of deliverance from their enemies, but only in the *name* and for the *sake* of *Him* whom *they had crucified.* They still refusing to humble themselves, and to look to Him whom they had pierced ; and having finally rejected the Lord that bought them ;—wrath

came upon their nation to the uttermost ; and, their case being hopeless, the Apostles left the land of Judea, and turned
to the *Gentiles ;* and while many of the wise and learned rejected the counsel of God, against themselves, multitudes of
the common people received the Apostles' doctrine, and turned
from their idols to the living God ; and hence, all the churches
mentioned in the New Testament, were formed in the main
from converted *Greeks.*   Yet still their philosophers and
great men continued *seeking after wisdom,* despising the simplicity of the preaching of the messengers of Christ ; as this
seemed *foolishness* in its *matter,* and, in its *manner* and *language,* opposite to every notion they had formed of what was
dignified and philosophic.   Thus, to multitudes the Gospel
was without effect, through *obstinacy* and *superstition* in
some, and through *pride* and *vain glory* in others.   As the
Jews saw no secular power nor worldly grandeur ;—so the
Greeks saw no rhetorical nor philosophic eminence, in the
doctrine of Christ crucified.

But was the word of God without effect ?   By no means.
God says that His word is either a savour of life unto life, or
death unto death, to them that hear.

Those who continued to harden their heart against the
highest evidence, were *hardened* by it : those who in simplicity
and godly sincerity received the truth in the love thereof,
were *softened,* enlightened, instructed, and built up by it.
Hence —

III. We are led to consider the application which St. Paul
makes of the above doctrine, in the twenty-fourth verse : *But
to them that are called, both Jews and Greeks, Christ the power
of God and the wisdom of God.*

1. We must first consider here, Who they are who are
saved by hearing the gospel.   They are, says the Apostle,
*They who are called,* Αντοις δε τοις κλητοις : *i. e.* those who
were *invited* to the *marriage feast ;* in a word, all those who
had the opportunity of *hearing* the offers of salvation by the
gospel.   For the κλητοι, *called* or *invited,* not only implies
those who *heard the call,* but them also who *received it,* and
*actually came ;* believed on *Christ Jesus,* and took upon them
the *profession of Christianity :*—it means those also, who
not only believed in Christ and professed His religion, but
who looked for and received its *saving influence ;* by which

they knew that *it* was the *power of God to their salvation.*
These blessings were *publicly* offered to ALL ;—both *Jews*
and *Gentiles*, that is, *all mankind.* The offer freely made to
*all*, by Divine authority, *all* might embrace: there was no
*moral hinderance* in the way of any man ; and God gave every
man a *power* to accept the invitation He sent. Those who
did receive the invitation, received it *freely:* as there was no
*restraint* in one case, so there was no *constraint* in the other.
Those who rejected it, might have embraced it: those who
embraced it, might have rejected it. Those who rejected it,
rejected their own blessedness: those who received it, received
present happiness, and with it, a *right to the tree of life.* God
has given every man a power to receive His truth, and come
unto Him. He who does not receive it, and continues in sin,
is he who has *abused* the power ; and for this abuse, and consequent rejection of the salvation provided for him, he must
stand and give an account at the bar of God. And it is because he rejected what he might have received but would not,
that he shall hear those awful words, *Depart from me ye accursed into everlasting fire, prepared for* (not *you, but*) *the
devil and his angels.* Ye have filled up the measure of your
wilful rebellion as they did ; therefore, be partakers of their
punishment !

2. What is implied in the gospel being the *power of God,*
and the *wisdom of God.*

The Δυναμις του Θεου, *power of God*, often signifies His
*miraculous energy ;* as we have seen in other places. And
it always means the *potency* of God, *in energy ;* not only a
*power* to work, but *actual working.* And we learn from this,
that the power of God ever accompanies the faithful preaching of His gospel. Where the gospel is preached, God works.
This was contained in the promise, *Lo, I am with you always,
to the end of the world ;* and as He was the same *yesterday,*
that He is *to-day*, and will be to the end of the *world :* therefore, the same effects will be produced by that Gospel,
wherever it is faithfully preached, and affectionately received.
There will be the same or similar conversions, justifications,
sanctifications and faith working by love, that were the fruits
of that *power of God* in the Apostolic times. Where these
*signs* follow not public preaching, *Christ crucified* is not properly or fully preached :—for where He is fully and faithfully

proclaimed, the mighty energy of God will accompany the preaching; so that the souls of the people who affectionately hear the call, shall become enlightened;—the power of their sins shall be broken;—the might of their enemies crushed;—the guilt of their sins taken away;—their hearts purified;—and on all that glory, there will be a powerful defence, *preserving* them through faith unto salvation. Thus they feel Christ crucified to be the *power of God.* This was the proper *miracle;* but this the Jews did not seek.

3. But they find this also to be the *wisdom of God.* The *Greeks* sought after *wisdom;* but whatever they found, or whatever they preached, had no changing power connected with it. It neither sanctified the *philosophers,* nor their *disciples.* The *plan* was not *good,*—the *teaching* was not *true.* As real wisdom shews the best *end;* and teaches that it is to be pursued and attained by the use of the *best means,* (and these also it points out;) consequently, the Greeks had not the true wisdom, for they never discovered the *best end,* nor the *way* to attain it.

Hence, the Apostle says here, *The world by wisdom, (its wisdom) knew not God;*—therefore, they continued under the *power of sin:* and by the teaching of the Gentile philosophers, not one soul was saved from its sins. But the Christian believers, found *Christ crucified* to be the *wisdom* of *God,* as well as His *power.* They could see a wonderful consistency in the *plan* of human redemption,—in the *mode* of its application,—in the *knowledge* which it imparted; and, as true wisdom is ever seen in discovering the *best end,* and suggesting the most *efficient means* for its attainment, they found the doctrine of the Apostles led them directly to God, the *Supreme Good,* through Jesus Christ, the alone available *Sacrifice;* and the change in their *views, hearts, passions,* and *lives,* proved the divinity of the doctrine, and the powerful energy of the Agent that applied it.

4. Besides, all that obeyed the *call* or *invitation,* found, not only their *minds enlightened,* but their *hearts* ennobled by it. Earthly things fell in their estimation, and *heavenly* things *rose.* They were taught that the animal nature was to be subjected to the *rational,* and the *rational* to the *Spirit of* God. Thus they rose in the *scale* of their own order of being; and were taught to answer the *end,* which the *wisdom* of God pro-

posed, when His *power* brought them into being. It opened
to them, whether they were *Jews* or *Greeks*, the only *source of
wisdom*,—the only *fountain of power* :—a *wisdom* ever at
hand to *teach ;* a *power* ever present to *save* and to *defend*.

5. The *Jews* sought after a *power* of a *secular* or *worldly*
kind, which, to this day, they have not received ; while they
rejected the *spiritual* power by which they might have been
freed, ennobled, and saved from sin and sinfulness. The
*Greeks* sought after a *wisdom* in the *teaching* and *writings* of
their *philosophers*, which gave no *true light* to the mind, and
no energy to the soul : all their boasted *wisdom*, left them in
the gall of bitterness, and bonds of iniquity.

6. All this power and wisdom was found in Christ—in
*Christ crucified*. Through Christ came the *teaching*, and
through Him came the *powerful salvation*. All true believers,
whether *Jews* or *Greeks*, found that God was in Christ, reconciling the world to Himself :—and, that to the Apostles, whom
they had before despised, He had intrusted the ministry of
reconciliation : and that, by what the *Greeks* had called the
*foolishness* of preaching, he saved them that believed from the
power, guilt, and pollution of sin. Thus they saw that what
they called *folly*, was the *supremest wisdom ;* and what they
called *weakness*, was the most *mighty power ;* and they saw
also, that by this *folly* and this *weakness*, so called, God had
confounded the *wisdom* of the *wise*, and the *strength* of the
*mighty*. In this the wisdom of God had appeared so signally,
that, the very things which they *despised*, and which they
called *base*, God had chosen, to bring to nought all their
boasted excellence. So that in a short time, their wisdom
was disgraced, and the whole system of idolatry brought into
contempt and ruin ; and the doctrine of the cross alone triumphed. Behold, how that which the wisdom of God has
*planned*, His *power* has gloriously executed.

But although the *Jews* and *Greeks*, of whom the Apostle
speaks, are long since dead and gone, yet they have left a
succession of representatives behind them, who have continued
through all generations to the present time. These may be
included in *two* classes :—

I. They who are of a *similar spirit* with the *Jews*.

II. Those who are of the *same spirit* with the *Greeks*.

I. The *Jews* professed to believe in the true God, to receive a revelation from Himself, to which they promised an implicit obedience: and yet looked for a *Messiah* and a *kingdom* that were of *this world*, and rejected the *true Messiah* when He came; because they saw that He was despised and rejected of men, they would not acknowledge Him to be the Redeemer of Israel; and, therefore, not only rejected, but crucified Him! They who are their representatives are all those, who are looking for, and steadily endeavouring to promote, a *secular state* of the CHURCH, and to give it *worldly power* and *earthly dominion*.

1. The principal representatives and successors of the ancient Jewish *sign-seekers* are the *heads* and *members* of the *Romish church*. They have raised to themselves a *visible head*, a *secular prince*, who, besides his own ecclesiastical territories, claims precedence of all potentates,—calls himself *Christ's Vicar* on earth,—assumes powers, dignities, and ascendancies, far beyond any thing Jesus Christ ever claimed. Jesus, the Creator and Lord of the world, had not where to lay His head: for though He was rich, yet, for the sake of man, He became poor, that we, through His poverty, might be made rich. Far from assuming authority and domination over all the kings of the earth, He even *paid tribute* to the Roman *heathen* government; and was obliged to *work a miracle*, so poor was He, in order to get the money necessary for the payment! Nor had his disciples more than himself; not even *Peter*, whose successors the popes of Rome pretend to be, had so much as *half a shekel* to pay for himself; so that the miracle was wrought both in behalf of the Master, and His disciple, in order to discharge the demanded tax! But the Roman pontiff and his adherents, that they might have the *sign* of secular power and worldly ascendancy, patched up a religion that was calculated to impose upon the judgment and understanding, by meeting the desires and gratifying the wishes of the *carnal mind*: for, as the world, as to matters of religion, had been divided among the *Greeks* and the *Jews*, and was now becoming *Christian*; they formed a multitude of ecclesiastical rites and ceremonies, agreeing with a number of *sensual dogmata*, out of the three great creeds, the *Heathen*, the *Jewish*, and the *Christian*, and thus they hoped to make *Christianity* palatable to the *Jew*, because he found there many portions of his own creed; and to the *Heathen*, because

he found the *temples* of his gods and goddesses devoted to Christian worship ; and, in many cases, the very same kind of *rites* observed—*feasts* that had belonged to the objects of his own heathen worship, offered to gods and goddesses, under the names of *male* and *female saints, virgins, confessors, martyrs,* &c. And the Christian, falling under the domination of this pretended vicar of Christ, and representative of St. Peter, dared not to dispute the determinations of one who was *supreme in power,* and proclaimed himself *infallible in judgment,* having authority to ordain rites and ceremonies, and to say, independently of the Scriptures, *what* should be believed, and what not : and, to support this anti-christian conduct, took away the key of knowledge from the common people, and gave them *tradition,* which spoke any thing its inventors and donors pleased, in place of the *Bible :* caused all the religious services to be performed in that *very language* and in those very temples, in which *Jupiter* and *Juno, Apollo* and *Diana, Bacchus* and *Venus, Mars* and *Flora, Ceres* and *Vesta,* had been worshipped with *rites* little differing from those. performed in honour of *disputable saints, canonized sinners ;* and, together with these they sinfully enrolled the Virgin Mary, as *Cybele, Queen of heaven,* and *Mother of God,* with a ribald bead roll of persons, called *saints,* confessors, and martyrs, with fathers and doctors, archangels and angels, &c. to whom prayers were addressed, libations poured out, vows made, and pilgrimages performed, in order to *make satisfaction* for sins, and create a *superabundant stock of merits,* which, being at the disposal of the church, might be given to those who had none, when they paid the church and performed certain *penances,* which should render them capable of appropriating the merits of those who had more than they needed for themselves ! And if any thing were left unfinished, or doubtful, a *purgatory* was feigned, for the refinement and cleansing of offences which had not been duly satisfied for in life : and even in this place, the *prayers* of the *church,* purchased by the *money* of surviving friends, were of sovereign virtue—to *alleviate* and *shorten* the sufferings of the deceased culprits, and get them a *speedier* passport from *penal fire* to the *paradise* into which all sent thither by the church, had an unalienable right to enter. And to keep this imposture from being perceived, the *Scriptures* were forbidden to be translated into the language of the people, who were called Christian; and even a Version, (indifferent enough in itself, but which had been authorized,) though in a *strange tongue*, was not allowed to be read. Add to this, the Pope and all his priests, assumed the prerogative of forgiving all manner of sins, and sold indulgences to the profligate, by virtue of which they might commit sins for a specified time: and this *space* was in proportion to the *price* paid for the indulgence.   Nothing more truly destructive and infernal could have ever been suggested, either by the profligate cunning of man, or the malice of Satan: and had not the *Reformation* taken place, it is more than probable, that pure Christianity would have been speedily abolished throughout Europe.  Thus the church of Rome out-did, by innumerable degrees, all that had been done in the *Jewish* church by the worst of its *rabbinical fables, puzzling genealogies, forged traditions,* and *false glosses* on the words of God.   And thus the worship of the true God was absorbed and lost in that of the Virgin Mary, and of *real* or *reputed saints,*—prayers were offered to them, and daily were they praised.  They had their offerings and their services, their feasts and vigils: and often whole classes of people were called by their names, instead of the name of Christ:—hence, *Dominicans, Franciscans, Augustines, Carthusians, Benedictines, &c. &c.,* who had become a whirlpool to engulph Christianity.  And what is called the Holy Catholic Church, was on the eve of becoming a *sink of Heathenism:* and if it have at all recovered itself from its sinful degradation, and travelled back on the records of salvation, it owes all this, under God, to *Protestantism:* to the *exposure* that was made of its superstitions, false doctrines, and abominable idolatries, by those holy and learned men called *Reformers,* many of whom were objects of the bitterest wrath, and most furious persecutions of that bloody church, while its supreme power and secular authority lasted.  And those men, from whom it was obliged to *take lessons,* and who were ultimately its *best benefactors,* it obliged to pass through the flames to the paradise of God.  In no nation has *this church* shewn more fellness and ferocity, than in *this;* the horrible persecutions under that most bad sovereign, Mary, egged on by *her* most inhuman prelates, were not only abhorrent from humanity, but also a scandal to the civilized world.  In the order of God's merciful providence, the worldly sceptre, which was in the hands of that church, *the sceptre of death*, was wrested from it; and since that time its remaining power has been variously broken, till its secular influence has become almost totally annihilated: and now, (1828,) in its last convulsive agonies, it seeks restoration *in Britain*, by claiming a right to *make* or *remodel our laws, sit on our benches of justice*, and *grasp* or *direct the sceptre of the prince;* that it may go out with strength renewed, from that country, the most potent in Europe, where it formerly had its *firmest seat* and *highest authority;* and where it knows, if it once more get ascendancy, it will soon be in a condition to give *its own laws* to a bleeding, death wounded world. May the mercy of God prevent these evils, and the mighty power of His grace *reform* and *regenerate* that church, that it may become as pure and as holy as it was when the Apostle of the Gentiles wrote his epistle to *the church that was in* ROME:—" *Beloved of God, constituted saints*,"—" *Whose faith was spoken of throughout the whole world*,"—and " *Whose obedience had come abroad unto all men*," And may it become illustrious in holiness, and reputable to the ends of the earth! It was once pure and holy; it may again become such. No genuine Protestant wishes its destruction. May it again become regenerated, its stones revived from their rubbish, its priests clothed with salvation, its children shout aloud for joy; and the whole, as a polished temple of the Lord, become a habitation of God, through the Spirit! Amen, Amen.

2. But the Jewish spirit of *sign-seeking*, in its succession, is not wholly confined to the *Romish Church:* most Churches, whether found in *Rome*, in *Paris*, in *Petersburgh*, in *Amsterdam*, in *Great Britain, Lisbon*, or *Madrid*, whatever the *form* of their *worship* may have been, and of what complexion soever their *creed*, have given no unequivocal proofs of this *sign-seeking spirit*—all have sought for *power:*—for *rule* and *authority*—a power above *gospel law*, if not above the *civil law:*—and by this how many of our ancestors have been driven through Smithfield fires to heaven! This is the bent, not only of *National Churches*, but of *all others*, where the body was numerous, and where their power of doing good had raised them to consequence in the land. Forgetting their *heavenly strength*, and that it was by grace they were saved, and *by grace they stood;* and that as the *love of God and*

*man* was their foundation, so was *Christ* their *Head;* have often attempted to act, not as *leaders*, but as *rulers* of the people; in which they have had no countenance either from Christ or His Apostles.    To all such Churches and people, Christ ever has been a stumbling-block.    Over Him, in His simplicity, purity, heavenly mindedness, and humility, they have stumbled, fallen, and have been broken.    The *image* that they worshipped, being set up in the holy place, fell on the threshold of the porch of His tabernacle; its arms, its hands, and its head, have been broken off: and still granting that again there may be a general apostacy, yet the tabernacle of God shall, though in a *wilderness*, be found among men.

It has been remarked also, that when such Churches obtained *power*, they became persecutors of others.    This must be granted as a *general fact*: but a most honourable exception, in respect to the English Episcopal Protestant Church, must be made.    Its *doctrines* are the pure principles of the gospel, and its *spirit* the mild and benevolent spirit of Christianity.    And for these it stands at the head of all the National Churches on the earth.    As a *Church*, it never persecuted since it recovered from the dregs of Popery, and I believe never *will*.

II. The representatives and successors of the ancient *Greeks*, who *sought after wisdom*, are they who, losing sight of the *spirituality* of religion—*knowing* nothing or *feeling* nothing of *communion with God*—the witness of His Spirit, and the necessity of maintaining a daily walk with Him, and of having a powerful spiritual ministry—endeavour to bring down religion to the *taste of the world*, and to find certain substitutes for all these things;—oppose the preaching of *Christ crucified*, unless all His work be confined to what He has done *for* us—without any reference to what He is to do *in* us.

In such circumstances, the simple and forcible method of preaching the gospel soon degenerates—and *rhetoric* or *oratory*, is studied much more than *divinity*.    A copious flow and elegance of language—words of splendid sound, imposing epithets, and striking figures and similes, are every where sought, in order to form harmonious sentences, and finely turned periods;—a fustian language, misnamed *oratory*, is thus introduced into the Church of Christ; but when the

T 2

words of this are analysed, they are found, however musically arranged, to be destitute of force; so that a dozen of such expressions will labour in vain to produce one single impressive *idea* that can illuminate the understanding, correct the judgement, or persuade the conscience either to *hate sin*, or *love righteousness. How forcible are right words*, can never be applied to such sermons; they may please the giddy and superficial, but they neither edify the saint, nor bring conviction into the bosom of the sinner. And what redounds to their reproach and discredit is, they are flowers meanly stolen from the gardens of others.

When Moses was appointed to bring the church through the wilderness to the Promised Land, he saw the utter impossibility of it, *unless God went with them.* Moses well knew that it was utterly impossible to govern and sustain such a numerous people in such a place, without supernatural and miraculous assistance. God, therefore, promises that *His presence shall go with them, and give them rest.* Exod. xxiii. 14, &c. And on the fulfilment of this promise, the safety of Israel depended.

The church of God is often now in such a state, that the full approbation of God cannot be manifested in it; and yet if His presence were wholly withdrawn, truth would fall in the streets, equity go backward, and the church become extinct. How strangely have the seeds of *light* and *life* been preserved, during the long, dark, and cold periods when error was triumphant, and the pure worship of God adulterated by the impurities of idolatry, and the thick darkness of superstition! This was by the presence of His endless mercy preserving His own truth, in circumstances in which He could not shew His full approbation. He was with the church in the wilderness, in its worst state, and preserved the holy oracles, kept alive the heavenly seeds, and afterwards shewed forth the glory of those designs, which before He had concealed from mankind, by commissioning extraordinary men to adopt extraordinary means, in order to revive those seeds, and call the people back to first principles, and to that truth, the sight of which they had lost. To this procedure of Divine mercy and kindness, we owe the present revival of religion in this land; the greatest, the most powerful, and most diffusive, that has taken place since the Apostolic times.

A *revival*, which continues to *revive :* at first, like the little cloud, no larger than a human hand ; but now overspreading the heavens, and pouring out its fertilizing showers of truth, holiness, mercy, and charity, over both hemispheres of the earth. May its *friends* never corrupt it ; for, as to its *enemies*, they can never prevail against it.

We have now seen who the *Jews* and *Greeks* were of the Apostle's time, and who may be considered their *representatives* and *successors* in the present day ; how the doctrine of *Christ crucified* was a *stumbling-block* to the one, and *foolishness* to the other. And that notwithstanding, this doctrine ever was, and ever will be, the *power of God*, to the salvation of all that believe. From this we may learn, that, to interest the power of God in the conviction and conversion of sinners, and the building up His church in righteousness and true holiness ;—to have His *wisdom* manifested not only in *teaching* His ministers and people, but also in the various *means* and *ways* used by Him to teach, save, and defend them ;—and to preserve a holy people on the earth who shall be faithful to His truth ;—is to preach CHRIST CRUCIFIED, and walk in His light ; as He alone is the *Way*, the *Truth*, and the *Life :* for no man cometh unto the Father, but by Him! Amen.

There is yet *another sense* in which it may be said that these *Jews* and *Greeks* still have *representatives* in the Christian church.

1. The Jews well knew that God had made a *covenant* with *Abraham* and all his *posterity*, taking him and them into His special protection, and giving them exceeding great and precious promises ; and also enjoining *circumcision* as the *sign* of this *covenant*—and had commanded them to observe certain *rites* and *ceremonies*, to distinguish them from all other people, and preserve them from idolatry. It is true, that all these things had *spiritual meanings* and *references*, with which they intermeddled little, but believed their state was perfectly safe as long as a well *kept genealogy* could shew them that they had *Abraham for their father*—that they had been *circumcised* the eighth day after their birth—and had conscientiously observed the *ordinances* of their law. Of a *spiritual religion*, and a *circumcision of the heart*, they knew nothing, and would know nothing ; but *depended wholly on those works of their law*, for justification and final admittance

into eternal glory. In short, their religion was no religion *of the heart*, but one of *rites* and *ceremonies*.

2. It is from this character and these pretensions of the ancient Jews being very similar to the character and pretensions of many who profess themselves to be Christians, that we are justified in saying, *they have, even now, their representatives in the Christian church.* There are multitudes of people who think all is right, if their *creed* be *sound :* and of this, whatsoever the creed may be, how few doubt! This nation was once *heathen ;* but, by the mercy of God, it became *Christian :*—true religion being corrupted, the nation was afterwards *Popish ;* but became *Protestant.* It is enough with many, that they are neither in their *profession*, nor in their *form of worship*, PAPAL. They look, with the highest respect, to the ancient *Reformers ;*—they see *Luther* and *Calvin*, on the Continent ; *Knox*, in Scotland ; and *Cranmer*, in England ; and these have they for their *fathers.* The *catechisms, creeds, confessions of faith*, and *liturgies*, or *directories*, of these eminent men, they have taken for their own ; and while they hold these, have no doubt of the soundness of the creed, and strict propriety of their mode of worship. And if they add to all this, a *regular attendance* on the *means of grace*, reverently hearing the word preached, and duly receiving the *holy sacrament*, and being *true* and *just* in all their dealings ; they are fully persuaded they have nothing farther to *do*, and nothing to *fear.* Now these, like the ancient Jewish Pharisees, do *make clean the outside of the cup and platter ;* and, so far, it is well and laudable : but is this enough ? Will not these acknowledge that they have *sinned*, and come short of the glory of God ;—that they have come into the world with a *fallen, sinful nature*—and that they cannot *atone* for the *former*, nor *cleanse* themselves from the *latter ?* If, then, it required the death of Christ to make atonement for the sin of the world ; if *it be impossible that the blood of bulls and goats should take away sin ;* is it not equally impossible that the observance of religious rites and ceremonies should be effectual ? That no human performance of any kind, how well soever it may be intentioned, can satisfy the demands of Divine justice, for sins already committed—nor can any thing but the blood of Jesus purge a guilty conscience, or cleanse a polluted soul. " But God

knows we are imperfect and weak; therefore, He accepts
*sincere*, in the stead of *perfect* obedience." But still, have
you not sinned? " Granted." Then how does it stand between Divine Justice and you? " Why, we must do the best
we can; and God, for Christ's sake, will accept us: and in
this way, Justice will have no farther claim." You mean,
then, that you will *do a part*, and Christ will *do the rest!*
Alas, for you! Such is the *nature* of *sin*, and the *holiness of
God*, that it requires an *infinitely meritorious sacrifice* to
purge the *slightest guilt*. Your attachment to your *creed*, if
it be sound, and your discharge of religious and social duties,
may be good evidence of your *sincerity*; and that you are
*seeking God* in *His own way*;—but they cannot *atone* for
what is past, *cleanse* your fallen heart, nor give you a *title* to
the kingdom of glory. Heaven and earth have not been able
to find out other ransom, sacrifice, or atonement for sin.
Jesus alone, and Him crucified, is the Lamb of God, who
takes away the sin of the world. No *outward thing* can
avail, no obedience can help, either to justify or sanctify.
The soul must be regenerated—all guilt must be purged
away, and the heart must be cleansed. " But we have been
regenerated, for we have been duly baptised." Baptism is
the *sign* of *regeneration*; but it is not the *thing* :—it is the
*outward and visible sign of an inward and spiritual grace.*
You must be *born of water*, and *of the spirit.* *Water* is the
emblem of the spiritual washing; but it is not the *washing
itself* :—*that which is born of the flesh is flesh*; and *that
which is born of the spirit is spirit*—is holy, pure, and heavenly. If your water baptism had been *spiritual regeneration*,
you would have a *heart cleansed from all unrighteousness*,—
free from *pride, wrath, evil desires, bad tempers, &c.* But
*you* who depend upon *this circumcision of the flesh*, have not
this; and you know you *never had it.* Therefore you want
the Blood that atones and purifies from all unrighteousness.
Your having the *Reformers* for your *fathers*—*baptism* for the
*seal* of *your covenant*—your *attendance on church and sacrament*, for the *foundation of your hope of glory*—can raise you
no higher than *Abraham* as their father—*circumcision* as the
*seal* of their *covenant*—*sacrifices* and *ceremonies* carefully
*offered* and *performed*, as the foundation of their hope of the
continuance of the Divine favour—did the ancient Jews. On

these things *they* depended ; on *such* things *you* depend. They
stumbled at *Christ crucified*, as *the only atonement* for sin ;
you stumble at the doctrine of *Christ dwelling in the heart
by faith*—and at having *the thoughts of your hearts purified by
the inspiration of His Holy Spirit*, so that you might perfectly love God, and worthily magnify His name. *You*, and
those *Jews*, are precisely in the same state, morally considered ; and of *them*, you are accurate *representatives*. Why
then live comparative infidels under the Gospel ? Go to God
by faith in Christ crucified. Plead the merit of His Passion
and Death alone ; nor rest till you feel Him to be to you,
the *Power of God*, and the *Wisdom of God.* Honesty, justice, integrity, and a strictly religious conduct, are all excellent, and are indispensable in the Christian character. But
they are not the *Blood of Atonement—the purifying influences of the Holy Ghost ;* nor can they be their *substitutes.*
In general, in the persons of whom we speak, they are but
the *semblance* and *shades* of those graces—*factitious* and *outside ;*—full, often, of pride, vain-glory, and self-seeking ;—
they spring not from God as their Root. But where the
*Atonement* is applied—the guilty conscience pardoned—the
heart purified by faith ;—there honesty, justice, integrity, a
strictly religious conduct—in a word, the *mind that was in
Jesus,* producing these fruits, and evidencing itself by love,
joy, peace, long-suffering, gentleness, goodness, fidelity, meekness, and temperance, the love of God, and the love of man,
as the fruits of the Spirit ;—these spring up with energy and
strength, and all produce their respective classes of effects,
which prove them to be of God : and such as never yet
sprang from any soul where Christ did not *dwell* by *faith,*
and *work* by *love.*

We may find *representatives* of the *Greeks* of the same
description.

1. The ancient Greeks *sought after wisdom,* and reckoned
the preaching of the Cross foolishness. There is a considerable class in the Christian church, who are thus embusied, and
with the same feelings. As the gospel is to be preached especially to the poor, it must be proclaimed in the utmost simplicity. It is a system of well attested facts ;—these should
be fully stated : there is a grand system of doctrines, or
teachings, built on these facts ;—these should be clearly

pointed out : there is a corresponding line of *practice* deducible from these facts and doctrines; this should be powerfully
urged; and urged too on the ground of the facts themselves :
*viz.* That man had totally fallen from God, and is utterly
unable to restore himself:—in his lapsed state he is not only
wretched, but exposed to the bitter pains of an endless death :
—that God in His mercy has provided a ransom for his soul,
for in His love He has sent His Son into the world—Him in
whom dwells all the fulness of the Godhead bodily :—that He
suffered and died in his stead—and that through this Passion
and Death there is a way made to the Holiest ; and that God,
though infinitely just, can justify and save all them who believe in Christ as crucified for them, and risen again for their
justification ;—and that this is the only way in which God
will save man, make him happy here, and glorious to eternity.

2. But the representatives of the Greeks which I have particularly in view, and who, above all others, affect to *seek
after wisdom*, boldly assert that, in the gospel scheme, as *we*
take it, there is *no wisdom :* it is not only *foolishness*, but
point blank *injustice* and *cruelty,* to cause an innocent person
to suffer for the guilty. However this may appear to them,
God has most positively declared it in that revelation which
they cannot confute. A revelation that bears His image and
likeness, and the authenticity of which He is daily sealing by
fulfilling those promises which have God's *yea,* and are *Amen*
in Him.

The preaching of Christ, as *dying, the just for the unjust,*
is that alone which God blesses yearly to the salvation of
myriads ; and this doctrine, and none other, does He ever
bless to the conversion and salvation of sinners. And we,
who preach Christ crucified, defy these *wise Greeks* to shew,
that God ever blesses the preaching of the *contrary doctrine.*
By this alone are the drunkards, liars, sabbath-breakers, unclean, dishonest, and wicked of every class, converted from
the error of their ways. By this preaching, those who were
pests of society, and a scandal to man, have become honest,
upright, decent, orderly, industrious, holy, and useful. In
preaching to the *heathen,* this is the only doctrine by which
they are affected, enlightened, changed, civilized ; and the
brute or savage, changed into a man, answers the end of his
being, and becomes a blessing to his fellows. If this be *fool-*

ishness, it is that *foolishness of God* which *is wiser than man.*
It is that *foolishness* by which men become wise unto salvation:—and while they learn an important creed, feel a deep
and most beneficial change—a change which proves God is
in the work; for neither man nor angel can cause such to
differ so essentially from their former selves.

3. Several *wise* and *benevolent Greeks*, of this description,
have attempted to convert the *heathen*, and especially the *Indians of North America*, by teaching them the *arts of civilization*. Satan, and the corrupt, untractable spirit of man, laugh
all such endeavours to scorn. The savage can be *civilized*
only by the *gospel*: and true religion and civilization always
go hand in hand.

4. Again, such Greeks as the above, lay the utmost stress
on human learning: nothing can be done without this: and,
provided it be a *learned ministry*, no attention is paid to its
*usefulness*. By their leave, learning neither opens the eyes
of the blind, nor converts souls. Even among *ministers*, we
do not always find that the *most learned* are either the *most
holy* or the *most useful*. Learning is good and useful in its
place, if it be used only as a handmaid to religion; but it
never *did*, and never *can*, convert a soul. In this respect also,
the gospel of Jesus, fully and faithfully preached, is the *power*
and *wisdom of God*, to the salvation of all them that believe.
Notwithstanding the *contradiction* of the obstinate and hardened *Jews*, and the *ridicule* of the proud and self-sufficient
*Greeks*, we must proceed as we have done, to preach Christ
crucified; as this is made, to all that obey the call, the power
of God, and the wisdom of God.

Therefore, unto Him that loved us, and washed us from our
sins in His own blood, and hath made us kings and priests
unto God and His Father; to Him be glory and dominion,
for ever and ever. Amen.

# SERMON XXVI.

## DESIGN AND USE OF JEWISH SACRIFICES:—THAT OF CHRIST THE ONLY ATONEMENT.

HEBREWS, Chap. ix. 13, 14.

13. For if the blood of bulls and of goats, and the ashes of a heifer sprinkling the unclean, sanctifieth to the purification of the flesh:

14. How much more shall the blood of Christ, who through the Eternal Spirit offered himself without spot to God, purge your conscience from dead works, to serve the living God?

THERE are certain ordinances of the Mosaic Law, to which the Apostle refers here, which should be noticed and explained, before we can see the force of his reasoning, and the truth of his conclusion.

I. The sacrificial offerings of *bulls* and *goats*.

II. What is called the ordinance of the *red heifer*.

I. When God chose the Israelites to be a peculiar people, and to make them depositaries of His laws, which contained a revelation of His will; and, at least, a typical representation of what was in His determination, necessary to be done, in order to save the souls of men; He instituted living sacrifices of various kinds, which were to be of clean animals of a certain age and the most perfect of their respective kinds; and being brought by the offerer, to the altar or place of sacrifice, who after confessing his sins, his hands being laid on the head of the victim, he delivered them to the priests, who slew

U

and poured out the life-blood before the Lord, and sprinkling part of it on the *altar ;* the act was considered an *atonement* for the sin of the owner ; and shewed, that as he had forfeited his life, by having sinned against God, the merciful Judge had accepted the life of the animal instead of his ; and that, by the sprinkling of a part of the blood upon *himself,* he should consider himself *dedicated* to God, and he should afterwards walk in newness of life ; having due respect to all the commandments of His Creator.

The most usual victims were the *cow,* the *goat,* and the *sheep,* with their young—*calfs, kids,* and *lambs.* These *three* kinds may be considered as comprised here under the general terms of *bulls,* or *calfs,* and *goats :* though in many instances, the *kid,* the *lamb,* and the *steer,* are mentioned as the proper victims in specified cases.

II. The ordinance of the *red heifer* was both singular and curious ; and was intended, no doubt, to typify the sacrifice of our blessed Lord ; and was probably chosen in opposition to an idolatrous superstition of the Egyptians. In this ordinance several curious particulars may be observed,—

1. Though *males* were generally preferred for sacrifice, yet here a *female* is ordered, in opposition to the Egyptian superstition, which held *cows* sacred ; for they actually worshipped their great goddess *Isis,* under this form.

2. It was a *red* heifer ; for *red bulls* were, by the Egyptians, sacrificed to appease the evil demon *Typhon,* worshipped among them.

3. This *heifer* was to be *without spot,* not only being *sound,* and without any natural *blemish,* but without any *mixture of colour ;* for, among the Egyptians, if there were a *single hair* either *white* or *black* found on the animal, the sacrifice was marred. The *spot* in the Text may refer to the *colour,*—the *blemish* to any *bodily* imperfection in the animal.

4. It was to be one *on which never yoke came.* Because any animal which had been used for any *common purpose* was by *universal consent,* deemed unworthy and improper to be offered in sacrifice to God ; for not only the Hebrews, but the Egyptians, Greeks, and Romans, forbade the sacrifice of any *kine* that had been used for *agricultural purposes.* The Egyptians borrowed their notions of sacrifice from the Patri-

archs ; the Greeks from them ; the Romans from the Greeks: but the *Hebrews* had theirs immediately from God.   No wonder, therefore, that there is a striking similarity in the religious rites of all those nations.

5. The *heifer* was to be slain, and her blood sprinkled seven times before the tabernacle by the priest.

6. The *body*, with all the *intestines* and their *contents*, the *skin, blood, &c.* were to be reduced to ashes, and while burning, *cedar-wood, hyssop*, and *scarlet*, were to be thrown into the flame.

7. These ashes were to be carefully collected, and kept in a clean place, at a distance from the camp, for general use.

8. If any person had contracted any legal uncleanness, by *touching* the *dead*, or *touching* a person who had been *murdered*, or a *human bone*, or a *grave*, some of these ashes were to be mixed with water, and sprinkled on the unclean person; who, after having been thus sprinkled, and his clothes and body afterwards washed, was considered as *clean* ;—might not only mingle with society at large, but was fit to take part in any religious ordinance.

9. The *water* in which those *ashes* were mixed, was called *the water of purifying ;* and as the ashes were carefully preserved, there was always at hand a mode of purifying the unclean ; and the preparation itself appears to have been looked on as a concentration of the essential properties of the *red heifer*, considered, as it should be, a real sin-offering : and to this mode of purifying, the people might continually resort, with comparatively little expense, little trouble, and almost no loss of time :—and as there were many things by which legal pollution might be contracted, it was necessary to have always at hand, in all their dwellings, a mode of purifying at once convenient and unexpensive.   And we learn from the Text, that these *ashes, mingled with water*, and sprinkled on the unclean, and which sanctified to the purification of the flesh, were intended to typify *the Blood of Christ, which purges the conscience from dead works, to serve the living God :* for, as without this sprinkling with the *water of the sin-offering*, the *Levites* were not fit to *serve* God in the wilderness ; so, without the *sprinkling of the Blood of Christ*, no *conscience* can be *purged from dead works to serve the living God.*   See the whole ordinance concerning the *red heifer*, Numb. xix. 1—22.

See also Numb. viii. 6, 7. where this water is called מֵי חַטָּאת *mey chataath, water of sin,* or *water of the sin-offering ;* shewing that the red heifer was considered a real *sin-offering :* and compare the Text with 1 Pet. i. 19, where, in reference to this ordinance, the *redemption of the soul* is referred to the *precious blood of Christ,* who, *as a Lamb without blemish and without spot,* had offered Himself unto God, and entered in *once into the holy place, having obtained eternal redemption for men.* And see Lev. xvi. 14—16, where *the blood of bulls and of goats,* is represented not only as *sprinkling the unclean* to *the purifying of the flesh ;* but, also, as being an *atonement* for the *sins and transgressions* of the people ; which places, sufficiently vindicate the assertion of the Apostle in the Text.

Having thus considered the Mosaic ordinances to which the Apostle refers in the Text ; and shewn that what he says of, and attributes to them, is a fair representation of what was intended by them in their original institution ; I come now to consider his argument ; viz. *If the blood of bulls and goats, and the ashes of a heifer sprinkling the unclean, sanctifieth to the purification of the flesh ; how much more shall the blood of Christ, who, through the Eternal Spirit, offered Himself without spot to God, purge your conscience from dead works to serve the living God :* with which we must collate what is said ch. x. 4, *For,* it is *not possible that the blood of bulls and of goats should take away sins :*—However these sacrifices and ceremonies, according to legal institutions, might *sanctify* to the *purifying of the* FLESH, they could neither take away the *guilt of sin,* nor *cleanse the soul from unrighteousness.*

From the whole, we learn that there are TWO *subjects* referred to here, which appear to engross the principal attention of men :—

1. One of these we *hear* of pretty GENERALLY and *always* SEE.

2. The other is *often* a subject of *discussion,* but is very *seldom seen.*

3. The former is with difficulty defined : and as it seems to subsist simply as a *negation,* can only be defined in reference to its *effects.*

4. The latter is a *positive quality,* and may be defined in *itself,* from its *tendency.*

5. The *first* is a poison which infects the whole *human constitution.*

6. The *last* is the *antidote* to that poison, and though often *exhibited*, is seldom *applied.*

7. The *first* is SIN :—the *second*, SALVATION from it.

8. As the *first* is *every where seen* and the *last*, but *seldom*, it is to be inferred, that the first *predominates*, and that the last has but a *limited and partial sway.*

Let us endeavour to examine these two subjects.

Sin, has been variously defined ; not in reference to *itself* as a *principle*, but as a *negative quality ;* yet producing *positive effects*, demonstrative of its *qualities*, and the necessary results of its *agency.*

SALVATION is defined as a *positive quality*, producing effects which are fairly deducible from its nature and origin : which effects prove its benign agency.

The definition of the *first* is four-fold :—

1st. Any want of conformity to the nature and will of God : or,

2ndly. It is the transgression of the law of God : or,

3rdly. It is to be defined from the terms used to express it in the Old and New Testaments : in the Old, חטא *chatah*, in the New ἁμαρτία : both derived from roots that signify *to miss the mark :* or,

4thly. According to Plato, *sin* is something both devoid of *number* and *measure ;* in opposition to *virtue*, which he made to consist in *harmony* or *musical numbers.*

Let us examine each of these definitions.

1. The *first* definition—*want of conformity to the will and nature of God*, cannot stand : for a *stone*, or *tree*, though both *perfect* in their *kinds*, are not in conformity to the moral perfections of God. But if the definition be restrained to *intelligent beings*, endued with *free agency*, created under a particular law, with *powers* adequate to its enactments, which powers they have in their free agency abused : the definition may stand in reference to the *angels* who kept not their first estate ; and to our *first parents* in Paradise, who abused theirs, and fell off from their allegiance to God. Those being partakers of the Divine Nature who had no written law but the *nature* and will of God, well understood and expressed, whether intuitively, or by an oracular voice.

2. The second is taken from the Holy Scriptures themselves ; for thus saith St. John, (1 Epist. iii. 4.) Whosoever
committeth sin, transgresseth also the Law ; *for sin is the
transgression of the law.* But even this refers to the *effect*
of the principle of sin, or the *sinful disposition,* in uncontrolled
agency, as to that immediate act : for the law of God having
forbidden all kinds of sin—*i. e.* acts, *mental* or *external,* which
are contrary to God's *holiness* and *authority ;* he that acts
contrary to this law, shews by the *transgression,* that he possesses the *unholy* and *rebellious* disposition ; which is what
we generally mean by the term sin.  The man has *transgres-
sed* the law : *sin* has led him to do so.

Now, sin being the *transgression of the law,* in the ordinary use of the term, supposes a previously *existing* and *published* law ; consequently, a law *well known :* this applies to
*Divine Revelation,* by which actions are weighed : the transgressions, therefore, of this law, are without excuse, because
this law in its promises and penalties, has been published, and
given to all as a rule of life, and is *acknowledged* by all, to be
*holy, just,* and *good.*  A pure law suited to such a being as
was made in the image and likeness of God.

3. The third definition, taken from those terms in the Old
and New Testaments, which we translate *sin : viz.* חטא *chata,*
and ἁμαρτια, *hamartia,* signify to take a wrong aim, to miss
the mark as in shooting or slinging.  So the 700 left-handed
Benjamite archers, every one of which could sling stones at a
hairs breadth and *not miss,* Judg. xx. 16.  To miss the mark
in aiming at happiness, Job v. 24, " Thou shalt visit thy habitation, and *shalt not sin ;*" *i. e.* err, miss of enjoyment, but
shalt find thyself happy in the comforts of life.  Thus the
*Hebrew* word ; and so nearly allied are the *disease* and the
*remedy,* that חטאת *chataath,* signifies a *sin-offering,*—*an atonement for sin.*

The *Greek* word ἁμαρτια, *hamartia,* SIN, from ἁμαρταω,
compounded of α, *negative,* and μαρττω, *to hit the mark,* is
the same in meaning as the *Hebrew :* and the same remark
may apply to this word, as to that above ; for ἁμαρτια not only
signifies *sin,* but also a *sin-offering ;* and is so used in numerous
places in the *Septuagint.*  It may, therefore, be truly said,
that sin causes *men to miss the mark of true happiness ;* for
all deviations from the law of God, prompted by the desire of

the flesh, the desire of the eye, and the pride of life, in search of that happiness, which is supposed to be found in *sensual gratifications*, are a palpable *missing of the mark* in reference to the attainment of *true happiness ;* which is found only in the possession and enjoyment of the Divine favour, *from* which their *passions* continually both *lead* and *drive* them.

4. The *fourth* definition is very singular, *viz.* " SIN is that which is *without* NUMBER and *without* MEASURE." This gives a strong meaning, which we might express by these *two* terms—it is that which is *discordant*, and that which is *extravagant*. It is *bounded* by no *measure ;* it is a whole system of *discords* without *concords :* it is *noise* without *harmony*. It possesses nothing like regular *progression*, as numbers do : nor can be brought by any collocation of *units* or *acts*, to express what is *even* or *regular*. It runs out into all *extravagant* actions, without *right direction* or *proper object :* it is *confusion* in *itself*, and leads to, and begets confusion : it *breaks* established *order*, and exists in *fragments* without *arrangement, definable form,* or *possible component parts :*— and as it is without *order*, or *possible composition*, so is it without *harmony, melody,* or *cadence*. It is worse than the *poetic chaos ;* which had the *principles* of *all things* without arrangement ; nothing *assorted*, nor as yet, *assortable*—

*Non bene junctarum discordia semina rerum.*

It is *darkness* and *confusion,—opposition* and *misrule :* It is a congeries of harsh, horrid, ear-breaking, stridulous sounds,—

*Bombalia, clangor, stridor, taratartara murmur.*

In short, to sum up with the Greek philosopher, " It is that which is without number, and without measure." And even this is not its worst : it is the disorder and curse of creation, the *disgrace* of the *body*, the *ruin* of the *soul*, and the *eternal perdition* of both.

Sin is a want of conformity to God,—the transgression of the law,—the erring aim that ever misses the mark of public utility and private happiness,—the numberless disorder, and the incommensurable confusion of inexpressible length, breadth, and thickness :—it is the pit of the bottomless deep, and the torment that has there its ever during reign.

But, leaving all definitions of the thing, let us look into that published law, the revelation of God, which refers to the *nature* of sin, the *extent* of its devastations, and its *fearful consequences.*

Let us hear it speak :—" Cursed is every one that continueth not in all things that are written in the book of the law to do them." Let us hear its declaration of its nature :—*The carnal mind is not subject to the law of God, neither indeed can be.* Let us hear it point out its devastations :—*The whole world lieth in wickedness,* and *the wrath of God is revealed from heaven against all ungodliness and unrighteousness of men.* And the termination is, *The wicked shall be turned into hell, with all that forget God.* THERE, *their worm dieth not, and the fire is not quenched.*

But cannot man raise himself out of this ruinous state ? No, for he is fallen—fallen from God, and has lost that image of God—righteousness and true holiness, in which he was created. In consequence, his wickedness became great in the earth ; he filled it with *violence ;* "for every imagination of his heart was only evil continually," But had he no redeeming quality, as the slang of novelists is ? No : there is no such power inherent in the human soul. All is darkness, insensibility, and opposition to God and goodness :—he is totally *indisposed* to every good *purpose,* and *incapable* of every good *work.* He has sinned, and can neither undo what is done, nor make an atonement for the past, He is, in a word, *guilty* and *sinful :* yea, *sold under sin.*

But if man be thus totally fallen, sinful, and helpless, How can he be *judged ?* How can he possibly be *saved ?*

The first question may be answered in a few words : though man, in his fall, lost all his spiritual light, power, and life ; yet, to make him accountable for his own actions, and to bring him into a salvable state, a measure of *Divine light,* has been *supernaturally* restored by Him who is *the true Light, lightening every man that cometh into the world :* and this Light shews him his *ruined state,* and *points* out Him, through *whom* salvation comes. So fallen is human nature, that without this Supernatural Light, none could be considered in a salvable state. *This Light,* uniting with the *light* of *Divine Revelation,* points out the *salvation* of which I have spoken : and that salvation comes by the person called *Christ*, or the *Messiah*, in the Text.

But *who* is He of whom such great and wonderful things are spoken? He is no less than GOD, *manifested in the flesh!* This is a most extraordinary case, into which even the angels desire to look. GOD might have been *manifested in* and *through* an *angel*, as He was in the patriarchal times. An angelic nature, pure and holy, could be no disparagement to God; for that spotless nature proceeded from Himself. God might have been manifested in the Jewish *Tabernacle*: that was a wooden portable temple, where a symbol of the Divine Presence was evident; for there could be nothing morally impure in the innocent *timbers* and *boards* of which it was constructed;—but for God to have been manifested in the *flesh*,—in that *human nature* that had fallen from, and rebelled against, the Almighty Sovereign, was the most extreme of all cases, and the most extraordinary of all wonders and miracles! Yet, such a manifestation, God found necessary : for, although the *rites* and *sacrifices* already explained were instituted by God Himself, yet He intended them to be considered as types; for He ever shewed that *it was not possible that the blood of bulls and goats should take away sin :*—and hence, a *body*, human nature, was *prepared for this Christ*, when the time came that *sacrifice, offering*, and *burnt-offering*, and sacrifice for sin, should cease, as things in which God had never delighted; and that *He*, in whom *God was well pleased*, should be born of a woman, and be made in the likeness of man; and that in that man all the fulness of the Godhead bodily might dwell.

But *human nature*, free from the infection of sin, must be provided : and how could such a corrupt source produce what is pure and holy? The Psalmist answers, *A body hast thou prepared me.* The *body* was *produced* by the Holy Spirit in the womb of a spotless virgin;—the *body* came from God,—not from *man*,—it was God's *preparation*, there was no *human act* in reference to generation;—the creative energy of the Divine Spirit alone, was that which was employed; on this point, the Prophets and Evangelists are express;—they declare this as a fact; and evidently with design that *faith* might receive this fact in the *fullest assurance :* and a *body*, thus produced, was a shrine more worthy of the indwelling of God than either *tabernacle* or *temple*, how glorious soever they might have been; and more suited to the sacrificial offering that was to be made, than any *angelic* nature could be, how pure soever that nature might be; for it was in *human* nature, not in the *angelic* nature, that the offence was committed and sin contracted. " Let," says reason, " human nature suffer, for it alone has sinned." But human nature, in its ordinary state, could not suffer in an expiatory manner, because it is corrupt, sinful, and under the curse: hence, the necessity of a *pure human nature*, pleasing to God, because pure and innocent; and dignified ineffably, in all its *actions* and *sufferings*, by its union with the Divine nature. Mr. *Burkitt's* saying on this subject can never be too often repeated: " Jesus Christ was MAN that He might have *blood* to *shed;* and he was GOD that when the blood was shed, it might be of *infinite value.*"

As, in the wisdom of God, the time of this manifestation was fixed, to bring about the great design; in the interim, God gave what is called the Old Covenant, or Mosaic Covenant. This word is not generally understood, and has been often badly applied. *Covenant,*—from two Latin words, *con,* together, and *venire,* to come,—signifies an agreement between two parties, who were either *unknown* previously to each other,—or were in a state of *hostility,* or *alienation :* and by what is called a *covenant,* they are brought *together,* and bound by mutual conditions to keep the agreement inviolate: and generally, in very solemn and important cases, a sacrifice was offered on the occasion; which being equally divided asunder, and the two halves laid opposite to each other, the contracting parties entering at each end of the divided victim, and meeting in the centre, took the *covenant oath,* swearing to be true and faithful to the contract then made: and intimating that he who should first break any of the conditions of the covenant, would deserve to be slain and cut to pieces as the victim had been.

The covenant between *God* and the *Hebrews,* though including many most solemn and excellent things, was summarily expressed in a few words: on the part of Jehovah, *I will be thy God :* on the part of the Israelites, *We will be thy people.*

In a covenant, the following things were chiefly to be considered :—1. The *contracting parties,* who expressed perfect willingness to enter into the contract. 2. The *conditions* or *terms* of the covenant, to which all agreed. 3. The *Victim* that was to be slain on the occasion. 4. The *Mediator* of the covenant, whose business it was, 1. To *witness* the terms of the agreement. 2. To *slay* the *victim;* and, 3. To *sprinkle* the contracting parties with the *blood.* The victim was slain *then* and *there*—his life's blood was poured out, and that blood caught by the mediator, was that which was sprinkled by him on the contracting parties. But where the covenant was made between *God* and the *people,* the *blood* was sprinkled on the *altar,* and on the *people:* the *altar* being the representative of the omnipresent, but invisible God.

The *mediator* was often a *priest:* Jesus is called not only a *Priest,* but also a *Mediator;* and in the covenant of redemption He is the *Sacrifice,* for He *offered Himself,* and was at once both *Priest* and *Sacrifice.* But in the context, the *Holy* SPIRIT is represented as the Mediator; and the text says, *Christ through the eternal Spirit offered Himself without spot to God,* ver. 4. It is the office of the Holy Spirit to *witness* to the conscience of man the covenant and its conditions—to apply the blood of sprinkling; and to take the things that are Christ's, and shew them to men: and it is His province to witness to the heart of the believing penitent, that by this shed blood, his *conscience is purged from dead works to serve the living God.* He is also the *sanctifying* Spirit; the *Spirit of judgement,* and the *Spirit of burning;* and as such, He *condemns* to utter *destruction* the whole of the carnal mind, and " *purifies* the very thoughts of the heart by His inspiration," enabling the true believer " perfectly to love God and worthily to magnify His holy name :"—and this same Spirit dwelling in the soul of a believer, *seals* him an *heir* of eternal glory.

From what has already been observed, we see what the blood of bulls and goats, and the sprinkling of the ashes of a heifer, *could not do* in reference to religion and salvation.

1. *They sanctified to the purifying of the flesh*—They rendered the persons legally clean that were before legally *unclean* or *defiled;* that is, those who had *touched a dead body,* or even any *bone of a dead body;* and were thereby unqualified to use any religious ceremony, or join in the public worship of God :—such persons, after offering the appointed *sacrifices,* and receiving the *aspersion* of the *ashes* of the *burnt*

*heifer*, mixed with *water*, were then considered to be *sancti-fied*, that is, *consecrated* afresh to God and His service :—but though by getting the privilege of using the means of grace, they were placed in the way of moral improvement and salvation, yet, no *moral change* was made in their minds, no sin blotted out, no holiness imparted by those ceremonies. They only *sanctified to the purification of the flesh*—from them the soul received no benefit.

2dly. Let us consider what those sacrifices and sprinklings *could do*. They were types of better things than themselves. They pointed out the true and available Sacrifice, that makes atonement for sin : that *Blood* shed, without which there is no *remission*, and that *sprinkling* of the blood of Jesus, by which the conscience is purged from dead works. This is all they either *did* or *could do*. All referred either to the purifying of the *flesh*—or the pointing out of the *Lamb of God* slain from the foundation of the world, and who taketh away the sin of the world.

And is there any *outward thing*, any *sacrifice, offering, washing, sprinkling, rite, duty, ceremony, religious perform-ance, fasting, abstinence, attrition, contrition, alms*, or *pilgrim-ages*, that can do more? In a certain way, they may sanctify to the *purifying of the flesh*, but nothing more : nothing can *pardon* but the mercy which flows freely through the Blood of the cross :—nothing can *purify* but the mighty Spirit of God, which comes through the passion, death, and resurrec-tion of Jesus Christ. Other *refuge* for the miserable—other *name* as the object of faith—other *sacrifice* as an atonement for sin—other *help* or *saviour*, is not found in the heavens above, in the earth beneath, nor in the waters under the earth. Through this, and this alone, God can be just, and yet the *Justifier* of him that believeth in Jesus.

The sum of the whole is, 1. That the blood of bulls and goats could not take away sin.

2. That it required the incarnation of Christ, and His sacri-ficial offering, to take away the guilt of sin, and reconcile us to God.

3. That what was procured by His offering, *viz. pardon, holiness*, and, in a word, *complete salvation*, must be applied not to the *body*, but to the *heart* and *conscience*.

4. That this application can be made by the *Eternal Spirit*

only; there being no substitute—none can come to the *Father* but through the *Son*, by the *Eternal Spirit*.

5. That the pure in heart only, can see God; and as the blood of Jesus cleanseth from all unrighteousness, so the Spirit alone can apply the cleansing efficacy of this blood.

6. We see from the text, that GOD the *Father*—CHRIST the *Saviour*—and the ETERNAL SPIRIT the *Sanctifier*, act together in this work of salvation: and so important and so difficult is it, that it requires the Holy, blessed, undivided, and glorious Trinity to effect it; for thus the Apostle—" How much more shall the blood of CHRIST, who through the Eternal SPIRIT offered Himself without spot to GOD, purge your consciences from dead works to serve the living God ?"

But shall we do as too many do, admire the goodness of God in providing a *Saviour* for them, and yet continue *un-saved?* They trust in what Christ has done *for* them, but seem comparatively unconcerned about what Christ is to *do in* them. This is the *common bane* of multitudes who hesitate not to rank themselves among *religious* people. No minister can be too earnest in warning his flock against this common error; which is very nearly allied to another error, not improperly called a *death-bed purgatory*—they vainly hope to receive in *death* what they neither *looked for*, nor *expected* in *life*, viz. a *sanctified nature*—a *heart purified from all unrighteousness.* Even their *state of grace* is problematical:—though they have often prayed to be *pardoned*, yet they have not *looked* for *pardon*—probably never felt the *pangs of a guilty conscience*, nor the *plague of their own hearts.* Though they have, no doubt, repeatedly felt *smart twingings* in their conscience, they have endeavoured to *quiet them* with a few such aspirations as these—" Lord, have mercy upon me. Lord, forgive me, and lay not this sin to my charge, for Christ's sake !" Thus, of the *work of repentance* they know little—they have not suffered their pangs of conscience to form themselves into true *repentance*—a deep conviction of their lost and ruined state, both by nature and practice—conviction *of* sin, and *contrition for sin* have only had a superficial influence upon their hearts. Their repentance is not a *deep* and *radical work;*—they have not suffered themselves to be led into the various chambers of the house of Imagery, to detect the hidden abominations that have every where been set up against the honour of God, and the safety of their own souls : when they have felt a little smarting from a wound of sin, they have got it *slightly healed ;* and their *repentance* is that, of which they may repent—it was partial and inefficient ; and its end proves this.   They have not through the excess of sorrow for sin, fled to lay hold on the hope set before them ; and refused to be comforted, till they felt that word powerfully spoken into their hearts, " Son !—daughter !—be of good cheer, thy sins are forgiven thee."    No man should consider his *repentance* as having answered a *saving end* to his soul, till he *feels* that *God for Christ's sake has forgiven him his sins ;* and the Spirit of God testifies with his spirit that he is a child of God.   Those who, by their preaching, cause the people to *rest short of this,* and to be satisfied with such a problematic *repentance* and *conversion,* are healing the hurt of the people slightly ; and crying *peace ! peace !* where God has not spoken peace.   All the advantage that such people have under such preaching, is, at best, no better to them than *the blood of bulls and of goats, and the sprinkling of the ashes of a heifer.*   They have not had the *work of re- pentance,* nor the *work* of *faith,* nor the *patience of hope,* and consequently are not able to perform to God or *man,* the *la- bour of love.    Their consciences are not purged from dead works ;* and therefore they cannot, by a loving obedience, *serve the living God.*

Reader, learn that *true repentance* is a *work*—and not the *work of an hour :*—it is not a *passing regret,* but a *deep and alarming conviction,* that thou art a fallen spirit—hast broken God's laws—art under His curse—and in danger of hell fire. Think also that the grave may be ready for thee ; that here, thou hast no continuing city—that *now* is the *accepted time*— and *now* the *day of salvation.    Now,* God waits to be gracious to thee, to *grant thee repentance unto life,* to blot out thy sins, and give thee an assurance of His love : and in that day thou wilt praise Him ; for though He was angry with thee, His anger is turned away, for lo, He comforteth thee. Henceforth thou mayest draw with joy, water out of the wells of salvation.    And if thou follow on to know the Lord, thou wilt soon find in addition to the pardon thou hast re- ceived, that the blood of Jesus Christ cleanseth thee from all sin.   Thus, thou wilt magnify God, for the work that Christ has wrought *in thee,* as well as for that which He has wrought *for thee.*

And now remember for what end God has purged thy conscience from *dead works*—works which procured not the *life,* but the *death* of the soul. It is, that thou mayest *serve the living God.* The phrase *νεκρα εργα, dead works,* is only used here, and in ch. vi. 1 : it refers to those *dead things* by which legal defilement was contracted ; and in both the above places, it seems to be intended by the Apostle, to point out such *works as deserve death*—the *works* of those who are *dead in trespasses,* and *dead in sins :* and *dead* by *sentence of the law,* because they had by these works broken the law.—— The *conscience being purged from dead works,* signifies the *forgiveness* of all those *sins,* the *sentence of death reversed,* and the *spirit of life* imparted, so that they might, having this *life* from the *dead,* and this inward *spirit of life,* serve the *living God* :—the *living God* requires a *living service,* performed according to the *light* of God and according to that measure of His *love* shed abroad in their hearts by the Holy Ghost. The experience of such, is beautifully sung by the poet,—

New *light* new *love,* new love new *life* hath bred ;
A *life* that *lives* by *love,* and *loves* by *light* ;
A *love* to Him, to whom all loves are wed ;
A *light* to which, the *sunne* is dark as *night :*
*Eye's* light, *heart's* love, *soul's* only *life* He is :
*Life, soul, love, heart, light, eye,* and all, are His :
He *eye, light, heart, love, soul ;* He all my joy and blisse !
                    *Fletcher's Purple Island ;* Canto I. stanza 7.

Heathens offered sacrifices, made vows, did services, and expected rewards from *dead gods,* idols of stone, wood, metal, clay, &c. ; gods who had *ears,* but could not *hear, eyes* but could not *see, tongues,* but could not *speak ;* wholly inanimate, and at best, only representations of *dead men,* or of *non-entities,* or of *devils.* Stones, trees, fountains, rivers, woods, mountains, the sun, moon, planets, and stars, were objects of worship among the nations of the earth ; and into this absurd worship of *dead things,* the Jews frequently relapsed, and followed the abominations of the heathens. The Apostle here shews what the *true worship* is :—its *object* is the true and *living* God :—Its grand *rite* is the *true Sacrifice,* the passion and death of the Lord Jesus.    It is *performed* by the influence of the *Eternal Spirit;* and its *end* is the purgation of the conscience from the *stains* contracted by the *dead works* above mentioned ; and the purification of the heart, that the living God might have a *living service ;* and that those who thus *served* Him might have *spiritual life* in the work; and this is agreeable to the exhortation of the Apostle to the *Romans,* ch. xii. 1.    *I beseech you brethren, by the mercies of God, that ye present your bodies a living sacrifice, holy, acceptable unto God,* which is *your reasonable service.*    Such a *service* is as *rational* as it is *divine.*    The *living* only, can shew forth the praise of, and render service to the living God.    And the true worshipper *lives* by his religious *service ;* for, *by these things do men live; and in all these, is the life of the spirit;* and this is agreeable to the gracious declaration of God Himself.— *Your hearts shall live who seek the Lord,* Psal. lxix. 32. Amos v. 4.    *I* LIVE, says the apostle, *yet not I, but Christ liveth in me ;* and *the* LIFE *that I now* LIVE, *I* LIVE *by the faith of the Son of God, who loved me, and gave Himself for me,* Gal. ii. 20.—The true believer lives to His God; and genuine Christianity is, *the* LIFE *of God in the soul of man :* and because Christ died for man and rose again, therefore, *they which live, should not live unto themselves, but unto Him, who died for them and rose again,* 2 Cor. v. 15.    And the true Christians can say, *Whether we live, we live unto the Lord ; and whether we die, we die unto the Lord : whether we live therefore or die, we are the Lord's,* Rom. xiv. 8.    Nothing can be more *high,* nothing more *noble,* nothing more *glorious,* than this CALLING : well may those who have got into it, " heartily *thank* their heavenly Father, that He hath called them into this STATE *of* SALVATION through Jesus Christ their Saviour : and *pray* to God to give them grace that they may continue in the same unto their life's end.

From all this, we learn, that a *genuine Christian* has a *right creed,* and a *right conduct.*    That he *hears,* that he may *learn :* that he *learns,* that he may *believe :* that he *believes,* in order to be *saved :* that he *receives salvation,* in order that he may shew forth the *virtues* of Him, who has called him from darkness into His marvellous light : and that he *walks* in the *light,* bringing forth the *fruits of righteous-*

*ness* unto the glory and praise of God, that he may be prepared for the *kingdom of glory*; and having overcome all enemies, and all difficulties, through the blood of the Lamb, he may sit down with Christ on His throne, as He, having overcome, is sat down with the Father on the Father's throne. May this be the happy lot of every Reader, for Christ's sake! Amen, so be it, Lord Jesus!

# SERMON XXVII.

## THE PRAYER OF AGUR.

PROVERBS, Chap. xxx. 1—9.

1—6. The words of Agur, the son of Jakeh, &c.

7. Two things have I required of thee: deny me them not before I die:

8. Remove far from me vanity and lies; give me neither poverty nor riches; feed me with food convenient for me:

9. Lest I be full, and deny thee, and say, who is the Lord! or lest I be poor, and steal, and take the name of my God in vain.

I SHALL first consider the short *history* which Agur gives of himself: secondly, his discourse concerning God and His word: and thirdly, examine his prayer, and the import of the different parts.

I. The history which Agur gives of himself.

This occurs in the *first*, *second*, and *third* verses.

Ver. 1. " The words of Agur the son of Jakeh, the prophecy the man spake unto Ithiel, even unto Ithiel and Ucal."

The first sentence, *The words of Agur the son of Jakeh,* has been supposed to be the *title* given to the succeeding words: so in my old MS. English Bible—𝔗𝔥𝔢 𝔴𝔬𝔯𝔡𝔢𝔰 𝔬𝔣 𝔱𝔥𝔢 𝔤𝔢𝔡𝔢𝔯𝔢𝔯, 𝔰𝔬𝔫𝔢 𝔟𝔬𝔪𝔭𝔱𝔢𝔯𝔦𝔫𝔤𝔢,—and then the chapter begins, 𝔗𝔥𝔢 𝔟𝔦𝔰𝔦𝔬𝔫 𝔱𝔥𝔞𝔱 𝔞 𝔪𝔞𝔫 𝔰𝔭𝔞𝔨𝔢, &c.

*Coverdale* makes this clause a regular heading to the chapter, *The wordes of Agur the sonne of Jake,* in his Bible, fol printed 1535: likewise in the Bible of *Thomas Matthew,* printed 1537—*The wordes of Agur the sonne of Jaketh.*   And nearly the same in *Edmund Beck's* Bible, dedicated to EDWARD VI. and printed in 1549,—*The words of Agur the sunne of Jakeh :* and so in the *Syriack* Version. But they make a part of the *first verse* in *Richard Cardmarden's* Bible, printed at Rouen, in 1566 ; and so in *King James's Bible,* 1611 ; in the *Geneva Bible* by *Barker,* 4to. 1613 ; and in all others since that time.

But the words *Agur, Jakeh, Ithiel,* and *Ucal,* have been considered by some, as *proper names ;* by others, who have translated literally, as expressing *qualities,* or *descriptive characters.*   With some, *Agur* is *Solomon :* and in course, *Jakeh* DAVID : and ITHIEL and UCAL, epithets of CHRIST ! Others think that *Agur* may here be considered a *Rabbin* or public *teacher ;* and *Ithiel* and *Ucal,* two of his *disciples.*

In some of the *ancient Versions,* the words are omitted ; in others, they are retained, partly as *proper names,* and partly as *epithets.*   The *Vulgate* only, has translated *all* literally, *Verba congregantis filii Vomentis : viris quam locutus est vir cum quo est Deus, et qui Deo secum morante confortatus, ait,—* " The words of the collector, the son of the Vomiter : the vision which the man spake with whom is God, and who is comforted by God dwelling with him, saith."—Now this is a meaning of the Hebrew : but a very little *reflection* might have given St. Jerom, the translator, to discern, that such a translation could never have been intended ; because he is obliged to have recourse to *allegory* and *metaphor,* in order to explain it.   The *collector,* (Agur,) with him, is the *preacher* of the *gospel,* (the *Ecclesiastes,* he who *calls the people together,*) for the *Church* is termed, the *assembly* or *congregation,* Ecclesia : and as the *father* of this collector, or Christian minister, is called the *vomiter,* (Jakeh,) it may refer to *David,* who in Psal. xli. 1, (made concerning his son *Solomon,*) begins with, *my heart is inditing (i. e. belching up) a good matter, &c.* The Christian minister dwells by communion, with God, (Ithiel,) and God dwells by inspiration with him, giving him *strength,* (*Ucal,*) without which, no man can understand the spiritual meaning of God's words, but will interpret them *literally,* or according to the *flesh,* &c.   Now all this has a shew of piety, but in the mean time where is the *true interpretation* of the words of God?—Could He ever have given a revelation

that was to be thus interpreted? Where the imagination, caprice, prejudice, and even the *ignorance* and *nonsense* of man,
may have equal right to propose spiritual meanings. The
*world* has been long enough amused, and the *Church* of God
disgraced, by such interpretations; and religion itself has fallen with many into contempt, on this very account;—no
wonder that on the erection of a certain *academical building*,
where all the arts, sciences, ancient languages, and even
trades, were to have their respective *professors*, Christianity
was proscribed, " because," said the superficial directors,
" we will have no professor of Christianity, till we know
what Christianity is !"—and yet Christianity taken from the
*Scriptures themselves*, is as easily *ascertained* as the science
of *geometry* is, out of the *elements of Euclid*. This was
thought a fine saying, was applauded, and the negative on
such a *professorship*, carried by acclamation. Poor souls!
how contemptible must they have appeared to even a boy in
the *first* forms, who had *read his Bible*, with suppose no
more attention than they were accustomed to peruse the *contents of a play-bill !* For the present, peace be with such *dis-
passionate* and *able judges !* we may meet them again, when
they venture next into *day light !*

To return, were we to translate *every word* here, the
whole might be thus rendered, keeping close enough to the
*letter*.

" *The words of the epistle of the obedient son :*" or " *The
words of the collector, the son of Jakeh :* the parable which
(הגבר *ha-geber*,) the mighty man, (or hero,) spake unto him
who is God with me : to him who is God with me, even the
strong God :"—or, as my *old* MS. reads, which follows the
*Vulgate*, 𝕿𝖍𝖊 𝖇𝖎𝖘𝖎𝖔𝖓 𝖙𝖍𝖆𝖙 𝖆 𝖒𝖆𝖓 𝖘𝖕𝖆𝖐𝖊, 𝖜𝖎𝖙𝖍 𝖜𝖍𝖎𝖈𝖍 𝖎𝖘 𝕲𝖔𝖉, 𝖆𝖓𝖉 𝖙𝖍𝖆𝖙
𝕲𝖔𝖉 𝖜𝖎𝖙𝖍 𝖍𝖎𝖒 𝖜𝖔𝖓𝖞𝖓𝖌, 𝖈𝖔𝖒𝖋𝖔𝖗𝖙𝖊𝖉:" or as *Coverdale*, who is more
paraphrastic, *The prophecie of a true faithful man, whom
God hath helped, whom God hath comforted and nourished.*

From this *introduction*, from the *names* here used, and
from the style of this chapter, compared with the other parts
of the book, it appears evident, that *Solomon* was not the au
thor of this prophecy; and that it was designed to be distin
guished from *his work*, by this *very preface*, by which the
*difference* is clearly marked : nor can the words, in which
the author professes his *ignorance* and *want of instruction*

in divine mysteries, (verses second, third, eighth, and ninth,) be at all applied to *Solomon*: they suit no part of Solomon's *life*, nor of his circumstances; at least previously to his most shameless apostacy, from which, we have no evidence that he was ever restored.

We must therefore consider the *words of Agur, son of Jakeh*, as an *appendix* or *supplement* to the preceding collection, similar to that which it is said *the men of Hezekiah, king of Judah, had made.* As to the names, *Agur, Jakeh, Ithiel*, and *Ucal*, I take them to be those of persons who *did really exist*, who are no where else distinctly mentioned in the Scriptures, and of whom we know nothing but what is mentioned here. I incline to the opinion, that *Agur* was some *public teacher*; that *Ithiel* and *Ucal* were his scholars; and that what he delivers to them here, was through the *spirit of prophecy*; and was what the prophets generally term משא *massa*, an *oracle*, something sent *immediately from God* for the instruction of man.

This, Agur seems strongly to intimate himself, speaking in relation to what he delivers here : surely *I am* more brutish than *any* man, *and have not the understanding of a man*, ver. 2. We have made this concession of Agur unnecessarily strong, כי בער אנכי מאיש *ki baâr anoki me-ish*, "For I am a boor, a rustic uneducated, when compared with great men, or scholars ;" ולא בינת אדם לי *v'lo binath adam li*, "nor is there to me the understanding of Adam." I have neither *intuitive* nor *acquired knowledge*. These words can be in no sense true of Solomon ; for while he was the *wisest of men*, he could not have said, as we translate, he was *more brutish than* any *man*, and *had not the understanding of a man* ;—rather may Agur be supposed to speak here in direct reference to *Solomon* the *wise*, and *Adam* the *perfect*.

It is vain for those who understand by *Agur, Solomon*, that HE *was more brutish and senseless than any man, independently of the divine teaching!* Had *he* said so, even by the slightest inuendo, it might be legitimate; but he does not; nor is it by fair implication, to be understood. If he could have been proved to have written this *chapter*, after his apostacy from God, then indeed he might say, he *had been more brutish than any man*, and *was destitute of the understanding of a man* ; but this is neither *proved* nor *pretended.* Agur

might have used these words, according to the sense I have
given them, for aught we know; for it is very probable that
he was a *rustic*, without any *regular education*, as was the
case with the prophet *Amos*, who tells us that he was not *the
son of a prophet*, not brought up in any of their schools, but
was *one of the herdsmen of Tekoa, and a gatherer of syca-
more fruit*, ch. i. 7—14; *but the Lord took him as he was
following the flock*, ver. 15: thus Agur intimates, that all he
knew now, was by the *inspiration of the Almighty*, independently of which he was an *uneducated rustic*. Hence, in
ver. 3, he says, *I neither learned wisdom, nor have the knowledge of the Holy*. The prophets and wise men, we know,
had *public schools*, and their disciples were called *sons of the
prophets;*—but he had never been brought up in these,
nor was he acquainted with any *eminent men*—those who
are probably meant here by דשקם *kedoshim, saints, holy
persons*.

The *Septuagint* translates this verse differently—Θεος
διδιδαχι με σοφιαν, και γνωσιν αγιων εγνωκα—*God hath taught
me wisdom, and the science of the holy ones I have known*.
This may refer to the *Patriarchs, Prophets*, or *holy men*, who
flourished *before* the days of Solomon; and these the *Septuagint*
might have had in view. My old MS. Bible translates thus:
I learned not wisdom, and I knew the kunnynge of Saints.—
*Kunnynge*, signifies *science* or *knowledge*. *Coverdale para-
phrases*, rather than *translates*, this and the preceding verses
conjointly—*For though I am the least of all, and have no
man's understandynge, (for I never lerned wissdom,) yet
have I understondinges, and am wel enfourmed in godly
things*. This amounts to what has already been said: and
to what St. Paul says of himself and his own acquirements, in
order that he might magnify the grace of his Lord: " Christ
sent me to preach the gospel, not with *wisdom of words*, lest
the *cross of Christ* should be made of none effect." 1 Cor.
i. 17. " I came to you—not with *excellency of speech*, or of
*wisdom*." " We have received, not the *spirit of the world*,
but the *spirit which is of God*, that we might *know the things*
that are *freely given to us of God:* which things also we
speak, not in the words which *man's wisdom teacheth*, but
which the *Holy Ghost teacheth*." 1 Cor. ii. 1, 12, 13. " For
though I be *rude in speech*, yet not *in knowledge*." 2 Cor.

**xi. 6.** As if he had said, "though, with you, I pass for a *rustic, ιδιωτης, unlettered man*, not adorning my preaching with fine *rhetorical touches*, yet I speak the *wisdom* which the Holy Spirit of God teaches."—This is in fact, what *Agur* says of himself—" Though I have *nothing from man*, I have *much from God.*"

And having disclaimed all human teaching and earthly advantages, he comes, *Secondly*, to discourse in the highest manner concerning the Divine Nature, God's government of the world, and the revelation He has given to man.

And first he calls upon his hearers to shew any man who had by human learning, study or science, found out the *knowledge of God*, His *ways*, or His *works :*—

1. *Who hath ascended up into heaven, or descended?*—As if he had said, "I have not the knowledge of the *Holy ones* —for how could I acquire it?—who is he who could attain to that? *Have any of you ascended to heaven*, to learn that science? *And who among you, has descended*, in order to publish it? Is the *science of salvation* one of those things which can be apprehended by *study?* Is it not a free gift of the mercy of God?"—Moses, after having shewn to the people the will of God, said : *This commandment which I command thee this day, is not hidden from thee ; neither is it far off. It is not in heaven, that thou shouldest say, who shall go up for us to heaven, in order to bring it to us, that we may hear and do it?* Deut. xxx. 11, 12. *Who hath gathered the wind in his fists?*—It is as difficult for a mortal man to acquire this divine science by his own *reason* and *strength*, as to *collect all the winds of heaven in his fists*—and who can command the *spirit of prophecy*, that he may prophecy when he pleases?—What I am about to speak, comes from Him, who is *perfect wisdom* and *unlimited power*—He alone, *hath bound the waters in a garment,*—He alone *hath established all the ends of the earth*—*What is his name?*—*What is His son's name? Canst thou tell?* Shew me the *nature* of this Supreme Being! Point out His *eternity!* His *omniscience, omnipotence, omnipresence.* His mode of *sustaining* and *governing* all things !—Comprehend and describe Him if thou canst! He will teach *as* He pleases—He will teach by *whom* He pleases. Out of the mouths of babes and sucklings He hath ordained strength. These are *mysteries* which ye can-

not *unfold*—*Depths* which ye cannot *fathom*—*Heights,* to which ye cannot *ascend.*—Be content to *know* Him as your *Instructor*—to *feel* Him as your *Saviour*—to adore Him as your GOD and your *Preserver.*

The words, *What is his son's name,* some copies of the *Septuagint* translate η τι ονομα τοις τεκνοις, *Or what is the name of his sons ?*—But in the commencement of this chapter, this *ancient Version* is all confusion. Many are of opinion that *Agur* refers here, to the *first* and *second* PERSONS of the ever-blessed TRINITY. It may be so :—but who would rest the *proof* of that most glorious doctrine upon such a *Text?*— to say nothing of the *obscure author,* of whom we know nothing, but what *he* says here of himself. Though this doctrine be *true*—*sublimely true;* yet it (like many other sublime doctrines) has suffered much in *controversy,* by having *improper,* or *dubious texts,* urged in its favour. Every lover of God and truth should be choice in his selections, when he comes before the public in behalf of the *more mysterious doctrines of the Bible.* Nothing should be alleged in reference to the point, that is not *clear*—nothing that does not *pointedly apply.* The man who is obliged to spend a world of critical labour to establish *the sense in which a text is to be understood,* which he intends to allege in *favour of a doctrine* which he designs to support, may rest assured that he *goes the wrong way to work.* Those who injudiciously, or incautiously *amass every text of Scripture,* which they think bears upon the subject they defend, often give their adversaries' great advantage against them. We may every day see many a sacred and important doctrine suffer, through the bad judgment of its friends. The Godhead of Christ—salvation by faith—the great atoning Sacrifice,—and other essential doctrines of this class, have suffered much, and are still suffering in this way. When the truth is assailed by all *kinds of weapons,* handled by *insidious cunning,* and *powerful foes,* its injudicious defenders may be ranked among its enemies. To such, I hope without offence, I may say, "Keep your cabins ! You do assist the STORM."

2. Agur having stated that he made no pretensions to any extraordinary knowledge, and shewn that he had not even the advantages of education, and that God could be known only by a *revelation* from Himself ; proceeds to draw the attention of his pupils to one of the essential *properties* of that revela

tion,—the necessity and advantage of faith in God, and the danger of corrupting His words by *pretending* a divine authority to make additions to them; and in stating these things he shews, what care and caution he had used in his intercourse with God, to report only what he had learned from Him; and that therefore the prophecy which he was about to deliver, might be confidently received as a communication from the Most High.

*Every word of God is pure.* The original is very emphatic, and should be carefully noticed, כל אמרת אלוה צרופה " *kol imroth Eloah tseruphah*"—*every oracle of God is purified;* a metaphor taken from metals,—every thing that God has pronounced, every law He has enacted, every inspiration which the prophets have received, is *pure truth*, without mixture of falsity or error,—there is no *dross* in it.—It is like *pure gold*, in which no trial by *fire* can detect any *alloy*, or *base mixture;* whatever trials the truth of God has been exposed to, it always, like gold, bears the fire, losing neither *weight*, nor *value*, nor *splendour*, by its action.   This meaning of the original is expressed with sententious brevity in my old MS. Bible, 𝕭𝖈𝖍𝖊 𝖘𝖊𝖗𝖒𝖔𝖓 𝖔𝖋 𝖌𝖔𝖔𝖉 𝖎𝖘 𝖋𝖎𝖗𝖊𝖉,—that is, *tried, as by fire:* men and devils,—friends and foes,—various circumstances, the changes and chances of life,—and even the providence of God, have contributed to try the truth, fidelity, purity, and unfailing nature of the oracles of God.—They are all *yea*, all *amen:* every word seems to say, *He is faithful who has promised, and will also do it.*   And as that word represents God as the Saviour and protector of men, Agur adds on this head, what he appears to have had immediately by divine inspiration, *He* is *a shield unto them that put their trust in Him:* which words are very emphatic in themselves; and peculiarly so in some Versions and many ancient MSS. which read thus: instead of לחסים *lechosim*, to them that trust, they read, *He is the defence* (לכל לחוסים בו *lecol le-chosim bo*,) TO ALL, or, *to every one of those who trust in Him.*   His faithful followers may have many adversaries, but they have no cause for fear: for as a *shield* protects the body from shots and thrusts—from the sword and the poisoned arrow,—so God protects them from all the fiery darts of the wicked one.—His truth is their shield and buckler.—But as it is the *shield of faith* that quenches all the fiery darts,—so the defence is promised to them that

Y

trust in him,—to them who take God at His word, knowing
that He can neither *fail* nor *deceive.*

Man, though considered the *lord of the earth,* is the object
of more persecution than any other creature. Ever since his
fall, that carnal mind which is enmity against GOD, excites him
to acts of hostility against his *fellows:* hence the *wars* and
*fightings* which have swept so many millions from the *face*
of the earth. But they who live a godly life, according to
the Christian system, must suffer persecution ; against these
the natural enmity takes a more studied and determined aim,
—hence have proceeded all the persecutions which have been
raised up against the Christian Church, and by which so many
have perished, both in ancient, and even in comparatively
modern times. Add to all these, that " *contention,*" of which
the Apostle speaks, Eph. vi. 12, " Against angels, principali-
ties, and powers, the rulers of the darkness of this world, and
spiritual wickedness in high places.'' And we are warned
against the *incessant attacks* of "*our adversary, the devil,* who
goes about as a roaring lion, seeking whom he may devour."
These make fearful odds against him. Now, all these things
considered, what need is there of the Divine protection ! It
is God alone that can shield us from such dangers. The
*power* of man is a sorry defence against *diabolic might:* and
his *skill* and *art* are *straw* and *stubble* against satanic *cunning,*
and the *wiles* of the *devil.* In no time, place, nor circumstance, is man secure : and because these enemies are spiritual, malevolent, and unseen, therefore are they the more
dangerous. Yet here is a promise of sure defence ;—but the
promise is *to them that trust in Him—to all believers.* Those
who do not confide in Him, are not entitled to protection. Is
it not strange when man's circumstances and danger are considered, that faith should be so little *in action,* that it is not
one of the most *popular,* so to speak, of all the Christian
graces ! and is it not one of the wiles of the devil, that per-
suades him that the exercise of this grace is *the most difficult
of all,* and, in short, almost impossible without a *miraculous
power ;* hence the saying, " We can no more believe, than
we can make a world." It is readily granted, that *without*
God we can do nothing ; but as He gives us power to discern,
to repent, to hope, to love, and to obey, so does He give us
power to *believe*—and to us, the *use* or *exercise* of the power

belongs. He does not discern, repent, hope, love, or obey, for us, no more than He *believes* for us :—by using the grace He gives, we discern, repent, hope, believe, love, and obey. Without the grace we can do nothing ; without the careful use of the grace, the grace profits us nothing. To every pre-scribed duty, God furnishes the requisite grace. The help is ever at hand, but we are *not workers together with Him*— hence, we are, in general, *receiving the grace of God in vain* : —and to excuse our negligence, indolence, and infidelity, we cry out, " We can do nothing !" " We have no strength !" " We can no more believe than we can make a world !" Our adversary knows well how to take advantage of such sayings ; and, indeed, they are issues of his own temptations ; there-fore, it is his business to persuade us that these are all incon-trovertible truths ! How strange, how disgraceful is it, that the words of the devil, and the wicked words of a lying world, and the antinomian maxims of fallen Churches or fallen Christians, should be implicitly believed, while the words of the living God are not credited ! He commands us to *believe*, reproaches us for our *unbelief*—tells us that if we *believe not*, we shall not be established—asserts that he who *believes not*, has made God a liar—proclaims *salvation* by *faith*,—and finishes the confutation of our infidel speeches, with, *He that believeth not, shall be damned.* Now, all this supposes, that He gives us the *strength*, and that we *do not use it.* Whose word so credible as the word of God ! and whose word has less credence ! Many are volunteers in faith, where there is *no promise*—for they can believe that we cannot be saved from all sin in this life—that we shall be saved in the article of death, and that there is a purgatorial middle state, where we may be cleansed by penal fire, from vices that the blood of Jesus either could not, or did not purge ; and that the Almighty Spirit of judgement and burn-ing, did not, or could not consume :—and where there are exceeding great and precious promises, which in GOD are *yea*, and in CHRIST *amen*, they can scarcely credit any thing ! How abominable is this conduct ! How insulting to God ! How destructive to the soul ! No wonder that many of our old and best writers have declaimed so much against this, calling unbelief *the damning sin*, by way of eminence ; and that which *binds all other sins upon the soul.* Men may treat the word of God as they list, but these truths of God shall endure for ever—*He that believeth shall be saved,* and *he that believeth not, shall be damned:* and, *He is a shield unto all them that put their trust in Him.*

To prevent men from making *creeds,* and *confessions* of faith for themselves, ecclesiastical *customs, &c.* of *materials* which God has not furnished, the Prophet gives this caution: *Add not thou unto his words, lest he reprove thee, and thou be found a liar,* ver. 6. The wise man may have his metaphor of *gold tried in the furnace,* still in view, as if he had said, " You can no more add to the value of these words of the Most High by any human additions, than you can add to the value of gold by *mixing other metals* with it." He *adds* to God's words, who brings in *spurious gospels,* which abounded in the early ages of Christianity;—and they who bring in *traditions*—*i. e. things* and *doctrines* which have been *delivered down* from *hand to hand,* from unknown or dubious authority, claiming not only the right to give particular illustrations of Scripture, or Scriptural doctrines, so as either to bring in peculiar customs, or supersede positive Scripture testimony relative to the customs, doctrines, and practice of the Primitive Church; such as purgatory, sacrifices and prayers for the dead, invocation of saints and angels, transubstantiation, omission of the cup in the Lord's Supper, priestly absolution, auricular confession, monastic institutions and orders, papal vicarage as proceeding from Christ, and image worship, with the long bead-roll of *legends* which pollute the words of God, as they encumber and disgrace the churches professing Christianity, which hold them.

Whatever is not plainly enjoined, whether in doctrine or practice, in the Sacred Writings, as essential to, or forming a part of genuine Christianity, is an *addition* to the *words of God;* and to be held in universal abhorrence;—for none of these can be produced by *plain testimony,* or *rational deduction,* from the *Hebrew* of the Old, or the *Greek* of the New Testament: therefore, no opinions of *Fathers* or *Doctors,* no *decisions* of *Popes* or *Councils,* should be received in reference to the *doctrines* which a Christian Church should hold, or the *discipline* which a Christian Church should administer. `ll such things are *additions* to the words of God; which, as \`fuge of lies, God will sweep away from the face of the earth, as He has already from several of the kingdoms and states of Christendom. The wise man gives this caution to such *Churches* and *people ;—lest*, says he, *He reprove thee, and thou be found a liar :—*the allusion to the *purification of metals* is still carried on—lest he *try* thy words by *fire*, as His words have been tried ; and it appears that, far from abiding the *test*, the *fire* shews yours to be *reprobate silver ;* and so thou be found a *falsifier* of God's word, and a *liar*. How amply has this been fulfilled in the case of the *Romish Church*—it has *added* all the *gross stuff* in the *Apocrypha*, besides innumerable *legends* and *traditions*, to the words of God. They have been tried by the *refiner's fire ;* and this Church has been *reproved, and found to be a liar*, in attempting to affiliate on the Most Holy God, spurious writings, alien from the dignity of His word, and discreditable to His nature.

A caution similar to this of Agur, may be found in the Book of the *Apocalypse*, ch. xxii. 18, 19. " I testify unto every man who heareth the words of the prophecy of this book, if any man shall *add unto these things*, God shall add unto him the plagues that are written in this book. And if any man *shall take away* from the words of the book of this prophecy, God shall take away his part out of the book of life, and out of the Holy City, and *from* the things which are written in this Book." These are awful words :—if any man, or number of men, shall make any *addition* to the *canon of Scripture*, or give, as *the mind of God*, any other meaning to any portion of His Book than that which He designs, on him God will inflict the curses threatened in His word : and if *he* or *they take away*, cut off *books, chapters, verses*, or *words*, from that book—endeavour to lessen their meaning, curtail their sense, or explain away the spirit or design of His laws, gospels, commandments, or precepts—he shall forfeit all his rights, titles, and privileges ; in a word, his hopes, and his final salvation, because he has dared to *take away* from the integrity of the revelation of God. Reader, take heed that *thou* do not any thing which this word *forbids*, nor *leave undone* any thing that it *commands ;* for this is *adding* and *diminishing*, according to the use and meaning of such words in Scripture.

III. Having considered what this Prophet says concerning

GOD and His WORD, I come now to consider, in the *third* place, his prayer to God, and the use we should make of it.

" Two *things*," says he, addressing his Maker, " have I required of thee, deny me *them* not before I die." It is not *now*, that Agur for the *first time* begins to pray. The petitions included in this prayer, he *had* desired of God ; he no doubt had often prayed for the same things : they had been objects of his *desire ;* and as being necessary to his well-being, he had humbly *required* them from his gracious Creator. Whatever we need, we may ask of God; and whatever He has promised, we may ask confidently; for God binds Himself graciously to fulfil all His promises to His followers. *Deny me* them *not before I die.* To his petitions, he wishes an answer now, that he may spend the rest of his life in the state he describes; for we are not to suppose that such a prayer as this could be offered up by any person who felt himself on the verge of the *grave :* it would rather appear that he was now *entering* upon public life, with a deep sense of his accountableness, and the dangers to which he was likely to be exposed in transacting the business of that station which the Divine Providence might assign him. The conduct of this man may afford lessons of prudence, piety, and caution, to all who are entering on the concerns of life, who wish to pass through them creditably, and who are properly sensible that this would be impossible without the blessing and direction of that God who is the *Author* and *Dispenser* of every *good* and *perfect gift.*

The text says, Agur asked *two* things from God ; but there appear to be *three* mentioned—1. Remove far from me vanity and lies. 2. Give me neither poverty nor riches. 3. Feed me with food convenient for me. But as the *first* seems to refer wholly to *religious* matters, and the two latter to the *concerns of this life,* and these constitute the essence of his prayer, the first article does not seem to be necessarily included in the prayer.

From the import of the original word שוא *shavé* and כזב *cazab*, which we translate *vanity* and *lies,* I am satisfied that Agur prays against *idolatry, false religion,* and *false worship* of every kind ; and is here to be understood as expressing his faith, the purity of his motives, and his sole *dependence* on the *true God,* to whom he is about to address himself for those things necessary for his *comfort* and *safety* in *life*. The word שוא *shavé*, is used for an *idol* or *false god*, Jerem. xviii. 15, " My people have forsaken me, and burnt incense to VANITY," לשוא *le-shavé*, to an IDOL. Psal. xxxi. 6, " I hate· them that regard lying VANITIES," הבלי שוא *habeley shavé*, vain IDOLS; see also Hos. xii. 11, " Is there iniquity in Gilead? surely they are VANITY, they sacrifice bullocks in Gilgal; yea, their altars are as heaps in the furrows of the field." The prophet here states, that Gilead and Gilgal were equally iniquitous, and equally *idolatrous*—their *idolatry* was universal, and their *altars*, the proof of it, were to be met with every where. The prophet *Jonah*, ch. ii. 8, uses the word in the same sense—" They that observe *lying* VANITIES, forsake their own mercy." That is, they, that trust in *idols*, follow *vain predictions*, and permit themselves to be influenced by *foolish fears*, so as to induce them to leave the path of obvious duty—*forsake their own mercy*, in leaving that God who is the Fountain of mercy:—but, says the prophet, I *will sacrifice to* THEE.

The word כזב *cazab*, which signifies a thing that *fails* or *deceives*, may well apply to the *vain pretensions*, *false promises*, and *deceptive* religious *rites* of *idolatry;* so Jerem. xv. 18, " Wilt thou be unto me as a liar," כמו אכזב *ke-mo acazob*, —like the *false, failing promises* of the *false gods:*—" and as waters that fail," לא נאמנו *lo ne-emenu*, that are *not faithful* —not like the *true God*, whose *promises never fail*. According to this view of the subject, Agur prays, 1. That he may be preserved from *idolatry*. 2. That he may put no confidence in any words, but those *pure words* of God, that *never fail* them, who *put their trust in Him*. In a general way, the words of the text may refer, 1. שוא *shavé*, to all *false shows*, all *false appearances* of *happiness*, every *vain expectation ;*—let me never set my heart on any thing that is not *solid, true, durable*, and *eternal*. 2. *Lies*, דברי כזב *dibrey cazab*, all *words of deception*, empty pretensions, false promises, uncertain dependencies, and words that *fail:* promises which, when they become due, are like *bad bills ;* they are dishonoured; because found to be forged, or the drawer *insolvent*.

It is right that in our addresses to God, we should have a proper view of the *benevolence* of His *nature*, and·the *truth* of

His *word*,—that we neither have *self dependence* nor *false dependence ;*—that we trust nothing to *fortune, chance,* or *speculation :* for all these are as deceptive as *idolatry,* and confidence in them, as criminal;—and that, with a clear conscience, we can approach our Maker, and declare our determination by His help, to avoid every *false way,* and use no *unfair, deceitful,* or *knavish* mode, in the conducting of our *business* or *trade :* or in transacting our temporal concerns with men.

These matters being settled, Agur prefers his TWO *petitions.*

I. *Give me neither poverty nor riches.* This petition consists of *two* parts ;—1. Give me not *poverty ;*—2. Give me not *riches ;* and for each of these, he gives a reason.

. The word which we translate *poverty,* רשׁ *res* or *resh,* has a great variety of meanings in the Bible. It signifies *head, chief, top,*—the *first* or *chief* of a kind,—a *captain,*—a *full sum* in accounts,—*poison,*—*gall,*—*deadly poison,* i. e. the *chief* of deleterious *plants,* or that of the most venomous *animals,*—the *head of a river,*—a *spring,*—*poverty, extreme poverty* or *indigence.* In short, it gives the idea of *precedence* and *priority* wherever it is used : but in this place, and in ch. vi. 11, it signifies *overwhelming poverty.* " So shall thy poverty come as one that travaileth, and thy want as an armed man." As we proceed, we shall see what connexion, on this subject, some of the several meanings of the word רשׁ *res,* have with the root רשׁ *raash,* which is composed of the *same letters,* and only differs in its various acceptation by means of the *vowel points.* The word *poverty,* we borrow from the *French pauvreté ;* which the grand dictionary of the *Academy,* defines thus : *Indigence, manque de biens, manque de choses necessaires à la vie*—" Indigence, want of substance, want of the things necessary for life." And in the same work, *Pauvre,* a *poor man,* is defined, *un mendiant ; un homme qui est veritablement dans le besoin*—" A beggar ; a man who is really in want ;"—no fictitious complainer,—one who has not the necessaries of life, and therefore, must *perish* if not relieved by the benevolence of others;—hence he is obliged to become *wholly dependent* on others, and beg from door to door, for bread and raiment, to prevent him from perishing. This idea has very properly occurred to the translator of my old MS. Bible ; *Two things I prepere to thee, ne denpe thou to me er I die.*

*Vanate and lesinge wordus far to thape fro me; beggri and richessis ne gebe thou to me.* Against *beggary* or the state of *absolute dependence* he prays, as the most *uncertain* in its produce, as the most *uncomfortable* to the *body*, and the most *ruinous* to that state of *mental independence*, which God has given to every man; and without which, man is capable of any villany. The *poor laws* in this country, though well designed in the beginning, have been totally subversive of this spirit, among the lower classes in the nation, on account of the successive, and now incurable abuses that have crept in by them. That nervous independent spirit which the *British yeomanry* possessed in days of yore, is nearly extinct. The profligate and the careless,—the man who no longer wishes to work, to maintain himself and his family, sees he can *claim* parish pay : and when he claims admittance into the *poor-house*, as he must *give up what he has*, in order to enter there, will expend his last shilling, sell off by slow degrees his furniture; and when he is to be received, is known to have sold his *clothes*, his *bed*, his *pan*, and his last *chair*, the price of which he has expended on wants, *created* by idleness, indulged under the conviction of the certainty of obtaining parish supply; and probably the public-house, the nursery of sin, has previously had one half of the price obtained for those articles. To the unacquainted with such cases, which are sufficiently numerous, such a case appears most pitiable,—for say they, " the family was found destitute of every thing, and ready to perish." I venture to state, that had it not been for the *beggarliness of spirit* induced by the *poor laws*, there would not have been *one* out of 500 cases of this kind, ever found in the nation.

Had such a man as Agur lived in our time, with such a spirit of independence as he enjoyed, he would have entered this in his prayer as a reason why God should hear him,— *Lest I should be tempted to claim relief from the parish, while able to earn my bread ; and lay down for ever at the threshhold of the poor-house, that independency of spirit with which thou hast endowed me ! and thus become capable of every evil work.*

*Poverty* has been divided into *two parts*, one *relative*, the other *absolute*. 1. *Relative poverty*,—the state in which a man has but *little*,—has *many wants*, and but *few supplies ;* is often *pinched*, and always *straitened ;* and is in such circum-

• stances, that he cannot relieve himself; and has no prospect of any amelioration of his condition. 2. *Absolute poverty:*— the state in which a man has neither *food, raiment,* nor *clothes,* and can earn none, either through total *want of employ,* or through *disease,* which has completely prostrated his strength.

*Relative poverty* possesses *a little;* but that little, in many cases, insufficient for the support of life.

*Absolute poverty,* possesses *nothing,* and has no prospect of a change of that condition. Against these, the prophet prays, *Give me not poverty;*—for which, he adds the reason, —*Lest I be poor and steal, and take the name of my God in* vain.

*Lest I become poor,* שרא ןפ *pen ivaresh*—lest, reduced to *absolute poverty,* and knowing no quarter from which I can obtain lawful help, I *steal;* and thus supply my pressing wants with my neighbour's property. My old MS. translates emphatically— 𝔄𝔫𝔡 𝔱𝔥𝔞𝔯𝔤 𝔫𝔢𝔢𝔡𝔢 𝔠𝔬𝔫𝔰𝔱𝔯𝔞𝔶𝔫𝔢𝔡 𝔰𝔱𝔢𝔩𝔩; 𝔞𝔫𝔡 𝔰𝔬 𝔣𝔬𝔯𝔰𝔴𝔢𝔯𝔢 𝔱𝔥𝔢 𝔫𝔞𝔪𝔢 𝔬𝔣 𝔪𝔶 𝔊𝔬𝔡. This clause is variously translated and understood. The *Versions* in general, translate as we do; or rather, our translators follow them; and *forswear the name of the Lord*—is the general sense given to the words; *i. e.* having fallen into poverty, and having in consequence of distrusting the Lord, put forth my hand and taken my neighbour's goods, and in order to hide, cover, vindicate or excuse my conduct, have *sworn* to my own innocence; or pleaded such pressing evils as left me no alternative but either to steal or perish. The original שפתת *taphasti, I catch at*—the name of my God—*lay violent hold* upon it—as many do, who reduced to their last shifts by overpowering testimony brought against them, *swear* the more *earnestly,* and the more *bitterly,* either that they are innocent—or that they took what they did, to save them from *death;* and thus, to cover one sin, bring forward another. Among the Jews, a man suspected of theft, was permitted to purge himself by an *oath;* and the accuser was obliged to accept of this oath, as a full proof, that the accused was innocent. See Exod. xxii. 11. To a false oath taken in this way, Agur doubtless, refers. Swearing and lying are frequently brought forward to cover fraud and deceit. Let us shew as much mercy as we can in such cases as these; I have known many decent respectable people, who feared a lie and trembled at an oath, who, when brought, either by failure of trade, sudden fall of some article of commerce, speculation in business, through the hope of what they considered honest gain, by which they might be enabled to pay every man his due—were led to forge bills—borrow money—impose upon even their own relations—cover one bad bill with another as bad, hoping that ere the time of payment they might, by the speculations or promises that were still in abeyance, be able to pay every one his due.　Now, here is the temptation, and here is the reason for the prayer—that had they not been brought into this state of pressing poverty, they would never have resorted to those exceptionable means, and what is called *dirty shifts*, and tricking conduct.　Reader, if thou be a man in business or trade, and art about to be straitened in thy circumstances, pray most fervently to God that thou mayest not fall into abject poverty, lest thou complete thy wretchedness, by lying, cheating, false promising, false swearing, and other dirty acts ; by which many, once respectable, honest, and upright, have been *drowned in destruction* of property, and *perdition* of *character* and *life* :—and so, the Lord have mercy on thy soul !—It was the knowledge I have acquired of men and things in the course of my long passage through life, that first brought me to form the purpose of writing a discourse on the Prayer of Agur.

2. But he seems to pray as earnestly against *riches* as against *poverty*.　*Give me not riches* ; עשׁר *âsher*, signifies opulence, or abundant property of any kind :—as, independently of the *vowel points*, it is composed of the same letters as עשׂר *êser*, TEN, it is supposed by some able Hebraists to be derived from this latter ;—*ten* being the rich number including all units under it.　No nation seems to have a higher numerical denomination than *ten ;* and as it includes the whole of the units, by combinations of which the greatest possible computations are made ; so *âsher* may be taken to express all those goods, property, wealth, &c. of every kind, that constitute *riches* or *abundance ;* so that the rich man is one who has all the *necessaries*, all the *conveniences*, and all the *comforts* of this life; and these in the utmost enjoyable quantity. Higher than this is to be *loaded*, not *enriched*.　For in these, all that is good or desirable is *contained*.

In vindication of deriving the Hebrew word עשׁר *âsher*, riches, from the root עשׂר *êser*, TEN, as the *rich* number, containing all the units, Mr. Parkhurst has the following note:

" In like manner, the Etymologists derive the Greek δεκα, ten, (whence the Latin *decem*, TEN, and English *decimate*, and *decimation*,) from δεχεσθαι, (Ionic, δεχεσθαι,) because it *contains* all numbers. And are not the Latin *teneo*, and the French *tenir*, to HOLD, (whence *contenir*, and the English *contain*,) and the English *ten*, all derived from the same origin. In an ancient language, containing little else than *simple terms*, and where each must admit of as many *shades of meaning* as might be sufficient to denominate other things, as far they could be referred to the *ideal* meaning of the primitive root ; it is not to be wondered at, that the term in question, for the reasons above mentioned, might be used, with different *vocal* sounds appended to the *letters*, to express *ten, tenth ; tythe*, a *measure* of *capacity*, that held the *tenth* part of an ephah ; an *instrument* of *music*, the *esur*, that was capable of expressing all *kinds of notes*, on its TEN *strings—*to express *riches, opulence, abundance*. And hence perhaps the *Sun*, which in Egypt was termed *Osiris* עור the *enricher* ; as the sun by his light and heat, was the means of *life* and *fructification* to universal nature ; and hence the *treasures* of the earth."

As the word עור *èser*, RICHES, is opposed to רש *res*, POVERTY, and both words seem to be taken in their *utmost* significations, we may conceive that Agur's prayer had for its object both *extremes—*Let me neither be *affluently rich*, nor *miserably poor* : and this is sufficiently evident from the *middle state*, (and in which there are gradations, verging upon comparative poverty on the one hand, and comparative riches on the other,) which he here specifies—*Feed me with food convenient for me.* He believed that both extremes were equally unfriendly to religion and happiness : and I have had occasion to remark, in many thousands of cases, during the observations of a long life, made in various parts, that *true religion* makes as little way among the *miserably poor*, as among the *affluently rich.* The *former—*full of *unbelief, baseness of mind*, and *pining bitterness—*neither pray to God, nor care to hear about the provision He has made for their salvation. The *latter—*full of *sensuality*, and *pampered* with the good things of this life—are only occupied with what they shall *eat*, what they shall *drink*, how they shall amuse and sport themselves, and wherewithal they shall be *clothed*, according to the endless changes in fantastic frippery fashions—are too busy or too brutally happy, to attend to the call of the gospel :—and because it would break in upon their *gratifications*, they hate religion, despise a crucified Saviour, and the men who proclaim salvation through His name alone

*Who* has been ever able to spread religion with much success, among the occupants of a *parish work-house ?* Who, whatsoever his authority might be, or his qualifications, has been able to make many favourable impressions on the souls of mighty, and, particularly, rich and opulent men, so as to stem the torrent of fashionable impiety, and to establish among them the *form*, or, if already *established*, imbue it with the *power of godliness!* A solitary example here and there, in the lapse of centuries of time, cannot overturn the fact : instances of real conversion are as rare among such persons as the *black swan* among birds. In short, the whole experience of the Church of God, and the ministers of that Church, goes to prove, that it is the *middle labouring classes* in general who receive the truth in the love thereof, with gladness of heart ;—and of those, mainly, is the visible Church upon earth constituted. The *poverty* and *riches* men, in Agur's acceptation of those words, although they form two widely different *communities*, in their *social* or *earthly relations*, make another kind of Church, one and indivisible. They are not the *living stones* instinct with the *life* and *power of godliness*, which are *builded up* for a *habitation of God through the Spirit.*

It must be granted, that there are *conditions of life*, some of which are favourable, others unfavourable, to a religious life : but in all such cases, there is sufficient help to be obtained from God, if it be earnestly sought. Where the faithful preaching of the pure gospel abounds, there is every advantage both to the *poor* and the *rich.* But none can calculate the disadvantages that they lie under, who are resident where the trumpet gives an uncertain sound, or where erroneous doctrines are preached ; or where the pure doctrine of salvation is not sufficiently preached, and pressed home on the consciences of the people.

If a person be in an unlawful calling, he cannot expect the blessing of God on his soul, whether he be rich or poor ;. or if he be employed in a *lawful business*, that is *unlawfully* pursued ; for instance, by the *breach of the sabbath.* There are many great men, who do not know the truth, because their chaplains, &c. do not know the truth themselves; and how then can they preach it!—or they are flattered in their vices; or their easily besetting sins are not at all, or but tenderly, touched.

Agricultural pursuits seem to possess every advantage for a religious life; and yet the *rich pluralist farmers* are often proverbially ungodly: they feed themselves without fear, and do not cultivate their minds, and therefore do not obtain the *wisdom* that cometh from above. Of such, an ancient wise man thus speaks:—

Τί σοφισθήσετι ὁ κρατῶν ἀρότρου,

Καὶ καυχάμενος ἐν δόρατι κέντρου,

Βόας ἐλαύνων καὶ ἀναστρεφόμενος ἐν ἔργοις αὐτῶν,

Καὶ ἡ διήγησις αὐτοῦ ἐν υἱοῖς ταύρων

Καρδίαν αὐτοῦ δώσει ἐκδοῦναι αὔλακας,

Καὶ ἡ ἀγρυπνία αὐτοῦ εἰς χορτάσματα δαμάλεων.

Σοφ. υἱου Σιραχ, ch. xxxviii. 25.

How can he get wisdom, who holdeth the *plough,*
And who glorieth in the spear of the *goad;*
Who driveth *oxen,* and is occupied in their labours,
And whose conversation is about *calves ?*
Who setteth his heart on the making of *furrows,*
And his watchful cares on the *fattening* of *cows?*

All these are important occupations, but what a pity that the *whole heart* should be set upon them; that He who causeth the grass to grow for cattle, and the corn for the service of man, should be forgotten in those very circumstances where His *power* and His *providence* are most conspicuous!

The *ardent pursuit* of riches, is as *destructive* as the *possession* of them is *dangerous.* The Apostle says, " the love of money is the root of all evil; which, while some coveted after, they have erred from the faith, and pierced themselves through with many sorrows :"—" For they that WILL be RICH, fall into temptation, and a snare, and into many foolish and hurtful lusts, which draw men into destruction and perdition." 1 Tim. vi. 9, 10. They *will* be rich, and being so determined, they utterly forget God and their souls.

For his prayer against *riches,* Agur gives as good a reason as he does for that against *poverty*—" Lest I be full and deny thee, and say, who is the Lord ?" My old MS. Bible is, as often is the case, emphatic here—𝕷𝖊𝖘𝖙 𝖕𝖊𝖗𝖆𝖇𝖊𝖓𝖙𝖚𝖗𝖊 𝕴 𝖋𝖚𝖑𝖋𝖎𝖑'𝖉, 𝖇𝖊 𝖉𝖗𝖆𝖜𝖊𝖓 𝖙𝖔 𝖉𝖊𝖓𝖞𝖊𝖓, 𝖆𝖓𝖉 𝖘𝖊𝖞𝖊𝖓, 𝖜𝖍𝖔 𝖎𝖘 𝖙𝖍𝖊 𝕷𝖔𝖗𝖉!—That is, lest having all earthly things at command, I should gratify all my sensual desires, and thus feeling no spiritual wants, be excited to deny that there is a God; and tauntingly and impudently call upon His followers to shew *Him* whom they call *Lord.* *Coverdale* expresses the *pride* and *naughtiness* of their heart, in his translation—*Lest if I be to full, I denye thee, and saye, what fellowe is the Lord?*—The general meaning is, " Lest I be full, and addict myself to luxurious living, pamper the flesh, and starve the soul, and so deny thee, the Fountain of goodness : and if called upon to resort to *first principles,* I say, *who is Jehovah?*—Why should I acknowledge, why should I serve Him ?—and thus cast aside all sense of religion, and all moral obligation."

But there is another clause that seems to make a separate prayer, though included in the preceding—*Feed me with food convenient for me,* expressed by *three words* in the original, הַטְרִיפֵנִי לֶחֶם חֻקִּי *ha-teripheni lechem chukki,* the meaning of which appears to be, " give me as *prey* my *statute allowance* of bread." The prayer of a *hunter* going out to the forest, to seek for venison. " Thou knowest I need a certain portion of food for myself and family ; so order it that I shall meet with such prey, as may be both *suitable* and *sufficient* for my wants." It is the same petition in *sense* and *substance* as that in our Lord's prayer, τον αρτον ημων τον επιουσιον δος ημιν σημερον, or το καθ' ημεραν, *Give us to-day our sufficient portion of food*—or, give us *each day* our proper *ration—i. e.* what is sufficient for our daily consumption.

There was great *moderation* in the prayer of Agur; he wished merely for what was *sufficient* for the *family support,* —just what was *needful,* and this was what Providence seemed to *prescribe;* and therefore it is termed חֻקִּי *chukki,* my *statute* allowance : that which is *marked out* as necessary for the support of life ; and this he asked not in advance, but day by day; and thus continual dependence on God, and continual gratitude for blessings daily received, were kept in full exercise.

This is a most lawful prayer : it can never be the design of God, that any man shall perish through the *want of the necessaries of life.* There is *bread* for all, furnished by divine

Providence; and *work* for all, by which they may acquire that bread : for it is in or by the *sweat of the brow*, that a man shall eat bread—this was God's original design; and hence the Apostle strongly asserts, 2 Thess. iii. 10, that *they who will not* WORK, *shall not* EAT : and hence he commands them, 1 Thess. iv. 11, " to study to be quiet, to *do their own business*, and to WORK *with their* HANDS." The *slothful* man shall be clothed with *rags* :—nor is there any thing in *providence* or in *grace*, to entitle him to expect a subsistence if he labour not :—in Agur's prayer, *he* can have *no part*. RICHES, in no sense, can he have, *who will not work*. POVERTY and wretchedness must be his portion ; with the disapprobation of God, both in time and eternity. But God will bless the hand of the diligent ; and he may not only have enough, but something to spare. Reader, should God not only give thee the portion necessary for thee, but something *more ;* remember, the *poor* is ever with thee, turn not away thy face from any poor man ; and so the face of the Lord shall never be turned away from thee. Add to this, the consideration, that God requires your help in behalf of His *Church,* and for the diffusion of His knowledge among the *heathen.* There are whole *nations* who have not heard of the Lord's Christ. *You* cannot get to them in *person*—go then in *proxy.* There are many holy men who have in this way consecrated their service to the Lord, and wish to be sent to those countries, from which a voice is come to our ears, and to our hearts, *Come over and help us !*—send them as your proxies and representatives.

Let the *rich*, who do not wish that their table should become a snare to them, expend at least a part of their surplus in this way : and this will be the means of getting the blessing of God on all the rest. Thus, between the *poor*, the *church*, and the *heathen*, there are so many open channels to take off all our superfluous cash, and consequently so many means of conveying God's approbation and blessing to our hearts and families. Thus the *rich* man may join in Agur's prayer with great fervour and success—*Give me not riches*, without giving me a *heart* to use them to thy glory and the good of mankind ! And thus, to use a plain term, that which God has *put into your hands*, you will never put *into your heart :* but will honour the Lord with your substance.

And now ye POOR : arise and shake yourselves from the

dust, and cry unto the Lord. Has not your present wretchedness proceeded either from your *slothfulness* or the *abuse of mercies* already received? God may bring back your captivity :—search your hearts, humble yourselves before Him—who knows, but He will return to you with mercies, and your expectation shall not perish for ever, He has promised " to deliver the *needy* when he *crieth; the *poor* also, and him that hath no helper." Psal. lxxii. 2. But remember, there is no promise of deliverance, where there is no *cry*. If you call earnestly upon Him, you will find the truth of this promise : " He raiseth up the *poor* out of the *dust,* and lifteth the *needy* out of the *dunghill."* Psal. cxiii. 7.

In the preceding paraphrase on the short history and maxims of Agur, I have endeavoured to point out the snares and dangers incident to the principal states and situations of life—the imperfection of human knowledge, the danger of self-confidence and presumption; the necessity of divine teaching and of preservation from *extremes* in reference to *poverty* on the one hand, and riches on the other ; the blessedness of a *middle state* in society ; the duties of the *rich,* the *poor,* and of those who occupy the *middle place* in reference to these two extremes—and the necessity of faith in God, prayer to Him, and contentment with the situation in which His wise Providence has thought fit to place us.

The prayer of Agur has been frequently quoted by many who attended very little to its meaning—and whose hearts were strongly set upon *gain,* who wished with all their souls to be as rich as the best of their neighbours; and who would have been glad to have been placed at the *head* of the community :—but as this was, in most cases, *hopeless,* they felt a desire to compound with Providence : and on condition that they were not to see *poverty,* but have all the *necessaries, conveniences,* and *comforts* of life, they would have been contented to have given up what they conceived to be *riches, i. e.* the state of *kings, great lords,* affluent *merchants,* wealthy *tradesmen,* and extensive land-holders ! For want of close *self-examination,* we possess but little of *self-knowledge ;* and often think we are very *sincere,* when in fact, we are very *ignorant* of the import of our own requests, and sometimes even mean the contrary to what we express.

The sum of all is, God alone is the Fountain, Author, and

Giver of all good. He loves man; and if, while humble, teachable, and dependent on Him, he earnestly and honestly put forth the powers which He has given him, steadily fleeing from sin to God his Saviour; that saving and merciful God will bless him in his lawful endeavours, and enable him to owe no man any thing, and to provide things honest in the sight of all men;—God will not very probably give him riches, but will save him from pinching poverty, and grant him the *food* or maintenance *convenient* or suitable to his state.

Whoever has received from God *food, raiment,* and a *contented spirit,* has received all that he should pray for, and all that any human being needs, to make him truly happy. What is beyond this, is generally an encumbrance, or a heavy charge entrusted to the possessor in behalf of the poor; and he has much need to pray for grace from God, to be faithful. He who prays for RICHES, prays for *snares, vanity,* and *vexation of spirit.* He who prays for POVERTY, prays for what few can *bear :* and should his prayer be heard, and he become *poor,* he will most probably *steal, and take the name of the Lord in vain.* For where a prophet of God did not feel himself safe, a common Christian would be very likely to fall.

Some pray for *poverty of spirit*—this is perhaps another word for *humility :* of this, no man can have too much. And some pray for the *riches of grace and glory :* by which they mean, an abundance of *faith, hope,* and *love.* This should be the incessant prayer of every Christian; for, without the *faith* that *works*—the *hope* that excites to universal *patience*—and the *love* that *labours* for the glory of God and the salvation of men—no man can be a true Christian, or ever expect, on the gospel plan, to inherit the kingdom of God.

# SERMON XXVIII.

## THE GLORY OF THE LATTER DAYS.

●

JOEL, Chap. ii. 28, 29, 32.

28. And it shall come to pass afterward, *that* I will pour out my spirit upon all flesh; and your sons and your daughters shall prophesy, your old men shall dream dreams, your young men shall see visions:

29. And also upon the servants and upon the handmaids in those days, will I pour out my spirit.

32. And it shall come to pass, *that* whosoever shall call upon the name of the Lord, shall be delivered.

This passage, as quoted by St. Peter, Acts ii. 17, 18, 21, stands thus—

17. And it shall come to pass in the last days, (εν ταις εσχαταις ημεραις,) saith God, I will pour out of my spirit upon all flesh: and your sons and your daughters shall prophesy, (προφητευσουσιν,) and your young men shall see visions, and your old men shall dream dreams.

18. And on my servants, and on my handmaidens, I will pour out in those days of my spirit; and they shall prophesy, (και προφητευσουσι.)

21. And it shall come to pass, that whosoever shall call on the name of the Lord shall be saved, (σωθησεται, *he shall be made safe,—be preserved.*)

Hope, "the expectation of good things to come," has a powerful operation on the human heart, in all states and conditions of life :—suppose it be *well* with us, we think it may be *better ;* and the bare *possibility* of the thing, is sufficient to excite hope that it shall be so : and hence *expectation*, which properly speaking, is hope drawn out into unlimited successive acts; and thus we pass through life, with, if not a *cheerful*, yet an amusing prospect of *future good*.

All expectation of this kind is legitimate in religion, whether it respect the *individual*, in relation to the Church of God, or whether it respect the *Church* itself. Every true Christian is hoping for better *days*, in reference to his own religious state; and for better *times*, in reference to a more extensive dissemination of the words of truth over the earth : and a larger effusion of the Divine Spirit to make the diffusion of truth effectual to the salvation of men.

In religious matters, these expectations are founded on the promises of God; and the descriptions, (often allegorical and figurative,) which the sacred writers give of the privileges of true believers, and the glory of the Church, considered as the spiritual body of our Lord Jesus : for as the HEAD is necessarily *glorious*, the BODY must be *consequently* so.

This state of mind and general feeling among Christians, every man on the whole should encourage; and though it is difficult to *correct* the exuberance of this hope; yet if got by misunderstanding or misapplying portions of Scripture, and carrying false views into acts of extravagance, this correction should be attempted, by shewing the *precise meaning* of such passages, and rigidly restraining them to that meaning : for, all religious feelings and expectations should be directed by religious knowledge : for even our *love* to God and man, must " abound more and more in all knowledge, as well as in all judgement or spiritual sense, that we may approve things that are excellent, be sincere and without offence, till the day of Christ; and be filled with the fruits of righteousness, which are by Jesus Christ, to the glory and praise of God." Phil. i. 9—11. Without this *knowledge* and *judgement*, expectation may be spent in useless hopes, and at last, end in bitter disappointment, which is most likely to be succeeded by a measure of unbelief in the promises of God; for it is natural to suppose that a promise from Eternal Truth should be fulfilled; and when, after having been strongly pleaded in faith by prayer, the answer appears to be delayed, and at last the heart is sickened by the disappointment of hope, doubts arise relative even to the *truth* of the promises on which the hope was founded.

Now all this was occasioned by taking a wrong view of the promise; applying it to that to which it did not refer; making that *general*, which was only *particular*,—or applying to *mankind* at *large*, what was only spoken of one *people*,—and often even of an *individual* in *peculiar circumstances*. But the greatest mischiefs have been done by applying that to things *yet to come*, that has had its fulfilment in things *already past*; and on this mistake, forming *arithmetical calculations*, relative to the *precise time* in which those great events, perhaps the children of our own fancy, should actually take place!

What disappointment and confusion have been brought into the minds of many, by calculations relative to the termination of certain empires, *Papal* and *Turkish* :—the *beast* and the *false prophet* :—Christ's second coming to establish a universal empire, the laws of which are to be administered by His presence corporeally manifested on earth :—and also concerning the time of the final judgement, and the end of the world! When a fancy is pursued, the line of pursuit is only directed by a sort of telegraphic phantoms, unreal land marks to unreal objects; and when the last *ignis fatuus* has terminated its uncertain dance by absorption in some other vapour by which it has been neutralized, we are left in sudden darkness, in the quagmire where all such mental aberrations must necessarily end: and thus prophecy is prostituted; faith and hope (improperly employed,) are disappointed; and religion itself discredited.

Leaving comparisons relative to the times and persons that now are, lest they might be thought invidious; let us go back to the days of the astonishing Lord *Napier*, the inventor of the Logarithms; who, deluded by an initial misapprehension of certain promises, and scriptural figurative expressions, began to calculate *time* and its *termination* in the general conflagration of the whole solar system, and the final winding up of the mortal story in the last judgement, when the irrevocable doom should be pronounced relative to the evil and the good, and their states rendered unchangeable, being forever shut in, by the deep driven bolt of God's eternal purpose. This great man, by his calculations on the *vials* or *trumpets* in the Apocalypse, found that each vial contained the space of 245 years, that the *seventh*, or last, began in A. D. 1541, consequently it would extend to 1786;—"Not," says this most eminent (though deplorably deceived) man, "that I mean that that age or yet the world shall continew so long, because it is said, that for the *elect's sake the time shall be shortened;* but I mean, that if the world wer to indure, that *seventh* age should continew until the yeare of Christ, 1786." But finding some data in the 1335 days of Daniel, ch. xii. and in the *times* of the *thundering angels*, Rev. viii. 9; from the former, he concluded that the *day of judgement* would take place in 1700; and by the latter, in 1688; whence, says he, " it may be confidently éxpected, that this awful day shall take place between these two periods!"—that is, Lord Napier brought the whole business within the certainty of occurrence in the difference (twelve years) between the above two pe riods! and thus our forefathers who lived in 1688, must be persuaded that within the space of twelve years " the heavens would pass away with a great noise, and the elements should melt with fervent heat, and the earth also and the works that are therein should be burnt up!" Alas for such calculators and expectants, we, who are alive 129 years after the utter failure of those laborious calculations, find the heavens and the earth in their original perfection; unchanged in their na- ture, without a hair's breadth of deviation in their various and multitudinous motions performed by an unseen guidance and energy in the vortex of space! and such has been and will be the issue of the schemes of all those who, in their cal- culations relative to a *millenial state of glory* just at hand, have been doing little else than tything mint and anise and cummin, while they omitted the weightier matters of the law, —judgement, mercy, and faith. How many mouths are full of the cry of the *approaching latter days' glory*—making their views of the subject the test of a sound creed, while those who differ from them, are reputed not much better than stubborn *heretics.*

It is strange that there should be so little caution used on subjects of this kind, where so many wise and learned men have been *deceived* by their *calculations*, and led *astray* by trusting to their own understanding: but adventurers in *pre- diction*, appear in every generation, every one supposing he has found out *the times and seasons which the Father hath put in His own power;*—and as *he* believes that to *him* the se- cret has been revealed, he is not deterred by the failure of his ~edecessors, as he *knows they* were *wrong*, because he be- ~s *he is right!*

That God, the great Sun of righteousness, is determined to shine *more* and *more* unto the perfect day; and that the light of Divine revelation is becoming more generally diffused, and that the work of righteousness in the earth is both extended and deepened—are truths which no friend to God and man would attempt to deny.    This is the *kingdom*, the *coming* of which our blessed Lord has commanded us to pray for, and strongly to expect : but even this kingdom of our Lord cometh not with observation; it advances slowly and silently along in that great way in which the Grace and Providence of God walk on with an even pace : but we want to see *portents*—we are looking for *wonderful appearances*—*we* want a different *shaking of the nations* than that of which God hath spoken; and we appear to be entering far into the *presumption*, that the path we have marked out, is that in which He must infallibly tread.    For, " the *glory of the latter day* is at hand, He hath promised to come, and we have proved that *this is the time;* and He is even *now at the doors.*"

The text on which these observations are founded, is considered a strong evidence on the subject; but without entering into the *manner* in which this text has been applied, and without touching the controversy that has lately been excited, I shall endeavour to give the *literal*, and what I believe to be the *only sense* of the inspired writer, and prove that the *great predicted* FACT has *already taken place ;* and that the *consequences* are still in manifest progression, and will continue to come on with the lapse of time, till mortality is swallowed up of life.    In doing this I shall—

I. Consider what is meant by the words, " It shall come to pass afterward."

II. The prediction—" I will pour out my spirit upon all flesh," and,

III. The consequences, " They shall prophesy," &c.

IV. What is the deliverance or salvation that shall be the result.

I. *And it shall come to pass afterward,* כן אחרי והיה *vehaiya acherey ken,*—And it shall be in the latter times, thus.

In the preceding part of this chapter, the prophet had predicted a terrible desolation of the land of Judea by the means of immense swarms of *locusts*, which should destroy all vegetation, and bring about a severe famine; but that on their repentance and humiliation, God would destroy those destroyers, and bless the land with an unprecedented degree of fertility, so that plenty should be restored, and universal prosperity should prevail in the land.

As the subject gave the prophet occasion, he passes, by a very elegant *transition*, into a prediction of the great blessings that should be dispensed to the *Jews* and to the *Gentiles*, in gospel times, by the unsearchable riches of Christ. *It shall come to pass after these things;* אחרי כן *acherey ken;* these words, says *Rab. David Kimchi*, always refer to *the days of the Messiah, the latter days;* and thus this prophecy is to be interpreted; and we have the testimony of St. Peter, Acts ii. 14—21, that this prophecy relates to that mighty effusion of the Holy Spirit, of which the Apostles were the subjects, on the first Pentecost after the resurrection of Christ. " But Peter standing up, lifted up his voice and said, This is that which was spoken by the prophet Joel, It shall come to pass in the last days, (εν ταις εσχαταις ημεραις,) saith God, I will pour out of my Spirit upon all flesh," &c.; and he goes on to quote the whole of this prophecy, applying it, by Divine authority, to the events that had *lately* taken place, and to that mighty baptism of the Spirit under which they then felt and spoke.

We see, therefore, that this prophecy of Joel related to *gospel times*—to those in which Christ was incarnate, dwelling among men, full of grace and truth, who being delivered for their offences, was raised again for their justification, and having received the promise of the Father, the Holy Ghost, He had shed forth that which they now saw and heard :—see as above, verses 22—33. So we have it fully ascertained, that the *latter days,* of which Joel spake, according to the interpretation of St. Peter, were those gospel times in which Christ was manifested in the flesh, lived, suffered, died, was buried, rose again from the dead, ascended into heaven, received the promise of the Father, and sent forth that baptism of the Holy Spirit, of which they were at that time made partakers: and that the prophecy does not refer to any *imaginary* manifestation of the Holy Spirit, which should take place more than eighteen hundred years afterwards. St. Peter's application of it to *those events,* and to *those only,* leaves us without doubt on the propriety of thus understanding the prophecy.

II. We come now to consider the PREDICTION—*I will pour out my spirit upon all flesh.* There is a good saying of Rabbi *Tancum*, though we know not the tradition from which he quotes; but he quotes in reference to this prophecy of Joel, " When Moses laid his hands upon Joshua, the holy blessed God said, In the time of the old text, each individual Prophet, prophesied : but in the times of the Messiah, all the Israelites shall be Prophets."

The term *Prophet*, among the ancient Jews, not only meant, (1) a man who could *foretel future events* by the direct inspiration of God, or by the information which *vivâ voce*, he received from Him ; but also, (2) a *teacher of* those *young men*, called *sons of the prophets*, who were to be employed in the service of the tabernacle; (3) one who instructed the people, a preacher; (4) one who acted as a *civil magistrate ;* and (5) a man of *faith* and *prayer*, who had power with God, and made effectual *supplication* for individuals, and for the nation.

By *Prophecy*, chiefly, was the will of God made known to men; and the whole of what is called *Divine Revelation*, came in this way. When *this* Prophecy was delivered, the greater part of the canon of the Scripture was completed; only *Ezekiel, Daniel,* and some of the *minor Prophets*, having not yet made their appearance. It is not, however, to what was farther necessary to be done, to complete the Jewish canon, that he speaks here; but to what *should be added* under the *Messiah :*—to what God would give in that *last dispensation* of justice and mercy, which He was to manifest in the world.

This dispensation might be emphatically called *The dispensation of the Holy Spirit.* The gifts and graces of this Spirit were but rarely given under the Old Testament. Few, besides *Prophets, Priests,* and some *Kings*, appear to have been made partakers of them. During the whole of the Mosaic economy, the *common people shared but little* in those gifts and graces. It was only under the *Christian* dispensation that the *kingdom of heaven was opened to all believers.* And this is what the Prophet means, when he introduces God, speaking thus: *I will pour out my spirit upon all flesh ;*

2 A

*i. e.* upon *mankind* at large ; no longer making those *distinctions* that prevailed formerly, where the great mass of the people were little noticed.

The word ‏בשר‎ *basar*, which is translated *flesh*, signifies properly the *human race ;* that *flesh*, or *nature*, which was the most *eminent*. See Gen. ii. 24. Psal. xxxviii. 3—7. And it is certainly used to express *all mankind*, in this prophecy, and in Gen. vi. 12. Isai. xl. 5. and other places. It is also used to express *good news, glad tidings ;* and by it the *term*, as well as the *thing*, which we call *gospel*, is designated in the Old Testament ; witness that remarkable passage, Isai. lxi. 1,—" The Spirit of the Lord is upon me, because he hath anointed me to *preach good tidings ;*" ‏לבשר‎ *le-basar*, to declare the flesh—the *incarnation* :—as if the *good tidings*, necessarily implied, *God manifested in the* FLESH :—and nothing could be so properly called *preaching*, or a *declaration of good news*, as that in which the *incarnation of Christ*, and the *end* for which He was incarnated, were prominently declared, and made the chief part of the subject. What can be called *good news* to a lost world, but the declaration of God's mercy in its redemption by Jesus Christ ?

As this *pouring out of the Holy Spirit upon all flesh*, is applied by St. Peter, as we have seen, to what took place at the day of *Pentecost*, when this dispensation was *first opened*, so its being *poured out on all flesh*, must have some particular relation to the *circumstances* of that case. For it is expressly said, " There were dwelling (κατοικουντες, or sojourning) at Jerusalem, Jews, devout men, out of every nation under heaven ;" who consequently were acquainted with the languages of the nations whence they came ; and they were now only *sojourning* at Jerusalem, having come up to attend at the *Pass-over*, or for the purpose of merchandise. And the *devout men*, ανδρις ευλαβεις, *men of good character*, respectable, moral men, were such as could be proper judges of what they heard and saw. They were either *native* Jews, or such as were *born* in the *countries* where their parents sojourned, or they were Gentiles, proselytes to Judaism, and were well qualified to give *credible testimony* relative to the *facts* that had taken place. At this time, there was scarcely a commercial or civilized nation under heaven, where the Jews had not been scattered for the purpose of trade, merchandise, &c.; and from all those nations it is here said, there were persons present at Jerusalem. Several of those nations are here specified : we shall consider them in order :—

1. PARTHIANS. *Parthia* anciently included the northern part of modern *Persia;* it was situated between the *Caspian Sea* and *Persian Gulf;* and rather to the *eastward* of both.

2. MEDES. *Media* was a country lying in the vicinity of the *Caspian Sea;* having *Parthia* on the *east, Assyria* on the *south,* and *Mesopotamia* on the *west.*

3. ELAMITES. Probably inhabitants of that country now called *Persia.* The *Medes* and *Elamites* were a neighbouring people, dwelling beyond the *Tigris.*

4. MESOPOTAMIA. Now called *Diarbeck,* in *Asiatic Turkey,* situated between the *Tigris* and *Euphrates;* hence its name—*the country between the rivers.* It had *Assyria* on the *east, Arabia Deserta,* with *Babylonia,* on the *south, Syria* on the *west,* and *Armenia* on the *north.* It is the same country that was called *Padan-Aram* by the ancient Hebrews; and by all the Asiatics is now called *Maverannahar; i. e.* The country beyond the river.

5. JUDEA. Whether this be meant to express the *Jewish Mesopotamia,* and that Ιουδαιαν should be taken for the adjective, read here as agreeing with Μεσοποταμιαν, *Mesopotamia,* learned men are not agreed. Vast multitudes of Jews were settled here; and Josephus says, the ten tribes dwelt in *Mesopotamia* in his time. Perhaps *Galilee* may be understood here, as that was a *part of Judea* bordering upon *Syria,* and we know that the dialect of the inhabitants of that province was so different from the other parts of Judea, especially about Jerusalem, as scarcely to be understood; and therefore might be specified here, as the miracle must also operate upon *them,* to enable them clearly and readily to understand what the disciples spoke, who either spoke pure *Hebrew,* or the *Chaldeo-Syriak.* For other particulars, see my Notes on this verse.

6. CAPPADOCIA. This was an ancient kingdom of *Asia-Minor,* comprehending all that country that lies between mount *Tauris* and the *Euxine Sea.*

7. PONTUS. Anciently, Pontus was a very powerful kingdom of Asia, and originally a part of *Cappadocia.* It was bounded on the *east* by *Colchis,* on the *west* by the river

*Halys*, on the *north* by the *Black*, or *Euxine Sea*, and on the *south* by *Asia Minor*. The famous *Mithridates* was king of this country, and it was one of the last that the Roman power was able to subjugate.

8. ASIA. Probably *Asia Minor*; it was that part of *Turkey* in *Europe*, now called *Natolia*, or *Anatolia*.

9. PHRYGIA. A country of *Asia Minor*, southward of Pontus, lying between the *Euxine* and *Mediterranean Seas*.

10. PAMPHYLIA. A country lying near the *Mediterranean Sea*, between *Lycia* and *Cilicia*: it is now called *Caramania*.

11. EGYPT. A very extensive country of *Africa*, bounded by the Mediterranean on the *north*, by the *Red Sea* and the *Isthmus* of *Suez*, which divide it from *Arabia*, on the *east*, by *Abyssinia* or *Ethiopia* on the *south*, and by the deserts of *Barca* and *Nubia* on the *west*. It was called *Mitzraim* by the ancient Hebrews; and now *Mesr*, by the *Arabians*. It extends 600 miles from *north* to *south*; and from 100 to 200 miles from *east* to *west*.

12. LYBIA, in a general way among the Greeks, signified *Africa*: but the south-eastern part in the vicinity of *Egypt*, bordering on *Cyrene*, may be here intended.

13. CYRENE. A country in *Africa*, on the coast of the *Mediterranean Sea*, southward of the most western point of the island of *Crete*.

There were present also at that time, several other people, distinguished by the names of the *places* where they had a temporary residence—*strangers of Rome, Jews,* and *Proselytes*: persons who had not been in Jerusalem before; but most probably *natives of Rome ;*—the Jews might be sojourners there; and the *Proselytes* were heathens professing the Jewish religion.

14. CRETANS. Inhabitants of Crete, a large and famous Island in the *Levant*, or eastern part of the *Mediterranean Sea*: now called *Candia*.

15. ARABIANS. Natives of *Arabia*, a large and well known country of Asia, having the *Red Sea* on the *west*, the *Persian Gulf* on the *east*, *Judea* on the *north*, and the *Indian Ocean* on the *south*. It is divided into districts, that have been denominated *Arabia Petrea, Arabia Felix,* and *Arabia Deserta*.

I have entered the more particularly into this *geographical sketch* of these places, because I am satisfied, that in the great work mentioned here, the prophecy in my text began to be fulfilled; and thus to shew how wisely it was ordered, that the miraculous *descent of the Holy Ghost*, called by *Joel* the *outpouring of the Spirit*, should have taken place at *this time;* when so many from various nations were present to witness it, and to be themselves subjects of its mighty workings. These, on their return to their respective countries, would naturally proclaim what things they had seen and heard, and by this the way of the Apostles was made plain; and thus Christianity made a *rapid progress* over all those parts above mentioned, in a very short time after the resurrection of our Lord.

2dly. I have entered into this subject the more particularly, to shew that, in the *variety of languages* possessed by men of various nations then present at Jerusalem, the prophecy in the text might be considered as having a most *singular fulfilment.*—The *Holy Spirit* was to be *poured out upon all flesh*—upon *mankind* at large; and here it might be said, the *human race* was present in their *representatives*. There was most probably not a *kind* or *national family* of man, which had not a representative among those *Parthians, Medes, Elamites, Mesopotamians, Jews, Cappadocians*, people of *Pontus*, of *Asia*, of *Phrygia, Pamphylia, Egypt, Lybia, Cyrene, Rome, Crete*, and *Arabia*. And there was not a *regular language* of the then known universe, that was not known by some or other of the nations here specified. The *three* great tongues in which it pleased God at the first to disseminate His Truth; viz. the HEBREW, the GREEK, and the LATIN, were here: among them also I can recognize the *Syriak*, the *Chaldee*, the *Abyssinian* or *Ethiopic*, the *Pehlevi* or ancient *Persian*, the *Coptic*, the *Armenian*, and the *Arabic;* and besides *how many* of the languages of *Asia Proper*, and *Asia Minor*, with *Greek, Slavonic*, and *Celtic dialects*, we cannot say, but we may presume not a few.

It was most probably through this, that we find *traditions* among all the great nations of the universe, relative to the true God, and the great Scripture *facts*. And this miracle thus predicted, was, humanly speaking, essentially necessary to prepare the nations of the world for the preaching of the gospel of Christ; and by these means, as we have already seen, was the way of the Apostles and first planters of Christianity made plain, not only through all the *land of Palestine,* but also through *Egypt, Syria, Asia, Asia Minor, Greece, Italy,* and probably through many *parts* of *Germany, France, Spain,* and the *Islands of the Sea.* And it is so managed now by the Providence and Grace of God, that to all the inhabitants of the earth the word of life is in the act of being *sent,* by translations of the Bible into the *different languages of the habitable world;*—and with these Bibles in *many languages,* Missionaries go forth to proclaim to those peoples in their own languages, the unsearchable riches of Christ. Now all these are *proofs* that the great promise contained in this most important *prophecy,* is in the *fullest progress* to be speedily fulfilled, even in the utmost sense of the words ; for, God is *pouring out His Spirit upon* ALL FLESH.

III. I shall now consider the *consequences* of this pouring out of the Spirit, and the instruments which He employs under the direction of this Spirit:—*Your sons and your daughters shall prophecy.*

We have already seen, that a *prophet* signified, 1. A *teacher of youth* in ecclesiastical matters.   2. A teacher of the *people* in the things that concerned their salvation; *i. e.* a preacher of righteousness.   3. One that had power in prayer, so as to become an *intercessor* for men.   These gifts and offices were, under the Mosaic dispensation, restrained to *particular persons,* chosen of God Himself; for the prophetic gifts were in no case hereditary.   But under this outpouring of the Spirit, there was to be no *selection* of *persons* from certain *tribes, families,* &c. ; but all who received this Spirit, and were actuated by it, were to be endued with those gifts and graces, by which they might be able to edify each other; and proclaim to those who were ignorant the unsearchable riches of Christ. They should be *exhorters, instructers, preachers,* and *intercessors,* so as to be able to edify the Church.   It intimates that the graces and gifts of the Spirit would be both *general* and *abundant :* and has not every age of Christianity been a proof of this?   There have, it is true, been many eminent *men* in Judaism :—prophets, priests, kings, historians, poets, statesmen, soldiers, heroes, and men deeply devoted to God ; but how few of these in proportion to the 2000 years' length of that dispensation, and the number of the people !   But leaving *Divine Inspiration* out of the question, what are they in their respective kinds when compared with Christians in all these characters, offices, and situations! There have also been some eminent *women;* but leaving out *extraordinary providences*, which worked in their behalf, what were they in number and eminence in comparison of the thousands in Christianity that have been great, wise, pious, and learned! But suppose we turn our attention to the *common people*, those who formed the aggregate of the Jewish church; and what shall we see? Ignorance and indevotion; they were rebels against God, and all legitimate rule; murmurers, complainers, malcontents, cruel, and vindictive; scarcely ever having the *form*, and more seldom the *power*, of *godliness*. On the other hand, look at the aggregate body of the Christian Church, and how convincingly true are the words of the Poet—

> *Men* in their own eyes, were *children* again;
> The *children* were wise, and solid as *men :*
> The *women* were fearful of nothing but *sin :*
> Their hearts were all cheerful, their consciences clean.

Without the aid of human learning, many Christians, male and female, became not only very respectable for their talents, but also eminently useful; and possessed so much of the genuine spirit of piety, and the life and power of religion, that they endured all kinds of hardships and persecutions, and loved not their lives even unto the death, that they might shew their invincible love to their God and Saviour, and unalterable attachment to their religion, in possession of which they enjoyed a happiness and foretaste of heaven, that absorbed all earthly and temporal considerations; therefore even the *women* braved death in all its terrific forms; and in the times of persecution, were all, at all times *confessors :* and multitudes of them *martyrs*. The *aged men* and *women saw their sons and their daughters* endued with the *spirit*, prophesying; not only visiting the sick, and ministering to the necessities of the poor, but also *Deaconesses* in the Church; teaching the truths of God to those who had not learned them, bringing by their good advice, and holy practice, Gentiles into the Church. In a word, " the *aged men* were vigilant, grave, holy, temperate, sound in the faith, in charity, and in patience."

" The *aged women* were in behaviour as became holy

women, not makers of strife, not intemperate, not false accusers, teachers of good things (καλοδιδασκαλους, good able teachers.")

" They taught the *young women* to be wise, to be lovers of their husbands, and lovers of their children, discreet, chaste, attached to their domestic affairs, good and obedient to their own husbands."

" The *young men* were also taught to be discreet, and of a sober mind."

" The *servants* to be obedient to their own masters, to please them well in all things, without contradiction or gainsaying—not defrauding or making waste of their masters' substance, but shewing all good fidelity." See Titus ii. 1—10. And all this was grounded on their having received " that grace of God that bringeth salvation to all men; teaching them, that denying all ungodliness and worldly desires, they might live discreetly, righteously, and godly, in the present world, looking for the blessed hope, and glorious appearing of the great God, and our Saviour Jesus Christ, who gave Himself for them, that He might redeem them from all unrighteousness, and cleanse to Himself a peculiar people, zealous of good works." Tit. ii. 11—14. Thus the Holy Spirit was poured out upon all, not only to save them from their sins, but to make them wise, holy, and useful. And while the Christian Church was faithful to its calling and privileges, *thus it was with them.*

And to the present hour, the same Spirit is poured out upon that Church in all its members:—for *also upon the servants and upon the handmaids He pours out His Spirit in these days;* and St. Peter, who lived to witness the initiatory fulfilment of this divine oracle, adds, και προφητευσουσιν, *and they shall prophesy:*—instead of being *slaves,* as they in general were among the *Jews,* they were the *freed-men* and *freed-women* of Christ; and were eligible to some of the most useful offices in the Church. For in the Christian Church, whether they were *male* or *female, bond* or *free,* (their grace being equal,) they were all *one* in Christ Jesus.

This prophecy may be considered as a general promise that the gifts of teaching and instructing men, should not be restricted to any one *class* or *order* of the people:—that God would call as *He* pleased, and qualify the men of His choice:

and should take such out of all ranks, orders, degrees, and offices in society: and would pour out His Spirit upon *them*, and endow *them* with all the gifts and graces necessary to convert sinners, and build up believers on their most holy faith.

And this God *has done*, and *is doing :*—He left the *line of Aaron*, and took His Apostles indiscriminately out of any tribe. He passed by the *regular order* of the *Priesthood*, and the *public schools* of the most celebrated *Doctors*, and took his Evangelists from among *fishermen*, *tent-makers*, and even the *Roman tax-gatherers*. And lastly, he passed by the whole of the *Jewish tribes*, and took converts from among the *Gentiles*, and made them *preachers of righteousness* to the inhabitants of the whole earth! The same practice He continues to the present day.

Yet He did not *then* pass by a man that was *brought up at the feet of Gamaliel*, no more than He would *now* pass by one brought up in any celebrated *seminary of learning*. He is ever *free* to use His *own gifts*, in His *own way ;* and when *learning* is sanctified, by being *devoted to the service of God*, and the possessor is pious and humble, and has those *natural gifts* proper for a *public teacher*, perhaps we may safely assert, that God would in many cases *prefer* such : but He will have *others*, servants and handmaids—persons from the common offices of life, as intimated in the prophecy, that we may see, that the *conversion of sinners* is not by *human might* nor *power, but by the Spirit of the Lord of hosts*. The *learned man* can do no good in the Church without His *Spirit :* and the *unlearned* must have its gifts and graces; without which the labours of both will be unprofitable :—and thus the *excellence of the power* is *of God*, and *no flesh can glory in His presence*.

It is said here, that when this outpouring shall take place, *The old men shall dream dreams, and the young men see visions*. On this passage, the Rev. John Wesley has a sensible note, *viz.* " In *young men*, the *outward* senses are most vigorous, and the bodily strength is entire, whereby they are best qualified to sustain the shock which usually attends the *visions of God*. In *old men*, the *internal* senses are most vigorous, suited to Divine dreams. Not that the *old* are wholly excluded from the *former*, nor the *young* from the *latter*."—In primitive times, such dreams and visions were frequent. The canon of Scripture was not yet complete, and supernatural interventions were requisite in order to conduct the Apostles, &c. in their work.

Something more particular should be said concerning the *instruments* which this *Spirit* employs in His great work.

The *instruments* which God used, in the primitive outpouring of His Spirit, for preaching the gospel among the Gentiles, are thus enumerated by Saint Paul, Eph. iv. 11, 12— "God gave some *Apostles*, some *Prophets*, some *Evangelists*, and some *Pastors* and *Teachers*, for the perfecting of the Saints for the work of the ministry, for the edifying of the Body of Christ."

And in 1 Cor. xii. 28, he mentions the same in the following order :—

" God hath set some in the Church, 1st. *Apostles*, 2dly. *Prophets*, 3dly. *Teachers ;* after that *miracles ;* then *gifts of healings, helps, governments,* and *diversity of tongues.*"

Thus we see that God established several *offices* in His Church, furnished these with the proper *officers,* and to qualify them for their work, gave them the proper *gifts.* On this subject St. Paul's reasoning is beautiful and appropriate. As the members in the *human body,* so the different members of the *mystical Body of Christ.* All are intended by Him to have the same relation to each other—to be mutually subservient to each other. He has also made, as in the human body, each member of the Church, necessary to the *beauty, proportion, strength,* and *perfection* of the whole. Not one is useless ; not one unnecessary. Paul, Apollos, Kephas, &c. with all their variety of gifts and graces, are " for the perfecting of the Saints, for the work of the ministry, for the edifying of the Body of Christ." Hence, no teacher should be *exalted above,* or *opposed* to another. As the eye could not say to the hand, I have no need of thee, so *luminous* Apollos could not say to *laborious* Paul, " I can build up and preserve the Church without thee." As the *foot* planted on the ground to support the whole fabric—and as the *hands* which swing at liberty—and the *eye* that is continually taking in near and distant objects—are all equally necessary to the whole, and mutually helpful to and dependent on each other ; so also are the `ferent ministers and members of the Church of Christ.— St. Paul's beautiful *apologue,* 1 Cor. xii. 12—27.

Now, as God has made evident distinctions among the members of the human body, (though all are necessary to its perfection and support,) so that some occupy a more eminent place than others! so has He in the Church: and this, the *same Spirit* which *Joel* predicted should be *poured out*, has Himself prescribed: therefore St. Paul, who was under this influence, enumerates to the Church at Corinth, the principal *offices*, and the *order* in which they should stand. Some of these seem to belong exclusively to the *primitive Church*, not being designed to continue, as not being necessary after the establishment of Christianity, and the completion of the canon of the New Covenant Scriptures.

1. APOSTLES are St. Paul's *first order*—Αποστολοι, from απο, *from*, and στιλλω, *I send*, from one person to another, and from one place to another. Persons immediately designated by Christ, and sent by Him to preach the Gospel, with the knowledge of which they were fully inspired.

2. PROPHETS—Προφηται, from προ, *before*, and φημι, *I speak*. Persons who, under divine inspiration, predict future events: under the Apostolic Church, there were several of these. But the word *prophet*, often, if not generally, means a *public teacher* or instructer; and is often applied to those who *preached the gospel*. See before.

3. TEACHERS—Διδασκαλοι, from the verb διδασκω, *I teach*. Persons whose chief business it was to *instruct the people* in the elements of the Christian Religion, and their duty to each other.

These were the chief permanent officers in the Church; those mentioned after were occasional, and not permanent in any particular *order* or *succession*—such as *miracles*, which seems to imply persons *endued with miraculous gifts*, such as those mentioned Mark xvi. 17, 18;—casting out devils;—*gifts of healings*—such as laying hands upon the sick, which being one of the most beneficent miraculous powers, was most frequently conceded.

*Helps*—Probably the *assistants* of the *Apostles*, who constantly accompanied them; baptised those whom they converted; and were sent by them to such places as the Apostles could not attend to, being otherwise employed. The *Levites*, under the law, were considered the *helpers of the Priests*.

*Governments*—Probably persons who formed the different

Churches, arranging them in religious Society according to their respective graces and gifts, and preserving them in a state of union by proper *discipline.*

*Diversities of tongues*—Persons who had a supernatural readiness to acquire strange languages; or, who had a miraculous power of speaking and interpreting those they had not learned.

*Discerning of Spirits*, is mentioned by the Apostle in ver. 10, of this same chapter: this probably means a gift by which the person so privileged, could discern a *false miracle* from a *true one*, or a *pretender* to Divine inspiration, from one who was really a *partaker of the Holy Ghost.* It probably extended to the *discernment* of *false professors* from *true ones*, as appears in the case of Peter, in reference to *Ananias* and his wife *Sapphira, Simon Magus,* &c.

It has been thought strange by some, that in this enumeration only *three* distinct *officers* in the Church should be mentioned—*Apostles, Prophets,* and *Teachers;* though he is professedly giving us an account of all the *officers* and gifts necessary for the constitution of a Christian Church: and that no mention is made of *Bishops, Presbyters,* or *Deacons,* much less of the various *officers* and *offices* which the Christian Church at present exhibits. That there were *Bishops,* Επισκοποι, *Presbyters* or *Elders,* Πρεσβυτεροι, and *Deacons,* Διακονοι, in the Apostolic Church, is sufficiently evident from other parts of Scripture. Perhaps *Bishops* are here included under APOSTLES: *Presbyters* under PROPHETS: and *Deacons* under TEACHERS: but in several cases *Bishops* and *Presbyters* seem to be the same order.

There are still in the Christian Church, those who answer to the character of *Apostles*—persons *sent of God*, to preach the gospel; and this sending appeared by especial Providences, as well as by the gifts and graces given to the persons, together with the strong and incessant impression on their own minds, that a dispensation of the gospel was committed unto them; and woe would betide them if they did not preach it.

*Prophets* may include the *ordinary ministers* of any Christian Church;—those appointed by that Church according to its own discipline, or peculiar customs, whether *Episcopalian, Presbyterian, Independent,* or *Methodist:*—but God will ever reserve to Himself the prerogative of sending *Apostles* or *extraordinary ministers* among, or from all those different classes; the success of whose labours will ascertain the certainty of their *divine mission*.

As to TEACHERS, or *Deacons*; they abound in all Churches; and about their office there is little dispute; they are under-ministers who visit and pray with the sick; help different departments of the Church with counsel and advice; examine the progress which those more immediately under their care; are making in the divine life; reporting the internal state of the Church to the *Prophet* or *Preacher* of that Church; that he may the better know how to suit his public ministrations to the necessities of the people.

In Ephes. iv. 11, St. Paul mentions *Evangelists*—those whose particular gift is manifested in their mode of preaching Christ crucified; shewing the nature, extent, worth, and efficacy of His Agony and Bloody Sweat, His Cross and Passion, His Death and Burial, His glorious Resurrection and Ascension, and His powerful *Mediation* at the Throne of God.

In the same place he mentions PASTORS and TEACHERS: *pastors* are those who *feed* the flock—*teachers* are those who *direct* it. Probably the *deacon* implies *both;* at least in many cases both the offices seem to be so incorporated, as to be discharged by the *same person.*

Such were the *officers* which the Holy Spirit influenced and directed in those offices, in which He designed they should act, for the fulfilment of the work of the ministry. But in process of time, the offices were greatly *blended*, till at last *distinction* was nearly, if not altogether lost; so that in the present day, we can scarcely dare to say such and such were the duties discharged by those officers whose official names we borrow from the Greek original of the new Covenant: such as, *Apostle, Prophet, Presbyter, Bishop, Deacon, Evangelist, Canon, &c.*: but this we know, that whatever *tended* to " the perfecting of the saints, for the work of the ministry, and for the edifying of the body of Christ; that all might come in the unity of the faith, and of the knowledge of the Son of God, unto a perfect man, unto the measure of the stature of the fulness of Christ;" was performed by those which are here called Apostles, Prophets, Evangelists, Pastors, and Teachers.

IV. I come now to consider the *deliverance* which the Prophet foretels, as the consequence of the pouring out of the Holy Spirit—" *For, whosoever shall call upon the name of the Lord, shall be delivered; for in Mount Zion and Jerusalem shall be deliverance as the Lord hath said,*" ver. 32. On this passage Bishop *Newcome* says, " This refers to the *safety* of the Christians during the Jewish and the Roman war." It may be so, but this would be a very poor consequence of such an event as the Prophet predicts here, were there nothing *more* intended by it. The pouring out such an abundance of the *gifts* and the *graces* of the Holy Spirit *upon all flesh*, can be but ill explained by the escape of a few *hundred Christians* from Jerusalem, at the time that *Cestius Gallus*, the Roman general, began to lay siege to that city. That such an escape took place, we have respectable authority to believe; and that this escape from the Roman sword might point out metaphorically, the *escape* of those who, by *invoking the name of the Lord Jesus Christ*, escape from the wrath of Divine justice, and the bitter pains of eternal death : and we shall find that we have *Apostolic* authority thus to apply it ;—" Whosoever shall call on the name of the Lord." The original will give us extra light on this passage—יִמָּלֵט יִקְרָא בְשֵׁם אֲשֶׁר כֹּל וְהָיָה *vehaiyah col asher yikra be-shem Yehovah yimmalet*—*And it shall be, that all who invoke in the name of Jehovah, shall escape.* St. Paul quotes this verse, Rom. x. 14. I shall take the context from ver. 9. " If thou shalt confess with thy mouth the Lord Jesus, and shalt believe in thine heart, that God hath raised Him from the dead, thou shalt be saved ;"—" For the Scriptures saith, *whosoever believeth on Him shall not be ashamed.* For there is no difference between the Jew and the Greek ; for the same Lord over all, is rich unto all that call upon Him. For whosoever shall call upon (επικαλεσηται, shall invoke,) the name of the Lord, (σωθησεται,) shall be saved." That *Christ* is the *Jehovah* here intended, seems evident from the Apostle's quotation, and that he understood *Joel* as speaking concerning *Him ;* and therefore his word, Κυριος, *Lord*, must answer to the prophet's word, יהוה *Yehovah ;* which by the way is no mean proof of the Godhead of Christ. If the text be translated, *whosoever shall invoke in the name of the Lord,* which translation the *Hebrew* will easily bear, yet still the term *Je-*

*hovah*, the incommunicable name, is given to *Christ;* because *invoking in the name*, signifies soliciting one in the *name* or on the *account* of another.—He who is *invoked*, is GOD: He, in whose name He is *invoked*, is JESUS the CHRIST, who is here called *Jehovah:* and then we see that the meaning of the Holy Spirit, both in the *Prophet* and *Apostle*, is, He who asks mercy from God, in the *name*, and for the *sake* of Jesus Christ, shall get his soul saved.  " God was in Christ reconciling the world to Himself—and, there is no *name* given under heaven among men by which they can be saved, nor is there salvation in any other."   And as the Prophet speaks of the days of the Messiah, and the outpouring of the Holy Spirit, he speaks of this salvation, for this is the sum and substance of the gospel.

The prophet adds, *For in Mount Zion, and in Jerusalem, shall be deliverance.*   Our blessed Lord first began to preach His gospel in *Mount Zion*, in the *temple*, and throughout *Jerusalem*.   *There* He formed His *Church;* and *thence* He sent His Apostles and Evangelists to every part of the globe; —*Go ye into all the world, and preach the gospel to every creature.*   Of the *Jews*, there was but a *remnant*, a very small number that received the doctrine of the gospel, here called the *remnant* whom *the Lord should call,* קרא *koré*, whom *He was calling.*   Many were *called* who would not obey; but they who obeyed the call were *saved:* and still He *delivers* from sin, and death, and hell, all those who call upon Him.

### CONCLUSION.

I have now taken a particular view of this prophecy, and of the several references to it in the New Testament; and have seen that it speaks of the *glory* of the *gospel times*, which are represented in the Sacred Writings, as the *last* and *latter day* or *days*—the *last times :*—that is, the *last dispensation* of *God's justice* and *mercy :*—that to which all the preceding dispensations referred—in which they are all completed—and after which no other is ever to take place; as this has provided every thing that the justice of God requires, and every thing that the fallen race of man needs, in order to its full restoration to the image of God, and its complete preparation for an eternal glory.

Of this grand event, *Isaiah*, ch. ii. 2, 3, speaks in nearly similar language: "And it shall come to pass, באחרית הימים *be-acharith ha-yamim*, in the LAST DAYS, that the mountain of the Lord's house shall be established in the top of the mountains, and shall be exalted above the hills; and all nations shall flow unto it. And many people shall go and say, come ye and let us go up to the mountain of the Lord, to the house of the God of Jacob; and He will teach us of His ways, and we will walk in His paths; for out of *Zion* shall go forth the LAW, and the WORD of the *Lord* from *Jerusalem*."

The prophet *Micah*, ch. iv. 1, &c. about fifty years after this, quotes this place of Isaiah at length, manifestly referring to the same times; and most likely the prophet *Ezekiel* has the same event in view, in ch. xvii. 22—24, and xxxviii.— *Hosea*, ch. iii. 1—5, manifestly refers to the gospel times, with a similar phraseology; see ver. 5;—"AFTERWARD, אחר *achar*, shall the children of Israel return and seek the Lord their God, and David their king, and shall fear the Lord and His Goodness, באחרית הימים *be-acharith ha-yamim*, IN THOSE LATTER DAYS." And all these have a reference to, and seem founded upon the prophecy which *Jacob*, Gen. xlix. 1, &c. delivered to his sons: "And Jacob called unto his sons, and said, gather yourselves together, that I may tell you what shall befal you, באחרית הימים *be-acharith ha-yamim*, IN THOSE LATTER DAYS:"—and in the *tenth verse*, we have that remarkable prediction of the *Messiah*, and the *glorious spread* of His *kingdom:* "The sceptre shall not depart from Judah, nor a lawgiver from between his feet, until Shiloh come; and unto Him shall be the gathering of the people."

St. *Paul* seems to have had all the above places in view, Heb. i. 1, 2—"God, who at sundry times, and in divers manners, spake in times past unto the fathers by the Prophets, hath IN THESE LAST DAYS, επ' εσχατου των ημερων τουτων, spoken unto us by His Son."

The beloved disciple, also, uses the same phraseology, speaking of the same things, 1 John ii. 18, "Little children, it is the *last time*, εσχατη ωρα εστι, and as ye have heard that Antichrist shall come, even now there are many Antichrists; whereby we know, οτι εσχατη ωρα εστιν, *that it is the last time*." St. *Paul* calls these times, *the ends of the world*, 1 Cor. x. 11.

Now the *glory* of the *latter days*, is evidently the *revelation of Christ*, and the *universal pouring out of His Spirit*: for, as HE by the grace of God, tasted death for every man, Heb. ii. 9 ;—and His grace, which brings salvation to all men, hath appeared, Tit. ii. 11 ;—so the HOLY SPIRIT was " to convince the world of sin, righteousness, and judgement," John xvi. 8 ;—to bear witness in the conscience, of what Christ delivered in His discourses ;—to purify the hearts of men, and make them habitations of God, Eph. ii. 22. As the disgrace of man in *all times*, was SIN and *rebellion against God*, so the glory of these *latter times* is the redemption of man from its power, its guilt, and its pollution ; so that faith working by love, should fill the whole life with a cheerful obedience. Nor are we in *any times*, to expect a greater or more efficacious *Saviour* than JESUS CHRIST ; nor a more powerful and energetic *Agent*, than the HOLY GHOST, the Spirit of judgement, and the Spirit of burning. Nor do I find in any part of the Divine Oracles, that there is any *reserve* of this Spirit in His gifts and graces for some future times ; nor do I find from these Sacred Records, that there is one ray of His light, or spark of His influence, that may not be had now, for all the purposes of salvation from sin here, and glorification hereafter, in as abundant a manner as can be expected, between this present hour, and that in which the angel shall swear by Him who liveth for ever and ever, that time shall be no longer.

I hold also, that those who are absurdly putting off the day of salvation, in expectation of *any outpouring of God's Spirit* that may not now be had through Christ, by faith and prayer, are rejecting their own mercies, are encompassing themselves with sparks of their own kindling, and shall lie down in sorrow in consequence.

It is truly an astonishing thing that men will prefer *hope* to *enjoyment;* and rather content themselves with blessings in *prospect* than in *possession!* Thousands in their affections, conversation, and conduct, are wandering after an undefined and undefinable period, commonly called a *millennial glory*, while *expectation* is *paralized*, and *prayer* and *faith restrained* in reference to *present salvation;* and yet none of these can tell what even a *day* may bring forth ;—for *now* we stand

2 B 2

on the *verge of eternity*, and because it is so, *now* is the accepted time, and now is the day of salvation!

These are the *times* in which Christ offers to dwell in the hearts of all true believers by faith, that they may be rooted and grounded in love, and prove with all saints, what is the *length*, and *breadth*, and *depth*, and *height*, and know the love of God that passeth knowledge, and be filled with ALL the FULNESS of GOD! Is there any thing *greater* than this to be expected or obtained on this side eternity? Can our hearts be *more* than *filled?* Can our souls be filled with *more* than *all the fulness of God?* These are the days of the Son of man—*now* is the Holy Spirit given in His plenitude—never were there times more favourable—never were spiritual advantages more numerous—never was the light more abundant —never were the Holy Scriptures more extensively dispersed —and never were their contents better understood. We have not *that time* which is looked for under the misapprehended title of *millennial glory ;* and yet the *whole earth* is in the way of being filled with the knowledge of God! Reader, lay these things to heart: *now*, arise and shake thyself from the dust :—we have seen the land, and behold it is very good ;— and are ye still? Be not slothful to go and to enter to possess the land! Awake, awake ; put on thy strength, O Zion; put on thy beautiful garments, O Jerusalem, the Holy City ; for henceforth there shall no more come into thee the uncircumcised and the unclean. Death is at the door ; but the power of the Lord is present to heal. O Thou, who dwellest between the Cherubim, shine forth! Amen.

# SERMON XXIX.

.

## SOME OBSERVATIONS ON THE BEING AND PROVIDENCE OF A GOD.

HEBREWS, Chap. xi. ver. 6.

He that cometh unto God must believe that he is: and that he is the rewarder of them
who diligently seek him.

I. METAPHYSICIANS and philosophers, in order to prove the existence of God, have used two modes of argumentation :—

*A priori*, proofs drawn from the necessity that such a Being as God is, must exist: arguments of this kind do not produce any thing in evidence which is *derived* from His works.

*A posteriori*, proofs of the being and perfections of God drawn from His own works.

### PROPOSITIONS à PRIORI.

Prop. I. If there be no one being in the universe but such as might possibly *not have existed*, it would follow, that there might possibly have been *no existence* at all : and if that could be so, it would be also possible that the present existence might have arisen from total *non-existence*, which is absurd. Therefore, it is not possible that there might have been no existence at all. Consequently, an impossibility of not existing must be found somewhere; there must have been a Being whose non-existence is impossible.

II. The *whole nature* of an unoriginated Being, or *aggregate* of His attributes, must be *unoriginated*, and necessarily what it is. A being cannot produce its own attributes; for this would suppose it acted before it existed. There is nothing in the nature of this Being that is *contingent*, or could have been *otherwise* than it is; for whatever is *contingent* must have a cause to determine its mode of existence.

III. The attributes of an unoriginated Being must be possessed by it *unlimitedly;* for, to possess an attribute *imperfectly*, or only in a *certain degree*, must suppose some cause to have *modified* this Being so as to make Him incapable of having that attribute in any other than an *imperfect degree.* But no cause can be admitted in this case, because this is the First of all beings, and the cause of all things. Farther, an imperfect attribute, or any.one that is not in its *highest degree*, must be capable of improvement by exercise and experience; which would imply that the unoriginated Being must be originally imperfect; and that He was deriving farther degrees of perfection from the exercise of His own powers, and acquaintance with His own works.

IV. The unoriginated Being must exist *every where*, in the same manner, He does *any where;* for if He did not, it would suppose some *cause* by which His presence was limited; but there can be no cause to limit that presence. See before.

V. This unoriginated Being must be a *simple uncompounded* substance, identically the same every where; not consisting of *parts*, for these must be distinct and independent; nor of *whole*, for this is the aggregate of parts; nor of *magnitude* or *quantity*, for these signify a composition of parts. This being must be as truly *one* and omnipresent as the present moment of time is indivisibly *one* in all places at once; and can no more be limited or measured by *time*, than the present moment can by duration.

Hence, this Being cannot be *matter* or *body*, because to these belong *extension, divisibility, figurability*, and *mobility*, which imply *limitation*. God and matter have essentially contrary properties.

God is not *material*. It has already been shewn, that

there necessarily must exist one infinite, unoriginated, and eternal Being. Now, this Being must be a *thinking* Being; for it is as impossible to conceive that *unthinking* matter could produce a *thinking* intelligent Being, as it is to conceive that *nothing* can produce *matter*.

Let us suppose any parcel of matter to be *eternal*, we shall find it, in itself, unable to produce any thing. Let us suppose its *parts* firmly at rest together; if there were no other being in the world, must it not eternally remain so, a dead inactive lump? Is it possible to conceive that it can add motion to itself, or produce it in other portions of matter? Matter, therefore, by its own strength, cannot produce in itself so much as *motion*. The motion it has must also be from eternity, or else added to matter by some other being more powerful than itself.

But let us suppose motion eternal too; yet matter, unthinking matter, and motion, could never produce *thought*. Knowledge will still be as far beyond the *power* of *motion* and *matter* to produce, as matter is beyond the power of nothing to produce. Divide matter into as minute parts as you will, vary the figure and motion of it as much as you please, it will operate no other way upon other bodies of proportionate bulk than it did before this division. The minutest particles of matter would impel, or resist one another, just as the greater do; and that is all that they can do. So that if we will suppose *nothing* eternal, *matter* can never begin to be. If we suppose bare matter, without motion, eternal: then motion can never begin to be. If we suppose only *matter* and *motion* eternal, then *thought* can never begin to be. For, it is impossible to conceive that matter, either with or without motion, could have originally, in and from itself, sense, perception, and knowledge; as is evident from hence, that sense, perception, and knowledge, must be properties eternally separate from matter, and every particle of it.

Since, therefore, whatsoever is the first eternal Being must necessarily be a *thinking* Being, and whatsoever is first of all things must necessarily contain in it, and actually have, at least, all the perfections that can ever after appear to exist; it necessarily follows, that the first eternal Being, cannot be matter.

VI. This Being must possess *intelligence* and *power* unlimited, and all other attributes that are in themselves absolute perfections.

Attributes are divided into *natural* and *moral*, or *primary* and *secondary.* The first, are those which essentially belong to the *nature* of a Being considered in *itself;* the second in its *manner of acting* towards *others.* All the attributes of God being *uncontingent,* must be unlimited; and, therefore, His knowledge must extend to every thing that *can be known,* and His power to every thing that *can be done.*

VII. There cannot be in the universe more than *one* un-originated Being; for as this Being is possessed of infinite attributes, let us suppose a *second* unoriginated Being. He must possess the same; for both these Beings are eternal, and necessarily the same, every where alike present, without any possible difference or distinction, and therefore one and the same. *Two* such cannot subsist; and the supposition of a *second* such Being is only a mental repetition of the being and attributes of the *first.*

VIII. All things owe their existence to their First Cause, operating according to its own free will. Absolute power does not act of necessity, but freely: the power may exist without exertion; if it did not, then it acts by *necessity;* and if so, *necessity* is the agent, and not the free power of the independent God. He can do what He will; but He will do only what is right, &c.

The like may be said of His *omniscience.* He knows Himself, and what He has formed, and what He can do; but is not *necessitated* to *know* as certain what Himself has made *contingent.* If God *must* continually act, because He is omnipotent, and know, because He is omniscient, then does not this imply that He must be constantly employed in doing or undoing whatever is possible to be done or undone; and knowing all that is, and all that can be, and what cannot be? Is not this absurd?

From the above we may infer another *Proposition,* which may serve as a connecting principle between arguments *à priori* and *à posteriori; viz. :—*

IX. God is a Being of infinite *goodness, wisdom, mercy, justice,* and *truth;* and all other perfections which become the Framer and Governor of the universe.

GOODNESS consists in being pleased with communicating happiness to others.

WISDOM, in making a right or beneficent use of knowledge or power; for no being, howsoever intelligent or powerful, is said to act *wisely*, but that which makes a *good* or *beneficent use* of knowledge and power. Hence *wisdom* and *goodness* must be ever conjoined to make any act of power perfect. As He is *wise*, He *knows* what is best to be done; *powerful*, He can do it; *good*, He will do it. Justice, mercy, truth, or faithfulness, are not distinct attributes, but denominations given to His power and wisdom, in their various operations on different occasions, in reference to His creatures.

God's *liberty of acting:* His power and wisdom being infinite, He cannot be prevented by any outward cause; His nature being essentially good, He can have no opposition from *within*. His power, and all His other attributes, being infinite, eternal, and consequently unlimited, can have no opposition from *without*. And His liberty consists in His being free to act or not act; or infinitely or limitedly to vary His operations according to His own wisdom, goodness, and truth. —See also the late *Bishop of Ossory, Chevalier Ramsay, Dr. S. Clarke,* and others.

### SKETCHES OF PROOFS à POSTERIORI.

#### Recapitulation of the preceding Propositions.

II. In the argument *à priori*, in order to demonstrate the being of a God, it was attempted to prove that there must have been a Being whose non-existence is impossible. In arguing on this subject it has been shewn,

1. That this Being was unoriginated.

2. That all His attributes must also be unoriginated.

3. That these attributes must be unlimited, and absolutely perfect.

4. That this Being must exist every where, in the same manner He does any where.

5. That He is simple and uncompounded; not consisting of *parts*, nor of *whole*; nor of *magnitude*, nor of *quantity*.

6. That He must possess intelligence and power unlimited; and all other attributes that are in themselves absolute perfections.

7. That there cannot be in the universe any more than one such unoriginated, simple, and infinite Being.

8. That all things owe their existence to this First Cause; operating, not according to any kind of *necessity*, but according to its own *free will*.   And,

9. That as, in all His operations, all His attributes must concur and combine; so all the works of His hands must bear the impress of *wisdom* and *goodness*;—of that *wisdom* which consists in making a right use of *knowledge* and *power*; *i. e.* using both beneficially;—of that *goodness* which consists in being pleased with communicating happiness to others.

Hence may be deduced CREATION; the plan of which proceeded from His *wisdom*; the execution from His *power*; and the result a proof of His *goodness*.

From these data we might proceed to prove the being of a God, and His beneficence and moral government of the world *à posteriori*, i. e. arguing from the *effects* to the *cause*.

And, first, a Being of infinite wisdom must be expected to form His works so as to evidence that wisdom, in their multiplicity, variety, internal structure, arrangement, connexions, and dependencies; and, consequently, that these works must be, in many respects, inscrutable to man.   And this, as they are His works, must be one of their characteristics.

Whether there be any other kind of beings than *spiritual* and *material*, and such as are of a *mixed nature*, we cannot tell: but we have no ideas of any other kinds, nor can we conceive the possibility of the existence of any other; as we have no ideas of any figure that is not formed of *straight* or *curved* lines, or a *mixture* of both.

God, the uncreated Spirit, manifests Himself by material substances.   Created spirits must be manifested in the same way; and, though matter may exist without spirit, and spirit without matter, yet, without the latter, spirit cannot become manifest.   Hence matter appears to have been created for the use of spirit or intellectual beings.

Creation, in general, demonstrates the being of a God.

The SOLAR SYSTEM, and plurality of worlds; magnitude, distances, velocity, and gravity, of the celestial bodies; projectile and centripetal forces; centre of gravity; ellipsis; double and treble motion; attraction; all demonstrate the wisdom, power, and goodness of God.

VEGETATION.—Plants; trees; circulation of 'nutritious juices; composition of ligneous fibres; dissolution and regeneration of terrestrial productions.

PRESERVATION of genera and species, is a demonstration of infinite skill, and of the wisest and most beneficent Providence.

MAN.—Life; nutrition; sleep; the senses, particularly vision; and muscular motion; each furnishes a series of irresistible arguments.

The HEART, and the *circulation of the blood*, afford the most striking proofs: and on this point let the reader particularly fix his attention.

In a healthy state, the heart makes *eighty* pulsations in a minute; and it is calculated that from two ounces to two ounces and a half of blood are expelled into the *aorta* at each pulsation; consequently, at least nine thousand six hundred ounces will be thrown into the *aorta* in *an hour*, which would amount to one thousand four hundred and forty pounds in *one day!*

At each pulsation, this quantum of blood is propelled *eight inches*, which amounts to *fifty feet* in a *minute!* The quantity of blood in a human body is, on an average, about *thirty pounds*, and passes through the heart about *twenty-three* times in the space of one *hour*.

A weight of fifty pounds, hung to the foot, the leg laid across the opposite knee, was raised by the action of the popliteal artery. Allowing for the distance from the centre of motion, this proves that the heart must possess a power of at least *four hundred pounds!*

The blood circulates by pressure from behind, occasioned by the action of the heart; which pressure, having propelled it, according to the laws of gravity, to the extremities, reconducts it, contrary to those laws, back to the heart. How is this effected? It has been supposed that the ARTERIES contribute much to the circulation of the blood; were it even so, it would be comparatively useless, as they cease where such an auxiliary power is most wanting, at the extremities, where their anastomosis with the veins takes place; and the veins are not supposed to possess any such propelling power.

But that the arteries possess no such power, *Bichat* has proved by the following experiment;—He took the arm of a

dead man, placed it in warm water, inserted one end of a tube
in the brachial artery, and the other end in the carotid artery of
a living dog: the blood circulated in the dead arm, the pulse
of which beat regularly by the action of the heart of the living
animal.   Is there not a wondrous and especial providence of
God, by which this is effected?

Others have attributed the pulsation of the heart itself to the
stimulating nature of the blood.   *Bichat* has disproved this
by the following experiments :—

1. Expose the heart of an animal, and empty it; apply a
stimulus to its muscles, and it will dilate and contract, as if it
were full.

2. Puncture all the large vessels connected with the heart,
so as to empty it entirely; and the alternate contractions and
dilations will continue for some time, notwithstanding the total
absence of the blood.

3. Remove two hearts of equal bulk from two living animals; place the fingers in the ventricles of the one, and grasp
the other in the opposite hand, and it will be found that the
effort of the latter in its dilation, is as forcible as the other in
its contraction.

*Incessant action of the heart.*—*Its unweariedness.*—What
exhausts all other muscles appears to increase its action and its
force!   Can any person conceive how it is possible that a
muscle can be in incessant action for threescore, fourscore, or
a hundred years, without any kind of weariness?   There is
nothing in nature that can well explain this.   Over its motion
the mind has no power.   This is wisely ordered; as many,
in momentary fits of caprice, despair, and passion, would suspend the circulation, and thus put an end to their lives.     .

*Providence*, or the economical government of God, in the
provision for men and animals.—Never too much; never too
little: the produce of the earth being ever in proportion to
the consumers; and the consumers to that produce.

*Redemption.*—1. As all things are intimately known to
God, He must know wherein the happiness of human beings
consists; and may, from His goodness, be expected to make
every provision for that happiness.

2. Every sentient creature is capable of happiness or misery.

3. No creature can choose a state of misery for itself, because no creature can desire to be unhappy.

4. If any being could choose that state for another, he must be led to it by some motive which may make it eligible or desirable ; and this must spring from his envy, jealousy, fear, or a conviction that the wretchedness of the other will contribute to his own happiness.· None of these can exist in God, the Creator; consequently, He must be supposed to have made man for happiness. His counsels never change ; and, therefore, when man had fallen, He provided him a Saviour : this might be naturally expected from His infinite benevolence.

The moral changes made in sinners, proofs of the being, agency, goodness, and presence of God.

Man's existence is a proof of the Being of God : he feels himself to be the *effect* of a Cause, and that Cause to be wise, powerful, and good. There is evidently no cause in nature capable of producing such an *effect*, for no operation of nature can produce *mind* or *intellect;* the wonderful structure of the body, and the astonishing powers of the *mind*, equally prove that God is our Maker, and that in Him we live, move, and have our being.

III. Astronomical phenomena, very difficult to be accounted for upon natural principles, are strong evidences of the being and continual agency of God.

### PHENOMENON I.

The motion of a planet in an elliptic orbit is truly wonderful, and incapable of a physical demonstration as to its commencements. From its aphelion, or greatest distance from the sun, or body round which it revolves, to its perihelion or least distance, its motion is continually accelerated ; and from its perihelion to its aphelion as constantly retarded. From what source has the planet derived that power, which it opposes to the solar attraction, in such a manner, that when passing from aphelion to perihelion, by a continued acceleration, it is prevented from making a nearer approach to the sun? And, on the other hand, what influence prevents the planet, after it has passed, by a continued retardation, from perihelion to aphelion, from going altogether out of the solar attraction, and causes it to return again to perihelion? Sir Isaac Newton has fully answered these questions in his de-

monstration that this phenomenon is a necessary result of the
laws of gravity and projectile forces : it is worthy of observation, that to account for a planet's moving in an elliptic orbit,
little differing from a circle, and having the sun in the lower
focus, the projectile force of the planet, or the power by which
the  projected body. tends to move forward in a straight line, •
is shewn to be nearly sufficient to counterbalance the planet's
gravitating power, or, which is the same thing, the attraction
of the central  body :—for, the demonstration, the particulars
of which are too complicated to be here detailed, puts us in
possession of the following facts :—if a planet be projected in
a direction exactly perpendicular to the line joining it and the
central body, with a velocity equal to what it would acquire
by falling half way to the centre by attraction alone, it will
describe a circle round the central body.  If the velocity of
projection be greater than this, but not equal to what the
planet would acquire in falling to the centre, it will move in
an elliptical orbit more or less eccentric according to the
greater or less degree of projectile force.  If the velocity of
projection be equal to that which the planet would acquire in
falling to the central body, it will move in a parabola ; if
greater than this, in a hyperbola.   Now, it cannot be demonstrated upon physical principles, that a planet should have a
certain projectile force, and no other ; or, which is the same,
that it should be projected with a given velocity and direction :
for it is a law of nature, ably demonstrated by Newton in his
*Principia*, that all bodies have such an indifference to rest or
motion, that, if once at rest, they must remain eternally so,
unless acted upon by some power sufficient to move them ;
and that a body once put in motion will proceed of itself ever
after in a straight line, if not diverted out of this rectilinear
course by some influence.   Every planetary body has a certain projectile force ; therefore, some previously existing
cause must have communicated it.   The planets have not
only a projectile force, but this power is at the same time
nearly a counterbalance to its gravitation, or the attraction of
the central body ; so that by virtue of these powers, thus harmoniously united, the planets perform their revolutions in orbits nearly circular, with the greatest regularity.   It hence
follows, that the cause which has originally projected the
planets with a given velocity and direction so as nearly to

produce an equilibrium in the centrifugal and centripetal powers, is infinitely intelligent; therefore this Cause must be God.

As all the planets move in orbits more or less elliptical, when they could have been made to move in circles by a particular adjustment of the attractive and projectile forces, the Divine purpose must be best answered by the eccentric orbit. The habitable earth evidently derives very great advantage from the elliptical orbit; for in consequence of it, the sun is seven or eight days of every year longer on the northern side of the ecliptic than he is on the southern; *i. e.* from the 21st of March, when he crosses the equator northward, to the 23d of September, when he again returns to the equator, there are 186 days; but from the 23d of September, or autumnal equinox, to the 21st of March, or vernal equinox, there are only 179 days. From this circumstance the northern hemisphere, which it pleased God should contain by far the greatest portion of land, is considerably warmer towards the polar regions than in similar latitudes towards the south pole, where an equal degree of temperature is not needed. Circumnavigators have not yet been able (because of the great cold of the south polar regions) to proceed beyond seventy-two or seventy-three degrees of south latitude; or, which is the same thing, to approach the south pole nearer than about 1200 miles: but the northern frigid zone, possessing a greater temperature, has been explored to within about 600 miles of the pole; *i. e.* to nearly eighty-two degrees of north latitude.

### PHENOMENON II.

The *double motion* of a primary planet, namely, its *annual* revolution and *diurnal* rotation, is one of the greatest wonders the science of astronomy presents to our view. The laws which regulate the periods of the latter of these motions are so completely hidden from man, notwithstanding his present great extension of philosophic research, that the times which the planets employ in their rotations can only be determined by observation. The first of these motions results from projection and gravitation, and depends on the velocity and direction originally impressed on the planet; the second results from a force acting on the planet in a line not passing through the centre of gravity, while an opposite force is ap-

plied at the centre to prevent a change in the progressive
motion.   The period of rotation will depend on this oblique
force, and be unvaried while uninfluenced by other causes, or
by forces acting towards the same parts on both sides the
centre.   Hence the rotations of the planets will be uniform;
but their existence and periods can be known only by observations.   The astonishing accuracy with which celestial observations have been conducted within the last one hundred
years, has enabled astronomers to demonstrate that the neighbouring planets very sensibly affect the figure of the earth's
orbit, and consequently its motion in its orbit.   Of this every
one may be convinced who examines the calculus employed
in ascertaining, for any particular point of time, the sun's place
in the heavens ; or, which is the same thing, the point of the
earth's orbit, which is exactly opposed to the place of the
earth in this orbit.   Thus the maximum that the earth is affected by Venus, is nine seconds and seven tenths of a degree ;
by Mars, six seconds and seven tenths ; and by Jupiter, eight
seconds and two thirds, &c.   But no astronomer, since the
foundation of the world, has been able to demonstrate that
the earth's motion in the heavens is at all accelerated or retarded by the diurnal rotation ; or, on the other hand, that
the earth's motion on its axis experiences the least irregulari-
ty from the annual revolution.   How wonderful is this contrivance ! and what incalculable benefits result from it !   The
uninterrupted and equable diurnal rotation of the earth gives
us day and night in their succession, and the annual revolution
causes all the varied scenery of the year.   If one motion in-
terfered with the other, the return of day and night would be
irregular ; and the change of season attended with uncertainty to the husbandman.   These two motions are, therefore,
harmoniously impressed upon the earth, that the gracious
promise of the Great Creator might be fulfilled : " While the
earth remaineth, seed-time and harvest, and cold and heat, and
summer and winter, and day and night, shall not cease."
The double motion of a secondary planet is still more singular
than that of its primary ; for, (taking the moon for an example,) besides its particular revolution round the earth, which
is performed in twenty-seven days, seven hours, forty-three
minutes, four seconds and a half; it is carried round the sun
with the earth once every year.   Of all the planetary motions

with which we. have a tolerable acquaintance, that of the moon is the most intricate : upwards of twenty equations are necessary, in the great majority of cases, to reduce her mean to her true place ; they depend on the different distances of the earth from the sun in its annual revolution, the position of the lunar nodes, the moon's place in her orbit, and various other causes, including the effects of the planetary attractions. Who can form an adequate conception of that influence of the earth which thus draws the moon with it round the sun, precisely in the same manner as if it were a loose or detached part of the earth's surface, notwithstanding the intervening distance of about two hundred and forty thousand miles; and, at the same time, leaves undisturbed the moon's proper motion round the earth ? And what beneficent purposes are subserved by this harmony ? In consequence of it we have the periodical returns of new and full moon; and the ebbing and flowing of the sea, which depend on the various lunar phases, with respect to the sun and earth, (as is demonstrable from each of these phases being continually contemporaneous with a particular phenomenon of the tides,) these always succeed each other with a regularity necessarily equal to that of the causes which produce them. These motions of rotation and of a secondary planet about its primary, clearly demonstrate the existence of a Supreme Intelligent Cause who first gave them birth.

### PHENOMENON III.

The impression of an inconceivably rapid motion upon the earth, without disturbing, in the smallest degree, any thing upon its surface, or in the atmosphere which surrounds it, is another instance of the infinite wisdom of God. That principle with which God has endued the celestial bodies, in order to accomplish this end, is called gravity, or attraction. The existence of this influence is easily demonstrable from the curious law which pervades all the bodies in the solar system, and probably every other body in the whole compass of space. This law, viz. that the squares of the periodic times of the planets are to each other as the cubes of their mean distances from the central body, was first discovered by Kepler, and afterwards demonstrated by Sir Isaac Newton, as the necessary result of a still more general law, viz. that gravitation is directly as the quantity of matter, and inversely as the square of the distance. Thus, if the distance of but one planet from the sun be known, and the periodic revolutions of the whole, the distance of each from the sun is easily ascertained. The mean distance of the earth from the sun has been found by the transits of Venus, in 1761 and 1769, to be about ninety-five and a half millions of English miles ; and the periodic times of all the planets are known by direct observation. Thus, to find the distance of Jupiter from the sun, nothing more is necessary than first to square the period of the earth, 365 days, 5 hours, 48¾ minutes ; and that of Jupiter, 11 years, 315 days, 14 hours and a half ; and divide the greater product by the less, to find the proportion one bears to the other ; then to cube the earth's mean distance from the sun, 95½ millions, and multiply the cube by the proportion between the periodic times already found ; and the cube root of the last product will be the distance required. By this means it was that the distances of the different planets from the sun, and of the satellites from the primaries, (for this law extends to the satellites,) have been calculated. From this law it is evident to every one that deeply considers this subject, that the planets revolve in orbits by an influence emanating from the sun ; for the nearer a planet is to the sun, the swifter is its motion in its orbit, and *vice versâ.* The singular phenomenon of a planet's describing equal areas in equal times, results from the inability of bodies to change their state, combined with a force directed to the centre round which the areas are described. Thus, if a planet describe in twenty-four hours any arc of its orbit, and the area contained within that arc, and two straight lines drawn from its extremities, and meeting in the sun, be ascertained, it will be precisely equal to what the planet will describe in any other twenty-four hours, the greater or less quantity of the arc described being continually compensated by the less or greater extent of the straight lines including the respective areas. We also find that, by virtue of these laws, the motion of a planet in its orbit is not decreased in arithmetical proportion to the increase of the distance from the central body : for the hourly orbitical motion of the Georgium Sidus, for example, is only about five times slower than that of the earth, though its distance from the sun is full nineteen times greater.

Every man may convince himself of the existence of gravity, by observing the phenomena attending falling bodies.
Why is it that the velocity of a falling body is continually accelerated till it arrives on the earth? We answer, that the
earth continually attracts it; consequently, its velocity must
be continually increasing as it falls. It is also observable,
that the nature of the influence on falling bodies is precisely
the same with that which retains the planets in their orbits :—
by numerous experiments it is found, that if the falling body
descend towards the earth 16 feet in the first second, (a
statement very near the truth,) it will fall through three times
this space, or 48 feet, in the next second; five times this
space, or 80 feet, in the third second; seven times this space,
or 112 feet, in the fourth second; nine times this space, or
144 feet, in the fifth second, &c. Hence the spaces fallen
through are as the squares of the times of falling; *i. e.* in the
first second the body falls 16 feet; and in the next second 48
feet: consequently, the body falls as many feet in the two
first seconds as is equal to the sum of these two numbers, *viz.*
64, which is 16 multiplied by 4, the square of 2, the number
of seconds it took up in falling through the first 64 feet.

The above is but a very brief account of the influence of
this wonderful principle, which is universally diffused through
nature, and capable of attracting every particle of matter under
all its possible modifications, and of imparting to each substance, from the lightest gas to the most ponderous metal,
that property which constitutes one body specifically heavier
or lighter than another. To detail all the benefits which result from it, would be almost to give a history of the whole
material creation. But it may be asked, What is gravity?
To the solution of this question natural philosophy is unable
to lead us. Suffice it to say, all we know of gravity is its
*mode* of operation, and that it is, like its Great Creator, an all-
pervading and continued energy. Therefore, that *it is*, and
not in *what* it consists, is capable of demonstration.

I gladly borrow the *Conclusion* of a very surprising and
deeply scientific work, just now published, entitled, " *A New
Theory of Physics, founded on Gravitation;* applied to explain
the Phenomena of Chemistry, Electricity, Galvanism, Magnet-
ism, and Electro-Magnetism. By T. Exely, M.A.''

" Of all the departments of natural philosophy, that of phy-

sical astronomy, at the first sight, would seem more than any
other to be placed beyond the reach of our faculties ; but it is
well known that there is none in which we have advanced
with so much success, and demonstrative certainty ; for this
we are chiefly indebted to our illustrious countryman, *Newton*
From the exposition of the laws of one single agent, the force
of gravitation, all the movements of the solar system are de-
veloped, as well those of rotation, as those which relate to
their periodical revolutions, and even the anomalies, and apparent irregularities, are under the dominion and control of
this power.    Now, since we are satisfied of the existence of
the principle of gravitation, and admit that it affects every atom
of matter, we ought to examine the actions of bodies on each
other at minute distances, with the view of finding what part
of these actions is attributable to gravitation.    Philosophers
seem to have agreed to discard the operation of this force, except at sensible distances ; but if gravitation be not the sole
agent, it must needs, at these exceedingly small distances, act
a very distinguished and important part, in producing the
changes which are constantly going on in nature.    Do not
lose sight of gravitation ;—and, by pursuing this thread, you
will be guided through the mazes of a most intricate labyrinth,
to a situation exceedingly near the seat of its activity.    Here
it will be seen that the whole mass of force presents its resist-
ance equally, uniformly, and with immense effect, on every
side ; consequently this centre has every property of a solid
substratum, and there is no imaginable use, as far as we can
perceive, for a solid nucleus, which is not answered by this
concentrated force, this itself forms the solid part of matter.
It is not here supposed that force acts against nothing, but
against another opposing force : we know nothing of *matter*,
but by the forces which it exerts, and which doubtless
constitute its nature.    Does any one ask—What is matter,
and what is force ?    It may be answered,—Matter is force
applied and exerted in a peculiar way : and reciprocally force
operating in a certain mode, constitutes matter.    Is the inquiry
pursued,—What is this force applied and exerted so as to constitute matter ?    We cannot tell what is its essential nature,
more than this, that it is a power acting against a similar
power, and may be greater or less than the other, or equal to
it, being, as far as it respects matter, a wonderful act of the

Ever-living God, who worketh all things according to the counsels of His Will. Every atom of matter, as will be seen from the view we have given of it, was created or brought into existence by an operation of the Almighty Power of God, and continues to exist by His continued act, either immediate or mediate; for the same power, which first produced this substance, is requisite to sustain or uphold it in existence. The inconceivable myriads of atoms, which are contained in bodies, tend to excite astonishment, and present before us an inexpressible sublimity. Here we see the act of creation and conservation; and, when we extend our views to the innumerable huge bodies, which compose the universe, and to the multiplied millions of millions of atoms in each, with the united actions of their concentrated forces; we are prepared to say, that Power belongeth to God alone.

"There is no less evidence of supreme Wisdom in the structure of matter: the law of force, which constitutes its actions, is adapted peculiarly to preserve the existence, and constant harmony of the universe. The same law of force is equally subservient to maintain the beautiful order, and motions of systems of worlds, and to regulate the various changes and modifications, which bodies and atoms are designed to undergo, in their connexions and combinations with each other. The all-powerful hand of the Creator could certainly have constituted matter with forces varying by other very different laws; but we can conceive of none, which could have so completely answered the great ends of creation in the constitution of the universe, and the regulations and organizations of its several parts. The same Wisdom is seen in the variety of the atoms of matter, and the proportions of each sort, none are in defect, none in excess; and from the nature of their constituent forces, there is a constant tendency to preserve the established order of things, according to an All-wise and Infinite design. We are easily led to perceive, that it was in the mind of the Creator to form beings more elevated in nature than mere matter; hence, He has superadded a principle, superior to that which has been the subject of this Treatise. I mean vegetable life. This, whatever it is, is associated with the seed of the plant, and directs the combinations of common matter, when put into suitable circumstances, according to the nature and species of the vegetable which is to be unfolded and matured.

The principle of animal life is still more dignified.   This principle is hid in the ovum, as that of the vegetable is in the seed.
It directs the growth of the animal, as well as the peculiari-
ties of its shape and organs; and the developement of these,
reciprocally aids the principle itself, which becomes capable
of supporting and directing wonderful movements, actions,
and instincts.   The result shews, that the Omnipotent Creator
had purposed to form a being, who should possess a nature
far more transcendant than that of the mere animal; one possessing an intelligent mind, capable of surveying His works,
and of rising from the survey of these to their Great Author.
This did not escape the notice of the Roman poet, as stated
in those well known lines :

*Sanctius his animal, mentisque capacius altæ—*
&ast; &ast; &ast; &ast; &ast; &ast; &ast; &ast; &ast;

*Finxit in effigiem moderantum cuncta Deorum.*
*Pronaque cum spectent animalia cætera terram,*
*Os homini sublime dedit; cælumque tueri*
*Jussit, et erectos ad sidera tollere vultus.*
                                        *Ovid. Metam.* lib. i. L 76.

'A creature of a more exalted kind
Was wanting yet, and then was man designed :
Conscious of thought, of more capacious breast,
For empire formed, and fit to rule the rest:—
Thus while the mute creation downward bend
Their sight, and to their earthly mother tend,
Man looks aloft; and with erected eyes
Beholds his own hereditary skies.'
                                        *Dryden.*

   " The material part of the earth is adapted to nourish and
maintain the vegetable world, and this serves to support the
animal kingdom, while the whole contributes to the maintenance and pleasure of man in his present state.   But the intelligent and rational principle is capable of more elevated
enjoyments and exercises in the pursuit of truth, and the discernment of right and wrong; and still more, in yielding due
homage to his Creator, and in presenting cordial expressions
of gratitude, veneration, and worship.
   " It is very observable, however, that some disorder has
affected the human race.   We search in vain in the book of
nature to ascertain either the cause or remedy of this evil.
Revelation alone furnishes this most important of all knowledge.   The Sacred Scriptures shew us the path of life, and

direct us in the right use and management of nature in general, as it respects the promotion of our present and future
felicity."

All these things prove not only that there is a God infinitely powerful and intelligent, but also kind and merciful;
working all according to the counsel of His will, and causing
all His operations to result in the benefit of His creatures.
They prove also, that God is continually present, supporting
all things by His energy, and that, while his working is manifest, His ways are past finding out. Yet, as far as He may
be known, we should endeavour to know Him: for, *he that
cometh unto God must know that He is.* Without this, it is
not likely that any man will serve Him; for, those alone who
know Him, seek Him; and they only, who put their trust in
Him, can testify *He is the rewarder of them who diligently
seek Him.*

The EIGHT PROPOSITIONS included in the argument *à priori,*
are formed totally independently of all considerations of the
Divine Being in reference to His *acts;* that is, to His attributes in *energetic operation,* becoming *causes* of certain, or
any *effects.* They discover His *Being,* and several of His
perfections, independently of His *works.* His *Being* and *perfections* argued from *creation, providence,* and *redemption,*
belong to the argument *à posteriori.* Now, though the above
mentioned propositions were conceived, stated, and argued,
as if there were neither *creation* nor *providence,*—nor even
the existence of a *revelation;* yet by them, His Being, eternal, unoriginated, and independent, with many of His essential attributes, are clearly demonstrated; and thus far, we can
go, being led by what is called *the light of nature;*—and it
must be as edifying as it is pleasing to find that the *Holy
Scriptures* assert precisely the same things of this Being.
So that we have not only those things from *revelation* which
we have been able to find out by *reason,* or the *light of nature,* but besides them, a multitude of others, which lie far
beyond the verge and limits of reason, or the light of nature,
—such as the *creation, fall* and *redemption* of man, the *immortality* of the *soul, future rewards* and *punishments,* &c.
&c. This is no mean proof that the *Bible* is from God;
and, that what is called the *light of nature* is a *ray* from the
*infinite splendour* of the *Eternal Sun of Wisdom* and *righte-*

*ousness.* And thus both *reason* and *revelation* illustrate each other, and conjoin to point out that Infinite Source of being and beneficence, who is alone the Supreme Good of man.

To shew, that without having any kind of reference to it, the Scripture proclaims those essential and important things found out by the arguments *à priori*, take the following examples :—

1. The Scriptures assert, that there is *one only God*, Deut. iv. 39. vi. 4. 2 Sam. vii. 22. Psal. lxxxvi. 10. Jer. x. 10, 11. xlv. 5. Matt. xix. 17. John xvii. 3. 1 Cor. viii. 4—6. 1 Tim. ii. 5. vi. 15.

2. That this GOD is a Being of all *possible perfections*, Matt. v. 48. 1 Chron. xxix. 11. Psal. viii. 1.

3. That this GOD is the *Creator of all things*, Gen. i. 1. Psal. xxxiii. 6. Acts xiv. 17. Heb. xi. 3.

4. That He is OMNISCIENT, *i. e.* perfectly *wise*, and *knows all things*, Job ix. 4. 1 Tim. i. 17. Isai. xl. 13, 14. 1 Sam. ii. 3. Job xxxvi. 4. xlii. 2. Psal. cxlvii. 5. Jer. xxxii. 19. Acts xv. 18.

5. That He is an *Eternal* SPIRIT, John iv. 24. Heb. xi 27. 1 Tim. vi. 16. Deut. xxxiii. 27. Psal. xc. 2.

6. That He is OMNIPRESENT, 1 Kings viii. 27. Psal. cxxxix. 7—10. Jer. xxiii. 24.

7. That He is OMNIPOTENT, Jer. xxxii. 17. Rev. xix. 6. Psal. cxlv. 3. Job ix. 4, &c. 1 Chron. xxix. 11, 12.

8. That He is IMMUTABLE, Exod. iii. 14, Mal. iii. 6. Heb. i. 10—12. Jam. i. 17.

9. That He is INCOMPREHENSIBLE, Job xi. 7. Psal. cxxxix. 6. Eccles. iii. 11. viii. 17. 1 Tim. vii. 16. Rom. xi. 33.

10. That He is essentially GOOD, Psal. lii. 1. cxlv. 9. Matt. xix. 17. Jam. i. 17. Exod. xxxiv. 6. 1 John iv. 8.

11. That He is TRUE and FAITHFUL to all His engagements, Numb. xxiii. 19. Deut. vii. 9. 2 Sam. vi. 28. Tit. i. 2.

12. That He is infinitely PURE and HOLY, Isai. vi. 3. xliii. 15. lvii. 15. Psal. cxlv. 14. Rev. xv. 4.

13. That he is infinitely JUST, Psal. xxxvi. 6. cxxix. 4. cxix. 137. Rom. ii. 6. Acts x. 34, 35. Rev. xv. 3.

14. That His PROVIDENCE is not only *general*, but *particular*, governing and preserving all things, Psal. xxxvi. 6. civ.

cvii. cxxxvi. 25. cxlv. 13, &c. Job xii. 10. Acts xiv. 17. xvii. 28. Matt. x. 29, 30.

15. That He *loves* MAN *especially*, and presses all the operations of all *inanimate* and *animate beings*, into His service, Prov. xvi. 33. Psal. lxv. 9, &c. civ. 13—30. cxlv. 15, 16, 33. cxlvii. 16, 18. Amos iii. 6. iv. 7. Job xxxvii. xxxviii. xxxix. For, all creatures, whether *corporeal* or *incorporeal*, *animal* or *spiritual*, not only owe their being to God, but they owe also, their efficacy to produce any effect, to the agency of a Divine Power in and upon them; as all creatures, every moment, depend upon God, for the *continuance* of their existence.

See *Doddridge*, and other writers, on this argument.

### SOME OBSERVATIONS ON THE DIVINE PROVIDENCE.

The providence of God in renewing the wastes of nature, and in fructifying barren tracts, so as to make the wilderness a fruitful field, and even the sterile rocks a vegetable surface, is a subject of astonishing beauty and contrivance; and as such is worthy of the contemplation of angels and men; and is a sovereign proof of the being and love of the Great First Cause and Preserver of all things. In order to set this in a clear and impressive light, I borrow, gladly and gratefully, the following observations from a late periodical work.

" Nothing can be more beautiful in itself, or more deeply interesting to a reflecting mind, than the proofs by which nature constantly produces an accession of soil, and an accumulation of vegetable matter to render it fertile. The process is varied so as to be exactly adapted to overcome the obstacles which the circumstances of each particular district present; but although the means employed are infinitely various, the final result is always the same. When the surface of a rock, for instance, becomes first exposed to the atmosphere, it is at once attacked by agents which operate on it, both *mechanically* and *chemically*. LIGHT calls into activity the latent HEAT; the pores become by that means sufficiently enlarged to admit particles of moisture, which gradually abrade the surface, and produce inequalities; upon these inequalities the seeds of *lichens* and *mosses* are deposited by the atmosphere; these forerunners of vegetation take root, and the fibres by which some sorts of these diminutive plants adhere to the

róck, concoct a vegetable ACID peculiarly.adapted to corrode
the substance with which it comes in contact, and increases
the inequalities which *heat* and *moisture* had already formed.
These diminutive plants decay and perish ; when decomposed,
they form a vegetable bed suited to the production of larger
plants; or, when the surface of the rock happens to present
*clefts* or natural *crevices*, they fall into *them;* and there
mingling with fine particles of sand, conveyed thither by the
atmosphere, or crumbled by the action of the *air* from the internal surfaces of the *crevices* themselves, they form fertile
mould.   Nature having advanced thus far in her preparations,
makes another forward step.   She sows the soil which has
been produced by the decomposition of vegetable matter, with
some of the more perfect plants which it has now become capable of sustaining.   These continue to be produced and decomposed, until a soil has been prepared of sufficient depth
and richness to bear plants of still higher quality and larger
dimensions,   The process of nature acquires accelerated force
as it advances towards its consummation.   When a sufficient
depth of soil has been formed to produce *ferns* for instance,
these annually decay and die : their decomposed materials
gradually form little conical heaps of vegetable mould round
the spot on which each plant grew.   When this has gone on
for a period of sufficient length to spread these cones over a
given surface, nature takes another stride : she sows *furze,*
*thorns,* and *briars,* which thrive luxuriantly, and by annually
shedding their leaves, contribute in the end to add greatly to
both the depth and fertility of the mould.   This species constitutes, in truth, the means which nature principally uses in
preparing a *bed* for the growth of the more valuable trees.
It is well known that these are the plants which make their
first appearance in *fallows,* or in *woods* which have been re-
cently cut down.   Into the centre of a tuft of *brambles,* is *ac-*
*cidentally* carried the seed of the majestic *oak;* meeting with
a congenial soil, it soon vegetates; it is carefully and effectually cherished and protected by its prickly defence, against
all injuries from the bite of the *animals* which roam over the
waste,   The larger trees having reached a height and size
which render *shelter* unnecessary, destroy their early nurses
and protectors, by robbing them of the *light* and the *air* indispensable for their well being.   The *thorny plants* then re-

tire to the outskirts of the forest, where, in the enjoyment of an abundant supply of LIGHT and SUN, they continue gradually to extend the empire of their superiors, and make encroachments upon the *plain* until the whole district becomes, at length, covered with magnificent *trees.* The roots of the larger trees penetrate the soil in all directions : they even find their way into the *crevices* of the *rocks,* fitted as these are already, by decomposed vegetable matter : here, they *swell* and *contract* as the HEAT and MOISTURE *increase* or *diminish.* They act like true *levers,* until they gradually pulverize the earthy materials which they have been able to penetrate. While the *roots* are thus busy *underground, boring, undermining, cleaving,* and *crumbling,* every thing that impedes their progress, the *branches* and *leaves* are equally indefatigable *overhead.* They arrest the volatile particles of vegetable food which float in the atmosphere. Thus fed and sustained, each tree not only increases annually in *size,* but produces and deposits a crop of *fruit* and *leaves.* The *fruit* becomes the food of animals, or is carried into a spot where it can produce a *new plant ;* the *leaves* fall around the tree, where they become gradually decomposed ; and, in the lapse of ages, make a vast addition to the depth of the vegetable mould ; whilst the decomposition of vegetables makes a gradual addition to the depth of the cultivatable soil, another cause, equally constant in operation, contributes to increase its fertility— the produce of the minutest plants serves to subsist myriads of *insects ;* after a brief existence, these perish and decay : their decomposed particles greatly fertilize the vegetable matter with which they happen to mingle. The period at last arrives, when the TIMBER, having reached its highest measure of growth and perfection, may be cut down in order that the *husbandman* may enter upon the inheritance prepared for him by the hand of the ALL-WISE and ALL-BENEFICENT Author of his existence. Such is the system which they who have eyes to see, may see. Plants which appear worthless in themselves—those *lichens, mosses, heaths, ferns, furze, briars,* and *brooms,* in which *economists,* forsooth ! perceive only the symbols of eternal barrenness—are so many instruments employed by perfect *Wisdom* in fertilizing new districts for the occupation of future generations of mankind :—

'The course of nature is the art of God.'

" The constant depasturing of cattle on *wastes* and *commons* counteracts the means which Providence makes use of in producing fertility ; and, in consequence, greatly retards the period when the soil becomes sufficiently deep for agricultural purposes.   There is not perhaps a healthy *waste* which would not become a *forest*, were the *commoners* restrained from setting their flocks upon it.

" It is a well known fact, that wherever trees of any *particular species* have fallen into decay, other trees of the *same species*, will not naturally thrive : for instance, when a forest of *firs* falls naturally into decay, it is never found to be succeeded by another crop of *firs*, but by *birch*, *oaks*, or other species congenial to the soil which the *fir-wood* had formed. Therefore, *oaks* should not be planted to supply the *place* of oaks already cut down from that place, no more than *wheat* should be sowed in the *same field* where *wheat* grew in the preceding year.   *Plantations* should be encouraged on all *waste* and *common* lands.   In such, we behold the most efficient means which could have been adopted towards covering these barren tracts with a depth of soil adequate for the purpose of *husbandry*.   Many of the trees ordinarily planted, and more especially the *larch*, are known to destroy the *heath*, and to afford a shelter highly favourable to the growth of *nutritious grasses*."—See No. 76 of the *Quarterly Review*, p. 438.

There is no land, howsoever sterile, which, by judicious *draining* or *planting*, may not become of the utmost benefit to man.   *Nature* is God's agent; but He has given man understanding to be a co-worker with this agent, and to direct and help her operations.   *Art* may not only embellish *nature*, but, by the assistance of *industry*, render her still more abundantly fruitful.

If God have said, " In the sweat of thy brow thou shalt eat bread," He has, even in this, strongly intimated, that the man who industriously plies his tillage, though to *lassitude* and *sweat*, shall have bread to eat.

Thus, then, the sun, moon, planets, rain, dew, snow, trees, herbs, shrubs, funguses, and vegetable excrescenses of every kind ;—all the smaller animals and most despicable insects ;— grass, corn, oil, water, fire ;—the brutes and the angels, which were all made by and depend upon Him;—are the servants of man.   And thus *reason* and *revelation* conjoin to prove that there *is* a GOD—that He is *good*—that He *hateth nothing that He hath made*—that He is *loving to every man*—that He *would have none perish* or be wretched—and that He *is the Rewarder of them that diligently seek Him.*—See Doddridge, Clarke, &c.

**END OF VOL. II.**

JOHN T WEST & CO. PRINTERS.

Lightning Source UK Ltd.
Milton Keynes UK
UKHW02f0850160818
327336UK00011B/946/P